Millennial Harvest

Millennial Harvest
The Life and Collected Poems of
Charles Greenleaf Bell

Helen Lane Editions
Lumen Books
Santa Fe, New Mexico

Acknowledgements

Here at the outset I gladly voice certain obligations, some already clear from the context. First, to my excellent parents: my father, Judge Percy Bell, outstanding lawyer-statesman of Mississippi—himself, late in his life, author of two unpublished books which I hold in my files—first, of great local interest, an autobiography called "Child of the Delta," ending with letters from the 1927 flood; second, a volume of searching thought, entitled "A Free Man's Worship," emphasizing the *free*, though he had led a Bible-study group at home and in our Methodist Church. Next, my mother, Nona Oliver Archer Bell, whose early poems are sampled in the first chapter, especially a graveside elegy for a loved nephew who had died early.

Let me here also acknowledge all the help of friends and family herein narrated, along with other supporters who have attended my St. John's Community Seminars and *Symbolic History* presentations, among them most especially Suzy Poole, as well as others who have read and commented on this book as a work in progress: Cynthia Green, Josephine Haxton (Ellen Douglas), Galway Kinnell, Richard Lenhert, John D. Nagle, Barbara Riley, and Suzanne Ruta.

I am also pleased to acknowledge publishers and publications that have previously issued my work: Indiana University Press; Michael Braziler, Persea Books; Norman S. Berg; *American Weave, Atlantic Monthly, Beloit Poetry Journal, Chicago Review, Chicago Tribune Magazine, Common Cause, English Leaflet, Epoch, The New Yorker, New York Herald Tribune, New York Times, Ladies' Home Journal, The Nation, New Mexico Review, Oxonian, Poetry, Poetry of Azatlán, Quarterly Review of Literature, Rio Grande Sierran.*

Among the most steadfast supporters of this project, without whom my work could not have reached this point, are the Witter Bynner Foundation for Poetry and the Frost Foundation, both of Santa Fe, New Mexico.

I also want to acknowledge the generous support of the Helen Lane Translation Fund of Lumen, Inc. as well as those who have contributed to the Danny Bell Memorial Fund for the publication of this book: Page Allen and Nat Owings, Sylvia and Dale Ball, Edward and Eva Borins, Stuart and Nan Boyd, Per and Barbara Mason Bro, Deborah S. Cornelius, David and Shirley Dayton, Ronald Christ and Dennis Dollens, Nancy Dahl, Eleanor C. Eisenmenger, Laurie Amory de Grazia, Darlene L. K. Kogan, Douglas Lee and Wilton Wiggins,

Erika Bast Little, Frank D. Moore, Ann Overton, Jane O. Overton, Marti Regio, Jamie M. and Cherry Whitener Rohe, Peter and Suzanne Ruta, Marcia C. Simpson, Lionel Soracco, Jr., Karen T. Walker, Virginia Westray, Kent Williamson, Ann B. Worthington, Mary Ruth Wotherspoon.

To which add, for this volume of my life and poems, an elegy:

I have suffered the loss of Diana (Danny), beloved and loving wife through fifty-five years, for whom, more than anyone else, I have harvested the prose and poems of this book. To bring Danny more clearly to mind at the very start, I will quote the first poem I wrote to her, in 1948, though the poem will be found at its appropriate place in the pages to follow:

WOODBIRD

Woodbird softly trilling from the maple spray;
Red leaves above quiet waters
In the webs of sun.

This fall is my spring; down the lost forest ways
Your frank eyes guide, the daughters
Of laughter run.

When I forget, my love, image of the light and spray,
Forget, eyes, earth, and waters,
And lose the sun.

Charles Greenleaf Bell
Santa Fe, 2006

Preface

*poetry celebrated
as integral to life*

This is a new book. In its main body I give an account of my life
story, meanwhile garnering from dozens of notebooks a lifetime of
poems not yet published in book form and now set into a chronological
fabric of event and comment that also overlaps and, I trust, enriches
certain poems in my published books, which follow this section. I had
attempted such a dual, prose/poetry account during my teaching days
at Princeton (1945-1949), first calling it "Sparks of Ego" (of course,
I pronounced it, êgo) and later, "The Old Life," in oblique, smiling
allusion to Dante's *Vita Nuova*, the first work, I believe, to situate its
poems in a context of autobiography. That earlier manuscript, though
encouraged by my mentors, the great refugee intellectuals then at
Princeton—Erich Kahler, Otto Benesch, Hermann Weil, Max Knoll,
and others—never found a publisher.

As to my three published books of poems, somewhat revised
here, I may briefly preface them: the first, *Songs for a New America*,
made rather a splash when it came out in October 1953 (Indiana
University Press)—a celebration of our national daring (though
potentially tragic: Cold War, Korea, Vietnam)—that is still for me
the vision of the Marshall Plan and Adlai Stevenson's first campaign
call to the people. In the second book, *Delta Return*, written (as if
dictated) later in 1953, though not published until 1956 (again by
University of Indiana Press), the affirmed westward flight yields
to a water-death and ebbing of the motion southward and home;
although, as with other underworld journeys, what is sought is not
death simply, but some ambivalent, regenerative sign. That book, my
largest single poetic utterance, projects a symbolic autobiography
onto a symbolic landscape—all caught in repeated five-fold lines and
stanzas: a Delta, or triangle, of three times five to the fifth power, so
that tireless revisions have had to work within that metric scheme.
The third, *Five Chambered Heart* (Persea Books, 1963), although
arranging poems of various lengths and versifications written over
many years, is effectively united by another grouping of fives: the
poems fall into numbered waves of the states of Love: (1) Love
simple; (2) Love narrowed as in Lust; (3) Love attached to things: as
Nature, say Earth; and, since such attachment mostly messes up the
scene, let (4) be Waste; there one might wish to start over again, but
one must first somehow transcend, so call the last (5) Soul. When this

sequence (Love, Lust, Earth, Waste, Soul), has been run twenty-five times through the whole book, it begins to appear that poems, not in themselves discursive, may form a canon of thought.

Charles G. Bell
Santa Fe, 2006

Contents

Millennial Harvest

Charles G. Bell, paternal grandfather, who
took his portable photographic studio up
and down the Mississippi River after
the Civil War.
Right, Charles, Ruth, and Percy Bell.
Overleaf, Charles Bell III (1918).

1. MISSISSIPPI, VIRGINIA, OXFORD (1916-39)

In Greenville, Mississippi, "Queen City of the Delta," where I was
born on Hallowe'en, 1916, my mother, who taught us some reading
and writing before we went to school, began with my sister, Ruth, then
five; I, although two years younger, joined in. When that sister, at six,
went to first grade (we had no kindergarten), I tagged along; it seems
no one could stop me. Though I was still four, I could read and write; at
my father's suggestion, the superintendent let me stay. Then my sister
said she wasn't going to sit in the first grade with her baby brother, so
she began the second and skipped the third. Three years later, it was
the turn of my younger brother, Percy, to take up the family tradition,
though it didn't work as pleasantly for him as for me. I enjoyed sin-
gularity, was always adoring some tall, long-haired girl, and the boys,
very brotherly, treated me as a mascot.

 Still, I came to a crisis in my second or third year. The cause
was my father's saddling us with his unrealized life ambitions—that
lost race for governor against the hillbilly faction of Mississippi's
despot governor, Theodore Gilmore Bilbo. My father's first move was
to keep our grades straight A's—what he called "passing." After sit-
ting all day in class, we were to come home and prepare tomorrow's
assignments, which he would hear when he returned that evening from
his law office. My sister and brother found no way out, though it was a
terrible drag on body and spirit—even on the brain, since the teachers
taught for the dullest, and if you knew the stuff already, you were being
trained to waste time. Both of them grew up fat, unexercised, allergic,
short of wind, physically handicapped.

 I was in despair, when a voice addressed me from the sky:
"You can give him the work you did during class today as though it
were tomorrow's assignment." That was all it took to make our public
education stimulating. From the third grade through high school, I used
the classes as they should be used. There was no time to waste. I ran
to school. No more dawdling in the halls. I flung myself into my seat
while the others were goofing off. Under the motivation of my father's
demand, I tried to do the lessons, solve the problems, and memorize the
poetry, before the teacher could discover I hadn't done my homework.
I found I could read a poem two or three times and know it by heart. Of
course such industry was conspicuous; a teacher would catch on now
and then that Charley was doing the assignments in class. The daily
grade would be marked down and, in a pinch, I might be given a note to
apprise my father that I had come unprepared.

 I walked home down an alley of old stables, garages, and

chicken coops. There was a knothole in a clapboard structure where I filed those messages over the years. "Old Judge Bell, independent as a hog on ice" (so *Time* magazine would describe him) was hardly to be buttonholed by a teacher.

Afternoons I was free to run and play, climb trees, pore over astronomy in the illustrated *Book of Knowledge* (to be supplemented, clear nights, from my twelfth year on, by a 2 1/2 inch refractor); also, as a Boy Scout, I enjoyed my Tom-and-Huck heritage of the river and swamp woods. Evenings, my father would hear what he thought was for tomorrow. When reports came in, the daily grades brought him to boil: B's, B minuses, sometimes a C+. But the exams were always A. He couldn't fathom it. A's I went to bed I would hear his voice from the study, addressing my mother in the great style of Southern oratory: "Suffering Mother of God, that I should be cursed with an imbecile son! He seems to know the stuff at night; he must forget it before morning. But then how does he pass the exams? That's a mystery that won't bear looking into." (Though his discipline was the mystery.) Smiling like Adam, "with superior Love," I fell asleep—and never told a soul.

Until I was finishing the University of Virginia (in my third year, with all As and a Rhodes Scholarship awarded), when I thought my father might enjoy my stratagem. Misprision! Never was a man so keelhauled: "That you could have deceived me all those years." I claimed necessity, and that it had been for the best, since I had acquired will and independence, not to speak of a healthy running, swimming, and tree-climbing body. He groaned, "But to have lied to your father!"

All that time, he had urged me to read Dickens and the rest, from a library rivaled in the state only by that of Walker Percy's cousin and adoptive father, Will. While I pursued the passions of science—astronomy, physics, evolution—there was one author we supremely shared: Mark Twain—those river books were more real to me than life. Of course I remembered the time Huck marvels (having never been in such a situation before) whether the truth, for once, might not be safer than a lie.

Another groan. "To have lied . . ."

"Tell it to Huck Finn!" I said. My father knew the passage as well as I. He could only laugh, and that was the end of that.

In those Greenville schools, we read poetry from the early grades—Longfellow, Whittier, folk ballads, etc.—and we were urged to compose such verse. In high school, I wrote ballads, not only for myself but also for the girls I was fond of. On such occasions, my father might tell a story about the father he adored, the old photographer for whom I was named, who died a year before I came along. There had been a time in that ancestral family when the daughter (my Aunt Bessie), in wall-eyed adolescence—and even my sour Kentucky grandmother—had a spell of reading Romantic verse and ohing and sighing over it. My father also seems to have been drawn in, evenings of those years when he first hung up his shingle as a local lawyer. But the old photographer must have found it so unreal that he interrupted one night after a dose of Keats, Shelley, or a later high-flown dreamer, intoning (as my father would tell me) a ditty of his own:

> Poetreé, poetreí
> On the wings of love I fly
> From groceree to grocereí.

So it was claimed we had poetry in our blood. Whatever truth there was in that claim should point more to my mother, who in her college years wrote moving poems; thus an elegy, one worked into "The Graves" chapter of my first novel, *The Married Land*. For what nephew was it written, child of a brother or sister, among nine, of whom she was the youngest?

> Last year you walked within this quiet place
> Where shadows cross the sunlit earth.
> And kneeling in your reverend tender grace,
> You laid your hand upon the springing grass.
>
> It hides you now. In the same place,
> With eyes half weary of the light,
> Dreaming again I see your face,
> Calm with the silence and the peace
> Of shadows on the sunlit earth.

For me, my first preserved "poem" was not assigned but volunteered; and already it turns the observed nature of a seeding dandelion into a symbol of death and transcendence. For that reason I do not shame to display it here. (The scrawled original—from about age ten (sixth or seventh grade)—appeared among my mother's papers in a tied box of the Virginia writings I had sent home, my name in her hand on the page.

HUMANITY

A puffball balanced on its stem
A dainty white and beauteous gem
While through its snowy head uplifted
Softly, slowly the breezes drifted;
This flower did gently fall and rise;
It was a happy paradise;
The winds of fate blew hard and strong,
The puff ball shattered and was gone
But its myriad parts in heaven blend
Carried on the wings of wind.

To illustrate further the obstacles my poetic fancy heaped upon itself: through the four high school years I would slip down to our family library in the secret depths of night to read and memorize Poe—until I knew most of the small leather volume of poems by heart. On the good side, we read at school a Shakespeare play each year after the seventh grade, and I loved to learn and orate those great speeches. Opposite, but I think also good, were the bawdy folk verses coming to us from the Black world:

Fire, fire, false alarm
Baby crapp'd in papa's arms.

Or thus from a version of "Casey Jones":

Casey was sittin in de house o'whores,
He heard de engine out o' doors.
He jump thoo de window wid his pecker in his hand:
Says: "'Scuse me ladies, I'm a railroad man."
(Chorus) Casey Jones, son of a bitch,
Run his engine in a hell of a ditch.
De boiler busted and de smoke stack fell;
Kill'd old Casey just as dead as hell.

Another dark innuendo floats up as from a blues-singing woman:

My man is a deep-sea diver,
With a stroke that can't go wrong;
He dive way down to the bottom
And he hold his breaf so long.

Here, since my scan of Delta sources has just welcomed bawdry from the Black world, I will mention an educational erotic source culled from our family library, the twenty-four-volume Burton translation of *The Arabian Nights* (with footnotes). Surely my memorizing Tom and Huck and even the lugubrious Poe would not have prepared me for the speed-browsing I was going to need in college. But about the time I discovered the Tarzan books and began to go through our great oaks more like an ape than Weissmuller could dream of, I also became aware of the erotica in my father's library. After exhausting Boccaccio, *Moll Flanders*, de Maupassant, I hit on those amorous *Nights*. For years I went through the volumes on the sly, perceptively searching and brain filing what was relevant—practicing, without intention, that scholarly skill.

Years later, at my father's death, I would inherit the set, and when my new wife, Danny, and I were at the University of Chicago, it was shelved high in the oak-paneled Tudor library of the Harper house.[1] I wrote there after everyone else was asleep. One night I wanted to refer to the story where a lady goes into the woods to couple with a bear. I climbed to the shelf and pulled out Volume Four. For the first time it opened to the back flyleaf, and there, in my father's scratchy hand, was a row of figures—all the page numbers of all the passages I had sifted so long and laboriously to glean. The same with every volume. What if I had hit on that in adolescence? I wouldn't have been ready for college, and my life would have been incalculably different. If what education needs is motivation, no wonder I have written (as these pages may testify) so many poems in praise of Eros.

Thus, having started first grade at the age of four, I went to the University of Virginia when I was sixteen. Despite this, as soon as I got on the dean's list and didn't have to go to classes—only take quizzes and exams, on which, by studying the whole night before, I could make nothing but A's—I decided to cram the entire four years into three. In the first, besides my chosen astronomy, physics, and math, there was required composition—where we read a good anthology of English literature, especially poetry, which I memorized by gobs, from Chaucer (as my mother had recited it to me) down to early Yeats. How much of Milton and the Romantics I would declaim to the woods on my long

1. William Rainey Harper (1856-1906) was the first president of the University of Chicago. Through his friendship with John Hey Vincent (1832-1920), an educator and Methodist minister who was instrumental in founding the Chautauqua lectures, both Vincent and I were invited to the University of Chicago. Vincent had come to know me through my lecture, "Mechanistic Replacement of Biology in Nature," which he admired. Because of these interconnecting friendships, the apartment on Woodlawn Avenue was rented to us for the price of a cold-water flat.

walks (and runs) through the Ragged Mountains!

Before Christmas-break of that first Virginia year, I won, by sheer luck, a very substantial scholarship—welcome especially to my father, whom the Depression, plus his laudable attempt, on his own, to wrest the governorship from a follower of Bilbo, had left him in such debt and mortgage, that my college costs would have been a burden. Here, my excellent Virginia teacher of composition and literature, for whom I had worked hard on weekly papers, recommended that I compete in an essay-writing contest—the prize, free tuition with some support for the remainder of one's bachelor enrollment. A bunch of us, brought together, were presented with a page of possible subjects from which each must choose and in a given time come up with an essay. We looked at the list and almost despaired at such unlikely titles as the one on which I focused: "Great Hills I Have Known." For a wonder, I seized on the eighty-or-more-foot levee holding the Mississippi back from our alluvial Delta—remembering its disastrous break of 1927, which drowned the whole flood plain under muddy depths of water. I subtly changed the title to "The Greatest Hill I Have Known," and, where everyone else was stymied, I, having lived through that memorable rupture, wrote as I had hardly written before. During that vacation, the phone call came saying I had won the award, designed to fund my undergraduate study—a present relief to my father though we could not foresee that Rhodes would add three graduate years abroad.

Still, on my earlier battlefront of sex, nothing had occurred. But now in my third and senior Virginia year, something surfaced, which, in my second novel, *The Half Gods*, would touch off a chapter called "In the Liver Vein"—see *Love's Labour's Lost* 4, 3, 74. The spur was a *University of Virginia Magazine* "purity test," on which a friend and I achieved so virginal a score that we ventured a two-week race, to see who could lose the most points in all categories. I won pants down. The story is extant (as Hamlet might say) and writ in choice English, so I do not retell it here. Yet something should be said of where I stood in the cloven matter of life's central drive.

On the purity test we had not counted kid-games. Of course little girls had come to our secret houses to make overtures with their apertures, and we boys had responded in our small way: eight-year-old Ginny, thrown back, dress raised, insistently pointing, "Put it in! Put it in!"—while we stared in baffled inadequacy. On the other hand, and with other girls, I hardly remember a time when I was not in love. One spring evening after school, my father found me sitting with a braided blonde under a mulberry tree, singing (he said) some adoring composition of my own. The rift was already there, to be widened in that South

to an ideal worship estranged from touch. Thus Victorian morality and the bawdy house. Indeed, without that house in Lynchburg, how could I have won the sin race? But where was the clue to a love-passionate mating procedure? What was required (as everywhere) was to knit the poles in a fabric of skill and luck, abandon and control.

Next, my Virginia experience with Milton is ripe for recounting. Yet first, I should say that in the perhaps remarkable Greenville High School, our senior English teacher, Miss Hawkins, whom we called "Hawkeye," had led us through "Comus," on which I wrote a paper and got the Epilogue by heart: "To the ocean now I fly," with the intervening songs, "Sweet Echo," "Sabrina fair," and the rest (not knowing how beautifully Henry Lawes had set them to music in the 17th century). But it was in the spring of my first Virginia year, one night, having finished my assignments, instead of taking up a Shakespearean play (as I often did), I opened the Milton I had just bought and began to read. The roll of that pentameter —"Of Man's first Disobedience and the Fruit / Of that Forbidden Tree whose mortal taste / Brought Death into the World, and all our woe, / With loss of Eden . . ."—so caught me that I read the rest of the night, went to the university cafeteria for breakfast, read all the following day, breaking for a cafeteria dinner, then all the next night; by that dawn I had absorbed *Paradise Lost, Paradise Regained,* and *Sampson Agonistes*—most of my Milton volume at a sitting.

Thereafter I could hardly write prose. When I tried, in essays, it came out blank verse, and even now, some clever friends, attending my *Symbolic History* shows, ask: "What's all that pentameter doing in there?" Whether my case of Miltonitis was curse or blessing is not mine to determine. Anyway, from those four years finished in three, with joyful study and such grades as won me Rhodes' bait of diamonds, there must be poetic attempts in my files; but I skip to the more consuming productions of my three Oxford years—though with some reluctance to present even those.

Meanwhile, before Fall and Oxford, it should be noted that the scientific drive which had held me at Virginia to a physics major had been complemented, from the first year (second semester), by my crowding into my three-year program Stringfellow Barr's course, History of the Ancient World.[2] His message, enforced by Spengler's *Decline of the West*, made me bold to go up to argue with him about the

2. Stringfellow Barr (1897-1982), who reappears later in these pages, was an historian, author, and former president of St. John's College in Annapolis, Maryland. Together with Scott Buchanan (who was also invited to St. John's in 1937 and served as the college's dean), he instituted the Great Books curriculum that he and Buchanan had previously

mechanism of his "simple harmonic" recurrence of cultural cycles. Barr showed me in four minutes that I was ignorant of history, about which I should not argue until I knew the "artifacts." His urging me to "widen my science to include man and all his works" must have been the most crucial stimulus in my education.

Already at Virginia my education had led from memorizing poetry to exploring art and music on my own. Now at Oxford, it hurled me from the dour small physicist assigned as tutor for my specialization to the only other field I was prepared to study: English Language and Literature, from Anglo-Saxon to our century, first with Neville Coghill and then with Edmund Blunden. Glory! I could spend my three European years learning languages and building a library of comparative literature, with art, plus the whole scope of music on records (especially of the early periods)—materials requisite for my life-work, *Symbolic History: Through Sight and Sound*, which will play a recurrent role in this autobiography.

Here I insert what in 1997 (then looking back over sixty years) I wrote for the *American Oxonian*:

> A Contrast of Teachers: Barr at
> Virginia, Coghill at Oxford
>
> I think, as I did long ago, that during my college student time (Virginia '33-36 and Oxford '36-39) I had two transforming teachers, utterly different in practice. At Virginia it was Stringfellow Barr (b. 1897, Balliol 1917, d. 1982). At Oxford, it was Neville Coghill, then tutor of English at Exeter, my asigned college. Barr changed me by his impassioned history lectures—or rather by my will to doubt yet explore the burdensome yoke of Spengler's *Decline of the West*. Barr's imperative to widen my

---

developed as a radical program for liberal education—centered on the reading and discussing of 100 of the great Western classics—at the University of Virginia, which shelved the proposal. Barr established and served as president of the Foundation for World Government from 1948 to 1958. In 1959, Barr, with Eleanor Roosevelt, Reinhold Niebuhr, and others, petitioned the U.S. Congress to abolish the House Committee on Un-American Activities. His many books include *The Will of Zeus: a History of Greece from the Origins of Hellenic Culture to the Death of Alexander, Voices that Endured: The Great Books and the Active Life, Mazzini: Portrait of an Exile, Citizens of the World, Let's Join the Human Race*, as well as the novel, *Purely Academic*, and *Copydog in India*, (a young reader's book about a French poodle).

studies certainly altered my life—as it may prove, from a likely success in science to hardly marketable arrogations of thought and utterance.

My Oxford scholarship was scheduled for physics. When I had warmed my feet a bit, and presented myself to the just-mentioned Magdalen physics tutor, I told him of my Virginia experience: how I had carried science with my good right hand and the whole of culture with my ambidextrous left; that since this was my great chance at languages, music and art, I aimed here to do the same.

"Eauo, Mr. Beyuh," he bowelled the vowels, "deaun't be faddish. Physics is a wery demanding subject. You will spend all your time in the laboratory." I countered that I would spend my vacations on the Continent, pursuing my heritage. We parted. Next day I had the luck of getting Neville Coghill, in my own college, as tutor of English Language and Literature.

I took to him from the start. He had the large Medici print of Botticelli's *Spring* on the wall; his shelves were full of books I wanted to read, records (as of Beethoven's late quartets) I was just beginning to know. He set me to compare Chaucer's *Criseyde* and Boccaccio's *Filostrato* in the parallel text, and to write a paper for our next week's session. Day and night I reveled in it. He had me read the paper, while he smoked, smiled, and said, "Very well. For next week, try *The Book of the Duchess*." That glowing Chaucer time, I was also working, on my own, to fathom Dante's Italian.

Against Barr's fiery proselytizing, Coghill's laconic sucking his pipe at a beginner's effort, his barely voiced (yet affirmative) responses seemed almost negligent—though perhaps his was the loose-rein incitement required to waft me, on my own, through Old and Middle English, through the Europe of great cathedrals, plus Dante, with the Incarnate wonder of Gothic into Renaissance.

By spring of '37, however, my younger brother, a freshman at Sewanee, had taken cyanide. So I spent the summer with my parents in the Delta:

At your death I was abroad; I crossed
The ocean to a sad home. A grief unhoused,
As from beyond the tomb, settled upon me.

I found myself, odd times, sketching figures
For poetic lines: "Bound on a wheel
Of fire . . . Tears like molten lead . . ." So I
Received your spirit. Brother of my blood,
You haunt not this house only, world-wounded shade.
(from *Delta Return*)

I had been absorbing my brother's poems and
pictures, and against his watercolor, "Soul Freed" (a robed
woman, like a phallus, being released from the hand), I shaped
a Michelangelesque male, as in Lear's "Bound on a wheel of
fire," so bound to life. Meanwhile, I swam across our partly
diverted Mississippi and back every day; plus probing and
mastering (for Coghill and myself) the inter-weavings of great
tragedy and bitter comedy. On my Fall '37 return, I gave my
tutor a distilled essay on tragedy—to become, ten years later,
my first University of Chicago lecture. I was the same "Mr.
Bell" who read it to the same Coghill, but he hailed me as
never before: "That's a first class paper! Let's drink a glass of
sherry, and you call me Neville and I'll call you Charles."

I had witnessed a second example of genuine teaching.
I sailed to England with another scholar who would enliven
the three years abroad and remain a lifetime friend, Rodney Baine.
(Though, alas, he has lately died.)
Our earliest tie (I learned later) was that Rodney's father had
proposed to my mother, Nona Oliver Archer, when they were both
young in the hills of northeast Mississippi. But she was starting college,
and it was to be years before she would consider marriage at all. A
generation later I met Rodney himself at the Rhodes competitions, state
and regional—on that perhaps unique occasion when two from Missis-
sippi were to be chosen.
We decided to save money, sailing not from New York City
with the other scholars, but on a $50 freighter from New Orleans to
London. After a Gulf hurricane and a mid-Atlantic storm, which drove
us south for days (while Hitler ranted on the short-wave as he took the
Rhineland—start of Europe's three-year build-up of crises)—through

twenty-three ocean days, Rodney's skilled playing of the violin, evenings, was a relief. We reached Oxford staunch friends.

It was then that Rodney, having been warned by his family not to come back with one of those prissy English accents, made a comical proposal: we must counterattack with what was known on the Delta as Black talk. I had talked such maybe more than White talk in the ninety-percent Black Delta, besides reading it in *Huck Finn* and *Uncle Remus*; so I agreed and, indeed, I started out that way; but when I shifted to English Language and Literature, I knew it would not work for Shakespeare. Besides, at morning chapel (attendance required in my college), I heard the British boys beautifully reading the *Book of Common Prayer*, marred by my dialect: "Ah' b'lieve in Gawd de Fader Awmighty, makah ob Heben an' Eart." I could only ask, what am I up to? Theirs sounds better. So I told Rodney I was going to relax and talk however it came to me. (Thus, after three years, one could hardly have guessed that I was an American, much less from Mississippi; though Black talk was still familiar to my tongue.)

But Rodney stuck to his resolve, not only talking Black, but corrupting the British language in every way he could. When I went with him to Marks & Spencer, which he called Marx & Spengler, to get some kitchen appliances, he confronted the salesgirl with, "Honey chile, have you got a little fun-hole? Cause Ah want to po wine in mah bott-hole"—pushing the glottal stops, to her astonishment. Then, where the Brits went from a penny to tuppence and even thruppence, he went right on up: fuppence, fippence, sippence, seppence, eppence, nippence, and so to a shiulin'—until making change was a shopkeeper's nightmare: "Ah give you shiulin' sippence, so you owe me thruppence hapenny."

The housekeeper who came with his college digs quit, no doubt baffled; but we teased him with what advances he must have provoked her. The next day or so, some of us invited him to tea. "Man," he said, "Ah'm so tah'd. Ah spent the whole mawnin tryin out new housemaids."

Of course I went with him abroad. In Paris, where we were looking around at churches, after examining a few, he confronted me, "Man, Ah doan know what de church o'God is coming to: dey got dat bad 'pussy here' [*poussez ici*] on all dese church doors." At a restaurant, having heard of a cheap meal at a prix fixe, he asked the manager, "You got de fix prick, man?" A year or so later, traveling together in Italy, we could catch only a local train from Florence to Assisi. Of course, all stations have restrooms marked "Ritirata," but at every station Rodney would crane out the window: "Man," he would say, "we mus' be on de wrong train. Heah we is back in Ritirata."

Rodney's boldest use of such talk was probably at our B.A. oral, Spring 1937. There was a certain don, named Professor M. L. Ridley, editor of the little Temple Classics of Shakespeare then coming out, and none of us (Northrup "Norrie" Frye or the rest) approved of his editing. However, Rodney ("inde-Goddamn-pendent") gave much of his Shakespeare exam to tearing into examiner Ridley, quoting from memory, text and footnote. For the oral, they called us in by threes, to sit in three chairs, each waiting his turn. Baine was before Bell, so I heard his viva voce, though I could hardly catch Ridley's almost whispered question. But Rodney spoke up loud and clear: "Well, Massah Ridley, when Ah wrote you wuz a fool in mah papeh, all Ah meant wuz that yo notes on *Othello* don't bear the mahks of a reasoning critter." Still, he got the degree, with the third year, and later degrees besides.

Returning with the war to the United States—a first marriage, two sons, vicissitudes of teaching and research, even a brief spell as an army technician—free again and wishing to serve his native state, Rodney took on the English department of Delta State College, where he protested its all-white segregation in a Black Delta. As he was booted from that bondage, a lucky road opened east to the University of Georgia in Athens, 1962. Visiting him there, we found Rodney a tenured and respected professor, though I observed that he had eased his Black talk to a cultured Southern drawl.

Finally, in 1987, when my *Symbolic History* had to go from slide/tape to video, and I hardly had the gumption or cash to start, Rodney ordered, for himself and for three institutions he espoused—Southwestern (name later changed to Rhodes), then Harvard, and Georgia—four prepaid sets, my delivery of them completed only by 1992.

Were I to live many lives, I would not hope (or wish) for a finer all-round friend than Rodney Baine.

At Oxford, Fall 1936, I made my first purchases at Parker's Book Store, adjacent to the college: the Nonesuch *Blake* and an Italian *Divine Comedy*. I had been drawn to Blake earlier, and the little Modern Library selection had been by me at Virginia. Now I made a frontal (by heart's) assault on the Prophetic Books. So it was hardly surprising that my first poetic conception and fragmentary creation should have been a visionary epic, in which the cycles of history (which I had fought and almost succumbed to) would reflect the symbolic contraries of Blakean prophecy. Of the sketches (as later typed and preserved), the first to be worked up was penned in Florence, the Christmas vacation of 1936-37. That Fall, a racking cough (curse of the English climate and of my attempt to swim weekends for the Oxford team in the public

pool, spat and otherwise performed in all week by the city's youth)
had deepened until, on the Channel boat, I thought I had TB—but
the condition yielded to Tuscan sky and sun in Florence, heart's best
home, with its Early Renaissance art of joy, Botticelli's *Venus* and
Spring—and the daughter of the pensione, Gabriella de Benedictis
(of the Blessed Ones), who in the evenings helped me read Dante ("al
tempo dei dolci sospiri"—"at the time of the sweet sighs"). No wonder
the following sketch flowed from me in neo-Blakean, mostly six-foot
lines—though it is strange how little delight besouls the adolescent verse:

> SONG OF THE RENAISSANCE, sung in the days
> of hope by Anthros, Child of God (December 1936)
>
> Let old men shout in the streets and beggars dance
>> with joy,
> For spring has come and all the birds sing "Resurrexit."
> Let sorrows fade; let men inhale the breath of flowers
> And draw new life from every freeborn breeze . . .
> There's not a bush or tree but some immortal being
> In it cries, "I live!" And pushes to the light
> With swift, green-springing joy.
> Rejoice, rejoice, O sons and daughters of Man;
> For you shall be clothed in beauty and in robes of
>> shining white
> And summer's sun shall lead you to the meadows.

Work on the never-to-be-finished "Book of Anthros" was as
complex and interrupted as my search for a free and passionate love
life. When I met Gabriella, she was recovering from what she had
thought to be an engagement to a fellow student, whose aristocratic
parents made him break off that middle-class relation—doubtless part
of the sadness then so moving in her. As a student and pensione helper
of her parents, she had no leeway for unchaperoned outings, much
less for erotic love. And in truth I, too, had already met at Oxford the
married woman who, three years later, would become my first wife.
Strange how that meeting had also hinged on Dante. Fall, in a fire-lit
college room, I had found myself seated by a dark-haired woman with a
face of longing. It was Mildred, come with her husband and his sisters,
the elder engaged to a scholar who was also at Exeter College. We
spoke of my studies, and I told her that in my parallel-text reading of
the *Inferno*, I had come to the most moving of all poetic love-stories:
of Paolo and married Francesca, blown forever on the dark winds of

their abandon. "Alas, what sweet thoughts, how much desire, has led them down into this place of sorrow!—Oh lasso, / quanti dolci pensier, quanto disio / menò costoro al doloroso passo!" Thus Dante, to whom Francesca narrates what brought them from the "time of sweet sighs" to that of "dubious desires." I had memorized the passage, which I quoted in my then bookish Italian, improvising a paraphrase. Here is my latest rendition of a passage I have been translating for sixty years:

> "One day, by chance, we read for our pleasure
> Of Lancelot—his love for Guenevere—;
> We were alone and without all misgiving.
> The page we shared would draw our eyes together
> And sometimes change the color of our faces;
> But it was one passage only conquered us.
> When the word, heard, quickened the desired smile
> Kissed by such a lover, this one you see,
> Never thereafter to be parted from me,
> Kissed my mouth all trembling. What Gallehault,
> What go-between, the book and he who wrote it!
> Upon that day we read in it no further."
> The while Francesca spoke, Paolo wept
> So grievously that, overcome by pity,
> I swooned away, like one who suffers death,
> And headlong fell, as a dead body falls.

> "Noi leggiavamo un giorno per diletto
> di Lancialotto come amor lo strinse;
> soli eravamo e sanza alcun sospetto.
> Per più fiate li occhi ci sospinse
> quella lettura, e scolorocci il viso;
> ma solo un punto fu quel che ci vinse.
> Quando leggemo il disiata riso
> esser baciato da cotanto amante,
> questi, che mai da me non fia diviso,
> la bocca mi baciò tutto tremante.
> Galeotto fu il libro e chi lo scrisse:
> quel giorno più non vi leggemmo avante."
> Mentre che l'uno spirto questo disse,
> l'altro piangea, si che di pietade
> io venni men cosi com' io morisse;
> e caddi come corpo morto cade.

Dante may have intended this passage as a warning against illicit passion, but the poetry works almost as a lure. And thus it would turn out for Mildred and for me, since our clandestine Oxford love, plus ten U.S. years of marriage, with three daughters, then divorce, sprang from that Fall '36 recitation in a firelit college room. But Mildred and her in-laws were touring Europe when I would be meeting Gabriella in Florence—Gabriella, with Beatrice (and Mildred), loves requiring sublimation.

What reams of sonnets sounded in my head that winter term of frustrated passion and darkening grief over the suicide of my younger brother. Whip all this into a brooding, still adolescent mind, and the shift of hopeful "Anthros" to "Lamentation":

THE HERESY OF ANTHROS,
in the days of darkening shadow

"Can Spring forget the birds that waken her with
            music,
Or Winter ignore the ice that freezes round his limbs?
            . . .
Am I to lie in sleep through all the nights of sorrow?
Where are the songs of the singers, where the faith of
            our fathers,
When Jehovah walked the earth and spoke with the
            sons of men?

"Heaven throw down your frowns and water earth
            with tears;
For the day is departed when sunlight brought forth joy,
And the night is over when pale stars held a charm . . .
I have fled from the woodpath,
Chased by flies that bloat the flesh of my body.
I have looked on the horror of cities where most pain is;
And out of the blackness of darkness,
Of corners, streets, and houses,
I have seen blank faces peering:
The face of Amenhotep of Egypt, set in sorrow,
Perpetual, inconsolable—
Gray granite faces, tight-skinned, brooding, full of
            silence.
In the press of people, overshadowed by towers,
I have seen voids of emptiness—

A wilderness of wasted beauty—
Absence, darkness, separation from light;
And the fear of a God who will never save."

It is clear that my Spenglerian flight from modern disillusion produced here a Romantic, somehow Biblical variant of the same. Meanwhile, a penned "Beginning of the Anthros Book" attempted a kind of neo-Blakean rewrite of cosmic and organic evolution, modernizing Genesis and Milton, spilling over into a poetic Earth to be grappled with later.

After the Delta summer with my bereft parents and a gray Fall Oxford return, the frustration of two loves (both absent and the reverse of sublimated) had begun, by December '37, also to overflow. At once "A Sonnet of Some Passion" (as if to a cold girl, imagined, perhaps English) was furiously dashed off. I sent it to Neville, my tutor and editor of Exeter College's *Stapeldon Magazine* (he had offered money for contributions), with this formal note: "Dear Mr. Coghill, I hope you will not hold it against me that money brings me to display what discretion might have kept hid. I have seen bad verse in your magazine, but none so foolish as this." He took it with more praise than it deserved. The five bright shillings, plus the pain of my crossed loves—I on the rack well into the Spring vacation of '38 for news from Mildred—her family earlier returned to Virginia—all crazed me. One night I beat my head against the wall; but getting poor satisfaction from that, I took up a block of wood serving as a doorstop and hacked it with my pocket knife into the face of a devil, my hands devilish raw. Next night, no wood offering, I wrote off a sequence of four more sonnets, to be expanded next day, with the first, to ten. When the new ones were also published, tutors and students seemed staggered—I suppose by the unleashed achievement of sonnet form. (In the following display of ten, the earliest written, stands as No. 5.) Next day, invited by friends Lou Palmer and family, I took off for the French Riviera.

A SEQUENT TOIL OF SONNETS

1

When we first met, if I had only known
One careless moment would beget in me
This brood of longings—sweet, I would have flown
Beyond the limits of the polar sea,
And in that climate tenanted alone,
Before surrendering up my liberty.

I did not long for love; I made no moan
Upon the night air. It has come to be
Without my asking. Should I now condone
The passion I have called infirmity?
I blame myself. I lay me down and groan.
Yet all my groanings cannot set me free.
Then do not add your censure to my own;
But let me come, and reap, though I've not sown.

2

Why must you meet with scorn what I propose
And turn to poison my expected bliss,
All things bestowing that augment my woes,
Yet stubbornly opposing me in this?
Your presence? "Welcome, take it if you please."
I know. My wit relieves your empty mind,
And my attention brings you that sweet ease
Which left alone your dullness could not find.
Your hand, your look, your kiss, you grant them well;
And when you've granted these, you think me blest.
But I must tell you, I consume in hell,
Because, loath love, you fear to grant the rest.
O leave your fear, submit to my control;
A part has pleased you, why not in the whole?

3

It is not thus you love me, you reply.
A stupid love, that fails to recognize
Its parent and its child! I know your eye
Feeds on my form with gladness. I surmise
By your fast breathing that this kiss has power.
Why will you flee the game you followed long;
Why close your eyes on love's most lovely flower?
If, as you say, you love me, do not wrong
Yourself, your pleasure, love, my love, and me.
We stand now on the summit of the world,
And time itself inclines to our decree.
In one bright garden lilies are unfurled.
O hear me, love, and come as I require;
The love we have is only love's desire.

4

How can the watery flame of your faint love
Wrap me about in such hard-bellowed fire?
Or how the sterile looks you proffer of
Beget in me such sturdy-boned desire?
You never spoke me fairer than your face,
Nor is your face more lovely than your form,
Your form's below your mind, your mind's a place
Where dullest notions live in dark and swarm.
You never can be loved, and yet my want,
Which is hard, lust-hard, for the deed of kind,
You scorn, and take it for a thing too gaunt
To lie beside your fullness. And so blind,
So mad am I, that still for you I call,
Despite your foulness, coldness, dullness, all.

5

If you deny me love, why call me friend?
Your friendship only plants forbidden seed.
Why do you smile on me when you are sure
Your smiling must revive the love you kill?
Why tempt me newly with a proffered lure
That wakes a hunger it will never fill?
The blessing of your presence is a curse
So long as presence adds to my desire,
And by a partial blessing renders worse
The torture of unconsummated fire.
It will be better for my peace of mind
To seek no more the love I cannot find.

6

If there are torments for me, let them rage;
If all the spiteful forces of the world:
War, weakness, famine, penury and age,
Can work me anguish, let them all be hurled
Upon my quivering flesh, till I cry out
In unreflecting agony of soul.
Let sickness plague. Let persecution shout
Around my serpent-serried form; and roll
My resurrected corpse in roaring hell
Ten years encompassed in a night of pain,
With never fading fires. Do! Do! Yet quell

The fiercer fires that riot in my brain.
All earth's affliction I would rather bear
Than living, searching, thinking, in despair.

7

Take me away on some deep-shrouded night
When I am sitting in remembrance bowed,
And bear me from the world of wished delight,
Cradled in the dark folds of a cloud.
Then set me down in silence where the loon
Alone gives answer, and the long night long
I shall not look to see the phthisic moon,
Or hear the nightingale's consumptive song.
Let my companions be the barred screech owl,
The gray moth and the bat; let no star stare,
But mist blow past me, while the low winds howl.
Let heaven be dark and the whole earth bare,
And not one tempting form that night appear:
Beauty and hope—these are the powers I fear.

8

Well, we have bickered, severed, gone our ways,
And found more torment in our life apart
Than all the burning of the lusty blaze
Of passion stirred to madness could impart.
Our days together were an age of pain—
Abortive twisting for denied content;
Our nights apart were shadows of disdain
Whose sleepless tongues rehearsed the days' dissent.
Each day out-damned the day that damned before,
Each night gave night a lease of sadder power;
And day to day and night to night wronged more;
I thought poor hell had squandered its dark dower.
Then absence came with worse—and I return
Begging for love: in hell, love, let me burn!

9

Through your neglect such torment I have known
As you must answer for on Judgment Day;
And through my cruelty you have undergone
Such griefs as, after life, I must repay.
Since all the sorrows that we bear alive

But tie our souls from joy, is it done well,
By damning disagreement thus to strive
With pains on earth to purchase pains in hell?
No. I will rather here be kind to you,
And you shall grant me all for which I yearn;
Divided joy shall so receive its due
And mutual blessing merit just return.
Thus I bestow on you and you on me,
Through present joy, joys in eternity.

10
Well, all is done. My love was nothing more
Than passionate necessity of flesh;
And, absolution granted, I deplore
The bait that lured me to this fowler's mesh.
My appetite, though tokened love, was pain,
And tortured me with lavas of desire,
Until my mounting passion could obtain
The satisfaction of expended fire.
Of this abortive love I had no joy,
But only wish to have and then regret,
That having had should recklessly destroy
The longing that importuned me to get.
And still I know that other wants impend,
Which I call love; yet prophesy their end.

Ten months later I had given up Elizabethan decorative
construction. I began to see the sonnet as a freer form of stripped ut-
terance, so condensed as to be almost cryptic. The influence of Donne
had been supplemented by that of Hopkins. Run-ons, half and internal
rhymes, with all devices of sprung stress and tensile syntax were used
to heighten explicit meaning. To exhibit such meaning, I will first para-
phrase such a sonnet, "On the Geometric Style," and later quote it:

The life of a late civilization is a voluptuous trespass
leading to world-weariness and spiritual hunger. Pardon,
with new faith, a new cycle, is granted only by the penance of
a Dark Age, which is thus spiritually desired, as it is
materially feared. For this reason Rome fell, initiating the
angular Byzantine, and Crete (or better, Mycenae) fell,
introducing the Geometric style of the Greek Dark Ages. In
the paradox of possession and non-possession, we should

recognize the penitential fall before us as life and blessing in disguise.

A cruise to Greece and the Aegean with Mildred, already widowed, during the Spring vacation of 1939, occasioned the poem just paraphrased—the sonnet itself would later be voiced, with slides, in the "Cycles" show of my *Symbolic History*. Here it is:

ON THE GEOMETRIC STYLE (February 1939)

Penance is, to pay for trespass, only
The path to pardon, and pardon's fullness not
Built but on hunger, wherefore Rome fell
And Cretan softness. Mournful stood many,
As when the whip strikes, self-wielded. Well
May the lash be longed for and lamented. What
Sage can affix our blessing, of pain or gladness?
Who gives his life finds it; paradox, such
Is our wisdom, and ends with grasping, lifeless
In conquest, as who runs and drops dead. Touch
No string of sorrow, the sweet sound rots
To the core. What is lost? Death. And ahead penitence,
Pain, crudeness, desert earth, or worse, bare plots
Of stone, now known our last defendence.

In Winter 1938 my reading of Marlowe, Shakespeare, and Webster had launched me onto a Biblical tragedy, in blank verse and lyrics, called "Justice to Dalilah," showing how she had sacrificed her love for Sampson and her happiness to the god Dagon; but my first attempt, the night of February 2, 1938, went so badly that I dismissed the whole thing with a bit of doggerel, easier to write than poetic drama:

Paper will burn if thrown on a fire,
But thrown on ashes it smolders away.
Had I been born to the age of desire—
But I am born to the present day;
I guess there is nothing more to say.
So goodnight all,
The curtain may fall;
There is really no need to attempt a play

Still, I had taken the project with me to the Riviera, and by that Easter (1938), returning via Solesmes Abbey for its Gregorian chant, I was planning to write fifty lines a day. But hardly had I stepped off the train from Paris when I was told there was not a room left to rent in the town. I went to Evensong anyway, where I chanced to meet some writers and musicians: one, an American pianist we had known in Italy as the Signora, another a French author called in my notes "The Girl of Solesmes"—I not paying attention to new names. She would turn out to be Simone Weil. I have told of this meeting, as it actually happened, in *The Half Gods,* in the chapter called "The Mansard." Here is the story of that first encounter:

As the Signora led me to her hotel for dinner, I sighted in the lobby a young woman of unbelievably severe intensity reading from a book that I recognized (owning just such a copy) as the complete Marlowe, opened surely to the *Faustus*. I began to quote the great closing soliloquy, which I knew by heart: "Ah, Faustus, now hast thou but one bare hour to live . . . ." She looked up. I continued in high style right to the close: "Come not, Lucifer; . . . I'll burn my books . . . Ah, Mephistopheles." She asked me—in an accent that pinpointed her problem—to keep quoting, since, she said, my recitation was that of a Greek rhapsode. For five years, I had been memorizing poetry, so all that weekend there was no chance of my running dry. Anyway, it was Simone and the American expatriate "Signora" who persuaded the hotel-owner to let me use his large furniture storeroom on the Mansard top floor of an adjoining building—no electricity, but plenty of candles for me to write my fifty lines a day. There the ladies would come up to hear me read by the great Mansard window, or evenings at the candlelit table. They were almost the first who graciously fostered my hope that I might have a lurking fund of poetic talent. In memory of them, and especially of Simone (whose identity and wartime fate were revealed in a letter to me, with her "Iliad: Poem of Force," which was later discovered and published), I risk "Fragments" from my attempted play. First, just before a scene between Dalilah and the Priest of Dagon, a Vision appears, to haunt Dalilah and to voice her fears:

JUSTICE TO DALILAH
Fragments of a contemplated play (April 16-24, 1938)

(*A room, Dalilah alone at the window*)

Dalilah: Once again the mists of night creep
In the vales, and rising blot the hills.
The woods are full of shadows. Brightness fades

From off the mountains; every crag hangs dark,
A sloping head athwart our charnel world.
The sky's friendly vault, blue-arched above,
With closer warmth of cloud, dissolves
Into a wide-hung lake of emptiness,
Eternal, silent, cold, and I remain
Alone.
Alone to will again what willed and willed
Weak will has left undone.
To live a beast, content with beast-desires,
Free to give passion rein, to lie in love—
Such needs a bestial brain. And yet to cast
Myself a mortal sacrifice before
The shrine of Dagon, asks a purer essence,
Saintly fire. Could I be earth or air!
But to be split, contested each on each . . .
What is the end? I ask, yet fear the knowledge,
Turn to hush reply. But no, it comes;
It comes in robes of darkness that strike death
Into my soul. Such fear filled Pharaoh's children
When the angel of the Jews stood
At the doors of Egypt . . .
Speak, Vision, though I fear you, I must hear.

Vision: Your life is a tale that is told. Whatever way
You move, the end will be the same. If you
Betray your love, the term of your regret
Will never come. If you forsake the service of
Your God, belief and love alike are dead;
You have outlived your joy, and now with all
The world, you drink the ever-during cup
Of sorrow. This is truth, for I am one
Who knows. I have appeared to you before,
And from this time, being of your substance,
I will stay with you, and fill your mind
With thoughts it would avoid, and even now
Refuses to believe.

Dalilah: . . . What are you? Say! . . .

Vision: I am the self you are to be.
I know all, doubt all, spurn all; look on grief

With eyes of coldness, and the world with scorn.
You fear me now; but there will come a time
When I will preach to you of earthly life,
Until you laugh at all your pain, though not
In happy laughter. Until that day, I'll play
A secret chorus to this comedy.
Prepare! Your tempter comes.

(*Vision, aside; enter the Priest of Dagon*)

Vision: Here's old religion, pointing out the road
To heaven, fearing in his heart it leads,
Like other roads, down hell's midnight valley.
He'll call a curse on love and set up bars
To keep the world from sweets he cannot share.
But all is well; sweets cloy the tongue, and prove
At last most bitter. Mark his words; he's angry.

Priest: Woman, what have you done? Delay, delay!
By God, you will delay till all the tribe
Has gone to glut this gobble-bellied Jew.
What! shall we leave the land, our soldiers killed,
Our temples and the altars of our God
Polluted with the touch of alien hands?
Or has the wanton stoking of your lust
Let you forget those purer fires that burn
Before the face of Dagon?
Was it not enough this Hebrew giant destroyed
The thirty friends of Timnath; burned the vines
And all the standing corn of Philistía?
Was it not enough to show his deadly nature?
Now a crime blacker than the rest
Fills our land with weeping—a thousand men
Slaughtered, and with the jawbone of an ass.
A thousand men!
But you delay. And for what cause? For love.
Distemper of the bowels. Heat. A lust.
A passion of today. The longing of
A belly to be filled. A rage, no more.
And for this rage you give your soul away.

Vision: He tells you truth, Dalilah; love decays.

It is a robe that molders from your arms
And leaves you sad and weeping. Cast it off.
But not in hope to save your soul. Your soul
Is less than love. It is a dream of nothing
And a pain.
For this good cause throw love away,
No love is worth retaining;
Throw next your soul, and all the day
You'll laugh without complaining.
Cast, O cast your soul away,
In sour laughter gaining.

Dalilah: Peace, fiend! I'll save my soul . . .

(*She declares her conflict—as earlier stated—to the priest.*)

Even so, I must decide. Return tomorrow.

Priest: Woman!

Dalilah: But now go! (*Exeunt*)

The next scene I give is of Sampson drunk, written after the
former (on the train to Oxford, May 25, 1938), though
preceding it in the play:

(*Enter: a host of Jewish revelers, with Sampson
drunk, led by his friend Michael.*)

Sampson: Michael, let be; you'll blight our joy.
I know I'm drunk, man; there's no need to say it.
And all my friends are drunk; I know it well.
I love you, Michael, yes; but I could wish
You puking drunk, big-bellied, tumbling, mad;
So you could be a devil with the rest,
And leave your angel scorn. I never saw
A good man yet, but goodness shut his heart.
Perfection's blind. Fill me the world with sinners,
Drunkards, whores: you'll see the night made merry,
Every street a carnival of laughter;
Day will rise, drenched in mists of wine,
And evening dance its shadows to the song

Of lute-tongued lovers; all the men of earth
Will smile on sin and wink with understanding.
This were a jolly world . . .
Michael: A jolly world, indeed.
Come Sampson, come to bed. Night yawns.
Come, come, I say; you've done enough. To bed!

Sampson: Talk of jealous lovers! Take note, world!
A lover's nothing to a sober man
Who looks on drunkards' pleasure. Lechery
That wants and is afraid, has built the bonds
Of marriage, branding freedom with the name
Of whore; and riches knit a veil of laws
To cloak cupidity; and now at last
The dull-eyed, dark-spleened prohibitioners
Stand up before the tipplers of the world
And tell us: "Drink is sin; abhor it you!"
I'll hear no such commands; I'll be most free.
Now, Michael, stand apart. Applaud our pleasure;
Let us dance a round.

(*They gather in a ring, drinking, singing.*)

Revelers: Hey, hey, Kathusalum,
Kathusalum, Kathusalum;
Hey, hey, Kathusalum,
The daughter of the Rabbi.
In days of yore there lived a maid,
Who carried on a roaring trade,
A prostitute
Of ill repute,
The daughter of the Rabbi.

Hey, hey, Kathusalum,
The harlot of Jerusalem;
Hey, hey, Kathusalum,
The daughter of the Rabbi. (*To which Sampson adds:*)

Sampson: Fill the cup beyond the brim'
Teach the belly how to swim;
Drink, drink, drink, drink 'er down.

(*Michael drives out the revelers; would lead
Sampson to bed.*)

Sampson: Here's a sight to tickle Dagon.
Here, here, look down, old king of darkness;
Look down on me:
Sampson, Sampson, the hope of the Jews,
The might of Jehovah, the light of the world;
Sampson, Sampson, hope of the Jews,
Led like a crippled child!
Am I blind, Michael? Am I lame?
Speak, Michael, am I blind? Why lead me then?
Let go, old friend, let go. I'll stand alone.
I'll predicate.
Fetch all the flop-eared fools of Philistía.
Quick, bring them in; stand off and let them stare.
Sampson's a dish to burn their watered tongues.
Come, you men of Gaza, hearken to
My words. I'll preach what is to come:
The Lord our God is a great God,
And yet he moves in a mysterious way.
And wine makes glad the hearts of men
And brings them laughter and dance and song.
But look, you fools of Gaza, who laugh to see me so:
I, who smile today, will frown on you tomorrow.
Wine is a dream of night; but the will of God must be done.
Go, then, and tell your friends to seek out caves
                    tomorrow.
Say I, whose birth the angel told,
Will come in angel fury . . .
Say this, and bid them fear.

   In the lonely time of February '38 I had written a maudlin
fable about love-disillusion. Then, April 26-27 about 2:00 AM, when I
was too sleepy to do anything but rhyme, I turned it into a ballad, think-
ing Dalilah might hear it from the Vision when she was doubting her
love. Vision leads off: "I'll tell a tale, Dalilah: Long ago . . .":

When I was young and happy,
In the morning of my day,
I walked along the forest
And I heard a lover say:

"I live a night of winter
And a day of burning flame,
In the cold of moral blackness
Or the heat of lusting shame.

"I seek a lasting morning
With its beams wide flung;
The sun above the mountains
Ever springing never sprung;

"The rose forever budding,
Never shattered, never blown;
Delight forever flitting,
Ever present, never flown."

The sound went through the forest
And the leaves turned pale;
Till an answer came returning
Like the sighing of a gale:

"Of joy, lover,
The time is never
That lovers ever
Seek to discover."

And the leaves fell in the forest,
And my hair grew gray,
And I slowly wandered homeward
By a snow-covered way.

In a note I proposed to expand this to a dream romance, as in Chaucer's *Book of the Duchess* or even Langland's *Piers*. By December it had spawned my (also fragmentary) "Triumph of Death," turning Gothic allegory toward the coming Nazi war. (See later "Withered Is the Garland of War" and "Triumph of Death.")

After the Solesmes Abbey Easter with Simone Weil and her companion, to whom I presented my Dalilah fragments, the latter, joined by her mother, had invited me—on my return through Paris toward Oxford—to favor them at a friend's dinner party. At the stipulated time, I found the place and was welcomed. There were several introductions during which cultured ladies offered me a cheek. An affable dame, when I kissed one cheek, counseled that I should always kiss both. When I asked, "Pourquoi?" I was struck by her answer: "Judas à baissé seulement l'une!" It was as if one would caution: "No treachery." Poor Parisian liberals—often converted Jews—a few years later, how likely some may have faced betrayal by the Nazi occupiers of their land and city.

Before I left, headed for my hotel, I tried, while thanking the hostess, to express (having drunk good wine before and during the meal) my need to reverse the miracle of Cana by turning wine into water. I stumbled for the polite French words: *toilette, cabinet, lavatoir,* even trying German *Abort* and Italian *ritirata,* to her puzzlement, until she caught on and hit the spot: "Vous voulez pisser, Monsieur, n'est pas?" I affirmed her premise and was guided to the convenience.

So, relieved, I set off, with repeated thanks, on my journey.

At Oxford, by the end of April 1938, with fond reading of Spenser and Drayton's "Nymphidia," plus years of *A Midsummer Night's Dream,* my poor wits overflowed again—this time in Spenserian stanzas, which, like the sonnets, seemed automatic. And conceiving a poem at least as long as Keats's *Fall of Hyperion*—what could I entitle the ten stanzas but "Prologue to a Fantasy"?—I wrote my parents of my sensuous joy as I penned the second, which I thought the best: how in the closure of my college room, and for the fifteen minutes I was scribbling it, I seemed to see and hear everything I wrote, the moon on the moss where I lay, the music, the pale forms dancing around me. When my father showed the copy to Walker Percy's father, William Alexander Percy, who was Greenville's Edwardian post-Romantic poet, he said he would have liked, in his youth, to have received such a vision. Let "The Prologue" be part of this record:

> In every world where poets' fancy lives
> There breathes the breath of spring; night meadows seem
> The haunt of fairies; for the poet gives
> Another life to insubstantial dream.
> Therefore in forests when the parting gleam
> Of mortal day has stretched out all the sky,
> Strange sights appear. At first with quickening beam
> The magic moon endews each petaled eye;
> Until that touch each one in filmy sleep must lie.
>
> Then blossoms open and from every core
> Of sweetness comes a shining form, more light
> Than woodland odors, while soft voices pour

Enchanted music in the cup of night.
Veils sweep the ground; and now the living sprite
Of mist breathes dew across the creeping thyme;
Leaves glow like candles; and to this delight
Comes sparkling Oberon with silver chime:
The fairies follow him, and flowers bend in time.

Among dim woods they move with subtle tread,
Tipping the loam like raindrops everywhere.
Some frailer still, of pallid star beams bred,
Incline along the regions of the air—
Soft as the down that summer breezes bear,
When dandelions unfold their feathered seed,
While green boughs wave above and flowers wear
New-woven colors, rich as cherub's weed—
With so much joy and lightness fly this fairy breed.

And ride upon the wings of middle air
So high that earth below, to their small sight,
Seems like a vision (or a village-fair,
Whose lamps the moving clouds disclose at night
To some lone watcher on a mountain height,
When darkness shapes the valley to appear
Another sky, where other stars give light);
So seem their far companions shining clear
To these high wanderers, that through shadows down
        ward peer.

Yet not so high they venture but the boughs
Bend still above their flight a shady zone:
Dark knitted spheres whose rustling voice endows
The dim vast air beneath with legends blown
On fairy zephyrs, played in fairy tone;
And to these tiny phantoms sailing so,
Night's leafy canopy seems vastly grown
Into a vaulted sky, whose reaches show
A cosmos spread above, a universe below.

To them the sad recesses of the leaves
Are dusky realms of magic and romance—
Faint otherworlds, where restless chaos heaves
Upon the bed of night. They coast askance

From these, intending down the dim expanse:
As when a host of bombers bend their way
Across beleaguered cities, while the dance
Of morning stars slows to the tune of day;
Bright in the waning night, they wheel their bold array;

Or like some cluster of assembled suns
That roam the curved immensity of space,
Where each perhaps draws whirling as it runs
A shadowy planet locked in close embrace;
There, breathing noxious air in noyous place,
Pale bulbous creatures move their wondering eyes,
Or in Cretaceous jungles saurians race,
Or on some dying world men old and wise,
Grown sad in wisdom, watch the deathly cold surise;

So fairies think their forms, but human eye
Would more conceive them like an open drove
Of woodland fireflies floating gently by
To lose themselves forever in the grove;
Even such as lure a lonely child to rove
Far in the forest as the dusk creeps on,
Till in some glade of alien shadows wove,
The white owl beats slow wings across the lawn;
He stops and darkling stands, like Night's affrighted fawn.

Thus blown about the world of brake and bog,
They take the paths that men can never know,
Plunging like stars in nebulae of fog,
With joy in joyful mystery they go.
And where night mushrooms thrust from earth below,
The denser fairies lead their dances on,
In moss beds treading till the shadows show
The coming freshness of the summer dawn;
Back then to flowers they creep, and all at once are gone.

The sun waves pound in light on earthly shores;
The moon, the stars, the blossoms quietly fade;
The cereus draws its alabaster doors;
The angel trumpets melt into the shade.
The nightly songs are silent. In the glade
A stillness hangs perceptive. Then a gleam

Of feathered scarlet on the leafy braid
Of trees, a trilled-out song, the crescent beam
Of day, and fishers' voices on the far off stream.

During the next days I forged ahead, turning to the elves and gnomes of the Fall, planning the Fantasy itself of their Hallowe'en battle to take the woods from the fays:

And rule—save on that hallowed eve wherein
The Prince of Peace was born; no goblin then
Affrights the world with misbegotten din;
But angels such as told good will to men
Turn fiery flight above mid-forest glen,
To wash the dusk with song. There soft below
The wondering Mother kneels, and in dark den
Of thatch near-by, close huddled oxen low;
While shepherds come with cherry bobs and mistltoe.

There I break off the "Fantasy" with my manifest love of 15th-century art and music. Had not Marcellus, early in *Hamlet*, assured us: "So hallowed, and so gracious, is that time"?

At this remove I can scarcely understand how in my third Oxford year I not only did all the research (days in the Bodleian or, sometimes, the British Library) plus the composition and writing of a book-length thesis, studying and editing Edward Fairfax, translator of Tasso, writer of pastoral poems, etc.; yet, on my own account, filled a notebook of verse, from short lyrics to long symbolic visions (unfinished, it is true; but too long to be more than sampled here). My mother and sister had come over to join me for the Summer of '38 on Italian travels. Mildred, too, her husband having died of pneumonia the Winter before, could join us in Italy, and then (on a widow's allowance) take an Oxford room not far from the apartment she found for me in the stone gardener's cottage of Worcester College. Trivial love lyrics record the change from her U.S. delay to her amorous presence that Fall. One of the delay poems uses a theme from the sonnet sequence:

FALSE EQUITY (Summer 1938)

You, who are clothed in loveliness
And beauty's banner bear,
Yet are not fair,
But where

You pity, and your looks a snare
For devils, but as you bless
With happiness,
And dress
The wound you gave in heartlessness.
No more
Do I implore
But justice, to restore
The peace you took from me before,
And gain, for right, the praise of kindliness.

This next, from after her coming, versifies my love-content in tricky stanzas of rhymes and off-rhymes:

HOW FAIR SHE BE (November 1938)

Fair are the maids of Castalie that dancing go
About the sacred fountain, under the shadow
The loved leaves of Phoebus throw.

And fair those three that Eris' apple stirred, to show
Them naked for an Idan swain, and sorrow
Brought with that far Greekish foe.

Fair too the quiet goddess that before the dawn
Stoops down to dewy Latmos, pays devotion
There, and sadly wanders on.

Yet more is fair to me a fair that's fairly mine,
And I more blessed with her than Jove with Aegin'
Or Dis adorned with Proserpine.

From the Summer had come a two-page poem on Paestum, with its "Windwashed temples jutting to the sea," as compared with the loved 15th-century art of Florence—"Arno-hills' eternal day . . . The cockle-curl of Aphrodite's shell"—thus attempting a sort of celebration of cyclical history:

Paestum, be still a guide and canon of the way
Where grace has passed, and when time has unfurled
New banners, should again return . . .
And O you gods of beauty, that have seen
The rise of Athens and the fall of Rome,

Teach me to bear the failings of this time
And weakness of my rhyme,
With patience, knowing well, that fresh to clean
The fields for wonder, and the wearied loam
For growth to purify, we fall, and all
Devices with us, ending being there,
Yea, even where
Beginning springs anew, and mending
Spirit, fast as our rich robes are rending.

My stance all that time was one of curious complexity, reared over opposites. There was no road to a fresh Age of Joy, but through those late-cycle wars and destruction, which I abhorred, thinking to oppose them with pacifism, as of early Christianity, the Sermon on the Mount, or, in our time, Gandhi. But the road to Christianity had led through a Rome whose imperial pomp also depressed me. Christianity itself had espoused the graveward descent of the catacombs, "enervate Origen," etc. Whereas my Oxford writings had robed themselves in Renaissance (even Romantic) sensuous form—along with Blake's radical revolt: "Energy is the only life and is from the body . . . Energy is Eternal Delight"—was all too deep in me to be denied; moreover, my Virginia Ragged Mountain forest walks partook of Thoreau and free America: "Olympus is but the outside of earth everywhere." And: "Not shrink philosophy into a Stoic vault or Christian tomb."

What I had yet to capture was *Symbolic History*, an affirming and dramatic polyvalent suspension (by multimedia quotations of thought, poetry, the visual arts, and music)—of everything that has shaped and articulated human culture. But by my third Oxford year, I was just assembling the huge body of material for such a slide-audio, then video, now digital epic. So these final pages of the Oxford record cannot avoid poems fragmentary and puzzling.

Fall 1938, as Hitler advanced the crisis-throttle toward the capture of the Sudetens and then of Czechoslovakia, I wrote a four-page poem: "Withered Is the Garland of the War." Upon its "Fruits of blessing: In autumn season, time of grapes / and grain" falls the "curse of feared war." That leads to prayer, and so "to the dew of rest . . . a sleep of dreams." But the dreams are of war itself: "thunder, flash of fire, plague, rain of poison . . . I fought a troubled age, I died . . . But rose in spirit . . . from where I lay . . . to view again the ravaged works of man. . . ." Once more the dreamer's substance fades; again he wakes to a tetrameter close of "time's immense war-frighted globe . . .":

Wasted effort, pain misborne
and ill-called sacrifice. . . . Not real
nor true life is, but as a worn
told tale, and I, one dead, look on
at things to come, nor sad nor stirred,
but empty, tired of ages gone
ere birth to death, and dumb ere heard.
God, grant earth new dawn.

On poetic grounds I later canceled a final religious statement of pacifism:

The voice of the lord God, declared unto his servant,
  who was in sorrow:
There is but one way to fight evil: with faith; one way
  to prove faith:
In martyrdom. Let this be the sword of the righteous.

Here, from the same crisis, is a short metric treatment, "On Our Last War":

Its waste was not of wealth but charity;
For the wealth, burnt there, had it been given,
Might have forbidden that war to be;

And that war's loss was not of life but love;
Had martyrs so many died for truth and kindness
As there for hate, what world might we now see?

By hate we have won hate, greed, greed, war, war.
Can submission kill more, or sacrifice waste more,
Or peace cost more, or achieve less than these?

Yet I also treated the same subject with a grotesque scoff at Cromwell:

"Trust in God," said Cromwell,
"And keep your powder dry."
"God is love," said Jesus,
"And love's humility."
What God was Cromwell trusting?
Belial the black, say I.

He drew the sword of anger,
And by that sword we die.

One, "On Armistice Day," blames the church-blessing of war-
riors; here a stanza:

> Preachers, how lightly, how sprightly,
> You sing: "By Christ in peace they are."
> Against Christ's word:
> "Who draws the sword . . ."
> Such priests mar
> The faith of prophets, and belie
> The sanctity of Calvary.

I skip others such as "Vision," "Martyrs" (False), etc. But a
four-page Gothic allegory, "The Triumph of Death," may be worth
sampling. With its sprung four-foot lines, mixed iamb and trochees,
rhymed in couplets as called for, it held me, a week or more, from my
research. Also the dream, shifting from John's Patmos to a hunt, based
on the great Pisan fresco marred in the last war—its corpses changed
to a deer, which, killed, becomes the Lamb of the Van Eyck Brussels
Altar—moved me at the time.

> A life I lived in Patmos; found
> Me in the woods, rock hills around,
> October leaves tossed on the ground,
> Bare limbs and trees with first frost crowned.
> The earth was dark, dawn in the sky;
> I heard the blown horn and the cry
> Of hounds, and knew that here the King
> Octavien would chase the deer . . .
> Louder the horn: "Hunt's up!" And I . . .
> Pight on a white horse in a blaze
> Of red, pursued, hard sped, a maze
> Of leaping deer . . . One, up a gorge dull
> As Golgotha, place of the skull,
> Turned, head up, and without fear
> Or anger waited death. He fell, and wet
> With blood and water all that plot
> Of ground. We came to the game, when lo!
> A lamb, new slain, yet living so,
> Received the voiced chant of a robed host:

"The Prince of Peace is come and home has brought
his lost."

At the end of the same notebook I find a modern "Shepherd's Calendar": Colin and Jankin, crazed as Charlie Chaplin from screwing nuts on cars. Also there is the start of a verse "Autobiography," noting my birth at the 1916 peak of the first Great War, and my writing at the 1939 likely start of the Second. I omit those. But we would not have plumbed the range of my twenty-year-old fancy without my attempt to decipher scribbles of a take-off on Milton: "Paradise Well Lost." The Dedication seems to anticipate today's rap-rhyme:

> To write my book a florid dedication
> Cannot procure its goodness more ovation,
> Or find its badness meed of commendation,
> Yet vanity must curtsy to temptation;
> So I begin without more conversation:
> I dedicate to all the whole creation,
> In order bound by Jahwe's regulation,
> To New Jerusalem's golden consecration,
> And sinning Man's complete regeneration.

The main text follows:

PARADISE WELL LOST (Oxford, 1939)

> Of the first great fall of erring man,
> (Who has fallen since the world began
> With charming regularity)
> I sing with modest clarity.
> I pray you if my song be coarse,
> Forgive me, I am very hoarse.
> Or if my tone suggest a frog,
> Condemn my parents of the bog.
> (For I have studied evolution,
> As well as Biblical effusion,
> And both of them I say are true;
> Deride them not, I conjure you.)
>
> Like Milton I invoke the Muse:
> (If you dislike it, best excuse;
> It's in the epic recipe,

And how to skip it baffles me):
O Muse, extend thy ulna to my aid,
Nor let the succoring radius be delayed,
Till mighty matters be to me conveyed.
I fall upon lean days; my powers fade.
O strengthen me that I may show displayed
The petulance of man, in goodness made,
But sunk through sin and sorrowfully decayed.
Enough of this. Six lines will serve:
It's all the Muses can deserve;
Besides, pentameter breaks the meter;
I'll try next time to be discreeter.
I had thought to begin in the very beginning,
Before the birth of death through sinning,
With the perfect all-enfolding God,
Who made the heavens and made the sod
(How heavily these verses plod.)—
In him no evil was discerned;
Whence evil came, I have not learned;
But I had scarcely started thus,
When Satan made a monstrous fuss,
And said with short perversity:
"Skip all that and begin with me."
So I have done as I was told
(So Milton did in days of old).

As this was droning on with rhymes of "survey" and "sway,"
"his throne," "and groan," it seems that Beelzebub broke in:

I am the great God Beelzebub,
As big as a barrel, as round as a tub;
I'm a beer-drinkin', smoke-stinkin' whale of a man,
And I follow the Devil as best I can. *Etc.*

What the "Etc." was meant to imply has been entirely
scratched out. What follows on the next page is an almost illegible
penning of short-lined Skeltonics—a bawdy bash on Sin, leading to the
Flood. To save space I set it up like prose, but with slashes to mark line
ends:

With many a scrub / and wanton rub / They began to
hug, / Mug to mug / In a kind of love, / Till each

belly did bub / With rub-a-dub-dub / On the belly
beneath or the belly above: / Sword in sheath, /
Pulpit-Jack, / Loaf in a sack, / The wedding ring /
And shake-that thing, / Are a kind of image, / To con-
vey this scrimmage, / This lusty battle; / But Tittle-
Taddle / Ran up to the Lord: / Says: "Look you, God;
they're at it hard; / Throw down fire and burn 'em up
quick!" / Says God: "Fire's short; but rain's the
trick." / The thunder bust in a hell-of-a-pother; / The
people shouted: "What a bother! / And look, look,
floods of water! / Holy Mother! I'd take it drier, if I
had my druther!"

Here page and text break off, though not without reminding
me of a pagan doggerel that popped into my head my first day at Exeter
College, and still lurks there sixty-four years later. I had visited the
library to consult some Gilbert Murray translations of Greek plays, hav-
ing left mine with my mother. A passage led me to the loves of Zeus.
What rattled my skull was:

ZEUS ON THE LOOSE

Saturn once I heard
Speak to Jove this word:
"You rotter, you prodigal toper;
You robber, you rape-a Europa!"
Jove replied with a nod:
"Necessity's my prod;
Danae denies de ninth;
and what's eight times to a god?
Later I lay you my Leda;
but now my business is greater:
I 'ope that I open Io!"
With Priapus I saw him go.

Finally from the crop of the bawdy verse, which has slid
from my tongue or frolicked from this pen over the years, I give some
samples. At Oxford, the Lady Madrigalists would sing, in a romantic
musical setting, a rather inane poem by Coleridge's poor son Hartley:

The lake lay blue beneath the hill;
O'er it as I looked there flew

Across the waters cold and still
A bird whose wings were palest blue.

For which I hatched a coda:

And as he flew he dropped a pill;
You can deny it if you will,
But surely it is very true:
The pill itself was palest blue.

(A pity the composer did not have that quatrain.)

Limericks were much quoted at the Oxford Sherry, etc. Parties. Nobody knew who wrote or revised them. I have variously quoted the one that Rodney Baine, my best friend, and I made as we began work on the third-year B. Litt. Thesis:

A Rhodes scholar wrote a thesis
On the nature and forms of feces;
It was only four words,
"All feces is turds";
The examiner tore it to pieces.

Why not unburden my memory of its retained dirty deftest, some of which I have touched up a little:

A man whose name was Perkin
Was always a-jerkin his gurkin
Said his wife to him: Perkin,
With jerkin your gurkin.
You're shirkin your firkin, get workin!

Next, two with English place names: first, Broome:

A fairy and a Lesbian of Broome
Agreed to share a room.
They spent the whole night
In a hell of a fight:
Who does what and with what and to whom?

Second, Chichester:

There was a babe of Chichester
Who made the saints in their niches stir.
When she paced the aisle
Her caudal style
Made the Bishop of Chichester's britches stir.

Or American, Cape Cod:

A pregnant girl of Cod
Thought she'd been raped by God,
Yet 'twas not the Almighty
Who lifted her nightie,
But Roger, the lodger—the sod!

Now of a friend's daughter at a Catholic college:

A charmer named Vanessa
Thought to consult the professor.
The force of his lesson—
Undressin', caressin'—
Sent Vanessa to her confessor.

Almost last, of a neglected craftsman:

An artisan named Dean
Invented a swyving machine;
'Twas both concave and convex,
Could handle either sex
'Twas a whiz of a swyving machine.

So to close—why not?—with something musical:

There was a Scot named Jock,
Who tied a gut string to his cock;
When he had an erection
He'd play a selection
From Johann Sebastian Bach.

The last thing I wrote at Oxford was neither bawdry nor parody, though the title, "To His Fair Mistress," reminding one of Marvell and the deepening of the whole "Gather ye rosebuds" provocation, might suggest as much, the poem somehow goes beyond that, since these six stanzas of six lines each, which Neville Coghill took up for his June '39 issue of *Stapeldon*, not only modernize the form by half rhymes and accent shifts, but turn the old love-plea to a broken search for truth, typical of my darker drift that year. As poetry, it may be my subtlest and best of 1939; so let it occupy the last Oxford page of this Millennial Harvest:

TO HIS FAIR MISTRESS (January 5, 1939)

When old age summons you into his graceless
Presence, lady, to grant you livery
Of a long and hard service, and you restless
Do roam his palace; seeing the vanity
Of gold there crusted, you will say sadly,
"Here is the gold of my tresses, long sought madly."

And over the wide bowls of pearls there hoarded,
You will lean complaining: "Behold the limitless
Wealth of my smiling, now lost and destroyed."
Delightful mirrors seeing: "Here lifeless
Are the rays of my glancing, and this vesture
Of smooth ivory my white hands texture."

Across the keys where other young hands lightly
Move, serving apprentice, look, a sparkle
Runs. Is not this life the freedom, lady,
Once of your body's motion? And the rustle
Of silks, too, and the clavecin's sound, your laughter?
And are not these, things lost and longèd after?

Where are they now, lady, the lures applauded,
Or what have left you but loss and mourning?
Is not the perfume of this place distillèd
From your breath, better days? True, my darling,
Age hath a rich house; but all his trappings
Are bought with youth, and then possessed with
weepings.

Spend then your beauties, lady, while the ardor
Of new coinage yet holds them lovely, making
For age this answer: "Long have I lived in pleasure."
Counsels so the songster. Yea, and what yielding

Comes of a spent harvest but hunger, even
On the wind of whose plenty grief is driven?

No, not of those jewels will you have comfort
Then, nor more of the vain pleasures remembered
That now you could take with me—in that desert
A mirage only, where palms are seen. Dissevered
From all hope stand, therefore; leave off your fair
Pride, and ragly clothed, seek truth somewhere.

Charles, Nona, and Mildred.

2. MIDWEST THROUGH IOWA (1939-45)

Still England, Summer of 1939, while I awaited the date set for the oral exam on my Fairfax thesis, Mildred and I cycled the island on a tandem (tantrum, sometimes), south to Salisbury, then north past Durham to the Roman Wall and back by the lakes to Oxford. There I picked up another degree (my fourth), and together we embarked on a German boat for New York. Half way over, the captain was ordered to return. He wheeled about—travelers alarmed, sure of war. But after what seemed a long hour, came the official countermand: "Go ahead, discharge your passengers, then speed back." We surmised that Hitler had delayed on Poland—but for how long?

     Landed, Mildred and I took the train to Greenville and the columned brick house of my parents' and my own youth. There we were married in the downstairs reception hall and drove the family car south over the Delta for a honeymoon night in the Leroy Percy State Park. In a cabin in a cypress swamp, our first child (a daughter, to be named Nona for my mother) was conceived. Of course the birth would occur the following Spring, in Carlinville, Illinois, hick town of a junior college where I would be teaching English—the job my Oxford friend, Rodney Baine (not then married or pressed to teach), had passed on to me. Meanwhile, returned to Greenville, next morning, in our second-story front bedroom, we heard from beyond the porch columns a newsboy yelling: POLAND INVADED, WAR DECLARED! For us, soon after, it was that two-year Blackburn College, unlikely place for a world-historical poetic aspirant.

     The stress of our union, jammed in a drear $35 apartment, seems recorded in contrasting poems of the Fall. One—looking back to an Oxford concert in a showy classical hall, October of 1938, our last year abroad—became in Illinois a dark Spenglerian brooding of the conscious mind; while the second—a playful "marriage" duet, dreamed to Mozartean music, as from *Don Giovanni*, the words, without music, scribbled as I waked—seems a subconscious escapist sport of the two. Begin with the cyclical, in which, as in Anglo-Saxon poems, later barbarians will wonder at our ruins, as our forebears wondered at the ruins of Rome:

AT A CONCERT (written October 1939)

When these walls, ivy-covered, stand in ruins,
Gray to the night of faintly altered stars,
And men beholding strike the savage harp

And sing the work of heroes, giants of old,
They will not know that in this crusted hall,
Where music wails the Specter of a Rose,
A man of peace leagued with an age of wars
Welcomed destruction, darkness, and the Plague
To find again—strength without compromise.

Next, the almost anti-marriage dream:

CHURCHWARD ROAD (November 1939)

John: A stile and a grove and a field beyond
(The field is full of clover),
A shadowed walk by the lilied pond,
Two miles in all, not over;

We'll come to the church at dusk of day
And set the bells a-ringin.
We'll have the parson wed us, May,
And home we'll come with singin.
Away, away,
To wed, to bed,
And home we'll come with singin.

May: Over the stile I'm with you then,
And to the grove beyond.
As I've tried before I'll try again
To pass the field and the pond.

But the road is hard for lovers to keep
In the leaf-bowered wood;
The field is soft, the clover deep;
The banks of the pond are good,
For sheep, for sheep,
Or lovers to sleep,
The banks of the pond are good.

John: I grant we've come this way before
And sung the marriage song;
We've tried to reach the parson's door,
But always stopped too long.

First we barely crossed the stile
Before we fell a-kissin;
Kissed a while and blissed a while,
And at the church were missin.
Fair, fair,
Sweet was the air,
When we at the church were missin.

May: The second night we reached the grove,
The third the field of clover,
Saw the sky turn pale above,
The darkness almost over.

Tonight we're on the road again,
But look, the moon shines for us;
Sure, we'll tarry as we've done;
We've still the pond before us.

Both: Yet let us sing,
For love's the thing,
And we've still the pond before us.

At Blackburn College, however, we had some good, hard-working, self-help students, whom I taught like a geyser, but so independently, that the two women who tried to boss their small department (me) luckily geysered me out. Yet it remained a crucial year, since Kodachrome, released that same 1939, launched me on a life-calling, with an Argus camera, beginning to photograph available art materials, toward a color-slide collection (now around 40,000) for my multimedia *Symbolic History*. Indeed, as soon as I had slides, Fall '39, I was thrusting my "correlations" on all new friends and visitors—Kodachromes, especially of the Gothic and Renaissance, projected, while I played the rare records I had brought from Europe, adding quotations from thought and poetry of each period. The Illinois state librarian, hearing of what I was doing, set up an adult class in Springfield, where for six months of the Winter and Spring I put together a sequence (from Egypt down) of the cultural epic to be expanded and enriched through the rest of my life.

Also my Blackburn dismissal would boost me to a bolder spread of the Prairie—Ames, Iowa—where I was to find intellectual friends: refugee Germans, with whom I could read Goethe and Hölderlin and speak the language; then a colleague, Richard Wendell, became a companion for Dante's *Divina Commedia* (an elegy to Wendell is in my first book). Other friends would meet for French: Racine to Baudelaire, plus talk; while least expected, Quaker economist, Kenneth Boulding, was prime for St. Augustine in Latin. Moreover, my scores of Early Music, plus my Dolmetch recorders, would attract student singing groups; last, Stringfellow Barr, with whom I was still in touch, had already sent me the St. John's list of Great Books, so I could dive deep into philosophy, perfecting my own Heraclitean celebrations of complementarity and ingredient causality. (Such will later appear as prose "Meditations"—voicing the poetic soul of nature and science, even of physics and cosmology.) But I have jumped forward from Illinois. There, as in the last crisis year abroad, my creative center remained a complex tangle—though darkened. On the furrowed flats of that corn belt ("Low light in the land of the living,/ have ye, plainsman, luckless plight"), it somehow seemed I had slipped to the bottom half of the world, while the European side I had come to love was being terribly tanked and bombed. Of course mind and spirit had still to dream toward peace and think toward truth, though under such handicap as shadowed my poems of the time.

It must have been when the "department" told me that the assigned paperback anthology (which I thought journalistic trash) was to be taught and that I should give up those mimeos of so-called Great Poems I had been providing for my classes—it must have been then that I scratched a little piece called "The Liberal Lost":

> Caught in a festered calm we shall go down,
> Old rotted hulls of ships that never sailed.

Or, from the same late Fall:

SOUL'S QUESTION

> And will it still be thus,
> The long nostalgia,
> Purposeless of living,
> Still in our death as lifetime?
> Will nothing come of it, our hunger;
> But the promise alone stand for fulfillment,
> And for the act, desire?

Also, after a two-hour faculty meeting, I wrote a diatribe in April 1940 (quoting Leopardi) "The World Is Mud," "Fango è'l Mondo,": "Nothing achieved—a feast on wind," concluding with my judgment of everything: war, society, etc. Plus a quatrain:

> What intellection rules
> In fancied paradise,
> Where earthly wise are fools
> And all the fools grown wise.

Three poems, however, from later in that school year turn conflicts of weather to dramas of spirit within *Symbolic History*. "The First Vision" (early 1940) explains itself:

> Into the bleak north of blown snow
> Breaks sunlight golden from the rim of dark,
> Melts in the drip of waters flashed to streams,
> Breathes up bending grass and feathered boughs,
> Sprung at a wing-beat to unearthly green,
> A glimpse of apples and one rush of song.
> Then down to night the brief sun plunging
> Draws the curtain, and a wind-swept snow
> Drifts back with polar whine across bare stones.

The other two (densened by Gerard Manley Hopkins) may require such clarification as I sent my mother. But let the poem precede comment:

> ON THE PROMISE OF PLENTY (c. 1940)
>
> Birth or death is as who judges it:
> So they that called the spreading steel decay
> (Of whom was I) turned to the Word,
> Believing that must flesh as flesh must fall;
> Thus of late winter we made early spring.
> But now the winds veer back and render us
> New harbingers of many weeks of cold,
> Which those not of our party hail with praise,
> Scheming to freeze a chrysolite of clay.
> But yet how bleak to us that dreamed past them,
> The long blue shadows of their mid-March snow.

I had not then, nor have I since, joined either Party or Church; nevertheless, from my high school days, when I independently re-invented socialism and won first prize in Mississippi for a Depression-brewed socialist oration; or later, from Virginia through Oxford and beyond, when I pored over the Testaments in Greek, Latin, Luther, and the King James—saw them enacted in great art and heard them set to music—I was dramatizing a complementarity of spiritual against material sway— the dynamic of my philosophy of history, as of the above poem.

The first line seems to grant a relativity of judgment, although I soon change sides: "I turned to the Word" (expecting a mystical thaw). But the symbolic weather veers, while world-flesh (whether capitalist or socialist) purposes to freeze a chrysolite (*Othello*, 5, 2, 43) of material well-being. Yet can cars and refrigerators (plus war) compensate for a mystical loss?

The next poem, a sonnet, is entitled: "Nostalgia of the Past and Future":

> Our late wind-clattered nights drive back the mind
> To leafing days of either self or Age.
> Where seems now beauty such, such peace we find,
> As had that been, time would have eased his rage,
> One moment soared to sure eternity,
> And we to this dissolving had not come.
> For even as some look forward and foresee
> (Unwittingly) longing's rest and home;
> Others invoke some golden past; both call
> Hope fact, call act, all not earth (spirit only) shows;
> So goes our stream source—hungry, mourns the fall,
> As if rise, fall, on earth, were of its life at all.
> Sun, moon, stars run, and fire, for rest eternal;
> Thus man, and yet thinks, fool, his hopes diurnal.

In sending this to my mother, I wrote an explanation, or re-statement:

> All nature, including man, longs for the infinite resolution
> (union with God, etc.) and therefore moves (lines 13 and 14).
> But since final grace is hardly found in the actual, man endows
> the partial with such properties, thinking what he seeks will
> be achieved in time (is diurnal). This error is of two sorts:
> in autumn nights of a private life, or of an age, one may look
> back to youth or to an early period (Renaissance, say, lines
> 1-2), investing that past with the beauty and peace each soul
> seeks, forgetting that had it been truly such, its blessing would
> not have been so subject to decay. Others, looking forward,
> may bathe a common future in eternal rays, calling "fact" a

social state they hope for, "act" what only spirit can bestow. Such are the modes of spiritual nostalgia: of the past and of the future.

With the drive to war threatening that Christian pacifism I had leaned toward from Virginia, through Oxford, and into the Nazi-Communist confusion of 1939-40, I wrote the third of such dialectic poems, this one contrasting the New Mystics of our time with the Old of the Fifth Century—ours often facing a choice of war or confinement:

> When you turned, Augustine, from that sad press
> Of Coloseums crashing, vast the domes
> Of rending Thermae, you found marked the road
> Through desert to the mountain—
> Its wound-assuaging fountain.
> Yours to follow; ours the weightier load:
> To be that voice of one in the wilderness,
> "Prepare the way," and mark it with our bones.

Was my "philosophy of paradox" almost ready to shift from Augustine's mystic reduction (as I had entitled a poem: "From the Arrogance of Humanism, O Lord, Deliver Us") toward a "field philosophy" aimed at describing and synthesizing (as Leibnitz did) man, earth, and cosmos? If so, the change to the spatial and human expanse of Iowa was timely. (Though my Iowa stay would hardly open with the bolder scene or the stimulus of European friends I have prematurely hinted at.)

Life was narrow. My first job in Iowa would be teaching freshman English to over a hundred mostly rural youths, each writing an essay a week—pages I had to mark, grade, and return for student revision. Moreover, there would be trouble before the Fall would bring me even to that.

I have anticipated the spring 1940 birth of Nona, our first child. For Mildred it was a terribly drawn-out and agonizing delivery, followed by a desperate post-partum depression, requiring weeks of sanatorium care, while my mother came to help me—she and I taking baby Nona to Greenville to be tended until Mildred could join us. Next I was under attack for a talk given in my father's Bible class, setting the Sermon on the Mount against our world of radical (or do-nothing) politics—the barber shops and town buzzing the next day with: "Young Bell, Communist, Nazi, Pacifist and Nigger Lover" (the last two accusations not unfounded). Then a Klansman, his ranks legion, spread the gossip to Iowa, so that I had a letter from the dean at Ames, abrogating my employment there. Only when my father took me, with a text of the talk, to his Mississippi Supreme Court friends, who phoned Iowa State, did I receive a cautious note reconfirming my position. (For the mob climax of this encounter, see *Delta Return*, "The Revivalist," with its narrative comment.)

Late Summer—our household goods, books, and records en route from Illinois to Ames—Mildred, baby Nona, and I detrained for a week in Chicago, I to copy early music scores in Newbury Library, racing my Oxford bike there on the Outer Drive. From those August 1940 days, two poems of post-Depression, mid-western realism issued from my pen. Here they are, in the order of composition:

CHICAGO BEACH

One whelm of life this beach is, and on me,
As with a surge of waves, breaks joyously
In light and energy.
The winds that cry in every corner, where
The block-cut stones cubistic lie, must wear
All objects clean and bare;
For so they stand: rocks bright with painted names,
Waves and their spray, clouds; the white sand claims
A kinship with the lake it frames.
All things are one, one substance, by the wind
Made sharp, honed to ecstasy; the bend
Of bodies is a blend
With all else here, black bodies carelessly
Stretched on the stones, or nuzzling fitfully
In love's enormity.

AN ENCOUNTERED BUM

It was in Chicago last night I met him:
The Scarecrow man; he haunts each turn. "Buddy,
A nickel, gimme a nickel for a bed."
"Where do you find those nickel beds?" I asked him,
Groping for my coins. "They ain't much beds,"
He whined; "But sure, they beats the ground." I had
Quarters only. "Well, take this," I said.
"And good night." "A first class bed!" he cried,
Hustling off. That night, on the train,
I gave the like sum for a pillow, which, late-

Waking, I could only beat, and find as hard
As this thought-question: "How, with both quarters,
Might the tramp have splurged? By joining, maybe,
An evening meal to a first-class bed? And would that
Have brought him comfort, or mere surfeit have done
            him in?"

We had just settled in Ames when males were summoned for
draft registration, October 16, 1940:

DRAFT REGISTRATION

The basement of a school, dim lamp above;
Light. Spreading, ageing; dropping,
Yellow with age, into lost corners—
Lying spent on the dingy floor.
The floor. I see only the floor now—
Peeled and over-painted, gray—
Battleship gray.
Then feet, crushing the butts of cigarettes,
And one cigar. Do the rich register? Strange.
Long steps are those leading back and up to the door,
Out of this dimness to the fields.
There the corn is standing; I see it sway: each leaf
And stalk fair yellow in the wind. I hear the rustle.
But that is too far. It is the sound of voices:
Low: "Your name, your father's name."
(Yes, he too fought in the wars,
And my grandfather, for the cause of the South.
Comical, it seems, now, reading, in books, and in school.
The basement of a school?
But that was blood of men.)

Outside, children run laughing in the sun.
I feel wind in the toss of their clothes.
Recess has come. Now sharp cries; a kids' brawl.
The teacher scolds: "Bad boys."
And here, below, their fathers:
"Your name, your father's name."
Two others rise; feet pass on the floor.
And outside: sunlight, air . . .
Look. One peers at the door, smiles.

Can we smile back, we men? Slouched here; each
one, alone?

I say, lean fellow, grease-face, gripped hands,
What have you come for? No answer? But your eyes—
Dull, causeless: God knows; . . . China maybe.
Next man! You rise.
Tell me there, student, democratic thinker,
Did you say yes? Did you say no?
When they passed the bill, did they say:
On the straight, here's what it's for, this war.
Is this what you want . . . to die, for this?
No answer? Fear to answer; fear to ask.
"Your name, your father's name."
And the bell sounds, cutting play,
No laughter now, but dead in line: one-two, one-two;
School must be. They see no why; but the bell
sounds,
And they go: causeless . . . Dull . . .
"Your name, your father's name . . ."
"Thank you, that's all;
Take this card with you, and be ready for the call!"

Soon grading essays began, late nights; also some marriage
problems. After work, I would slip off to an old bed in the attic tak-
ing *Don Quixote* in Spanish and English and, as I read, laughter would
seize me. That gray time, looked back on, is still quixotically joyful.
Even when the first Winter storms blasted, in a way I had not yet expe-
rienced, how could the very flesh of such a spanner of polarities as I but
greet them with: "Hail!"

Ten below is a good cold. The tread
Snow rings to the sole, sheer crystal song;
The arm-swung body melts to glow,
And the stirred blood wakes in a flow bubbling as wine . . .

Of course there were negatives. Take music: against the
Oxford college choirs singing in Gothic chapels those many-voiced an-
thems and masses by Byrd, Gibbons, and the rest, we had at Iowa State
a Music Department Head who seemed to oppose all genuine musical
possibility.
Our English department building, those years, confronted

that of music over a stretch of lawn. Warm days of Fall or Spring, the windows would be open. I would often be reading Dante with Dick Wendell, while the Head's voice students sang. From prairie farms and towns, healthy voices had been enrolled—appropriate to the motet and madrigal groups that would gather at my house to read such scores as I had acquired in Europe and was then hand copying. I had even offered the Head some, but his students were destined for Grand Opera; so when the howls of the Valkyrie were impossibly stretching some girl's voice across the campus, it was agony for us, but surely worse for the victim. One of those times I saw that stubborn Head walking below, accompanying a musical visitor. I craned my head out of our window and shouted: "For God's sake, give her a Caesarian." It did not improve my already doubtful relation to the Head.

He also managed the Gymnasium Concert programs to which the college community was strongly "invited." I limit myself to two concert anecdotes. From one also came a poem but, first, the story. My German friends had joined me (with my *Symbolic History*) in the love of special music from Medieval, through Renaissance and Baroque, to the best of Bach, Mozart, Beethoven, and down to Berg and Bartok; but the Head favored such post-Romantics and pseudo-Moderns as so weep on your shoulder that you instinctively try to shrug them off. My Germans had taken up that shrugging gesture, with another even more expressive: remembering Poussin's *Martyrdom of St. Erasmus*, where his gut is being rolled out on a spool, I had only, when we were wallowing in a musical bog, to glance at them across the aisle and make a rotation with my hands, as if I were the disemboweled saint. I doubt if the Head was apprised of that, though it occasioned tittering.

Twice, however, when visiting orchestras drooled their way through a "Post-Romantic Concerto," and later "A New Symphony," I let loose in two poems—neither successful, though if I cut and join them now, I may bring 1943 and '44 closer to the intended mark:

> He vaunts himself like an old lecher
> Who lechers the harder to hold him young,
> And only remembers now and again in the shadows
> With a long sigh.
> I see the spirit of Leonardo smiling,
> Too wise for pity, as one smiles
> On a blustering child,
> And over the strings of his fantastic lyre
> Sweep the fingers of a 1500 chord,
> Resolved in mystery, equivocably sure.

What has the Precursor precursed?
Yet his wisdom, even at this, might have smiled . . .

This wretch whines at the close; his maudlin cries
Make even the Reaper turn his face for shame,
And strike the fouler blow for covered eyes,
While the poor spirit sputters like damped flame.
I can bear much; but not the uncontrolled
Fevered flinchings of the meager-souled.

The next incident produced only an anecdote. The Budapest
Quartet, being by chance in Iowa, was nabbed by the Head, but only for
the least-demanding of programs: early Haydn, an Opus 18 Beethoven,
then Brahms. In the break, I went up, told them I had from England
their Society Recordings, and that to give us their best, they should play
Beethoven's *Grosse Fuge* as an encore. They were humorously amazed,
but said they could not so defy the Head. A few months later, when I
had been called to my Princeton research, I attended the first concert in
a Budapest series of all the Beethoven Quartets, and for a wonder, they
closed with that very fugue. I went backstage afterward; the jolly cel-
list, Mischa Schneider, nudged the others: "What do you know! Here's
the man who wanted *Die Grosse Fuge* for an encore." I cheered: "And
now I've had it! Hoorah!" The next meeting would be a still friendlier
one, in Santa Fe, after 1970.

But we have digressed from Ames of the 1940s, its pluses
and minuses. Not only in music had that Winter prairie slid down from
Gothic Europe. Sample here a late Fall poem:

Night of the day, night of the year . . .
Hear the cold single cry,
Wolf or dog lets creep up the black vault,
To die in the slow toils of a wasting sky . . .

Thus entropy, thermodynamics' second law (in the same
poem) burdens the crystal song:

The frost of breath a reminder:
Death is not confined
To the particular— . . .

down to the closing couplet:

Space is a bubble, and the mouth withdrawn,
Wilts back into the bowl whence it was blown.

Meanwhile, those European friends, plus the tensile polarities
of *Symbolic History*, spurred and deepened my "Meditations":

> The life of humanity is a mansion too large for all
> parts to be kept in repair. Who would raise one wall
> must draw from the ruin of another. Thus creation
> destroys and destruction builds, and of every action
> there will stand opposing views, each just and sound.

After Pearl Harbor (December 7, 1941), the Navy's V-12
program, created to provide college-trained officers for the projected
invasion fleets, sent units to Iowa State for schooling. I was detailed to
teach them physics—giving me a draft deferment as well as a stirring
return to earlier studies—and, on my own account, the challenge of
grappling with the St John's classics of science, which Barr had helped
me get from the bookstore there. Result? By the March thunderstorms
of that time, my journal would record thought's entry into the core of
an organic cosmology:

> I walked into the woods and climbed a large oak,
> clouds boiling above, batteries of lightning bursting
> around—sat with my shoulder to the twisting trunk
> and pondered the astonishing world. Having per-
> ceived the dilemma of Newton's laws, that mass
> resists motion only by moving—where inertia and
> acceleration are counterfaces of the same stress—;
> having extended this through all realms of energy,
> observing the self-contradiction of Carnot's law of
> decay, except as met by its validating antithesis, a
> creative buttressing of energy against its own fall—
> thus weaving from smaller ephemerids more embrac-
> ing wholes—it came to me in that wind and downpour,
> that here was the key, the creative field in which man
> and universe are strung. Returning home I wrote:
> "All matter, systems, worlds, and living things
> express the need of energy to buttress against its own
> decay. In this sense cosmic history is a heightening
> and unfolding of the perceptive ambivalence
> of energy: that its activity is the fall by which it dies,

its life in time a transcendence, using and used by the destructive urge."

A while back, my Illinois account jumped the gun, foreseeing the bolder prairie expanse of Iowa and with it, the bounty of new intellectual friends—Kenneth Boulding and Richard Wendell as well as some cultured French readers—though most crucial for my later Princeton Deutsche Gesellschaft, and thereafter for the blessed Fulbright to Munich, was the Iowa State crop of intellectual German refugees. Strange that we Americans could have owed to the hated, ranting, maniac Hitler, of yearly crises and global war, such a wealth of remarkable Jewish friends. Here I would like to give color to the families who refined my German by reading Goethe and Hölderlin ("Still in dämmriger Luft ertönen geläutete Glocken") and speaking their rich language through all the times we were together—even when the teenage youths would join me cycling over that incised corn plateau and down its stream-cut valleys to romantic landscape vales. There were two intelligent widows of forty or so, the first with two sons: Professor Kaethe Mengelberg with Rainer, wild transcendental dreamer, and Stefan, future pianist and conductor; the other, Lily Wendel, with her reliable, eighteen-year-old son, Helmut. In the sketches I was then trying to set down and shape into an international fiction, the Helmut passages are filed in a notebook labeled "First Novel." These may give a touch of reality to those Iowa-transported Teutonic companions. What Helmut spoke in German, I have rendered as faithfully as I could.

The story goes too far back to be told entire; start when Jewish Frau Wendel and her then seventeen-year-old son, Helmut, had gone to Brussels—she separated from her German husband who was still working in Berlin, running his own war-critical factory, though he kept Lily supplied with a plentiful bank account. Then came the bombing and attack of German Panzer divisions—cutting the English and French forces, which retreated to the sea for the famous evacuation of Dunkerque. But for Frau Lily Wendel and her son there was no way but to buy visas through France and into Spain. She was sent to a black market adjunct of the Spanish consul called Professor Rugenegri, a shriveled remnant of a man, originally German-Italian of Jewish descent, who by teaching at a Castilian university had somehow slipped into a position of power with the Spanish consulate. He, taking their passports, plus ten thousand francs, delayed almost too long; but at the last moment, and for another considerable bribe, gave her the visas. By then, the German army was blocking all roads. There was only the train to Paris and from there to Spain.

At the Spanish border, Frau Wendel was told she could cross, but that her son must remain. German men of sixteen to thirty-five were forbid passage. The two found rooms in a French border hotel. Helmut knew they could be detained there until France fell, and all the former flight would come to nothing. Going to the lavatory, he wrote his mother a note: "I am stealing across the border and will meet you in Madrid at our family office. Go at once. You serve no purpose here. Helmut." Putting the paper in his pocket and returning to the room, he lay down in his clothes. This was an act so frequent as to cause no concern. At about one o'clock he got up, took a small bundle of toilet things, five one hundred franc notes, and, leaving the letter, quietly slipped away.

He issued into the street of the mountain village, a youth alone in a strange land. The narrow alley bore him up rising ground, while houses fell away on either side. Soon he was in open fields, emptiness above him, and winding ahead into a rising, ominous valley, his road, dusty gray under the moon. The mountains were jagged and bare, like craters of that dead world riding the sky. It seemed strange that these stones should stand here, stable in desolation, a boundary to the boiling flood of passion and hate that was Europe. As though this were a foretaste of the silence that must follow when the cold should creep down and the air slip away and life freeze from the rocky deserts of a changeless earth.

But as he walked up into the shadow of the gorge, a wind moaned from behind, clouds billowed on the horizon, shot with lightning, heavy with distant growls of storm. He thought only of the symbol: the violence of Europe—washing across France, overpouring these solitudes, as though men should extend their wars across the dead lavas of the moon. Little did he know this storm would save his life. For individuals there are turning points, great divides; chance may throw them here or there. In the moonlight at three o'clock that night, Helmut would have been seen, taken up, returned to France, and in two years his shoes would have stood in the salvage heaps of Lublin. But the storm came, broke over him in a glory of thunder; forked lightning fell with searing flame on the piled rocks of the gorge; the stream surged into a torrent leaping and crying, bearing boulders down with a grating roar to the alternate tides of the sea.

When he passed the border hut, rain was falling in such sheets that a liquid seemed interposed between him and the lighted windows. No one was on guard. In the house Helmut saw a man moving about, but he felt no alarm. It was as though he were a fish peering into the porthole of a bathysphere, undisturbed by those motions in another element. He plodded on, dripping and cold.

A terrific bolt of fire crashed upon a rock a hundred feet away. By what chance had it avoided him? The rock was higher. Some poet had written on this: the dangers of high places. But it might have struck lower. "Probability," he murmured. The jagged path of that lightning, seared on his eye, came to him as a type of man and the world. Why did it swerve where it did? Chance. Yet swerve it must somewhere, following a zigzag course to the ground—each swerve the chance of an accelerated leader-ion, like those populist Napoleons of history. But always to the ground—as if there were indeed a cosmic will, a prevailing drive of the whole. And how else to explain the evolution of nebulas, suns, worlds, of life up to man? Was this the whole life problem: to find and serve a world directive? Yet not the sort he had seen in his world. He splashed on, downhill, in slackening rain.

By dawn, gray in the faint after-drizzle of the storm, Helmut entered the Spanish border town. In the café early workers sat at the counter taking their liqueur or coffee before commencing a hard day. Or had they worked all night? They were dirty, unshaven, swarthy, glum, worn. A stove stood in the floor-midst, its chimney pipe winding over the room before making a forlorn exit in the smoky rear. Helmut came in dripping a broad swath over the floor, as though a mop were dragged across the boards. He stood by the stove shivering. "Tea," he said, in French, "with rum." The men glanced at him furtively, whispered among themselves. One left the café. "Pay first," said the host with suspicion. Helmut took out a note for a hundred francs. "Give me change," he said. "But that is French money, and this is Spain." "Well, you know the rate," said Helmut, "cash it for me." The owner delayed. "Not at par. Seventy percent, eh?" Another vulture, thought Helmut, who feeds on the dead. "Well, do it," he answered.

At this moment the slinking fellow who had disappeared returned, leading two gendarmes. "Here he is," he pointed, "maybe a spy or convict. He's come over the border, that's sure. I should have a reward, eh?"

"To hell with your reward," said the first gendarme; "you do no more than your duty." He was short and dark with a curly mop of hair. He talked as in passion.

The second, behind him, was lean with a long, wise face. His hair was straight and blond, his skin dry and crinkled, giving him the appearance of a Swiss mountaineer, a strange type for Spain. "Reward?" he questioned. "You have enjoyed it too much without that." The dry irony of his tone blended with his mien. He stepped ahead, speaking in French to Helmut, "Your passport?" He turned the pages. "Well, yes . . . you have stolen over the border?" Helmut nodded; the play was done. "I must take you to headquarters. Come quietly." Then to his companion: "You stay on duty, Pedro. I shall get this fellow in alone." Pedro objected. He had rather be the escort himself. "We shall toss," said León Aguillera, "heads I go with him, tails I stay." He took a large coin from his pocket, spun it deftly in the air, slapped it to the back of his hand. "Heads," he said. "Come now with me."

He led Helmut down a dusky, deserted way. After several blocks were passed, he peered cautiously behind, turned into an alley. "Look at this," he said. In his hand was the coin. Helmut took it with an unreal stirring of wonder. Heads. He turned it over. Heads. "It's all heads," said León, and he chuckled with the sound of a cracking board. Helmut felt a rising wave of fear. Was the fellow mad? "What do you mean? What are going to do with me?"

"I shall help you," said León. Helmut looked at the gendarme with wide eyes. The dry wrinkled face wore an aged smile. "Help you." The world seemed melting in a thaw of kindness. "I shall help you," he repeated, and chuckled again. How pleasant his laugh, how restful a sound, as in Fall woods the friendly chatter of a squirrel.

"Come to my house," he went on. "You can hide out there until night. You have no money? This is French money. I shall change it. Where do you want to go? Madrid? At 11:40 you shall get on the train."

(This man seems to have been a humane convert of the Civil War. At any rate, without him, Helmut could not have joined his mother and come to America where I met him at Ames.)

    Ames still, where teaching physics drew me, of course, from the doldrums of utilitarian "teachers-college English for farm-youths," into a science group livelier than I would have hoped for. The alert and friendly department head—name lost—was a Rhodes man, helpful in every way. Around 1942, he took me with some of my German-speaking exiles to a party at the house of John Atanasoff, who was inventing (and constructing) the first electronic, digital computer He was ranked as the intellectual and humorous star of the lot, but on a research stipend, which barely kept him in house, food, and party-drink.[1]

    For some while the college students of our German families had been cycling with me over the corn-plateau and (as already mentioned) down wagon roads into the wooded valleys of that incised typography. It was fine to descend slopes forested against erosion, to streambeds with spreading sycamores, maples, elms (not yet blighted). We were talking of that to Atanasoff at his party, where he served good whiskey, though I drank only a little wine. Anyway, Atanasoff, excited, wished that he could afford a bicycle, to join us on those scenic and life-giving rides. The teenage Mengelberg boys, fans of Beethoven, Goethe, and Hölderlin, teased Atanasoff: "Why don't you give up whiskey, and you could buy a bike?" Atanasoff voiced his computer brain: "Give up whiskey? What would I do with all those bicycles?"

    In January of 1944, before its March thunderstorm vision, I

---

1. John Vincent Atanasoff (1903-1963), the son of a Bulgarian immigrant whose name was altered at Ellis Island, and Clifford Berry, a graduate student in electrical engineering, built the Atanasoff-Berry Computer, the world's first electronic digital computer at Iowa State University from 1937 to 1942, where Atanasoff had come in 1925 on a teaching fellowship and later became a professor of both mathematics and physics.

    Their invention, known as the ABC, incorporated several major innovations in computing, including the use of binary arithmetic, regenerative memory, parallel processing, and separation of memory and computing functions. A lengthy court case challenged Atanasoff's proprietary claim, but in 1973, a federal court decided in Atanasoff's favor, naming him the inventor of the electronic digital computer. In recognition of his achievement, Atanasoff was awarded the National Medal of Technology by President George H. Bush on November 13, 1990.

    A few lines from the Iowa University website will substantiate the anecdote I tell about him: "The obsession of finding a solution to the computer problem had built to a frenzy in the winter months of 1937. One night, frustrated after many discouraging events, he got into his car and started driving without destination. Two hundred miles later, he pulled onto a roadhouse in the state of Illinois. Here, he had a drink of bourbon and continued thinking about the creation of the machine. No longer nervous and tense, he realized that his thoughts were coming together clearly. He began generating ideas on how to build this computer!"

had written "Augustinian Wisdom," the last and richest of my cyclical poems. Indeed, its quality made it the earliest piece chosen for *Songs for a New America*. Here our poetic Life begins to circle toward the time of that early book's gleaning. Turn to the text of the poem, and I will clarify a few matters: Spengler is implicit; where others have fought the war, I have been teaching in Iowa. But even here we have borne the art-glooms of the age: *The Waste Land*, Gorky's *Lower Depths*; we have put up with teachers who think Russian communism will (like Rome) "Goad the world to order!" But when materialist dogma and tyranny fail, as I thought they must, we should pray that ingredient faith might alchemize suffering into wisdom.

By April, I was applying the cosmic polarity the March storm had given me to the wealth of Spring: "Patterned Evening," second Iowa poem to be taken up in that first book, but not simply as a Romantic praise of nature: "winding stream . . . budding trees . . . wind-spread cloud . . . flock of birds . . . vastly volute in that radiant air!" Already, as in Schrödinger's little 1943 book of lectures, *What Is Life?*, there is a complementarity of inert and vital, entropy and anti-entropy—summoning a new meter, variable as in Dante, to the cosmic celebration—thus, the close:

> Image of the world, mirror to all time:
> Cloud, winds, and waves of light, senselessly beautiful,
> Flung from high to low, seeking repose;
> And birds, bearers of life, that sing and soar,
> Fired with a god-like will, breasters of the wind,
> Beating bold wings up a torrent sky,
> Feeding the sweet blaze of eternal desire.

The third and last Iowa poem to strengthen *Songs* was "In the Time of the Italian Campaign" (of July 1944). A first title, "Friedrich's Brown," made that artist's russet stippling of green meadows (with blades of desiccation) a metaphor for Job's moral problem: why such death and outrage on God's earth?

By the next spring (of '45), it was time—having taught physics strongly, and helped Atanasoff at his Herculean task (he had a huge lab space, shelved all around with what looked like disemboweled radios; and, whenever the computer went awry, volunteers had to check whole areas of wiring, tubes, and condensers to find the flaw and repair it)—it was time I should be recommended for a place in Palmer Lab, Princeton, doing electronics research on a war-time telemetering project. Leaving my family, I would go to be interviewed—arriving, as it would turn out, with the weekend free.

But here, before I bind up the sheaves of those Iowa years, two crucial trials, or darkenings, overhang the portal: one real: the 1942 death of my father; the other fictional or poetic: to shape from known incidents of wartime Ames a prairie romance, actually sad, yet soulfully radiant.

As for my father: from *Delta Return*, one may learn something of his double battle: first of body, against what Hopkins called "fatal four disorders": in his case, diabetes, with stones; tobacco-induced emphysema, causing a flabby or "enlarged" heart. Then for the battle of mind, see *Delta*, "Liquidation Sale": "The life dream torn/ By politicians [Bilbo's gang] and a failing farm, / Private loss and Hitler, our world-betrayal"—that global curse working even then to a Europe of explosion and flame. Meanwhile he was trapped in the Greenville hospital, saved from pneumonia by a new sulpha drug, but bed-bound for a month on oxygen, the mortgaged house and mortgaged life insurance both threatened by mounting costs—he powerless either to live or die. That was when I was called to him from Iowa, and he importuned me to bring his little pistol, and I did, and waited that night for the phone call.

Hardly matter for a poem, then or later. It took almost twenty years of transmuting it, so that it could be framed in a novel, *The Married Land,* of a new, life-giving love (mine for Danny), in which the remembered death of the father would become a focal tragic encounter, to be so far surmounted that its chapter might bear the title "Let There Be Light"—though the setting of that recovery is fifteen years later, when it is the father's unmarried younger sister, old Aunt Bets, thrown by a car crash into the same hospital—where my task, to get her out and cared for in her own house—revives events of the father's sacrifice, against a marriage bridging poles of our land: my "great American novel," though it has not yet been so acclaimed.

A lyric, however, did come from an Iowa autumn, which joined my father's remembered crisis to that of the fire-girdled world—from the fall of France to the Battle of the Bulge. I revise from my notes of the 1940s:

SACRIFICIAL FALL

The long slow twilights of July have fled.
These eager banners catch the fiery stream,
Hold it a blaze of passion and are sped;
While trees, scarlet and gold, lift tongues of flame,
That cry to heaven—the clouds' antiphonal.

Here now before these filaments can fade,
We feel three Passions weave to one death-braid:
The mortal struggle of our world and way,
The wine-red offering of Fall,
And this, the burning sacrament of day.

Such is the first Iowa darkening mentioned above. The second is almost fictional—a short story, like the 13th-century romance of Aucassin and Nicolette, in alternating prose and verse; mine, a love-poignancy called "November: Cross and Swan" (the Northern Cross, of sacrifice, high in the autumn sky, mythically named Cygnus, the wing-spread Swan). I wrote this story as if it were my own, and in a sense it approached that, so who could doubt its place in this Life? I knew the girl—a mother, also church organist, here amorous heroine. She had shared in my poetry reading groups, as well as singing soprano and sometimes playing the virginals for my motet and madrigal evenings. Thus she would be caught up later in that first novel, published 1962, where my Daniel "self" discovers that "women will fall for any halfway-daimonic man"—that they had been falling for him, and wanting him to take them, as when Dan and she, after longing and sighing through the Summer and Autumn, finally converge in the Winter woods with almost a foot of snow on the ground and more falling.

I would have known the "Cross and Swan" character's blacksmith husband, Johnny, but he was drafted to the Pacific as I entered Iowa. I did know the Conscientious Objector lover from the Quaker camp: he has picked up so many of my walking, running, and tree-climbing traits that I can almost stand in for him. Her Nietzchean brother had recently died or killed himself, I never knew which.

NOVEMBER: CROSS AND SWAN

Dante, who witnessed heaven and hell,
Found both fashioned out of flame.
In the passion of this calm,
Feel love's keel wake worlds of pain.

I

She was riding the secondhand bike of her nine-year-old son.
The father had chosen it before being sent overseas—his
choice, surely his brand. What had been called streamlining
hung on it, weighty and battered—a chrome sham. The man
she was to meet had gone by the back road, racing a light-built
Raleigh. Two months ago he had laughed at her boy's bike,

dragging those heavy plates of what had been advertised
for speed. "Typical," he said, "for a false show, to inhibit
freedom." That was the Quaker voice, scornful of pre-
tense. Now he had phoned and asked for a secret meeting,
and she had agreed, despising secrecy.

It was bleak November. She pedaled out of town,
fenders rattling. The tin-roofed service station and yellow
diner slipped behind her. This end of town was a Depres-
sion hangover, holding on through the war, waiting its
turn. Mulatto squatters and wallowing runts of pigs, crazy
fences, unpainted collapsing sheds. The plain fell away
to the river. Incised topography. Here the gullies began,
sallow mud of the prairies, the garbage dump in a smok-
ing field, tin cans and filth to earth recalled, not without
stench and flies. She gathered speed with the slope; lean-
ing forward she shot onto the iron bridge, its wooden floor
rumbling. A car. She swung to the rail, almost hiding her
face. Then up on the other side in the loose gravel, her
heart loud. Well, let them look. She had a right to ride.

> Or what is right—
> Her thought pursued—
> When the right of one
> Is the other's goad?
> Or where is right so insular
> That another need not fear
> The exercise of our desire?
> If good is reasoned out of wrong,
> What is good
> But the will of the strong?
> She recalled her brother
> Before he died,
> The haunted one—
> That talk they had:
> He asked if Lucifer or Christ
> Was the sacrament of God,
> And if both those and Faust
> Met in him, and were mad?
> It was a family mark
> To see themselves
> A type of the world,
> Western travelers,

Demigods of the dark.
When the lightning has been hurled
Can we find Eden again?
She dreamed, yes.
Eden—at most,
The barred gate we pass.

II

The walnut grove by the stream was mostly cut down.
She could not deny memory. Ten years ago it had been
a virgin stand. She had lived with her mother then and
was halfway through high school. She would steal out,
much as now, afternoons or nights, sometimes to the park,
sometimes to the walnut wood. Slipping through Summer
leaves by moonlight—bullfrogs croaking in the ponds,
high weeds loud with katydids and locusts—the luminous
warmth opened to one life, fraught with fear and desire. A
beating roar of quail—something broken in the dark, not
to be restored. Let it go. For in the open glade (and the dry
tongue cleaved to the mouth), from his swimming bare,
a tanned pillar of flesh out of the fronds of fern—beauti-
ful body, but why yield to him so?—dull-witted Adonis
and fisherman's spawning—stood indiscriminate Johnny.
Not Adonis really; he was hardly reluctant. The initiator
rather; call him Mars. So she had been caught in the toils.
But those were of Vulcan. Well, he had taken a turn at the
forge. Now at any rate he was of the Martian calling.

The unwillingly voluptuous pages
Of June night and naked Johnny,
What surrender a girl offers,
Closed in bitterness.
She stood to the handlebars
And forced the hill, panting.
On stump-littered acres
The last hollow tree
Spread stripped branches
In the corner of her eye:—
The brown field to the crumbling
Bank of the river,
The dark earth
Down with the water,

Robbing the land,
To pollute the sea.
An old hawk banked
On tattered wings.
Let the past perish.
He might be killed on Bataan.

III

She was before the quarry now. A group had gone out to-
gether a year ago. It was a church picnic, a sacred weenie
roast, given for the Conscientious Objectors of the neigh-
boring camp. The church promotes young loves—beyond
its will. That was three months after Johnny had sailed.
Some had painted in watercolors. "Quarrelsome Quarry"
her C.O. named his. An unexpected violence of style. She
had joined him where he sat under the haw bushes. The
red berries, hanging on the branches or spilled over the
ground, had given a flaming accent, not only to the picture
but to the afternoon. They had come with the rest; they
left as two. He had ridden home with her along this road,
as a moon they called their own had brightened against
the dying glow. And a pheasant had flown up whirring—
eyes reaching for the glint of gold.

There was dynamiting at the quarry these days,
and it was like bombs. Everybody was looking for bombs.
The overpass where the railroad and the highway crossed
they took for the strategic center of America. And the hun-
ger that drove her son over town to play at shooting (or
dreamed what seemed impossible but as a dream: war's
madness gripping the world) urged involvement: swas-
tikas glimpsed at every beating in the sky; or—windows
rattling from the quarry blast—mind's hostile tread heard
in staggering crescendo. Life had always been catching at
moments in the storm.

There was not one thing that could be separated
from another. Desire in the walnut wood, the unwanted
and alarming child whose bicycle she rode, the patched
marriage of a pregnant schoolgirl to a thick-witted
Adonis, who had worked for a time at the profession of
Vulcan and must now wear the horns—past and present, it
was of a single piece.

Her grandfather too had broken the land
Girdling trees and burning for corn
In fat valleys of the harvest home.
And her westward father had gullied the soil
And loved her mother on his whistling hill,
Then poured blood east in a wilder cause
And returned a "Veteran of Foreign Whores,"
To sear her memory with houseless fire
In the trailer camps of his wandering;
So gathered force and veered off west,
To bring other and successive wives
Cuttings of his tree of waste.
That was her father's war and this was hers;
Those were his gullies and these were hers;
And she was his orphan and she remembered hers.

Of swift autumnal changes is the day.
Piled clouds to cumulus tufts
Blow sudden shadows across the clear.
The stream under the hill
Wrinkling runs silver with light.
The old hawk veers, bracing into the wind.
The world is redeemed by the passion of air—
Flying leaves on the russet of Fall.
Over the next slope and around the bend
She would find him by the second tree.
Do eyes create or perceive?
Look, look there in the valley,
How the long, dying grass
Races in waves like the sea.

IV
At the top of the hill she fell back on the seat, tired.
It was an awkward saddle with a bent metal cowl.
The quick hurt piercing and returning brought in its train
Threefold memory on a dwindling scale of pain:—

Closing her moon of honey she sits at the stone wall
In the bare county jail, waiting the answering cable,
While such pangs, but worse, increasing, rise and fall.

White highways with Johnny stretch out behind,
Haystack nights and hitchhiking, days—swollen
With wantonness, an amorous vagabond;

Until the reply comes promising fees and fine,
And they rush to the hospital, no less bare, as the
        wounding son
Is ten minutes from his first, her fiercest pang.

So *pain* goes *round* in its circuit of empty *walls*.

Those were prints of memory as the hurt rose.
Its weaker return brings the second of her sorrows:
A dead time, when death of passion overthrows

The will of bearing, and life annuls its own—
He then consenting, without occupation—
In a third bare room a druggist works the wrong.

Glittering noose of wire. Life's blood is wild
To waste with its cast fruit, and fever kindled
Burns at the stem, until a doctor called,

Restores, *holding* his *tongue*, although he *knows*.

That was the second, to flesh diminished pain.
Like a reflection in an open pipe of the organ
She plays Sundays to the indifferent throng—

Not from the closure, but the orifice—
The pain that has gone once up and down, rallies,
Revives, climbs faintly again and dies,

Trivial as the first (yet worst) when she took her fill
In the summer fern bed, and for a grass-stained kirtle,
Abandoned music and books, college and all,

And *fell* to *serve* the cooperatives of *ruin*.

V

Where the road crossed the spur she could look over the
valley. She was opposite the country club, golf links and
wood, but higher. Behind and to the left she could see
the edge of town—a tall stack, and dwarfed below it the
church where she played, then a scurf of frame houses
spreading to the park and fields. The Friends Service
Camp was out of sight, over the ridge, beyond the school.

War had strained them out, these souls of convic-
tion, and nothing was stranger than that the dedication to
peace should have gathered such a youth of passion. The
spiritual sword. Though it had not taken a C.O. camp to
tell her that only energy can make its way against the clan.
And the unsheathed and shelterless of her and hers, what-
ever had flung them generation after generation to clear
a new soil, felt its kinship with that power. But it was
kinship with a difference. Two centuries had cradled his
in the paternal rest. Her force was the thing itself, his self-
limiting. Without understanding how the paradox could
be resolved: that desire itself could form its own outward
bound, she sensed that the answer was somewhere in
tradition, the containment to which she had not been born.
That they had waited a year had been no choice of hers.

And yet she had waited, secure in something
she did not reduce to words: that freedom's law springs
from within, and that he would not live by outward rule.
So there would be a new world, errors redeemed. She had
never felt that her actions were merely private. As she
looked over the bowl of the valley, it was like surveying
a symbolic stage. Today was the turning point, not only
for her. It was her brother who had argued that this second
war would be the culminant extravagance of the Western
dream . . .

Over there and to the right, at the bend of the
stream, stood the wooded bluff he and his German friends
had called Beethoven point. They had planted all these
memories like seed in the land:—

> The golf links spread to the wood;
> And we are running at the field's edge,
> Where tall corn slopes to the ridge,
> And a barn and silo, glimpsed between

Splotched yellow and brown, are red on green.

Now the voice I love: "Apples." He runs to the orchard.
A spring, he is in the branches. We gather
Below: "Throw me a good one." Arms are reaching
White through the boughs, and eyes are laughing.
We bite the skin and suck the cider.

Leaping to the earth, "To the Point," he cries.
The Germans and I are faithful spirits.
Vaulting a barbed-wire fence he goes dodging trees;
He breaks through a thicket, arms over his eyes.
Momentum carries him out across the gully,

To mount the next slope. Where it fails him, he waits.
I come up with him first. The leaves at our feet
Are a pool of gold—such gold-wind—rippled.
We look above, where the low sun strikes
The flaming leaves of a tremendous maple.

> (But had she forgotten,
> Above the trees,
> In the light that lay
> Like a golden fleece,
> And through those skies
> Of cloudless day,
> With what sharp cries
> Dipping swallows
> Took their prey?
> She had heard.
> Had she understood:
> Peace is partial,
> Islands of calm
> Beat round by ocean's mother flood?)

"Watch him," Friedrich yelled; "between here and
        the Point,
I bet he falls three times. I saw him last week
Jump without looking, turn two somersaults
And come up running. I swear you'd have thought
It was just the regular way to walk."

(She had known such ways
Of walking too,
Where falling is an emblem
Of being you.
The thing is to rise,
The hopeful phase
Of the soul's drama.
This day of all days,
Blown November,
Let hearts compelled
Sign and seal.)

VI

On the brown leaves where she lay in the mild candor
Of flesh, she apprehended her more than surrender:
Clinging and continuing, she beat like the wings of a bird.
And he shocked at the utter abandon—

Elements aflame and will appalled—
In spirit was withdrawing, afraid to be taken
In the act of being what by blood we are.

Like Ariadne she stood on the shore,
Or wild Medea, when impassioned fear,
In windows of confronting eyes,
Read the fate of diverging ways;
Her eyes in his took images:
Patterns of ancestral hills,
Stone walls, proprietary fields,
Georgian houses, broad stairs and porches,
Parents settled, children courteous,
And in the cool and cultured quiet,
The foreknown presence of a heart
That would never lunge far, whether for right or wrong.

So this was either mistake or game.
She seized as always—like golden plumes—
At the moment retreating, the flying bird.
And once more he returned, body, eyes, and voice.
Neither. Not game. They were not playing.
If mistake, there had been no choice.
She saw herself as a life he was passing through,

Something of world-abandon they hated and loved:
The western dream and wasteful real.
She was supreme in the same measure
That her force was a self-destroying seizure.
Two centuries at the fathers' hearth
And sheltered East his flame had been nursed;
And where was her hearth, where that of her fathers?
Or what hearth can hold the fire of forests?
She pondered it all as the dark air cooled:
If fire must burn
Within a custom or destroy its own,
It is the quality of fire
To reduce its natal sphere,
And by that act assume
The life in death of flame.
She saw him through her tears, a myth maintained
By some hypocrisy of the mean.
He would go; Johnny abides;
The land would gully and wars succeed.
The next age might bring him again . . .
She held it in her open palm:
The time at the hearth is a frail time
Before both hearth and house burn.

VII

They rode over the hill as lights brightened in the town.
He must go left, she ahead. They laid the bicycles down,
the trim and battered, and stood waiting, as on that other
ride of a year before—while the moon rose over the river.
A living year between two cratered moons. Four motors
beat above, pursuing the last glow. Forest and field, the
broad earth turned, always the retreating curve—dropping
into night. Forever night dotted with random flaming stars.
The noose of Solomon where all is platted. Seeing it now
before and after, in the moment of time that gathers past
and future, her eyes wept and lips smiled. She affirmed.

> (In the lightning, brother,
> That comes at last,
> You saw clearly
> How Lucifer and Christ,
> In the cloud reaches of our West,

Burn the Eden
That is always lost.
Them the enigma
Blasts by sheer power,
To the devouring vision
Of priestess and priest.
Priestess at last
At the sacrament of a god
Dying and born
In the always of time,
On lips that are the world
I set my sign and seal . . .)

The speech unspoken, silence, the soul's mark.
To the west, clouds beat up across the sparse
Low light. Wind sings in the dry grass.
They go separate ways into the dark.

Wait. Over the empty hill the constellations are
            forming:
Behind gathering clouds the summer Crown is
            declining;
The seven mysterious Sisters are riding up the east,
Pursued by an arrow of flight, the rainy Hyades;
On the eastern horizon under the moon's phos-
            phorous wake
The armed Hunter is lifting; he will lord it over
            the world,
The red eye, Betelgeuse, glinting on frozen fields.
But still, high overhead, almost at the sky's peak,
Cygnus, the Swan, plumed image of the raised
            Cross of the north,
Widens starry wings above the November earth.

William Carlos Williams responded to this romance, of which
I had sent him a copy revised in Annapolis, on February 23, 1960:

Dear Charles, you know the secret of enlisting my undying
interest in a story; it is to have a courageous young and
adventurous American woman who throws away her virtue
for love of a man she can attain to, such as did the Virgin
Mary in her place and day. . . . She's a hot baby but not vulgar,

purely a woman, which for any of us who have seen, spells
the defeat of the male. For such, we who are poets send up
hymns of praise. . . . A wonderfully successful piece of
composition. . . . The form, switching from prose to verse,
grips me from the start. . . . Does not let me go. Catches me
right by the balls.

Farewell to Iowa. In a long-misplaced clamp-binder of my
typed diary notes from 1940 into 1948, I find (with the record of an
April '45 trip from Ames, to see my mother in Greenville—as it turned
out just before the phone call inviting me to Princeton) a page-long
impromptu homecoming poem, surprising source of *Delta Return*
suggestions, to be carried in my head and developed in that book eight
years later—especially in its graveyard close. (Note: the second stanza
below became the last six lines of "The Beacon" in *Delta Return*):

HOMECOMING

Toward home. Under gray trees and the moon
We grow into loneliness—
Down to the bones of earth as roots to the ground,
Up through heavy air under stars that are worlds,
Taller than all trees to the night spaces . . .

Between black cedars, peaked as in Val d'Arno,
Gleams the white angel cut of Carrara. O dark-haired
Mother, child of Palermo, what old hunger
Of blue waves and olives sent back over far seas
For this girl of home, you homeward, here to stand,
The phare and beacon of your waveless harbor?

"Here lies the infant son" . . . Across this stone
I played an infant. First now the letters move me.
What we know, we feel, ask pity's alms of sorrow.
"This mother left three sons" . . . So worlds and all
Drop into the night-glistening like dew
That runs down grass to the whispering ground—
Myriad as tree frogs billowing dark with cries,
And each as lonely, lost within its void.

In the town I was dispossessed; on strangers beat
The vagrant knocking of a beggared mind.
Here almost I grow to heritage,
Here, in the presence of my father's tomb.

This little village glimmering down the stream
And sweeping yellow flood by gibbous moon
Drop in the shift of leaves—sad withered time—
And all turns one; my father's ghost am I,
No longer of these cells, strange clutch of hands,
Nor touch of beard or brawn or clothing skin,
But clean non-sentience poured through all those orbs
And weaving spaces of the buttressed worlds—
All forms and woes and loves in essence, without
The tyranny of place or tegument of days . . .

Who has not been all time in one time
And all places without place would not believe
Either of the glory which for him is dark
Or of the fear and inexpressive pain,
Torn growth of April crying back for snows.
This life is as a death into whose pangs
I am not wombed yet to be born,
Nor home can turn until all time's time turns.
Homeward rather to the stranger place
Whose columned flutings bore my stranger days.

Well, we shall not live always in the trivial shell.
Who has seen the walls once waver knows from then
That they are stage set, canvas lightly daubed,
Till curtain, and they change, or drawn away,
Leave night forever, all a blaze of stars;
And we who glimpsed home grow to homeward arms.

Top: Danny, Charles, Barbara Mason Bro (Danny's sister), and Per Bro. Spring vacation, 1945.
Insert: Charles playing the recorder. August, 1945.
Bottom: Charles, Charlotte, Deedie, and Nona. 338 Nassau Street, Princeton.

3. PRINCETON (1945-49)

So I was called to Princeton, Spring 1945. Arriving there on a Saturday, I hit first on the Parnassus Bookshop, unacknowledged cultural center. Keene and Anne Fleck ferreted out that I was writing philosophy, poetry, fiction, and cultural history (using music and slides). They asked me to their mid-day meal, a walk by Carnegie Lake, and then a piano performance, by some great European, of Bach's *Art of the Fugue*. I launched into German with a couple sitting beside me—comparing the last unfinished fugue we were soon to hear with the destinate past and unpredictable future of Hegel's *History*. The man turned out to be Paul Frankl, art historian. The next evening we met at his house to begin reading Hegel's *Die Philosophie der Geschichte*.

The Frankls told me of Erich Kahler, the cultural historian who had just published his great book, *Man the Measure: A New Approach to History* (1943), which Ashley Montagu called "the best history of the rise of man of humanity," and they invited me for the next night, to join the local European community which was to gather at Kahler's place. I went, talked with Erich, my host, who seated me by Einstein, idol of my youth.[1]

---

1. Erich von Kahler (1885-1970) was born in Czechoslovakia and studied literature, fine arts, history, sociology, and psychology at universities in Vienna, Munich, Berlin, Heidelberg, and Freiburg, before earning a Ph.D. at the University of Vienna in 1911. Up until 1933 he traveled through Europe as a writer and lecturer, abandoning Germany after Hitler's rise. He immigrated to the United States in 1938, taking citizenship in 1944, and marrying Alice (Lili) Lowey.

In Vienna, Kahler and his first wife, (Jose) Fine von Kahler moved in the same social circles as Freud; and Fine, to whom Friedrich Gundolf's famous biography of Goethe (1916) is dedicated, was the sole woman in the Georgekries, the literary group that gathered around Stefan George. She became friends with Hermann Broch and remained close to him after they both had relocated to Princeton.

An immensely prolific author—of such books as *The Tower and the Abyss, The Meaning of History, The Jews among the Nations, The Germans, The Inward Turn of Narrative, The Disintegration of Form in the Arts,* and *Reason and Science*—Kahler also taught at The New School for Social Research, Black Mountain College, and Cornell as well as Princeton, where he was a member of Institute for Advanced Study. He was the center of a large group, which I dubbed the Kahlerkreis, that included Einstein, Thomas Mann, and Broch, who wrote *The Death of Virgil* (1945) in Kahler's home. His correspondence with Thomas Mann, *An Exceptional Friendship,* demonstrates his closeness to Mann and to his family, which Kahler preserved after Mann's death, while his writing about Mann's work distinguishes him as a literary critic.

In addition to studying history and man's changing relation to the world, as well as science and technology, Kahler's writing often embodied his political commitment. He supported the Zionist movement and was active in the Committee to Frame a World Constitution, the Emergency Civil Liberties Committee, and various antiwar, antinuclear bomb organizations.

Astonishing, that the lower floor of an old house on Mercer Street, which I rented the next day, turned out to be across the street from Einstein's. My family arrived, and I began my research. Nona, my first daughter, about five, was favored by the genial sage. He was her teacher in the lore of the pendulum clock on his stair landing. Einstein (opening the clock): "What is it. Nona? And how does it work?"

Our telemetering job was to find at what points fighter-jets should be strengthened, so they would no longer come apart as they were forced beyond the speed of sound. We were putting strain gauges on the crucial joints of automatically piloted planes. The signals these planes emitted had to be changed from waveform to flattop, then scanned in sequence, broadcast over a single channel, and reconstructed on the ground as continuous readings from each strain gauge. Our plane-borne broadcaster had to be tested under stratospheric low temperature and pressure. How much ice and dry ice we lugged into our pumped-out chamber, to test our wave front; what dull times of waiting we had, as if stalled at the end of a vacuum tube; though by the end of the war we had put a jet through the sound barrier. Meanwhile, I had my papers: poetry, philosophy, and an autobiographical fiction too much like Wolfe's *Look Homeward Angel*.

At Princeton I completed poems sketched in Iowa, still in touch with Boulding and the pacifists' camp near Ames that wartime summer of 1945, but reworked now. The first, "Lost Empery," describes such a stallion as I had seen framed on the wall in my aunt's Greenville attic (it had been my father's in his youth). I applied the picture to our war-rabid world:

LOST EMPERY (June 1945)

Fire of flint-stone flares at his hooves,
He towers above us blotting the stars;
On the black fell, are foam-fleck bars
And the eyes glint flame as he moves.
What ebon flag on the gusty wind
Severs the night—his cleaving mane!
Bring us the curb bit, whip and rein;
A stallion's heart is steel to bend.
Silver rein, silver rein, and the golden bells—
Are these the crop and snaffle for a steed
Whose force, to will, knits thews for giant war?
Poor soul, you shall be thrown; no breathing dawn
Will find you master of this beastly brawn.

Another page of Iowa notes gave me, as by planned contrast, a summer landscape:

SUNSET UNDER CLOUDS (August 1944 into '45)

Strike, strike once more upon the fore-struck string:—
If the earth so often brings dawns and evenings
And never repeats or tires devotion,
Why then should I fear to tread in her traces,
If the glow that gilds me but wreathe my branches
With the tithe of its riches endlessly changing?

Here was a new evening for the world,
Closing a day of thunder. When I looked
West under clouds, corrugate, bulky,
Toward the long streak of an ocean-blue,
As if the mortal veil had split and parted;
I ran to open fields and orchard hills,
With apples crowning weed-enfeathered vales.

Believe me, as I stood here by the stream,
Behind me pines upon a slope of green,
And a sudden sun broke on the plain,
Pointing each needle, sharp as flame,
I laughed like a child in a waterfall
When the spray hits; for the sky was a pall,
And the sunlit trees were crying even
That earth is a brighter place than heaven.

Dying Helios, who mourns the loss
That burns this instant heritage?
Here now, with dusk and shadows gathering,
Strike, strike, once more upon the fore-struck string,
And ask that evening bring again
Such validation of a day of rain.

Sometimes the lab scribbling would give way to my photographing for *Symbolic History* in the splendid art library (the sun slanting through wide plate glass); so enriching my slide collection for the multimedia shows I was giving weekly at the Parnassus Bookshop to an audience of European colleagues, including Kahler and Einstein, plus some top students (Galway Kinnell, W.S. Merwin, William Arrowsmith, etc.).

Since then, whenever a show has drawn a small audience, I say: "For years I've hardly needed any audience, since at Princeton I had a great one. But I thank you who do come, since if I had been working at this, all these years, in solitude, I'd be even wackier than I am."

At the Princeton Art Library: frequently an art-plate would also touch off a poem: thus with a 1200 Christ on the Cross:

HERACLITEAN CRUCIFIX (May1945)

Long-dead mourner, whose tensile finger
Carved the Gothic mastery of this sorrow:
Bone and writhing tendon,
Hung in the vortex binding earth to heaven—
As if from cloud, lightning should fall sinuous,
And there hang timeless, a taut string of being,
Racked from rock to sky for the song of men and angels.
He who would sing the peace eternal
Must tune his harp in the war of its fibers.

On another day the library took me forward to the gleaming Night Nativities of 1500 Flanders and Germany, source of a four-stanza poem (here cut to the first and last):

RESIDUARY LEGATEE (April 1946)

Man, who was once a walking spirit,
Divinity clouded with a little clay,
Will not rest content as clay forever,
Cradling a little breath of spirit.
In these things too the old recurrences
Assert themselves—a yearning heart
Claims Maria's Yuletide smart!
. . . .
If life inhere in spirit's serfdom,
Not ours to shirk the pilgrimage of living.
But when shadows fall on the world-evening,
Sweet is the light that beckons from
The casements of home, and sweet the old
Song of angels, shimmering the dusk with gold.

Peaking the sacramental mystery of Renaissance night-lighted land-scapes and Biblical scenes, I found in volume five of the great *Mc-*

Graw-Hill Encyclopedia of World Art a moon-lit *Agony in the Garden*
by Flemish Gossaert, called Mabuse, about 1512, now in the Berlin
Staatliche Museen—the sort of magic that could have influenced
Altdorfer of the same years. I made a slide, of course, which I comple-
mented, Spring 1945, with this poem:

> It is a warm still night. Close the air
> And heavy hung as musk. Do voices break
> From glowing pools and hollows of the dusk?
> Night's body stirs with life. What Lazarus wakes
> Under phosphorescent groinings of the moon?
> Is it foxfire in the forest burns?
> Out of the glistening, grows a cup,
> (Down laurel leaves, dew-pearls drop):
> "Father, father, in my agony,
> Thy will be done, eternally."

Since my first showing of *Symbolic History* to an Illinois State Library
class, Fall '39-Spring '40, I had been trying to add to my 20th-cen-
tury slides and to strengthen their interpretation. By 1941, in Ames, I
had hardly glimpsed my later insight that, from the Fauves, through
abstract, Dada and beyond, the earth-and-art-program was to crack
civilized forms and stabilities, for a liberation of energy—to loosen
restraints and consume resources in a population burst and life-display
as huge, indulgent, and awesome as the ecological and global threat—a
real and symbolic gradient against which, for more than a century, it
has been hard for art to contend.

Though my Princeton Kodachromes revived for Cubism an
almost playful poem:

PICASSO LOQUITOR (1941- 45)

> I tell you, friend, I have seen more than most men,
> For I have seen this thing and that thing,
> Not seeing two things,
> But one,
> Which is cause of confusion.
> Gothic Paris bred me;
> I grew when Thames was silver,
> Plain air and Arno hills around me;
> I have lived in the painted ivy,
> Clasping the ruins of a classic stable.

But I have held a grain of sand
And pried within to desolation and the waste of spaces;
And a single shell bursting
Has made youth and beauty
Crumble to lost shadows.

There is no word for confusion but
Confusion.
This is the *why* of cubism.

As I moved into the middle span of our culture, I studied varieties of
the 17th and 18th century, from late Renaissance to Revolutionary; and
besides photographing, I would try to express the art-styles in verse. So
with Poussin's French classic *Realm of Flora*, painted 1631:

A fair world, dream world, World of an Age of Gold;
Where those unliving live, robed Gods, with Goddesses
Melodiously unrobed; where woods and meadows
Overflow gaiety of flowers, guessed odors, breezes
Blown, and song. Though strange, how sadly here
Immortals linger—not in pain, nor abandoned,
Either to grief or joy, but pensive, leaned
Above a rose, whose petals, curling, fall.

How different from the great sacred Baroque (Rembrandt's light and
shade), where space itself, as in Newton's *Optics*, is God's Sensorium.
Or from that, how radical the stripping to Goya's fiercely hardened
vaults of prisons and madhouses. In my Princeton files of that time are
five or so trial renderings, variously called "The Great Baroque," "The
Tenebrist Vault," and "The Lost Glory of Baroque." All stabs at an
ambitious philosophical poem, stretching from the simple experience of
staring out under lowered lids and brows; then of sounding the irradiat-
ed dark of Rembrandt's sacred vaults—tied in thought to the axiomatic
certainty of Spinoza: "Extension is an attribute of God," and "Reality
and Perfection I understand to be one and the same"—and finally, a
consideration of Whitehead's blaming the equational determinism of
Cartesian and Newtonian science for its "Error of Misplaced Concrete-
ness." Whitehead, all the while, whipping the antidote of Uncertainty
into his "Body-Soul-Event."

Having thus laid out the scheme for a poem, which never quite
drew itself together, what's to do but retrieve from those sketches a

cluster of verse-lines:

> Shag down your lids and squint against the light.
> What is the cloudy vault in which you find yourself,
> Under the spatial bondage of the skull—
> As if we saw all things through chinks of our cavern?—
> Goya made prisons and mad houses so;
> But Rembrandt had besouled his vaults with light:
> Thus Newton's optic space, Milton's "Offspring of
>   Heaven, first born!"
> Extension such, to the God-inebriated Jew,
>   Though destined like his God to Thought's axiomatic laws.

Going from great Baroque to ironic Rococo, *Symbolic History* had to face Voltaire as precursing Revolution, even Romantic—a complicity to stir a darker poem:

VOLTAIRE'S LAST SMILE

> From the pearl and pink and cockle-shelled
> Pastel volutions of the gilded walls,
> The wreathed salon of mirrors and the clavecin's
>   laced trill,
> From the polished floors that image what of petticoats
>   and slippers,
> The delicate hair-balance of a wig-embroidered sentence,
> The viciousness and ennui that it fosters, festers, fathers,
> And on itself unleashes in a withering of scorn;
> Yet scorn, still polished to a jeweled bright precision;
> From the food in more than plenty and warmth of
>   robes (what texture!):
>   I shall break, cut, burn me,
>   Tear it off like cobwebs,
>   And myself too that am of it,
>   Bruise, crush, devour and kill;
>   Till phoenix out of flame, by that self-engendering,
>   Stripped flesh, I stand to moonlight, in the
>   shivering of wind,
>   From time's earth yearning—let it waste, stand
>   ruinous:
>   Never for a moment can the least cup be filled.

And fools will write in histories that the hunger of
    the masses
Bore me down—fact-foundered fools who turn
    blind eyes
To: "No, death does not kill life, but life dies."

A contrasting Iowa-to-Princeton transplant speaks the agrarian wonder, in metaphors of Dawn and Spring, Birth and Resurrection:

HODIE, HODIE (1944-45)

Who plows at evening
  Sows by night,
    In darkness closing
      Seed of light;

Dies when the bell
  Has tolled its twelve;
    Spiders spin;
      They spade him in.

Lost is the land
  He never knew . . .
    Out of his vault expands
      The dew—

Touches the iron
  Bars of earth,
    Melts the barren
      Into birth.

Darkness scorning,
  The grain at dawning
    Wears the wings
      And shafts of morning.

So we come to a poem first sketched in Palmer Lab, Princeton, where, pursuing electronic war research, I read of the atom bomb (August 6, 1945), though remembering Ames, Iowa (1940-44)—our house, there by a railroad trunk line of the continent:

EXTREME UNCTION
(August 6, 1945—lately revised)

Five years at the nation's heart I lay,
And heard the pounding night and day—
Blood of earth, down railroad veins—
Death-freighted transcontinental trains.

Winter dawns I watched them go,
Predestined vortices of snow;
Summer nights I saw the reel
Of sliding lights on lanes of steel.

War wrung the world; each hour we knew
Man's internecine fury grew:
When Gatling-pistons plunging beat
Our saturation-raids of hate.

I was a man of peace, and should
Have felt remorse temper my blood;
Yet still I rallied to an age of wars,
As to the tread of dinosaurs.

When long flat-cars went crashing by,
Heaped with lend-lease armory—
I swear my heart astonished me,
Drafted to new savagery.

Climax night: in a sun-flash,
Hills of White Sand fuse to glass;
While cloud on cloud of mushroom flame
Shroud the atoms of our shame.

The banned fruit falls; a stench of worlds,
Round the nuclear cosmos, curls;
From Hiróshima to Cold War, I wheel:
Where bright, as terrible, in burnished mail,
Retributive Justice turns, and lifts the flail.

(The later terrorist attack, September 11, 2001 with Bush's misguided
bombing of Baghdad, continued the threat I foresaw.)

It was between the end of the War and the start of the Cold War, that I observed my three children, with a friend, clustered over a magazine. My closer approach engendered a poem called "Mad Heritage" (about 1945-46):

> This, my children, is steel in the heart's sanctum:
> The book you bend above is nothing other
> Than LIFE, a magazine of pictures;
> But it draws you to the bud of such
> A blossom, I pluck back your pliant petals:
> To discover atomic bombs and rockets—
> All the fever you may live and die in,
> Children—heirs to wars we leave you,
> Mad earth's poor foundlings.

Now that I had growing daughters, innocent domestic rhymes would pop into my head: one, "From the Stultifying Stool" (in what the kids used to change from "bathroom" to "baboon"):

> No intrusion on my seclusion
> Go back, go back, you fool!
> I want no eyes of peeping spies
> When I am on the stool.

Also I would make rhymes for little children:

> Wake children, dawn breaks,
> Up the portals of the east;
> Song recovers day's delight:
> Bright now, brighter, now most bright.

At the same time poems came to me inspired by Hölderlin and late Beethoven, to celebrate the Transcendental Now. Here is one called "Holy Song of Praise," with a German caption: "An den Heiligen Dankgesang":

> Vision is no more than this,
> Time's opening on eternal bliss
> A moment splits; time gives way,
> Bringing together night and day.
> Within, all moments are become
> Co-partners in Elysium—

Where once dull and heavy hours
Glow like clouds sunlight devours;
Then time is two-fold mystery:
Time's quest and time's eternity.

When vision sleeps we come again
Into the busy fold of men
But vision's core, our life, our soul,
Inhabit worlds ageless, though old;
So Phaethon tumbled from the sky
But the blaze of search that could not die
Burned the heavens with his cry.

By the Fall of 1945 the war was over. To mark that event, I squeeze in
three stanzas of a poem just dredged from my files (that paper Sargas-
so)—grim comment on the Princeton Peace-orgy:

ON V-DAY: 1945

Degenerate people—through these war years,
Festering with and of you, have I heard
Such yelps of joy as now your dogtooth tears
(Hounds at the kill) flesh of the living prey—
Your beastly passions stirred
By draughts of hot blood drawn from half a world at bay.

Nor blood enough to craze, you needs must add
Your liquid fires: each pimply foppish boy
Bearing his bottled god to make him mad
In ecstasy, and these poor painted drabs
Whose reliquated joys
Tomorrow will drape shrubs and fleck the lawn like scabs.
. . . .
Still, still these autos blare; this drunken crowd
Mills in the street, wasting vital stores
Four years of war had drained. Not yet the proud
Prodigal turns eyes home. How should he pine,
Here, with his swill and whores,
Not sensing yet, poor fool, he wallows but with swine.

So I was released from my physics research and joined the
English faculty; but the next event to occasion a dated poem was the

January 25, 1946 Annapolis report of a radar beam bounced off the moon (feeler for rocket exploration). My poem seems of that July and, by my notation, appeared in the *American Oxonian* (also Fall 2002, in *ecopoetics*, J. Skinner, Buffalo, NY):

ON PLANS FOR PEACE AND
RADAR TO THE MOON

When Rome, like some blind beast, turned the water
        shed
Of its groping years, and coasting from the height,
Took the westward plunge for the rock, the seething
        bed
Of a wasteful ocean, and the shores of night—
Lucretius, sensing ruin, only perceived
The expected fall of man, his ultimate achieved.

While we of the West (Incarnate) claim divinity:—
When the Christian heaven crumbled, we became
Sparks of all-soul, kindling eternities
Of self-perception on worlds evolved from flame.
Now Super-science fancies satellites
As bending conquered heads before telluric wars.

Here on the brink of destruction, still the swallow
Flies for the spirit south and halcyon
Summer. Atoms open vales of Valhalla
Even as the gods overwhelm with thunder. And man,
Wasting his own world in the blown typhoon
Of its rape, wafts herald radar to the desert moon.

(Already a pivotal care is global ecology.)

Meanwhile, it was sharing such earth-concern that Professor Frankl of the Institute for Advanced Study had invited me to join him, with Erich Kahler, Hermann Broch, Hermann (Peter) Weyl, Einstein and others, in a group to plan for a just peace, a world constitution, etc. Giuseppe Antonio Borgese (to become a chief friend at Chicago) would join us when he could.[2] Our first aim was to ease the threat of a

2. Giuseppe Antonio Borgese (1882-1952), who married Elizabeth Mann, Thomas Mann's youngest daughter, served as the secretary of the Committee to Frame a World Constitution. He was principal author of the Committee's Chicago draft in 1947.

nuclear arms race, with cold and then hot war between Russia and the West. Einstein's motivation was the responsibility he felt for the Bomb. For me, I had just spread around a mimeographed essay based on that provocative talk to my father's Bible Class, its title "Studies in the Future," a realistic projection of our drive toward the worst. I saw that it troubled Einstein, most wishful and naïve politically; whereas Kahler, following his *Man the Measure*, could weigh dire possibility against a kind of post-Hegelian calculus of progress—insisting: "The property of spirit is transcendence."

After our first year in Princeton, Mildred bought a big house on Nassau Street, and we left the rented one across from Einstein to find ourselves next door to Erich and Lili Kahler, with Hermann Broch in their attic. One day, Broch—admired author of *The Death of Virgil*, who is thought by some to excel Thomas Mann (and for stream-of-consciousness obscurity, whether in German or translation, that can be granted), came over to beg my help with his first English task: writing an introduction to Bespaloff's Homer. He hoped I would correct, smooth, and shorten his attempt. The revision (stemming from *Symbolic History*) turned out to be as much mine as his). But the shortening took weeks. Every time I would cut something, he would close his eyes and say dreamily: "Add this!" Then, in a trance, he would deliver pages of clouded improvisation. "Put that into shape," he would nod, "and we'll look at it tomorrow." I hardly know how we finished the job; but we did.

Though my most memorable discussion was not with Broch, but with Einstein about his rejection of Heisenberg's Quantum Indeterminacy, which his own early articles had anticipated and which seemed to me essential to a modern organic philosophy. I began with the classical prototype: How Democritus' merely material atoms gave Epicurus, two centuries later, no way to make his philosophy a "medicine for sick souls," since such souls could not change their atomic destiny. So Epicurus had to endow his atoms with the power to "swerve" on their own (each, as his follower Lucretius would say, "sponte sua"), for how else could human choice be grounded in nature? I pressed the point: "The

---

Borgese was born near Palermo, Italy. Taking his Ph.D. from the University of Florence in 1903, he taught at the universities of Rome and Milan from 1910 to 1931. He immigrated to the United States in 1931 in opposition to Italy's Fascist regime, teaching at Smith from 1932-1935 and the University of Chicago after 1936. Borgese's philosophic, poetic, and political work was informed by his concept of spiritual unity or what he termed *syntax*. His works of criticism, fiction, and poetry include the Italian novel *Rubè* and, written in English, *Goliath: the March of Fascism* (1937) and *Common Cause* (1943). Both Elizabeth Mann and Borgese reappear in the Chicago chapter.

Ancients followed philosophy, which our empirical physics did not take to, so Descartes and Newton could hardly escape the mechanism Whitehead would later accuse them of. For us, as Moderns, it was only optic experiment which would enforce our wave-particle antinomy, the lack of which had driven Kant and even Hegel into a rift between body, as if bound, and mind, as if free."

I closed with "How can we fail to accept the probability underlay of perception and response which science has given us as belonging to energy itself?" Einstein answered amicably: he could understand how philosophy and even religion might take advantage of Heisenberg; yet he rallied, as if his own luckless search for a total mathematical field-equation were threatened: "I see it philosophically; but it's not physics!"

Erich Kahler, however, was for me the nearest, best, and wisest center of that intellectual refugee circle—the quality and range of which may be surmised from the list of contributors to the Festschrift dedicated to him in 1951, he then sixty-five: Charles Bell, John Berryman, Giuseppe Antonio Borgese, Hermann Broch, Albert Einstein, Robert M. Hutchins, Rudolf Kassner, Victor Lange, Ben Shahn, Thomas Mann, Frenk Jewett Mather, Jr., Wolfgang Pauli, Roger Sessions, Herbert Steiner, William H. Woglom, Kurt and Eleanor Wolff, with a photo portrait by Trude Fleishman.

Let my own feeling conviction be voiced in my tribute—which comes first, thanks to the alphabet and my Bell name. Written after my move from Princeton to Chicago, the pages I insert will resume some Princeton and Black Mountain sequences.

KAHLER, THE MEASURE OF MAN

One cannot ask acquaintance in life with more than one Socrates; seven years ago I discovered mine. I had come to do war physics in Princeton, when what I wished for, and spent my nights on, was philosophical and cultural history. About that time reviews appeared of *Man the Measure*. I skimmed the comments. Hegel I was studying with the aid of Professor Frankl. He first took me to 1 Evelyn Place, and it was on the way that I made the connection, Kahler, *Man the Measure*.

The house was a mecca that night. An ancient German was performing poetry, mostly of the showy kind, Biedermeier and ballads; but the event was symptomatic of pre-war culture; I think all intellectual Princeton was there. The verse pleased me as little as others—I had hoped for Hölderlin and

Goethe—but the atmosphere was something else. On the walls were remnants of an art collection, in the bookshelves, the wealth of a European library. There was richness in sitting among so many minds saved from the violence then sweeping the West, in absorbing the scene, while beside me mused Einstein, idol of my science-loving youth, with his parchment face and corona of hair, a resigned and sphinx-like wisdom, between the Saint Bernard and Angel, as if he had lived the whole rise from brute to human, and was himself the record of that trial and achievement. But it was after the reading, when my host, physically different but with curiously kindred face, came forward through the crowd to welcome me, that I met my Socrates, the living master.

Years later, not long before leaving Princeton, I sat in Erich Kahler's upper chamber, having cleared from the chair piles of books and clippings which settled like snow on every object there, while he conferred with me on *The Meaning of History*. He was to give a lecture at the Institute for Advanced Study; as often, he did me the favor of hearing him talk it over. Not that I was in a position to help him at all, but as a man likes a friend on an expedition he could just as easily make alone. Besides, being a born teacher, he knew what these sessions gave to me. What Erich meant by "the meaning of history" was a thing shallower moderns are apt to call old-fashioned, though it belongs to the future as much as to the past; human history, that is, as a phase in the evolution of spirit, the evolution which the new and organic sciences are also the study of. This was universal history with a vengeance.

Erich did not sit to talk; I do not believe he can possibly think sitting down. He stood and paced the cluttered room, glancing at the floor and then at the ceiling, not absently, but with the determined energy of a man calling up daimons; and the harder he thought, the more explosive and Germanic his speech became, and the more he moved and distorted his face:—"But that is just what it is; they miss the whole point of spirit; it is TRANSCENDENCE!"—walking always more violently, running his hand over a noble skull through tattered hanks of hair and tugging at them as if in the labor of birth, and the words stammering and then rushing out grandly mouthed, the giant-speech of the Wessobrunner Gebet—*Dat gafregin ih mit firahim*—until the creating-Jehovah gesture on "transcendence" topped the whole picture of beloved quaintness and power.

I tried to sit in the chair to answer and talk, but as I looked up at Erich I remembered the past years, Black Mountain especially, where we had been most together, an otherwise hectic span that he redeemed. I saw the rocky pool in the stream where we plunged in the heat of an afternoon, Erich, splendidly unaquatic, poised in the center, punctuating philosophic discussion with a burst of enthusiasm; "Wuaagh! Wundervoll! Marvelous! Aargh"—splashing and blowing, surrendering, as to that clean stream, to those rivers of thought in which he lived and moved. Then there was evening, and the rough pine hall where he lectured—sitting with volumes of notes as if he were speaking to himself, burying his head sometimes in his hands and lowering his voice to an awful whisper, with the sad wisdom of one who has himself endured the whole of Western hope and ruin—tracing "The Crisis of the Individual in our Time." And always there followed a discussion, with Erich the provocation and center of a tangential battle, the wakened animosities of rival minds winging like bats through the raftered room. But peace and richness crowned those wrangling sessions, when Erich and I would stroll to Jollowitz' for the pagan ritual of his nightly beer, and then with the beautiful Trude of the Gypsy face across that lighted valley under the reigning full moon, the far-off mountains melting into mist; when Erich would quote an old geography he had studied as a boy:

> Die Nacht ist ja die schönste Tageszeit
> (And surely night is the fairest time of day).

So to a ridge, from which we looked down (as Dante from the eighth sphere upon this "little threshing-floor") we, on the hub, in the midst of that silence, of so much agitation and pride.

All this and more rose before me as I sat in Erich's study while he paced up and down, tugging his hair and vehemently stammering of transcendence. He was a droll and wonderful sight, and as I gazed at him, remembering the years together and that they were now at an end, I found concentration dissolving between laughter and tears. So I rose, and paced around too, my eyes on the floor, and in this way could hear only and understand, while great insights opened and spread around me like realms of light; for there is no one else who can talk like Erich Kahler.

Curious, that the next Princeton poem in my files is of October '46, and dashed off "as three atomic researchers (not Einstein or Szilard) spoke on the world." My poem was published afterward in *The Bulletin of Atomic Scientists* and stirred hot letters pro and con:

TITAN CHAINED

This first, a choleric fool, swollen with pride
Of war-loosed atoms, beats a general tongue
(So Plato warned us) over things to come—
Vows he will save the world, bone, flesh and hide,
If men like atoms will be loosed and tied.

This next, by the scientific attitude,
Discovers what the wise have known two hundred
Years—external power grows, sundered
The bonds that held man's rebel self subdued.
His word: let these by science be renewed.

This last, more sound, perceives the mortal soul
A substance scarcely mastered, itself against
Its own, not apt to be distilled, condensed
And mollified at will. He draws the stole
Of sad retirement round his arsenal.

And these are men we wished salvation of—
More blind than all—still mad Prometheans,
Or broken drudges, working death's weapons,
Irrelevant what cause. So all props prove
At last abortive, built of the crumbling tuff.

If any sage of science yet was strong
To search his cell, spy out and speak his wards
(He once sought truth)—baffled pragmatic lords
Of cold-war nations, he might build for song
High tragedy, though not, slave, right his wrong.

(A note which I wrote to my mother deplored, with Thomas Mann, the mass-praise of "practical science"; it also blamed, with Socrates, men, who, trained in one field, will rant in another, however foolishly.)

By now, at Kahler's, I had also been introduced to Giuliano Bonfante, Princeton head of Italian, who, at my urging, formed, for special Europeans (art historians, etc.), a Dante reading group at his house. We became friends, and he gave me extra sessions on the poet-revolutionaries surrounding 1600: Michelangelo, Bruno, and Campanella. It was from the long-imprisoned third of these, whose sonnets I was translating late-night, the same October, that a poem of my own seemed dictated in his praise:

ON CAMPANELLA (Princeton, October 1946)

Study is sweet, and sweet by night to commune
With the living dead, who sustained like heart and spoke
Like thoughts before us. Campanella held me,
In whom I greet my sire. Midnight tolls
A distant warning, filtering through the world
Of leaves and moon . . . Blotting the lamp, I rise
And to this open door walk as in dream;
Stand, while the last bell billows waves about me,
Over the gray floor of time's war-troubled sea.
We breathe a single spirit . . .
                                             As the moon
Links Autumn leaves to one perception, so
Fountain soul, in the double prison of
His flesh and Rome, broke on this musing man,
As now it breaks upon our age and me . . .
Tears tell the eyes it is for God they witness,
And the earth they weave, a love-gift for
His hunger, his requital of our need.

Campanella, who bore all racks and pangs,
Two dozen years of creed-inflicted shame,
As you have fathered in this night of calm
The peace of thought, sire action in our storm:
When last evening over a shattered wood
Wounds cloudy west with presages of blood,
Pluck then the chords of courage, that we don
The mail of strength, which you have nobly worn.

At this point, such a poem of historical re-creation is so like and dependent on verse translation that I think to sample my renditions of three sonnets from the poetic revolutionaries mentioned above. First, Michelangelo's "Giunto è già 'l corso della vita mia, / Con tempestoso mar per fragil barca . . . ."

> Already now across tempestuous seas'
> Uncharted course my brittle bark has blown
> To the common port, where all come to own
> Account and cause of goods and trespasses.
> Wherefore the loving fancy's subtleties,
> That made of art an idol and a throne,
> Break in deception-snares, too late known
> Such bitter sweets as to damnation please.
> Amorous thoughts, long since proved vanities,
> What are you now, if double death incline,
> One sure, one doubted, both foretasted harms?
> Not any mastery of paint or stone
> Can ease the heart that sees how love divine
> Spreads on the cross, to gather us, his arms.

The Italian close:

> Nè pinger nè scolpir fia più che quieti
> L'anima volta a quell' Amor divino
> Ch' aperse, a preder noi, in croce le braccia.

For Bruno, take the sonnet mostly attributed to Tansillo but which Bruno appropriates in his *Heroic Furies—Degli eroici furori,* or *Heroic Enthusiasts* ("Poi che spiegat' ho l'ale al bel desio"); so Tansillo's "Icarus":

> Since first my soul beat wings to the high desire,
> The vaster sense of air beneath my tread,
> The swifter pinions to the air I spread,
> Till spurning earth, toward heaven I aspire.
> Not Daedal's son warns with example dire
> That I descend or bow my threatened head;
> For though with him I plummet earthward dead,
> What is life's candle to this funeral pyre?
> I hear my heart's voice through the dusky air:
> Whither, O fearless darer, would you dare?
> Not without wreck this giant temerity.
> Fear not, I answer, what the ruin may be;

> Hold secure to the clouds and calmly die,
> Content if heaven allow a death so high.

This Tansillo, Bruno accompanied with daring poems of his own on the infinite universe, a vision which (breaking the crystalline spheres) brought him to his 1600 pyre. Here is the sestet of such a sonnet:

> Quindi l'ali sicure a l'aria porgo;
> Nè temo intoppo di cristallo o vetro,
> Ma fendo i cieli e a l'infinito m'ergo.
> E mentre dal mio globo a gli altri sorgo,
> E per l'eterio campo oltre penetro:
> Quel ch' altri lungi vede, lascio al tergo.

And here, my translation:

> And so I spread wide pinions on the air,
> Nor fear the impasse of glass or crystal sphere,
> Piercing the heavens to the infinite.
> And as I leave this globe and mount the vast,
> Beating my way across the ethereal waste,
> I lose the care of every common sight.

My chosen Campanella begins "Udite, amanti, il mio cantar" and ends "Dunque insieme adoro / Possanza, Senno, Amor, Primo ente e Donno" (literally: Power, Wisdom, Love, First Being and Lord), but I translate the whole poem:

> List, lovers, to my song: Before time was,
> Was universal Love; for it was He
> Bade God shape earth, not force or destiny.
> And Power into that operance did pass
> Because, encircled in Her infinite sphere,
> Primal Wisdom (my song's dwelling place)
> Foresaw potential essences spread there
> Of every finite kind,
> And with a word—"Be planted"—sowed out space.
> For Love, to whom each being is the fore-
> Thought good (which is truth to the Mind,
> Life to the Power),
> The pre-envisaged possible did fill
> With His own instant Love, the which, so fired,

He rendered back to Mind and Potency,
Which cannot move but if Love light the will . . .
Thus I adore that Trinity above
Of Power, Wisdom, and of primal Love.

For me a great Princeton happening was the appearance in my 1946-47 English classes of Galway Kinnell, who chose me also as his advisor. On an early visit to my house he noticed a poem on my desk, conspicuously entitled: "Confessions of a Late Romantic." Here, as often with Eliot, I made my own progress of spirit express that of Western culture. Of course, when Kinnell wished to read it, I agreed. Moved, he asked me, as his adviser, to be his mentor as well in poetry. At the same time he joined my *Symbolic History* audience.

CONFESSIONS OF A LATE ROMANTIC (1946-47)

Born of ambitious fathers, I inhaled
With the first breath of life the maddening flame
Of lust for glory and ephemeral fame.
I pierced the earth and pried the secret ways
Of power, clutching at elusive bays.
So worn with seeking, from the fever of
The world I asked redemption in the arms
Of love and solitude, romantic song—
To find, alas, that fever of the world
A mere quartan to the quotidian agues
That racked me now, of sick romantic soul
Self-pitying, self-absorbed, self-deified,
Playing the heart-wrung hero's conscious role
Before the impassive synod of the gods.
Thus worn at last with acts Promethean,
I sought extinction of the self in all,
Beat frenzied hands upon the long-closed doors
Ghiberti sealed—believers' paradise—
Implored the heavens to open and some god
But swallow up this one tormented cry
Into the vast night of his clasping arms.
But found the frenzy of romantic self
A guttered candle to the scoriac rage
Of self-afflicted, spirit-seeking soul
that moulds its own secretion-ooze of wounds—
Into the wished immortal ghostly balm,

And soiled with lust, leaps the inviolable One.
So all paths lead me to my self and home;
And but for some faint whispering from the eaves,
Some half-spelled message of the Sibyl's leaves,
I would quit hope. One promise holds hope green:
In the rank of its own bubbling, filth grows clean.

Years later, when I was composing a modern *Symbolic History* show called "The Atomic Age," I joined a concentrate of that poem to a sequence of seven slides—as on the script page here excerpted. Identifying the slides, without indicating their precise place in the shortened poem, may hint how extended in date (from 1200 to 1900) and dramatically heightened the cultural multimedia experience might be—if only we could display the images here. They are:

First, a compound slide of

Six sculpted heads: French Gothic 1200; Parler, c. 1385; Vischer, c. 1515; Puget, c. 1670 (?); Dannecker, 1805-10 (of Schiller); Wildt, 1908;

then the same singly, plus two by Lehmbruck.

(These depict Gothic mystery, Chaucerian pilgrimage, a Christian saint in humanist pride, French-Baroque cradle of irony, ego as defiant hope, pain on the road to abstraction; it is then in Lehmbruck that the modern grows clean; though at a life-cost).

That consciousness speaks in the compressed poem, "Ego as Incarnate West":

I, Flame of God, took flesh in the flame
Of earth's delight—pride, glory, fame.
With earth unsatisfied, the bleeding heart
Spent itself in romantic passion's part.
Worse-fevered now, passion beats at the gate
Ghiberti sealed, lost paradise of faith—
Last delirium, where self-pitying soul
Licks its own secretion, ooze of wounds,
Into the wished immortal ghostly balm,
And soiled with lust, leaps the inviolable One.

So all paths lead me to my self and home;
And but for some faint whispering from the eaves,
Some half-spelled message of the Sibyl's leaves,
I would quit hope. One promise holds hope green:
"In the rank of its own bubbling, filth grows clean."

Curious, for that "Romantic Confession" of January 1946
to trigger, in my memory (now, November 2000), another neglected
poem, "Road to Emmaus," also from Easter 1946, when I, new to the
Princeton English Department and advised "to sharpen my professional
axe," was revising, for learned publication, chapters of my Oxford
thesis on Edward Fairfax, translator of Tasso's *Conquest of Jerusalem*.
I must have been typing its stanza (II, 56): "Emaus è citta cui breve
strada / de la regal Gierusalem disgiunge . . ." etc—with Fairfax's
almost literal pentameter equivalent:

Emmaus is a citie small, that lies
From Sion's wals distant a little way . . .

The following ballad-like poem of spiritual polarity came to me—a
kind of Biblical complement to my deepest organic and cosmic philoso-
phy of science:

ROAD TO EMMAUS (Easter 1946)

Emmaus is a city small
That lies outside Jerusalem wall
      Distant a little way;
A man who rises with the dawn
May to that city wander on
      Ere the third hour of day.

The years have drifted down like snow
Since Easter day, long days ago,
      When pilgrims, sorrow-led,
Slowly to that town did go;
Saw one they knew and did not know—
      The living and the dead.

The snowy years have sifted down,
Covered field and covered town,

And grayed the hearts of men;
And faith that was a living stream
Has chilled and wears the frosty sheen
Of mental discipline.

I know how consequence and cause
Go linked in never-changing laws;
And I have felt the pride
And spacious grandeur of a world
Where planets round the center hurled
On smooth ellipses glide.

Nor shall I quit my cosmic creed;
Wherefore the cerebral master need
Not turn his face and lour,
If I from his allegiance plead
Release in hope, if not in deed—
Yet vassal to his power.

Though in my dreams I wander still
To seek the stranger on the hill;
Yea, like the wounded man,
Whom thieves abandoned by the way,
I watch and weep and witless pray
For my Samaritan.

From half a century ago, the exact time order blurs, but it was surely about 1946 that I would take the children on the train to New York City for the Museum of Natural History—those dioramas plus the old shellac record we heard in the museum library: "Sounds of an African Watering Hole"—from which I jotted my title: "Sounds of an African, or Prehistoric, Watering Hole," lately revised:

NIGHTLY TERROR

Our cruel and kind is nature's—think of old,
Crotched in a tree beside a watering hole;
Dark: slow damp dripping from the rock,
The gurgling of the stream. Here they stalk
All night, carnivore, for the thirsty game.
One by one, gazelles (hear the cautious tripping).
You see no more than where the ripple

Swells the reflex of a star. And then
The lion's roar. Harvest of carnage: whinnies
Of fear; plashing hooves speak where
They are; a crashing as great bodies tear
The circling brush; the beat of paws; a groan
And yelp of anguish where one fell. Then the long
Slow crunching of the bone. And now you mark
Across the silence of the plain, the last
Retreating hooves fade in the dark. And now
Again, the drip of water to the stream;
And dawn breaks golden on a world of green.

While I am with the children, let me take up again my old Oxford bike, seats now before and behind, so we can cycle and then walk in the fruitful and maple-shaded suburbs of Princeton, where—Autumn mornings and evenings—one could see deer feeding off the apple trees. Of course I scribbled notes for poems, and it is striking how different from those of the Iowa plateau these of garden-rich Princeton are; and yet, like my "Meditations," they as well employ philosophical thought. Here are two:

TREES BY NIGHT (March 1946)

Strangely still across the valley
Broods the misty shroud,
And the moon above glows palely
Veiled by cirrus cloud.

Strangely strewn with light is heaven,
For the rays creep down
As though poured through water, riven
To a green ocean ground.

And a mystery is teeming
In the wide womb of earth;
Some insensate germ of meaning
Presses to its birth.

Tangled skein of forest fingers,
Into what strange prayer
Do you weave your folded branches
In the moon-gray air?

I am told that you are thoughtless,
For the brain, where thought inheres,
Has not wrought in you the tissue
Of our hopes and fears.

I assume that you are senseless,
For the nerves, where sense appears,
Have not laced you with the conduits
Of our joy and tears.

But as sure as these your branches
Break from the common core,
You and I have burgeoned
From life's mother spore.

And the laughter of your leafage—
The musing of man's mind—
Bear such latency in matter,
As sight bears in the blind.

Wings of oneness waft your language
To my ear and eye:—
It is spirit, to live spirit,
We have linked voiceless cry.

And the cry itself builds answer,
Wherever shards are curled
To the calm eternal trances
Of our space-encompassed world.

CYPRESS LANE (May 1946)

Living in a time subject to accident,
I shun the accidental;
Growing under the shadow of particular failure,
I would transcend the particular.

This moonlit lane, plumed with peaks of cypress—
Beyond, the dogwood, whitening dusk of hillsides—
Strange, that all its momentary beauty,

All that makes it one and singular,
I count abandoned treasure,—

Holding to eternals only:— light and shade,
Which were, and are, and will be;
Space, perspectived motion, lines that meet before
And fold their limbs behind me;

The multiplicity subsumed in one,
The broken one distributed in many;
Plants, upward building in the tension
Of inward force and downward destiny;

The claimed pervasion of the starry spheres
By unheard music of concordant airs—
As if the radiance of eternal spirit
Alone could lift the limited to merit.

Next, for a show I was giving to my Parnassus audience on the Promethean phase of Renaissance entitled "Giants in the Earth" I used, for its visual start and close, Giulio Romano's terrific fresco of *Giants Thrown Down* (in the Mantuan vault, Palazzo del Te). The resonance spawned a variant poem, where the revolt of the old Titans is translated to the dangerously luring expanse of America.

WESTWARD GIANTS (1946)

Now all whom superstitions of the dark
Had thundered down for daring: Icarus
Sun-melted, Phaeton Jove-destroyed,
Prometheus of fire, morning's Lucifer,
Hunter Nimrod of the tower, thirsting Tantalus,
Old Laöcoön snake-harried with his sons,
Niobe made tears and Semele love-burning—
All rose divinely, winging west with the dawn:
Tall timber on the hills, unsullied streams,
Central valleys virgin to the plow,
Wind-washed grasslands boundless as the main,
With herds of bison shifting under clouds
Of soaring thunder-heads, cloud shadows they
In moving magnitude; rock mountains northward,
Snow-flanked, verged with fir; down shoreward granite,

Redwood trees—to the gull-clipped blue Pacific:—
That was a land for risen giants and demigods
To act again Shinar and Pelion.
We feel the fatal angels strike the tower,
Or through rifts of Titanic rock-hurled hail,
Glimpse dreads of distance where our running kind,
Seared with lightnings fall and the mountains drown.

About this time in Princeton, as I browsed Leonardo's Notebooks,
lately bought—remembering from 1938 a discussion of its stained-wall
passage (with Norrie Frye and Rodney Baine in a cheap Italian hotel,
where mottled walls haunted us with shapes from the Sistine Chapel,
seen the day before)—I puzzled the Leonardo into a meditation called:

SHAPES ON A WALL (March 1946)

"Within the mottlings of this ancient wall,"
Said Leonardo to a friend of craft,
"You may discover all the shapes of art:
That lift of shoulder, loom of lip and brow,
Rock recession of a strataed gorge,
With monsters, marshes, sky's spiral storms,
Or tumbling tumult of Jehovah's flood—
Shapes not to eye explicit, nor to thought, or dream,
Until some reconstructive mind, with sudden
Lightening, links them here, caught, between loss
And possession, in the vagaries of a wall."

I was not there. I would have asked him else,
"Whence grow the forms?" For aimless stipplings
Bear no such intrinsic life, nor claim alone
To weave the limbs of beauty, and they wear
For each new viewer still his private air.
Not from the wall then? . . . Should we say from mind?
Why then employ the wall? —
Which yields imagination (spoke the sage)
Far richer fruit than her own seed supply,
And strangely guides her power.

Ah, then we should have seen at one bright blow,
Both sage and I (and smiled a Gothic smile)—
All life is such a studied interplay—

Where non-existent, disembodied will
Imprints the unformed, non-existent clay
With all the changelings of incarnate skill—
The protoplasms of a cosmic day.

We should have seen the evolving globe
Sprout incremental mind, and that in turn
By bare becoming, spin the earth a robe
Of clouds and colors, rays that flash and burn
Down spacious torrents of the glistening air,
And trees and whorling leaves and close-curled fern;
Then these, enriched by mind, to mind repay
The eternal debt of spirit's interplay.
We should have seen all contrarieties
Blend in the birth of nature's mysteries—
And found a symbol for it all
In the suggestive mottlings of a wall.

From this same time, I here insert excerpts of a poem (the whole, as Polonius complains, "too long," and Hamlet quips "It shall to the barber with your beard"), a piece so imitative of the Eliot I was currently teaching, reading, and inevitably memorizing, that I excluded it, years later, in Chicago, when *Songs for a New America* was going to press. Indeed, the poems from my Iowa and Princeton 1940s, which made it into that collection ("Augustinian Wisdom," "Patterned Evening," and "Proteus' Song") surpass this Eliot-smart addition; yet those expressions of my own mind and voice were rejected by *Kenyon Review* and the like, while the pastiche got such favorable comment as made me think it had almost broken through. Here is a sample of what was rejected:

FORCED PHYSIC (c. 1946)

The long days shrink,
Curl, are gone.
On this brink
We stand alone,
Lay your light hands down and moan
Fingers knuckling to the bone
To the tendonous cords that roll
Like hump-backed colliers bearing coal . . .

Voices fall
From beech and wall
Crossing like many-colored wires
That weave our age its strange attires.
Follow, follow,
Out of the hollow,
Voice of the thrush, whirr of the swallow.
And at our backs the rusty weight
Of night like a clanged portcullis gate;
But the nightingale sings all night long
Transmuting dark to the cordial of song . . .

We have lived for this blow; living we have fought it.
It has come and we know how dearly we have bought it—
Not having found the meed for which we sought it.
Long years and patience yet must wear this burr
To the alien pip and seed, our comforter.

Then over some wide sweep of Indian land
Will break the singing of an angel band
(Superstition, we the wise will know);
But to those starving men that hear it so,
The Second Coming's coming is at hand.

(Here ends my anti-Quarterly Demonstration.)

That same '46 Fall, our great old German shepherd, Dammit, whom
Mildred brought to our marriage, having failed in the hips and likely in
the heart, died. I wrote: "Death, like the moon, shows one face to the
world." And then:

DOG-EARED DAMMIT

Men I have seen, and dogs, die, and observe
Little distinction. Both drag limbs, slip to the verge
At times, win back with a sigh,
As who would wake and cannot sleep deny.
They droop much toward the close
And wear a look that knows and nothing knows,
Yet is a look of pain. Their minds revolve
From wish to apathy; perceptions dissolve
Either before or after or in sleep,

To leave a failing or disabled wreck,
Of which no spirit postulate is made.
But if man has soul, dog has; life-absolutes
Before that threshold are obliterate.
If we go out of time, why go or come
Within time's predication?
So men die like dogs; like dogs, rot flesh
Into a beastly kind of dreck.
Only this difference I have descried:
I've seen as yet no canine suicide.

Having broached such a theme, I risk another salvo, recalled
from my youth.

DANCE OF DEATH

My grammar school was like a prison or a ward
Where the state kept crazy men. In the yard
We danced our games. Northward against a tree,
Coughed one long lean poor soul; it was whispered
          me
He should rest there, because he had T. B.
I see him dressed in black, as who should play
Two roles in one, dire death and death's dire prey.

A third, "Adagio," came in a dream of the obolus, that coin a Greek
soul (or corpse) had to pay Charon to be ferried over the River Styx.

In the dark water, waved long tendrils of an algous
          green.
The wharf I stood on was of rotten wood,
Slimed with the plash of waves,
Smooth, somber waves, preternaturally slow.
Mist lay before me, from whose depths,
Unseen, came the sweep of oars.
I touched my hand and in the darkness
Felt an oblate coin.
A flood of memory came and left me cold.
It was the obolus.

As I dreamed of waiting for Charon, the obolus in my hand,
life-events of diverse kinds were crowding in, touching off strongly

conflicting poems. No doubt most central to my life was the sequence of loss and love, shaking down one marriage and by1949 blessing me with another. Perhaps the Iowa "Cross and Swan" of Chapter 2 anticipated such trials as any love or marriage might be subject to. But the guns of personal loss first spoke for me after love's usual dread discovery, in a June 1947, six-line poem, "This Little Vigil" in *Songs for a New America*. (Moving through pangs, the first "bitter-sweet," the last "bitter," and leaving "the waste of fore and after desert.") Indeed, by that August I had struck off a related poem, previously unpublished, though it ends with hope

AUROREAN PRAYER

The gods who paced beside me lithe and strong
Over the hills and through the fountain dawn,
The gods are withdrawn—
Revisit eyes that have invoked you long.

Ten years of bickering in the north and west,
Bore the long encroachment of the waste—
To time and woman as I played the beast;
Return to the troubled heart, swallow of grace.

Who beckoned up the clouds, if thus you see
Your sometime darling, weep the infirmity;
Think after: you in me
But raze your wasted house to build more spaciously:—
Wake, winds of dawning, sing in the blasted tree.

At Black Mountain College, summer of 1947 (peak of the anguished rupture of my first marriage), I hit on an earlier sketch of mine, which took me back to when I came home from Oxford to comfort my bereaved parents; and, as I browsed our vast glass-cased library—being then myself in love with a married woman, Mildred—noticed a small red-and-gold bound *Love Classics* tenderly inscribed to my father, who told me of his own ship-board romance with a wealthy young wife from New England—he a dashing lawyer returning from first travels abroad. That affair had been tearfully broken off, but it was for the best, he said, since the next year he met my incomparable mother. In some of my own such ups and downs as attend the rupture of a marriage—for me, say, that turbulent Black Mountain summer—I was stirred to discover, as if from my father, a meditation of my own, though I did not

work it up until the romantic unravelings of my first union initiated the
quest that would lead to Danny:

FORFEIT GOOD (1947)

Perhaps all men should have some forfeit good
Some Heloise, or Laura, lost, abjured,
For whom desire might lead beyond desire
Into a space of light. It could appear
Love was blessing us, that time your eyes
Closed in parting, and my lips left yours,
Sighing, for a last touch of those eyes.
Loss may turn to good. But what reward
Will take away the salt taste of your tears?

This is not the place or time to hint at the broils that climaxed in that
pre-hippie North Carolina experiment fictionally treated in the "Dark
Love" chapter of *The Married Land*. Memory strips it to a moment,
as I stood in line for a blood test. And when the nurse needled me, the
plunger broke, and my blood spurted over the room. "You see," said the
beautiful Trude Guermonprez beside me, "you can't even give blood
like a normal person, but there has to be a mix-up and explosion."
From that summer's scribble, I spit out one satiric piece, its
motto from *Inferno* I, "In the time of false and lying gods":

IDOLATRY
nel tempo de li dèi falsi e bugiardi . . .

In this Black Mountain cottage
Our looking glass is low;
So every morning
You kneel at the chapel
Of your face, my darling.

And I too might kneel, adoring,
Did I not I fear that hell-circle
Of fired tombs, where souls suffer,
Who, worshiping, have bowed
To false and lying gods.

The Black Mountain climax of 1947 would arrive soon enough. I had
still to share with my first family the summer of 1946 on Long Beach

Island, in a house by the shore, which Mildred had rented. She had gone there, late spring, with a French couple she had come to know, while I was still tied to grading Princeton exams. For me, the solitary (almost deserted) nights proved a time of defiantly affirmative creation, spilling over into the Fall of my 1946 return to teaching, with the midnight rhapsody of "Proteus Song," to be caught in *Songs for a New America* and surely the six-stanzaed pantheistic outpouring—its thirty-six lines all tuned to a single "O" sound, is as loving a hymn to the cosmos of life and dying as I have managed. But the earlier and longer solitude of Spring 1946 gave me a notebook of pentameter sections of my long-delayed "Earth Epic," with an "Invocation" akin to the "Proteus Song."

"Long Beach Island," the chief poem of that 1947 Summer spent with my first family and even with my sister and her daughter in our beach retreat, was published in the *Songs*. To that poem, I now add two others. The first, during a wave-crashing storm, voiced somehow defiance to whatever loss was threatening.

LEARN FROM LEVATHAN (June 1946)

Sooner or later a man
Must come to terms with what we are,
Slug it out with the mad persistence
Of that storm ocean on this shore.

A more diverting poem is called "Harvey Cedars Point" (with a German motto):

Wer je die flamme umschritt
Bleibe der flamme trabant!
Stefan George, "Hold to the Flame"

On Harvey Cedars Point, beat by winds,
The Presbyterian Conference stands.
Here I come evenings to observe the day
Beat last wings over the bay.
As God works wonders here across the sky
In a dark hall they wail and cry
Their drooping dirges—"Lead, Kindly Light"—
While light is hurled
In vast innundance round the receptive world . . .
If such dark come, that these fools' song

Should show them right, and show us wrong,
Be ours still the nobler claim
Of those who worship at the shrine of flame.

This reminds me of a later church poem—though about a singer in my hometown:

OFFERTORY

In the Baptist barn the old singer puts
A tremolo voice through paces of
"The Lord's Prayer."
Coins strike the pewter: "clank!"
A rough road to God
For any Christian with a musical ear.

Compare a new Judgment preacher at that same church who tried at first to be genial but found his audience and tithes falling off, so broke into his "Fire and Brimstone Curse on a Generation of Vipers," all to be hurled into the pit of Hell where there will be "fear and trembling and gnashing of teeth. You will sense nothing but fear, trembling, gnashing of teeth." To which a withered parishoner raised his hand as he bared his gums, "But Preacher, what about us that don't have any teeth?" The doomsday voice roared down all opposition: "Teeth will be provided!"

The long solitude of the Spring 1946 yielded my Earth Epic. First, the "Invocation":

INVOCATION—FOR THE EARTH EPIC
(Princeton, c.1946-47)

What winds wake in the trees, now sweep the strings
Of inward music! Powers that press the stars,
Set heart and hand in motion! Plume the night
With glimmering quills of brightness! And ye souls
That on the shapeless severance of things
Tie cords of spirit, binding globe with globe,
Until the waste of air billows with wings
And trill of birds, then bells, and leaping joy
Buds up like crocus in the crescent time—
Plain words weave now into the weft of song.

Fools, fools, who feel no pulse of the living heart

That feeds the fronds we are. Who rests in God
Knows him; thought requires no proof beyond
Us of the breath we bear.
And I, who unresisting ride the blue
Waves of the over-spatial ocean, know
That even this act I will welled up in me
From out of me, not mine. How strangely strikes
The world upon itself, and strikes through me,
Down to this anvil me, this me the steel,
While off-struck sparks of mine still star the night
With untold glints of promise.
                                        Melt in me,
Eternal sun-thaw of the vernal earth,
The cerements of snow; lure these late seed
To upward veins of leafage and of bloom,
That I may tell what forming fire within
Wakes into artistry the willing stone.

No wonder my notebook of Earth Epic fragments remained unrevised,
unrealized. I was attempting in blank verse what *Symbolic History*
had already begun to express in the multimedia resonance of words,
images, and music. The very astronomy with which I thought to begin,
has required, besides its mathematical science, sensuous translation into
the marvels of telescopic photography—as in my first ninety-minute
show, "Nature: A Heraclitean Celebration and Synthesis of the Modern
Organic Cosmos." Of the 1946 blank verse prototypes, I sample only
suggestive lines—first, "Stars Are Suns" (*Delta Return*):

It was as if I had been born again,
When, in the depths of space, I saw the stars.
The Book of Knowledge had told me through that day
How stars are other suns. Late night I climbed
Our tallest oak. Above the last leaves spread
A dome of burning worlds, then first seen
When day's new knowledge taught the sky to loom.

I skip the next section, on the origin of the solar system, since my
youthful reading of James Hopwood Jeans had launched me, against
my better thought and theory, upon his drama of near collision with a
passing star, an event he reckoned so unlikely as to make ours perhaps
the only such habitat in the universe; whereas I, having learned that
stars condense from seeded nebulae in varying clusters, preferred the

likelihood of multitudes of planetary systems. Since my Jeans debate did not help the poetry, I rather present a sequence from "The Geological Ages":

> Six times since life began has the deep earth shaken
> Down to the core, and revolution thrown
> The curling waters off the vaulting stone:—
>
> First the Laurentian, when the Canadian shield
> Of slow-built sea-bed felt the interthrust
> Of fluid fingers, and the Greenville lime—
> Under the bay-trough of the Eastern Shore
> (There the first germs had formed it, grain on grain),
> Warped and uplifted-rose on the lifeless air,
> Rearing the mountains, whose eroded trunks
> After interval vicissitudes,
> Once more exalted, score their stream-cut shelves
> In Adirondacks (or the Catskill Range,
> Where Rip van Winkle down rekindling dawns
> Slept half his life away).
>   Second the Algoman,
> After a long encroachment of the seas,
> Wrinkled the crust, and on the southern scarps
> Of Canada, and where lake vessels ply,
> Flung barrier cliffs and Alpine peaks of snow.
> Again the wind and waters in their long
> Ablution of the aerial shores, cleft rocks
> And pinnacles, and wore this splendor to
> A gentle plain—but bare and earthy, yet
> No greenness clothed the heaving billows of
> The rounded highlands, but working cells in every
> Vale of loam and cranny of the hills
> Foretold the vital power; and standing pools
> Mantled with algae, which beached in the sun,
> Died in the want of roots they labored on.
> So rose the seas and covered all this plain
> With sandy depositions called Huronian;
> And glaciers from the north bore down the earth
> With groaning green of ice, grooved granite mounds
> And shallow beds of bays, while over wastes
> Of trackless freezing, borne on the sterile wind,
> Dry snow, like gray sand, winnowed on the world.

Then gradual uplifting, central fires
Broke from the fissured crust and loosed their storms
Of ash and lava over barren plains,
While magma from below pushed molten heads
Of hot intrusion, wombs of cupric ore;—
So to the third upheaval, named Killarney,
Rearing new turrets for the sun's bright dawning.

All these are Cryptozoic, lie like dream,
Unknown, behind the metamorphic veil.
But for the paltry half-a-billion years
From then till now—earth bears the fossil scroll
Of her spawn's breeding as of her own throes.

Three-fold the eras, each begun and closed
By vast orogeny-seasons of change:—
Emergent earth shakes water from her loins,
And girds herself with glaciers, drains the pools
Of indolence and ease, beats stagnant forms
Of settled fatness reeling off the globe,
And thrusts new blood, churned at the heart of strife
Through the transfigured veins. Meanwhile no records
Write the tale; earth rather is eroded
Than receives the general deposition.
After years, when on the mountain roots,
Now sunk and worn, the next detritus falls,
Bearing word again what stalks the sphere,
We see all creatures altered, plant, beast, bird,
As if behind a curtain, both the scene
And cast of players had spun with the age
To act new fictions on the starry stage.

These times bear names of Early, Middle, Late:—
Paleozoic, after Killarney's peaks
Had worn to monadnocks, saw the seven-fold spread
Of inland seas over recessive lands
And seven-fold emergence, while each later
Spread records new leaps of life:— the Cambrian
With trilobites and brachiopods;
The Ordovician with first vertebrates;
Silurian of warm seas and coral reefs

And giant sea-scorpions feared of armored fish;
Devonian of first forests, tall tree ferns,
And lobe-finned fishes sloughing through the slime
To mould amphibious limbs; then Mississippian
With epeiric seas again advancing:
Teloists and sharks, the land subdued
To the creeping kind; sixth Pennsylvanian,
Rich in steamy swamps whose carbon formed
Our coal-jungles of spore-bearing trees,
Where droned great dragonflies above the bogs
Of croaking roof-heads, and first reptiles crawled
Out to the hills they kept watch on alone;
And last the Permian, as the quivering earth
Rose slow by years to more volcanic throes
So dried the land, and down the desert steppes
Drove ice and glaciers, and the sodden beasts
That held their swamp homes, felt the steely thrust
Of the cruel nurse that reared them and now killed.
The red-beds of the flood-plains tell what trials
Lashed sprawling sail-fins into Cynodants,
Keen, swift and dog-toothed, our mammalian sires.

There ends the Paleozoic at the wall
And sheer rock cliff that buckled all the world
In folded mountains—Appalachian, fourth
Of revolutions.

       When the curtain draws
(Two-hundred million years before our birth)
We breathe the Mesozoic, the Middle age —
A drier clime; the seed ferns are swept clean;
These rocky hills mantled with conifers,
With pine and redwood and with cycad palm,
Stand over gullied fields of grassless plain.
But in the highlands, answering the demands
Of plunging seasons, flowering plants and trees,
Divergent cycads, forge deciduous power
To gird the world, like some new phalanx, up
From the torrid zone to battlemented snows,
Before this era finds erruptive close.

Here was the time of reptiles, a warm-tempered

World, under the genial sun, and once
Again of spread embayments down the sloping
Plains. This era speaks three periods
Each cut from each by smaller mountain building:—
Triassic, yet of highlands, when the ruling
Reptiles rose upon hindquarters, leaping
Over trails of far-flung promise, pressing
Tracks in time as the mad living flood
Boiled over muddy shores; Jurassic with
Toothed birds, winged lizards, and the Sundance Sea
Withdrawn to marshes, in which beasts of dream,
Huge brontosaurs were feeding, and through fog
Long necks curled upward from the water's womb;
Last the Cretaceous, with the ultimate spread
Of armored reptiles, clawed, horned and fanged:—
When evening beat up wings across chalk walls
Of the Niobrara sea-way, filled with spawn
Of wild sea-lizards foaming past the shore
Where beasts of prey waged elemental war,
Hissing, crying, eating, destroying—the air
Dark with bat-like vanes of reptile sky-wolves,
And the Tyrant King, shaking the rock-shore
Of that dismal main—O then what cowering
Mammal in the trembling trees preserved
Our nascent blood? How many seasons threatened
Nursed a life of sputtering casuistry?
But earth again is folded, faults again
In crustal warpings and volcanic pangs.
Laramide this, whose revolution curled
The western sea-trough from the round of land
Five miles in air, whose sunk roots, reared again,
Piled the front ranges of the Rocky Chain.

When first the mists of transformation clear,
The Cenozoic morning warms a world
Altered like magic from the ruddy plains
Of leaping dinosaurs. Leaves, rustling leaves,
Mottle the forest beds and grassy glades
With shifting shadows, and the golden rays
Of filtered sunlight spill down vaulted bays
And aisles of greenness. Meadows round the highlands
Clothed with ripening grain. Here breeding mammals,

Ever-changing forms, build with maternal
Care propinquities of soul—till sprung
To conscious act they coruscate our globe
With Christian piety and atomic war.

Such the Cenozoic, which contains
Six ages—Paleocene, with tribes of rude
Archaic mammals; Eocene of the new;
Oligocene, with great apes in the trees
And venturing to the ground; mild Miocene,
The golden age of elephants and herds;
Then Pliocene, with winds of future cold,
And human traces; last the Pleistocene,
Closing that period with the mountain throes
That peaked our Himalayas, Alps, Cascades,
And in the rigors of a glacial world
Forged the dire faculties of man.
In such a manifold of altered ages
We mark, of global life, the vital stages.

That lonely Princeton Spring, then Fall, when my overweening
epic would stagger to a pause (midnight, say), I could feel the chill seeping
into the old frame house. What could I do but huddle closer to the grate?
In fact, from my Greenville youth, through the Oxford years, to that very
Princeton clapboard, grated fireplaces had kindled coal with wood. That
night, as invention stalled, five lines versified my service at the hearth:

PATIENCE

The March wind shakes the soul's dark house.
No oracle. I give the fire
The last slash of kindling and a chunk of coal.

How long that black rock waited in the seam
To touch the live wood, and be flame.

The following four neglected pieces review my attempt at a poetry of
thought: from the short Illinois exile (1939-40); through Iowa (1940-
45) and into Princeton, advancing from small Pascalian doubts, like
searchings for a lost faith-world, through a suspended complex of yes
and no, as if complementarity—Blakean or the wave-particle physics of
light—should express wholeness. Here is such a series:

Heresy: I have lived heresy and bear the print of it
          Not for one day, but day by day, in life and
              living.
          I have lived heresy and I surfeit of it.
          I have lived heresy; but where is the truth?

Spring: By thawed ponds I have seen,
          Hung to the water, willow wands, first
              green;
          And I have broke black earth
          And furrowed it and spread the seed of birth
          And watched the fat air bring
          Innumerous spawn to woodland pools of rain.
          Yet Oh, how many times must lusty spring
          Leap on the ragged earth and I creep
          To the truth in vain?

Resolution: I believe all things and disbelieve all
              things;
          I am all contradiction in one, all faith, all
              question;
          And the arguments of life stir me not a straw;
          For each resolves to this:
          That our being is infinite and infinitesimal,
          The world a shambles and glory ineffable,
          The life in us multitudinous and one,
          Incomprehensibly defiled and fine.
          Therefore I give thanks for the spirit
          That lives in me and beyond me,
          That shall live forever, bodied and disembodied,
          To eternal afflictions of joy.
          For these words grow not of this flesh,
          Hand or pencil, which they stir to life,
          And which sink to death behind them.

Let the last in this search for the abstract take us to 1948, when heavy hydrogen mushroomed over Bikini Atoll, and earth's atomic voice broke upon me again, but in such a fury of Satan, prehistory, and Christendom as baffles me still, after more than fifty years.

BIKINI (August 1948)

When a scheduled blast of mass opened under ocean water
The lighted cave of death, one of protean generation
Wallowing in the hot ooze at the blue wall of the cavern
Spoke to Amerigo Vespucci:—

What madness is this in the veins of your westward children,
In the spring-thaw and lilac and fullness of the land
To nurse prurience of murder like coals of an old fire
To the feared and wished birth of killing perversion? Is it an
African savage you love, who moves in jungle fastness
Feculent hips to the drum-tempered sickness of loins?
Is it a memory of that morning in the jungle Gobi .
When you leapt from the light branch on the fear-
        halted gazelle
And took warm blood, crusting the beard of body?
        Deeper still . . .
There stalked in the bush beside you, and you sprang
        to the tree,
One of your ancient kinsmen, mouthing, the
        saber-toothed tiger.
You had many rivals then in killing who usurp now
The whole lease of office, forgetting you are only puppet
Agent of the lord Lucifer whose cruelty thews his motion.
You have a mother it is true of different nature, mild, benign
With whom once played in the beast-hemmed cradle Christ,
While real or imagined angels sang the hope that has blessed
Your procreation. And you will hunger to live her
        sweetness
Of which even the wish plumes war. For the mad
        father who fell
From the sky's hell and gathered in the brute arms of
        his burning
Her sin-conceiving beauty, runs in your limbs like fever;
And your kin and kind you know and greet with the
        kiss of Judas,
Knowing, betraying, hating, loving. World enigma wounds
Your fallen self. From the brunt of matter and beast-tearing
Down into death and spirit's rearing—all will be accomplished;
And not your peace or terror is worth the salt of your tears;
For bridging the cleft bides One you thought to

partake too much of,
Who has pressed wine of your ruin the years' instant
of his music,
Drunk on hills of space the must of your immolation,
Singing the song that shakes your heart with triumph
and despair.
Atoms of his tumult caught a flash in waves of his
warfare,
Plunging destruction you burn his voice rivering the hills.

To which Vespucci idling the tide whispered in answer:—
You who are of protean generation speak as if you
thought me
Man and earth mother and a bridge over the cleft of time—
Forgetting I am but a bone-wraith lackeyed on the flood.
And to what I am will come my children, when your protean
Heart will question no earth-mother but first mother of stars.
And I, who am barely bones, will know as much of
the answer
As that life-drunk giant you have dreamed, shaking
eternal hills.

At Princeton that year, events were pressing toward a change
of jobs. Gerould, sensitive chairman of English, who had received
me from wartime physics, had retired, giving way to Donald Stauffer,
who told me (in regard to *Symbolic History*), trembling all over: "Your
larger studies constitute a liability in this department." I pointed out
that I had published (from my Fairfax thesis) as much as most of them
lately; besides (though I did not mention it), I was admired as a teacher.
But nothing could compensate for my avoiding the gossiping Eng-
lish Club (I knew English already), or worse, arrogating beyond my
competence in the shows (as if anybody had a secure competence in
anything). Besides, I had earlier vexed our senior professor, Old Root,
arguing with him that a core of Blake's prophetic works should join
our required reading list and be studied in class. To which he stormed:
"Blake's prophecies will enter the assigned readings over my dead
body!" Recklessly, I replied: "That might not be a bad idea."
Now, indeed, I went hog wild, and when it came my turn to
address the English faculty, instead of presenting some normal Fairfax
criticism, I gave them (without benefit of slides or music) the densest
abstract of my Philosophy of Paradox, with its overflow into an Outline
of Period Styles. That same Root, who read his lectures from notebooks

falling to pieces, left, crying: "Bell is mad!" Though I was not half as mad as I needed to be.

Kahler and John Berryman, however, were so moved that we went to Erich's and drank wine and talked much of the night; and John, without sleeping, got on the train and went to New York to tell the John D. Rockefeller people, whom he knew, that they had best give me a postwar grant, which they did, without my even applying. By the Spring of '48, I was given leave to go abroad, photographing, now from the originals, for my Epic of Culture.

Before that departure, I return to what I might earlier have called "the accelerating tug of lust, loss, and new love," since in addition to the seven poems there mentioned as printed in *Songs* I have uncovered in the Poetry Notebooks a variety of other verses from the same years and range of places, which range also in message, from bitter misogyny, hardly to be defended, to extravagantly reaffirmed passion. For the instruction of troubled couples, and to confront the paradoxes I weathered more than fifty years ago, when a first marriage was tearing itself to pieces, let me pluck samples of that acid fruit:

DELIVREZ-NOUS, SEIGNEUR

Speak of constancy to the wind,
Of friendship to the foeman,
Speak of pity to the wolves,
But never to a woman.

Look for bitterness in gall,
For lying in the showman;
Count on the littleness of all,
And the cruelty of woman.

Spare children from the wars, O Lord,
Spare foxes from the yeoman;
Shelter dream from truth, good Lord,
And shield my heart from woman.

EROS NIKETOR

"We are too wise in this afflicted age,
Too conscious of the cost; we dare not wage
The spendthrift life of love. The guardian angels
That spread healing wings above the charnels

Of rent hearts have flown. Our fragments fall
To ruin. We cannot, lady, cast our all
Upon a doubted loss. Timid we've grown.
Such is the fever saps us to the bone."

So mumbling, self-secured, I sensed the blow
About the heart; and down the undertow
Of bewildering tides witnessed the wild god's glow
And learned his leaping voice: "Fool, fool, now know—
Whatever loss the spinners at their loom
Have spun your lingering days, you bear the doom
Of my dire will and desperate martyrdom."

TO A WISHFUL WIFE WHO TOOK FLIGHT
(Princeton, 1948)

Diotima, you I sing
Lovely, cold, sepulchral thing—
Shrined in your Platonic sphere
Like Guenevere upon a bier,
Tell me, though: did Guinevere
Sweeter fancies discover,
Above, or here?

Her pupils were less fortunate—
Love she took, and heaven as well,
But lost Francesca wings in hell
For welcoming the importunate
Sweet kiss that binds her still.

We though have learned a new device
To lethargize our love on ice,
Nor know from first to last
If it has come or passed.
Therefore, Diotima, dear,
We'll hymn Platonic songs upon our amorous bier.

DARWINIAN LOVE

Trust no sirens but in bed;
Aim at maidenhead.
That's the art to clip their wing—
Leave them bound and you go sing
In the sweet spring.

Love, like all affairs of life
From life to death is a strife;
And if you come with honest gentleness
They take your heart to dress
For their hearts' mess.

I do not laugh as I write this,
For I sealed love with a kiss
And we who are of docile nature know
Only beasts of prey can go
Safe from the foe.

Despite the sour realism, it remains true that the sullied Eros of our
marriage never spread bolder sexual wings. Who would have believed
that the Black Mountain-to-Rockefeller-year of mutual infidelities,
would also have produced, after a long woodland coupling, a poem
clearly addressed to the same first wife and invoking that Ganymede
whom early Goethe made a symbol of physical love raised to enrap-
tured transcendence ("Ich komm, ich komme! / Wohin! Ach wohin? /
Hinauf! Hinauf strebts / . . . / Mir! Mir! / In eurem Schosse / Aufwärts!
. . : "I come, but where? / Upward, upward . . . / Clouds of the sky /
Bend to me, / Me; I am here, / Seizing, seized—/ All-loving Father—/
Upward on your breast") Goethe soared; yet my own "Transcendental
Ganymede" (Princeton, Fall 1947) seems to have come from the final
desperate sexuality which, over that year, had singed the page with the
misogyny quoted above.

> Not that we reach, mounted, beyond ourselves, but
>   that gods
> Descending take homes in us, as doves
> In late bare trees. Who knows these moments, nods
>   Their mastery.
>   But not doves only (love's
> Peaceful possession)—hawks too, or bright air's

Eagles, Zeus-birds, rend the blue. Our hearts
Greet sensuous seizure.
                    This the title bears:
"Transcending self," and is the highest part
Of man as spirit. Spirit is it sure,
When such mere body's touch as late with you,
Long my life's love, sounding hearts' overture,
Summons antiphonal reply—this hue
And cry of Amors, that with panting prey
Beat broad plumes skyward in flesh-caressing day.

Opportune that on the Italian boat steaming to Mediterranean ports I met a man, U.S.-Florentine, long in the States and just divorced, who was going back to manage his town house and country estate. He boasted that he had found the secret to lasting happiness in marriage: "Get a new wife every year." I dashed off a poem shallow enough to please him: "Perennial" ("love's bittersweet had all come back"):

Leaves, leaves.
What is this talk the dead revive?

They do, they do;
But from another branch or stem—

As every spring love's bittersweet
Returns, but kindled by new eyes.

And indeed, my crisis of marriage had stamped me with such hunger that through all the early 1948 wandering I was caught in the magnetism of looks—only to back off, determined to weather and regain my family.

The peak of that nostalgia struck in war-ruined and impoverished Naples, where disguised rogues, pleading for help, tricked me out of money I could hardly afford to lose; though I got most of it back by a counter-plot as I have narrated in a yet unpublished short story. The mood of Naples would be caught later in the last poem of *Delta Return's* Love dialectic, "Dark Caritas." Anyway, my final poetic appeal to Mildred (as the Blacks would say, "a fart kicked from a dead donkey") reached out from the Bay of Naples—rephrasing Arnold's "Dover Beach." Such my "Letter from Naples," March 1948, in *Songs*, with a now-added reprint of the Arnold.

Consider, I had sailed February 25—a month already of

traveling, with the Naples American Express as my address. Of course
I had written home, but no answer had come. When the young Goethe,
in a love-depression short of suicide, purged it in *Leiden des jungen
Werthers* (*Sorrows of the Young Werther*), a romance which took
Europe by storm, the book generated a wave of suicides, which Goethe
had, as it were, exported. I, in the depression of Naples, set down
sixteen lines, with a title from Dante's *Inferno* vii, 123, oh the wrathful;
though if wrath was my trouble, it seems to have been self-wounding:

PORTANDO DENTRO ACCIDIOSO FUMMO
(Bearing within acid fumes)

We have lived too deep and lived too long:
It is time, Lord! Let fall
Some culminant displeasure. That wrong
And right and all,

Together hurled, like clay handled
With hope, be wrung in rage;
So sick love sours in us a vandal
Hate and sacrilege.

And as the flush of maudlin music wanes
To one poor pipe that trembles
Heart's nursed pain—
Then breaks to brass and cymbals—

Break in us this sigh of wounding wish
Into the blast and flaming wars
Of your clean force, that moves
Cosmic fingers down exploding nebulae of stars.

Of course Mildred had made up her mind, even then (thank God), that
our marriage was irrecoverable.

From Naples, radiating escape, I went to Florence, where Ga-
briella, as always, was lovingly platonic, though her vivacious younger
sister, Lilla, began to think she too was falling in love with me. In sub-
conscious response, I dreamed of our meeting on the pensione balcony
over Florence ("La Giostra", *Songs*, a poem whose last line came to me
in Italian: "La Simonetta ardente mi riprienava le braccia," "the burning
Simonetta filled my arms"—thus demanding the rest of the poem). I
confirmed, however, that I had to leave next day for Le Harvre, and the

boat of return to my family. How could Lilla know that on the train I would write a playful tribute to our fondness?

> Young of face, my heart is old,
> Begs for alms, the love of youth.
> When hearts are changed, I find for cold
> I have her fire, but she my winter's ruth.
> There is no way, when one heart's done,
> Changing, to make two of one.
> Now burning with her heart of flame,
> I see her eyes glazed in my snow;
> And of that fire and cold, call back again
> My ancient heart and let her sweet heart go.
> So now I have this heart of stone,
> And she burns love, and burns alone.

From that 1948 stay in Florence, there was a memorable complement to the pensione fondnesses in my introduction to Bernard Berenson's Fiesole garden and Villa I Tatti. It was a fine Spring day and B.B was helped around the garden and later into the art-loaded house by the usual devoted lady attendants, among them the charming librarian and secretary, Nicky Mariano.

Berenson greeted me cordially, and treated me, with others, to an account of his life on that beautiful hill over Florence, waving at the garden with its new-grown spires of Italian cypress, assuring us that he and his wife (with Nicky) had planted those trees what seemed ages ago. I scanned it all, marveling, then said, "You must feel like a creating God in this paradise." His finely-shaped, grey-bearded face went poignantly sad, "Yes," he said, "God also suffered disappointments in his Garden of Eden." I guessed the chief such for B.B. was the 1945 death of Mary, that life-companion.

After the smile of Florence, Paris seemed to load both sight and scribbled responses with decadent rancor, especially what seemed the lecherous Luxembourg:

> A bald old man and married girl
> On a bench in a park weeping;
> Colors of evening dance in the wind:
> "It's a long time gone since we were young."
>
> I sit beside them on the bench, alone.
> Under the bushes four fat legs are twined.

> If love is rightly to be called a pearl,
> It often has been cast, I say, to swine . . .

> Another runs to the dappled path, opening skirts
> Behind her. Is that a buttock
> I have known? Let it go . . .

But what neither the specter (or flesh) of Mildred, nor I, or anyone else, could foresee was that when my Havre boat would dock at Southampton, Friday, July 9, 1948, Diana Mason (Danny) would come aboard, and that, by a chance of seat assignment, I would find myself across the table from her maiden grace and naturalness. Later, we drew deck chairs together through a quiet crossing, while I read her Shakespearean plays. Of course, I told her of my family, and though we knew we were in love, when her mother met her in New York, we parted as if forever.

Mildred wanted the house solely in her name. Why—God knows?—That left me wondering at first: all the trouble we had had with it—making apartments in the unused wings to help my poor Princeton salary pay the mortgage and tax. In the course of which an odd incident occurred. In one room there was a big built-in cupboard; I think it was a storage place off the kitchen. But a new lavatory was being put in to serve a planned apartment. Our plumber, named Hubbard, had found no way but to cut into the cupboard for a drain and vent pipe. The result I expressed in a lousy rhyme:

> Old Mister Hubbard
> Cut up the cupboard
> To put a stink-pipe there;
> When the pipe was in
> He said with a grin,
> "That cupboard's past repair."

So I had wondered why a wife would want single title. Of course, I agreed. We went down town on our bikes. After the papers were signed and sealed, she told me, now the house was hers, I should get out. So I went to the Parnassus Bookshop where the Flecks rented me an attic room with board. That was September 12, 1948. I need not be ashamed that the first night or so I wrote the bitter "Locus of Love" in *Songs*. Then I remembered Danny's talking of her home, Little Pines Farm, Darlington, Maryland; so I wrote, asking to visit and meet her parents. After a weekend of walking the river hills, the poem, "Woodbird" (my simple best?), was written Sunday evening on the train returning to Princeton.

Here, leafing my Poetry III notebook, ranging from Princeton to Chicago, I find a page dated 1948-49 offering three poems: one is that same "Woodbird."

WOODBIRD (for Diana)

Woodbird softly trilling from the maple spray;
Red leaves above quiet waters
In the webs of sun.

This fall is my spring; down lost forest ways
Your frank eyes guide, the daughters
Of laughter run.

When I forget, my love, image of the light and spray,
Forget, eyes, earth and waters
And lose the sun.

But another accompanies it, of which I had missed the context. Rereading now, I see myself in the poignant role of "A Broken Sea-Bird," This poem also is dedicated "To Danny":

All day the wind drove westward foam-gray cloud
Out of a cloud-foamed sea. At evening furled
Spent wings in the harbor-home a sick bird, cowed
By what malignance reefs a vessel world.
A girl of the orchard bore him to the warm.
He droops tattered wings that have plumed earth-
Defiance. She strokes that head. What life-storm
Has beat this broken sea bird to love's hearth?

But by now Mildred was fighting to delay the divorce or make it punitive; so Danny and I had to separate until the plaintiff would take her lawyer's advice and go to Reno. The poem for that "October Parting" I publish here for the first time:

Under the drift of cloud gold maples down
The last days' leafage to the rain-mired ground,
Baring the boughs which—mingled gray and brown—
Wail winter's coming, with the fall wind's sound.

Where are the days, daughters of the sun,
Of pear and grape, red leaves and yellow corn,
With long evenings of the harvest moon?
From their rich ruin this lonely winter's born.

Well lost, well loved. When last we plighted eyes
And turned off homeward, each to some far home—
If moon took fog, and with the dull day's rise,
Dead leaves were rattling in the veered wind's song—

We knew we'd lived such autumn as would warm
Seed of return beyond the snows of our harm.

Still, as I wrote in "The Brief I Am": "It was a long winter,
with all the pangs of legal action and inaction. When Galway brought
a Princeton sweetheart up to my heaped attic to meet the professor, she
looked at the book-stacked bunk and refused to believe I lived there.
"Where do you sleep?" she asked. "There, on that cot," I told her; "I
clear the books off at night." She thought she had me. "Where's your
pillow?" she demanded. I never used a pillow those years; but what I
said was: "My pillow is care." Galway told me that when he took her
home she ran into the house crying: "Oh Mother, Mother, I've met a
man whose pillow is care!"

One other Parnassus happening relates to a dream I had in that
same attic, sleeping on that cot (right by the wall). As I have written in
"The Brief I Am":

In my third and last year at Virginia, for required
gym, I submitted—as my father urged—to the noble
art of fisticuffs. I had been dieting for years, not to be
fat like the rest of my family, and now, living on one
meal a day, plus milk and apples, I used to weigh in
at about 117 pounds. I could not tell until I got on the
scales the fate of that day. Below 118, I was
Bantam and sparred with a little Creeping Jesus even
lighter than I, whom I could beat around. Over the
mark it was Featherweight, and I was paired with a
heavier and tougher Italian who would mostly pound
me. Every boxing day was like a Last Judgment
weighing of the soul. How well such libation attuned
me to the unaccountability of divine will.

Now, past midnight on that Parnassus cot, I dreamed
I was with Danny, and that same tough Italian was
making vile remarks about her. Of course I hauled off
to swat him with my powerful left to the jaw, and as
sleep can sometimes break into action, that left of
mine (I was lying on my right side, facing the wall)
delivered a desperate blow to the wall itself,
bruising the knuckles of that hand. When I told
Danny of my dream and showed her the fist, it was
about when her loving great-uncle had tried to
persuade her, while there was time, to give up a man
who had lost his first wife and was losing his
Princeton job. He hated to see her married to a loser.
If she had been moved at all by him, the memory of
my fist, almost broken dream-fighting for her,
confirmed her loyalty.

So the next two poems in *Songs* lead us
through the Spring wedding, source of a twenty-
two-page chapter, so named, from *The Married
Land*. Naturally, it occurred in the beautiful summer
garden of Danny's English mother. My wardrobe
being tied up in the forbidden Princeton house, I wore
a white linen suit of Danny's father. For my best
man, Erich Kahler, my fictional Loewenstein, was
driven down by Max Knoll, another of those exiles
and the inventor of the electron microscope. As Diana
(Lucy of the novel), quaking, left her father's arm,
she might hardly have made it, but twelve white
ducks she had raised and fed came around the corner
of the house, waddling and quacking and fell into line
behind her:

> So she took strength, and with that train of
> gabbling
> bridesmaids she walked pale to the altar,
> which was a bank
> of lilies, and standing, white as a lily, a duck,
> a swan, she
> opened her trembling bill and spoke the fatal
> words. While
> the gaudy peacock her Quaker father, for
> some reason or other

liked to keep around the place, that bird of
luxurious male

pride, spread the iridescent fan of his tail,
and violated the
whole yard and farm with the raucous
assault of his cry.

Earlier, in Princeton, my philosophic-scientific
meditations (after exciting studies with biologist John
Bonner—he then rich with organic insights won from
his slime molds) had come to focus in a four-page
essay published in *The Philosophy of Science*
(January 1948) called "Mechanistic Replacement of
Purpose in Biology"—showing that such analysis of
essence into relationship, while it may suggest
channels of research, is inadequate for the
philosophic synthesis of the organic. Near the close, I
summarize:

The axiom here is only this, that the sum of any
interacting and organized thing, from the electron to
the cosmos, transcends as a unity the parts which
construct it, and if examined rationally must be found
to exist as well in toto, in essence, in spirit (a shocking
word) as in the no more solid particles, the relationships
and dependencies. If this is metaphysics, make the
most of it. It is only what physics presents us, in a
world where without this not only we ourselves but
the universe throughout dissolves into nothings
within nothings, every substance to the last
electron melting into mystery, a trail of
manifestations only, the essential void crowning
a phenomenal field.

Princeton coda: A curious little poem called "Poetic Choice," or
"Choice Reneged" (from my Poetry III Notebook) came to me as I
was walking east of Princeton, below Carnegie Lake dam, along the
Delaware (rather dried up by the dam) and paralleled by the old Dela-
ware-Raritan Canal (formerly much used, and with locks to keep it full,
though stagnant). As I followed the narrow ridge between the two, I
somehow envisaged Nature as a Muse, with this verse result:

When I was younger, Nature came to me
In shape of woman, framed fantastically.
Her eyes were pools beneath long braids
Of trailing vine, her brows were of stone
That moss and flowers curled upon;
Her breasts gold haycocks mantling glades
Above the swart abysm her belly shades.

She found me writing. With the smile of one
Who has loved men, but now loves none,
She spoke these words prophetical:
"You come in a bad season," I heard her voice:
"The wet-mould or the dry-rot, take your choice."
I stared incomprehension. "Well,"
She said, "I cannot speak except by parable:

"Between that dry stream and this stagnant canal
You sit a-fishing. In yonder bed
You take no fish; here many, but they stink like dead."

Against her beauty's scorn I bowed my head.
Held to my scriving. She divining there
Else fool or madman, left me to my care.

I must say that in a search for examples, I thought to propose,
for contrast, a proportionality:

Bell : lush canal : : friend Berryman : dry stream

but I could not maintain it, since he (though avant-garde hermetic)
was prolific and acclaimed, while I (though attempting grand mat-
ter in grand style) was unpublished and unknown. So I shifted to the
most literary student pair, both my friends, and viewers of my shows:
Galway Kinnell, post-romantic; Bill Merwin, as occult and mysterious
as any Surrealist artist. But if I liked them both, how could it fit the
parable? Then I realized that symbolic poles admit of countless vital
blends. Thus any fisherman would hope, neither for a skeletal gar nor
a fat, stinking carp, but for a fine trout or bass. It seemed the exampled
choice had to be reneged. But, what then could the vision mean?

Wedding Day, July 24, 1949. Diana Mason and
Charles Greenleaf Bell.
Left: Wedding portrait of Danny.

Charles Bell teaching the Great Books at St. John's Annapolis: *Treatise on Light* (Newton, Huygens) edited by Robert Maynard Hutchins.

4. CHICAGO (1949-56)
(with Frankfurt; Clearing, Wisconsin; and Puerto Rico)

The move, with Danny, to Chicago was my first venture into the air, as described in the Preface to *Songs for a New America*—how the title-poem of that book had its improvised origin in my blank-verse account of our flight from Baltimore to Chicago's old Midway Airport. From there a taxi took us to 5728 Woodlawn Avenue, where our new Harper friends—Isabel (born a Vincent) and her daughter, Jane, married to George Overton, lawyer—greeted us; but sadly. Paul Harper, a lawyer living next door with his wife, our patroness, Isabel, was in the hospital, dying of a ruptured appendix, peritonitis, plus heart failure. The family soon left to be with him—our job to look after the children of Isabel's daughter, Jane Overton, on the second floor of the house of which we were to occupy the main floor.[1]

Weirdly enough, as we sat in that place, dark and strange to us, I was reading aloud James' *Turn of the Screw*, and we had reached the climax encounter with the evil spirit on the stair—probably the most hair-raising moment in our literature. Just then, through the kitchen door adjoining the hall where we sat, an alarming noise of fierce rustling broke out. Dropping the book, I sprang up, throwing back that kitchen door to find the whole floor covered, after wall painting, with newspapers in which veritable armies of rats were rushing, tumbling, fighting, tearing, and tousling the paper. When I charged in, shouting and flicking the light, they scrammed; though it was hard to resume James' fiction of the ghost on the stair.

In the next days, after I had begun to teach, I realized how deep a demand on time and mind the Hutchins Chicago Plan—emphasizing the Great Books and measuring achievement by comprehensive examination rather than time spent in the classroom—was going to

---

1. How we came into relation with these distinguished families bears explaining. William Rainey Harper (1856-1906), one of the most extraordinary figures in American education, founded and served as first president of the University of Chicago 1890. Harper was also active in the Chautaqua movement, which was co-founded by the Methodist bishop, John Heyl Vincent (1832-1920), father of George E. Vincent (1864-1941), first president of Chautauqua and a student as well as, later, a dean at the University of Chicago. John Vincent, son of George and brother of Isabel Vincent, later read and took interest in my four-page essay, "Mechanistic Replacement of Purpose in Biology" (*The Philosophy of Science*, January 1948) and thus, in 1949, through intermarried Vincents and Harpers of New Hampshire and Chicago, my new wife, Danny, and I won a honeymoon summerhouse in New England; and in Chicago, the library floor of the Woodlawn Avenue Harper House—plus Harpers and Overtons for lifelong friends. To our children, Sandy and Carola, Isabel was always "Granny Harper."

make in preparation and teaching of great works, with a committed faculty, and to excited students. Possessed, almost daunted, by this demand, yet stirred by teacher friends—our Humanities I leader, Gladys Campbell; artists Jim Gilbert, Hal Haydon; and others—I resolved by a creative thrust of my own to reaffirm some poetic imperative. Right away, I wrote my first Chicago verses never before published (though with a fine motto from Coleridge: "of such hues / as veil the Almighty Spirit, when yet he makes / Spirits perceive his presence.")

KNOWN AND NOT KNOWN—CHICAGO

Who has not sat with pen in hand or with brush,
To be quietly surprised by a stranger angel
Lighted at the threshold? You who witness here
The first unfolding of this patterned world; think
It saluted me with just that touch of usurpation:
Some free-verse flower discovered in
The woods. I too have seen it, beckoning
That I should call it mine and not mine,
As you who read, or as Abraham the angels.

We do not ask the blind the color of sun,
Or how the moon is shattered on the waves,
But live the light we are. Vain to confirm
The substance of things believed: dawn openings,
Through windows of the heart, into what,
As we breathe of it, earth-cosmos is—
Every spirit is known and unknown;
Here on the word crest you ride,
(The same that lifted me) both now dissolve,
Quit the stage, to leave in their stead,
Smiling immortal diffidence, the Gods.

In Chicago I stood at a turning point; this early autobiography defines it well:

SPARKS OF EGO (1947)

If I am not destined to create, then there is madness in me, for I have never a moment doubted the augury of my stars. It is with the utmost humility and good humor I make the admission;— This is my peculiarity, as that of the Don was knight-errantry; I describe it no less frankly than I would an extra toe, or any other deformity. That I have it is a fact, nothing more. All men perhaps may feel the same; I believe my father did. In him, one might say, it proved illusion; and so it may in all. Every achievement (beyond what instantaneous spiritual values there are in life itself) is no doubt trivial in the last analysis. Our sense of destiny is only the common voice of the god in us—whatever shorn god has been tricked into mortality. One moment I scoff at my consecration, calling it the nightmare all must suffer; the next moment I cherish it, holding it for the voice of inner oracle. But cursed or loved, in any event it is mine. I admit the possession.

I was plagued with such ambition in disembodied form before I knew what aims to attach it to. I know the feel of it in itself, existing like a Platonic idea without particularity. I trust it is more than a festering of selfhood; though that seems an affliction of our time.

I have run through many states of being, but one thing has united them all: the claim of fevered ego. Until my thirteenth year I read no fiction but of Tom and Huck, Burroughs' *Tarzan*, London's *Before Adam*, and the like; I spent my life on the River or swinging through trees, dreaming of the Mesozoic age and wishing I was an atavism. When I fell in love at eight or ten, I thought no one had loved with that passion before. My second year in high school, when I invented socialism, no man, I would have sworn, had ever dreamed of such a system. I intended to reform the world at once. No money, no classes, no poverty. But first the world must be conquered, lashed into submission. I would be a socialistic Napoleon. I would invent secret weapons—death-rays and rockets. With one strange friend I carried on my dark conspiracies. He left town. We wrote letters that I have since been told were insane. Then he moved again and we lost touch. Earl Sensing was his name, though in my *Delta Return* I turned it to an anagram (Lear Nigssen). I have often wondered if he came to a tragic end; as we both might have—witness that *Delta Return* poem, where we climbed into the chemistry lab of the failed Academy to make nitro-glycerin, see # 4 in the "Book of Knowledge" section: "The Bomb."

Drunk with the poetry of time and space, I feasted on all sciences. Three years I gave to equations and amazing stories, peering at stars, grinding a six-inch mirror, attempting to conceive a three-dimensional sphere turned inside out. At this time I became a violent agnostic—"Religion," I cried, "must be destroyed. The whole world is opening; it will yield like an oyster." I saw all things flow to meaning. We had only to be bold, free, absolute Faustians. Whenever I could, I defied tradition, police, and the law. I raced the car, swerved, cut in, took risks with joyful abandon. I did not know this was the Futurist creed, the faith of a thousand lost, egoistic stirrers of the First World War—at the crux of which I was born.

Many a Summer's night, pondering in my head the bending of space and the formation of galaxies, I peered into the lumpy convolutions of the Milky Way in Sagittarius (as intently as earlier I had peered at a cat I was determined to hypnotize), feeling myself on the verge of vast revelation—one moment and I would catch the key, unravel the knot forever. Napoleon was abandoned. Let the stupid world stew in its own greases. I would enter science, discover high truths, and be content. How could death trouble me? I was cosmic spirit. To live for meaning—a life of gods. I did not know that every romantic from young Goethe to mad Scriabin had been so siren-tempted—the shallow ones hanging over the abyss, until suicide or lunacy took them, and successive wars their world:—

> Until "a subtler Sphinx renew
> Riddles of death Thebes never knew." (Shelley)

In the schools I did nothing. To tell the truth, there was no need. We sat all day in the stupid grades, while the teachers taught for the dullest. The only economy I found was to be among them [I have already told in Chapter I how I would give my father today's assignment as tomorrow's, lowering my daily grades to B- or C +, though my exams were always A. Also how he would groan about "a feeble-minded son; but how on earth does he pass the exams?"] To such pretenses a self-willed person of reasonable intelligence is pushed in this abysmal system we call educational.

Say the fault was my own. I was slow to obey arbitrary demands. "If reasons were as plenty as blackberries I would give no man a reason upon compulsion" (Falstaff). By some rare luck I was sent to the University of Virginia. There, cut off from home and friends, girls and all life's trammels,

left in freedom to make or mar, dared indeed by the society
I had derided, I set like a crystal into a seemingly new form.
I grew diligent to a degree, caressed my work into order,
performed three times what was suggested. I loved to read
through the night—to walk out in the first dawn, the air filled
with robins' song, while the sluggish world was sleeping. Most
of my freshman anthology of poetry was soon memorized. I
read on my own 20,000 pages of listed books the first year,
30,000 the second. In these numbers I took an American joy.
My work in mathematics and the sciences was rational and
meticulous. This lasted long enough to impress my teachers
and get me a good start. Then I became a romantic again—but
at least a hard-working one. I cut almost all my classes, as was
my privilege there, finding them a bore and books more full
of matter. Thoreau I canonized, and worshiped on long walks
to the mountains where I would climb trees and recite poetry
aloud. Science meanwhile led to the dead end of a vacuum
tube. These betrayals were disheartening; but the world of the
arts and philosophy opened its arms.

My whole being was contradiction and anomaly. The
universe of reason and matter in which I so absolutely believed
seemed at times melting away. Spirit and will became every-
thing. That faith could move mountains I accepted. Yet how
could anyone be a dialectic materialist and Berkelian idealist at
one time? I attempted it, knowing neither Marx nor Berkeley.
When I read O'Neil's play of the man who became Christ, I
was convinced that with faith and daring all could do likewise.
Often in walking the street, seeing a cripple or a blind man,
I was pulled by a wild impulse to lay hands upon him say-
ing, "Be whole." If once I could take the step, cast off fear,
and act—I should be that in which I believed, he that which I
desired him. I never took the plunge; and now laughing I say
that if I had, the man would have remained a cripple. But this
would not then have convinced me, nor should it now, since
the test was never made.

So I proceeded, welcoming all extravagance, sus-
pending antinomy, inflating myself with the wildest illusions.
Whatever I thought or did, no one had done before. I discovered
Platonism and a hundred things. It was long after that I found
every fool for a thousand years had been aware of these novel-
ties. Like a true romantic I repeated the errors and follies of
history, under a fond presumption of originality and greatness.

Meanwhile I wrote. In the act of writing I wrote always nobly. It became trash afterwards. The romantic existence is a carnival roller coaster—up and down at sickening speed, manic-depressive forever. But I was seldom depressive. Manias followed too rapidly one on the other.

Even while in the grades, I crept out of bed one night (having just discovered words can be rhymed) and with my sister slipped downstairs at perhaps one or two in the morning to write verses, until my father tenderly—we had feared with rage—lured us to bed. It was then I wrote some nature symbols of a kind, with rhyme, about dandelion seed, etc; but the teacher said they could not be scanned. I proceeded to scan them, employing not only anapests but feet with three shorts and a long. The meter I believe was four beat, so this was primitive stress rhythm. But I was told there were no such feet. I did not write verse again until I was in college. I was a scientist, after all. My last year at Virginia I did some awful stuff. The professor wrote: "If you work all your life, you may learn to write prose; but you will never write poetry, to that I can swear." He may have been correct; it hardly concerns me. I have gone on writing as impulse seized me, then and now under the momentary illusion of worth, and with the still beckoning hope of achievement.

My younger brother, Percy, was the true poet in our family. He developed early. At the end of high school he had written volumes—modern in form, tormented, increasingly schizophrenic. He also painted, in a style between Blake and Nijinsky. I was utterly commonplace beside him. If I wrote verses at all, they were old form and heavy. I did not much paint. It is a misfortune that he was too delicately poised for life, plagued by fat, asthma, thoughts, and countless afflictions. When he bowed out in 1937, I somehow inherited the whole poetic responsibility of the family. I have been writing ever since, generally without exhibiting the product. I have wished to do two things: To develop a living, modern, integrated philosophy, and to express it in classical form. The first of these, I have almost achieved; on the second, I have made a little progress. Though I am now more modest about the excellence of my immediate production than I was when that production was poorer; as regards the future I am mad enough to believe I shall make my synthesis and express it in fit form. But this I must believe, in order to work; and so let it be.

My present (1947) proposal is to publish samples of the verse I have written. Of the worth of his own creation no modern poet can pretend to judge. For the liberated ego and the liberated doubt wage a battle in his mind. One moment he sees the beauty of his progeny, the next moment he would scotch them all. Of one thing, however, I can be fairly sure: this verse will not prove exactly what the poetry-reading public has come to expect. Mine is an emotional and romantic diction different from that of our avant-garde contemporaries (say, my Princeton friend, Berryman). I seldom employ symbolist and imagist veilings. Here you will find direct statement rather than oblique, rhetoric openly indulged in, straightforward didactic and philosophic utterance. Most of these modes, today, are repudiated. However, it is my belief (and my fear) that the modern love of precocious and ingenious verbalism has become a flight from directness on the part of a world which has little direct to say; and I count it as much a disease of our time as "gaudy verse" was of the eighteenth century. My first concern is with communication, and since the average reader may find it difficult enough to understand what a poet has to say, even simply stated, I see no need to obscure my message with devices of the time. Both now and later I should prefer to follow in the steps of Dante, Michelangelo, Bruno, Campanella, Milton, Wordsworth, Goethe, and Blake.

I have even undertaken to explain myself when confusion might arise. This has been done by Dante in so direct a set of poems as those of the *Vita Nuova* and, after him, by Campanella and others.

Having begun to float my verses on a stream of prose, I intend to weave both into a spiritual biography of myself and the age. This has opened my book at once to experiments which could scarcely have been admitted on their own account—particularly to the works of my student years, often adolescent, artful, or out-moded, yet of interest as historical documents in a testament to our time. It is to set off my poems in this light that I have begun and plan to continue.

So I wrote half a century ago and so I take up the task again, though now I have *Songs for a New America*, soon to be published (1953), to refer to.

If we examine that book, searching for principal themes through the Chicago years, from Fall 1949 through 1956 (though the

Spring of '52 would go to the Frankfurt exchange, and the last year be spent on loan to Puerto Rico), the earliest poetic impact is of the Indiana Dunes, where our painter colleague, Jim Gilbert, would entertain us, from the first, in his leased cabin. I tied that remnant wilderness to pioneering history, with the ecological threat of today: thus "Pioneer Fragments," and "These Winter Dunes," lately reprinted by the Santa Fe Sierra Club. In this case, Galway, soon to join us, and I were working almost in resonance—so his "Westport" and his "First Song" (taking a hint from Burl Ives).

A variant of the landscape theme took root a little north and west, at Isabel Harper's country place, "Wind Farm." Its poem, "Nova" (November, '51) will be found somewhat trimmed and improved in *Songs*. Here, I sample my Dedication, with her reply, also the first verse paragraph, affirming the landscape, and the last, protesting suburban development—even to the threat of the "Nova" close.

NOVA (Chicago, November 1951)

For Isabel Vincent Harper, our Libertyville Hostes
who replied: "You have caught the very look and feel of
my country . . ."

Two days of rest from the city; they are welcome.
Afternoon: the sky relaxing holds the horizoned land;
Fields and oaks are brown, the elms are bare;
One sycamore lifts tattered leaves, gold
In the long light, over the whiteness of boughs.
On gusts of wind, clouds are forming and dissolving,
Through which, in slower recurrence, brightens the moon.

South and west a freight train rumbles;
A flight of jets crosses overhead.
They are not even gainful wings of commerce,
But trainers of war from the Glencoe base.
Tomorrow we return to the soar of the city.
Two days of quiet, an island in space and time,
We watch the winter woods and enduring sky,
As we dream in the eddy of an exploding star.

Pursuing the Harper tie, I include a somewhat later poem based on my pruning a row of elms, now part of the same farm, and published in *The London Magazine*, June 1955:

WIND FARM

The old must have incentives
To play the part of the young
(Praise to the fruitful need);
This row of elms wants pruning,
So like a boy I have come
To the swinging top of a tree.
The low sun coins the leaves;
Through fall-gold windows
I watch the lengthening rays
Cross the foreground stubble,
Touch the white hives of the bees,
Where cornrows are standing.

Along the river Des Plaines
In the dark mass of the wood,
Ash and maple turning
Show first yellow in the green.
Beyond is the sweep of the prairies.
It was here that Indians
In the memory of our fathers
Burned the dry grass of winter,
For the sweet forage of spring—
A lure for wild buffalo;
Braves in the wood by the river
Waiting, loosed their arrows.

That brick house at the crossroad
Was built on one of frame;
At the core is a log cabin,
Once the trading post for skins.
The old man who lived there planted
These elms, from the top of which
Swaying, I note these things.
He laughed, years back (says Isabel),
As he leaned on his spade and said:
"A boy, I cleared the land,
Ploughed the first furrows;
Now I plant trees again."

Cycles return and are changed,
Ours and the land's. Who raped,
Rues the loss—our plundered earth.
So I to the sport of a boy,
Come with creaking knees;
Climb the swaying branches
To prune these hard-earned trees.

I recall that from Granny Harper's farm it was a short walk to
Adlai Stevenson's neighboring place. So I leap to his 1952 campaign,
or, just before the election, to a meeting of Bell, Kinnell, and Gilbert in
Gilbert's Dunes cottage—from which to conjure my pre-election poem
written for Adlai.

But before advancing to that doomed espousal, I must cel-
ebrate the extended honeymoon which, by 1963, would produce the
spun polarities of my first novel, *The Married Land.* As Isaiah says,
"Thou shalt no more be called forsaken, for thy land shall be married";
and Augustine: "The beauty of the course of this world is achieved by
the opposition of contraries, arranged as it were by an eloquence not of
words but of things." And indeed, wife Danny and I had exercised our
passion so boldly that by October our first child, to be called Carola,
was begotten. Over the same span, my professional urgency was to give
what I could to the varied teaching of college humanities in Hutchins'
University of Chicago.

It was amazing, in that line, how quickly things got moving.
My reception into the near family group of Humanities I—a study of
choice art, music and literature—was genial from the start. Soon the
Chicago readings, joining those of Virginia, Oxford, and Princeton,
brought into focus a sketch begun at Black Mountain during and after
my cultural shows. Its title, at first "A Modern Sequence," has become
"A Century of Voices."

My Own: "The order you observe is broken; they bend
Across like comets, fiery, burning; we no
Longer control them; it is a sign of the time."

Melville's: One arched in blaze about me, blighted brow,
Lips of lean defiance: "I am Ahab,
I have my desire"—plunged to the ocean
Of proud destruction, flying the crimson hope
Of despair.

Conrad's: Another leapt above me like
          A hound baying the trace, a lurid light
          Linked to an ebon star: "I am Kurtz, I
          Have my desire. From the Walled Sepulcher
          I seared the dark; my victory is horror."—
          Wound in the night he died a desperate yellow.

Faulkner's: "All fruit of knowledge tastes of gall;
          The free heart's hunger, mark, is cannibal."

T. S. Eliot's: Explosion yields to aimless wandering stars
          Beneath a shifting banner, on this side
          Of the Acherontian river, slackers and trimmers.
          One lackeyed the lazy tide: "I am Prufrock,
          I have no desire. In the dearth of will is nothing,
          Dust of the field . . . Emptiness is the way."
          He faded upon the distance, lifeless, gray.

Against the general fellowship of Humanities I, the college seemed split by the Aristotelian rigor of Richard McKeon, dean of the division of humanities and a noted classics scholar, opposed to the forced analytics he imposed, especially on the texts of Humanities II. "Yet surely," I thought, "I have been as much drawn to philosophy as to anything." I sent him an offprint of my biological essay from *The Philosophy of Science*. An appointment followed, at which I was amazed by his hostile warning that my organic thought was as far as possible from that of the Stagyrite, which informed the college program, and to which I should adjust my way of thinking as soon as possible.

I did not tell him that I had tried his introductions the night before and found them mostly soporific. But even without such confession, I felt myself almost booted out of his office. Our meeting had broached what time would confirm—that the teaching delights of Chicago were cleft by the dominance of McKeon as dogmatic Aristotelian. Indeed it was less McKeon himself than the competitive rivalry of his sycophantic followers—for all the world as if the big lobster had commandeered a school of crawfish, and even down to shrimp, all working their lesser claws with the same rhythmic assent, urgency, or threat as the big lord of the reef. Clearly, to break into those committee sessions with a counter message was to strike at one's professional chances. I witnessed several over the years who, going either modern or Platonic, were relegated to the larger fishpond—as I would, surely (and soon) have been, but for the backing of European and American friends. Of course I wrote a poem about such displays, though I didn't publish it or even pass it around. It enacts a collapse to the "I" of soul's "Windowless Monad."

I shall go up into my room again.
In all walks of life are the little men
With grasshopper jaws and dry, small spirits;
They have the shifting eyes of ferrets.

I shall go up into my room.
Theirs is the scent of rodents; if you come
A stranger here, they snarl you back;
It is a kindness in effect:
Their presence is a poison cup.

I shall go up.
Darker than ever—but within, dark breaks
To unmeasured mountains where sun strikes
And an eagle soars in the dawn glow.

I shall go.
And no insects alive. When the powers call,

I shall
Respond to the cry—

I.

Having spat that out, I come to Chicago's counter-blessing, the vital immigrant Europeans urged by those of Princeton, especially Erich Kahler, to search us out and bring us the solace of fellowship. Surely the greatest European of that Chicago was a fugitive from Mussolini, Giuseppe Antonio Borgese, whom Hutchins had met on an Atlantic crossing and, without consulting his professors, had invited into the language department. When those professors champed at the bit, Borgese was put in charge of The Committee to Frame a World Constitution, with its journal *Common Cause*. Though he was also giving Dante readings where his thrust-out jaw and lip seemed to make him the most defiant sinner in hell: "Vedi la!—Look there, Farinata, who has raised himself up!"

It was one of our first Sunday afternoons, when he appeared at the Harper dwelling with his wife, Elizabeth, youngest daughter of

Thomas Mann. As it turned out, I had met them before, at Erich's of course—a reception after their Princeton marriage. (Her father had also been there, looking younger than the Italian husband.) Now the two arrived as I was unpacking and shelving my books in the mullioned Jacobean library of the Harper House. And Borgese read a three-language poem he was working on: of his Italian youth, German college years, and now American exile—having fled from a Europe of Fascism, war, and post-war.

Since it is one of the great poems of our time (though known, if at all, because I showed it to Rolfe Humphries, who published it in his first Ballantine anthology), I appropriate it here, exercising, perhaps, a minor right, since Antonio (though the English of his own close is consummate) preferred that Galway and I provide translations of his Italian and German passages.

EASTER SUNDAY (1945)

O Sicilia, o Toscana, ove sostai
fanciullo, o dolce pian di Lombardia,
misurato dai gelsi, ventilato
dalle piume dei pioppi, io dunque più
non premerò le vostre vie, levando
il ciglio ai borghi bruni in cima ai olivi,
ai fidi vespri reduce cercando
le tue guglie marmoree, Milano
che il respire dei paschi inteneriva
di volubile nube; non più:

(O Sicily, O Tuscany, where I
In boyhood paused, O sweet Lombardy plain,
Measured by mulberry-trees, fanned by the feathers
Of poplars, where no more I tread your ways,
Lifting my eyes to townships brown along
Your hills, or, coming home to trusty evenings,
Seeking the marble pinnacles of Milan,
Made softer by the breathing of the meadows
Where the cloud lingered. Now no more.)

                    dich
nicht, Deutschland, Erde meiner zweiten Frühe,
wo klare Ströme rauschten durch den dunklen
Duft der sachte weichenden Waldungsnacht,

Geranien aus erwachenden Geländern
mit tausendfält'gen Mädchenlippen lachten,
ich aber einsam wandelte von Berg
zu Berg, stieg auf ur-rote Glockentürme,
lauschte den Tönen, die die Tiefe barg,
die fremde Schöne mit verliebtem Auge
fasste: night mehr:
O Tenebrae! O Aceldama!

(Nor thee,
Germany, land of my second prime, where clear streams
Rushed through the fragrant darkness of the night,
The slowly yielding woodland night, and flowers,
Geraniums, from balconies at morning,
Laughed like a thousand girls, but I went, lonely,
Wandered from ridge to ridge, climbing bell-towers
Of immemorial red, listened to music
Enclosed in depth, and with my loving eyes
Held that strange beauty. Now no more!
O Tenebrae! O Aceldama!

You passers-by who stop and wonder
what I in uncommuning sounds lament;
it is as if I had left home at noon
and looked homeward before sundown; I see
the barns aflame, the house a rump, the trees
writhing in desperate embraces; death
with claws of strangling smoke grips ground and air.
The silence is one shriek, one chasm Languages the paths.
So let me step westward; my shadow is long.

I noticed at once a triple wonder of Borgese's poem: the linguistic skill that could write of his classical youth in the style of Manzoni, then of the university years in a German redolent of Goethe and Hölderlin, and finally, in a blend of Shakespeare's sonnets with post-Yeatsian modernity, could master our poetry and period style—to all of which was added an amusing turn, in that one who had such command of the written languages, when he read the piece aloud, brandished throughout the Italian accent of his origin. Finally came the substantial marvel of the last line; the affirming length of the exile's shadow comes exactly from the burning world behind him: "So let me step westward, my shadow is long."

I need not, or rather cannot, express how crucially those two, Antonio and Elizabeth, added to our Chicago stay. (Racing along the outer drive with Elizabeth at the wheel, going from a wine tasting to our house, I hatched my finest expression of the tragic glory of Adlai's dreamed America—"Diretro al Sol"—the title drawn from Dante's great passage of Ulysses sailing "Beyond the Sunset"—to his doom.) But that poem would initiate the fall of 1951.

Meanwhile the 1949-50 school year had ended. For those early Chicago summers, Danny and I would return to her family at Little Pines Farm, Maryland—that year for the birth of Carola. Once East, I could manage art jaunts to Washington, Baltimore, New York, even Boston, staying with kith or kin and not only seeing but turning the seen into verse. What American museum could so foster art and myth as Boston's Isabella Steward Gardner? I scooped up what I could for the scribbled first draft of this dramatic monologue, "The Museum: Isabella, Widowed, to the Family Lawyer" (Summer, 1951):

> "Up at a villa, down in the city," here
> We take them both in one:—under Boston's
> December sun, the glass vault culls Venetian
> Spring. Leaves and blossoms. On those trees, gold
> Fruit of the Hesperides. Peeping statues
> Out of vines: the marble faun, the brazen
> Swain. And the smooth grace of Hellenic line
> Teases a pleasure out of pain. Casements
> Triple-arched are here, from the hills
> Of Tuscany. But the great thing arrived
> Today. Come, my dear. Here at the fountain
> Mounts the stair. (Red is the tile; silks rustle
> On the balustraded aisle.) Up again,
> And so you see: the Titian purchased by
> B.B. I think now I can pass in peace,
> Holding that play of color. I saw it first
> In Venice at the Casa d'Or, where cockroaches
> Ran on the marble floor; and it is rich
> In memories, like every chair and stone.
> They have all known the good times gone, when Europe
> Sang—its season of birth, when I too would have wished
> To be born. Observe the court. That little Pan
> Was our first loot, the first we carried Westward.
> Take my hand. The things I have seen: I cannot
> Bear it, old. I called you here to say

This will of course be public, a museum,
And they will share it all, all but the dream . . .
That rattle on the glass. Our Boston rains.
But the blown robe of Europa brightens the gloom.
Now only the descent remains. My dear friend, come.

It was another fine European, Arnold Bergsträsser, Chicago
Head of German, who having lost an eye in the First World War, but
shunning Hitler before the Second, had come to America and been ad-
vanced by Hutchins; he, learning of my love for Goethe and Hölderlin,
came weekly to the house for such readings—which gave me another
boost forward, especially for my European photographing—since by
late January '51, Arnold and I were friends, and he had decided to send
me, with Danny, on the Frankfurt-Chicago exchange of Spring '52 to
teach the American Literature Program (using German conversation).[2]
Five poems from that term, with its Easter vacation, found their way
into *Songs*; others from that varied span have now to be gathered into
this Life.

When I turn, however, to my Poetry Notebook for datings of
the time, I am reminded that the Fall of '51 should first be dealt with. I
have mentioned "Diretro al Sol" (September '51) as my most glowing
American celebration, though like Thucydides' praise of Athens, my
paean has a tragic cast. And how else, when those years heightened the
Fascist threat of McCarthy; while our European refugees flocked to the
university common room television, dreading lest we were hatching
an American Hitler. No wonder my poems of the Chicago notebook
variously precipitate a nightmare counterpale, as of Apocalyptic vision.
Here is one such from that October 1951:

DREAM OF THINGS FEARED

We were walking down the rock scarp of the hill
In the decline of day, as light waned
Under a dark omen of cloud. Our eyes scanned
The looming threat of horizon and sky, then fell;
Bent to the road, as if walking would quell
The voice of alarm, some dread of ruin at hand.
But crisis delayed ebbs; we proceed the same,
Forget our fear, push on, trust all is well.

---

2. In 1949, with the idea of introducing the Chicago University model to Germans as a
means of training them for a new democracy, Borgese and Bergsträsser had organized a
program to send Chicago faculty to the Goethe University in Frankfurt.

When lightning now takes the roadside elm,
A shelter of the past. We look again
To see the neglected great mushrooming cloud
Advanced over all the sky—incredible.
And we can only pace down the same road
In the first drops of apocalyptic rain.

In December, Gladys Campbell, born in Chicago before 1900,
narrated what she had seen that day, while I turned her account to a
kind of pseudo sonnet: "Show Us a Sign":

Through two wars I have watched this city. No bombs
Have struck here; I saw no blocks destroyed, no flood
Of fire. We traveled for the witnessed harms
Of history—this land mercifully spared.

But yesterday at the corner of Third and State
A trolley turned blind in a blinding rain
Crashing a truck of gasoline. The whole street
Exploded; buildings, people, what could remain?

Today the charred-out roots of torn walls,
Recalling London, Milan, Cologne; the crowds
Gathered to witness, pressing and appalled,
Stunned to silence; only the headlines loud—

Teach us, in the space flight of our pride,
The intrinsic peril of the powers we ride.

Strange that though my hatred of McCarthy's rabid anti-com-
munist conspiracy, hostile also to Adlai, was such as compelled me
to tear him to pieces, under the pseudonym of O'Malley, through a
whole chapter ("Conspiracy") of *The Half Gods*, it has left in my verse
mostly oblique ironies:

FOR A CHILD OF THE NOBLE SAVAGE
IN TIMES OF INVESTIGATON

The man-trained willow
Bends to the ground,
Obsequious, mellow,
Over-inclined.

Trees of nature,
Tall as strong,
Lightning may blast
On the hill's crown.

To the time's temper
Give regard:
Plant the weeping willow
In your yard.

Though I recover a poem stronger, perhaps, which turns the descent of night on the city to an image of political rigor:

NIGHT CITY; CHICAGO; TIME OF McCARTHY

Strange in the park beneath our sky-tall city
To watch daylight ebb, night lights appearing;
Earth's calm glow of land, cloud and azure
Hardening to glints in darkness. Cars,
Driven by men of human form and feeling,
A woman now and then of memorable beauty
Sharpen to extremes, abstract speeding flares;
A glaring cauldron is a place of meeting,
Vanished the subtle shadings of our liberal city;
Skeletal white-on-black repacing loved humanity.

Historical motion, engendering symbolic fear.
Deliver us from the zeal of radical polarity:
Neon and steel, stripped years of the modern;
Vision power-wrenched to ruthless reality.

But now the new year gave me what is probably my most precisely imaged expression of modern organic science. February 1952 I was walking around a university playing field when a man riding a fine horse sped by on the cinder track. What I saw and scribbled became "The Rider," one of the last poems in *Songs*, searching a mystery: how the will masters matter by subtly guiding natural forces. Its last line: "Perceptive spirit rides with loosened rein."

Memory now assures me our vessel was French, since Carola, then nearing two years, confined her eating mostly to the ever-present tray of cheeses. At Plymouth I hailed "The Humanist Island," which had gallantly weathered the war. Here are phrases:

> Night. The long path of the moon sways
> On calming water. The pulse of motors ebbs;
> Lights, then slow dawn. Chalk cliffs;
> Dapple-crowned with gardens. All the worth
> You poured into the world has earned a name
> For joined folk endurance. I greet you—
> Loved island in your sheltering sea.

From Plymouth we bussed north to Tintern Abbey—scene of Wordsworth's poem, memorized at Virginia—scene also of the ridge trail, which I had hiked with a friend when we cycled from Oxford, 1938. So I begin:

TINTERN REVISITED (March 1952)

> Fourteen years have passed, summer and winter,
> And here this first of spring I stand again
> On the tall rock over a curve of the Wye—
> The Abbey ruin below in its green field.
> But listen! East of the ridge on the Chepstow side
> Comes a roar of tractors—that forest betrays
> Harvest of power-saw run wild. I recall
> The stripped Appalachians and Ozarks of home:
> "The time," I said "has come; our New World disease
> Spreads contagion on an earth gone mad."
> And then I thought "Why ours? Why now?" These Isles
> For centuries could hold their treasured forests—
> Exploiting those abroad—till Britain's wealth
> War-wasted, the chain saw gnaws at Robin's wood.
> Back then to the rock: north and westward stretch
> Pastoral reaches of the poet's praise.
>
> Let the tractor snarl on gullied trails . . .
> It is only at my back; before me swathed
> In luminous mists of grass-valleyed streams
> A broad sun sinks over the mountains of Wales.

From Tintern, we bussed north to Danny's wonderful cousins in their Queen Anne house at Elmley Lovett in Worcestershire. Hardly for long enough, since Danny and Carola went to London to visit the

beloved Aunt Ev and then flew south to Aunt Sally in Provence. I head-
ed for Frankfurt, but by a southern loop of photographing in northern
Italy. From that April swing, two Lago di Como poems came into my
Songs: "Tremezzo," "Villa Carlotta." On the following pages, the first
Frankfurt poem tangled with some drunken soldiers of our post-war
Occupation.

Meanwhile Carola in Provence had contracted diarrhea (the
direst rear in the country), exacerbated by local treatment, from which
she might have died, if Danny had not brought her to Frankfurt and an
American doctor. There, I thought I had secured an apartment—rather a
feat in a city so bombed and occupied. But when Danny arrived, a nurs-
ing mother with a fluxing child, to wash fluxy diapers and hang them
on the veranda, the home owner luckily advised us to commute north
to Bad Homburg, where Hölderlin stayed when his love for a Frank-
furt banker's wife (his "Diotima") had got him fired from teaching the
banker's son. We found an agreeable pension near the Kurpark where
we could walk and drink the mineral waters, inscribed to noble ladies,
as if their waters had tasted just so. Walking the other way, west and
north, past the ruined castle, we could enter the Forest of Taunus at the
walled limit of the old Roman Colony. It was there indeed that Danny
and I enjoyed a picnic which produced a visionary poem, as if sleep
and storm had revived Nazi war:

IN THE WOODS OF TAUNUS

The young beech leaves dance gold against the darker
Fir—a wind-blown weaving. We have slept
An hour, a shift of sun and cloud, while birds
Sang from their towers, and brown bread and wine
Mingled, breeding dreams, first calm, and after
Thunder: planes in the air, drifts of acrid smoke,
As burned from flesh and rags—all birdsong silenced.

I do not know the cause of these eruptions,
Peace into war; why God being nature, us
And now, having this leaftime cannot rest
At ease, sharing his sweetness. It is the question
Satan, waked in fire and touched with visions,
Whether dreamed or real—peace beyond that storm—
Put to his maker: "Why not have kept us there?"

God feeds upon that asking. And yet in sleep
Or love, those troughs of action, you may find
By your side a fair wife smiling; or glimpse above
Fir trees in the play of clouds, whose threat of thunder
Waits under the hill, such past, such now,
As when—more would deny the opposites we are—
Lucifer of the morning dances with his God.

After a spell of teaching, a short break took us east and south
to the rural beauty of the Neckar, with Tübingen and the tower where
Hölderlin, greatest rhapsode since Pindar, first neglected and then mad,
closed his life. My notebook offers two poems, "Dawn in Tübingen"
and "Hölderlin's Tower"; let the latter suffice:

HÖLDERLIN'S TOWER

In the park by the Neckar
The morning martin
Sings over the river
From Hölderlin's tower.

Can the soul of the poet
Who watched at that window
All the years of his madness
Take a glad martin's voice?

No. Come at night rather,
When reflecting water
Cradles the moon
In a darkness of trees.

And a nightingale
Grieves the silence,
That caged nightingale
Whose partial call

Is the bare planctus
"Tereu" and "tereu,"
Which swelling and ceasing,
Sighs and fails—

Gone the "dug, dug" trills
That even a night bird,
Born to nature,
Sings with its kind;

Yet that disabled
Lamentation
Says more than the "chuck, chuck;
Good year and good luck"—

For us, too, whose life-word,
Like his, unheard
Abides long years
In soul's windowed tower.

After "Hölderlin's Tower," during my next bout of teaching in
early July, Danny thought it best to bear our second daughter, San-
dra, at home. The weekend before she left, Lulix von Simson, wife of
Otto von Simson (our Chicago friends), staying in her ancestral great
"Frankenstein" house, invited us there. One poetic piece, stirred by the
night cry of a bird, seems a symbolic search into the validity of my (or
anyone else's) wartime pacifism:

FROM A CASTLE NEAR THE IRON CURTAIN
(Night of July 9, 1952)

The sudden screech of a bird fills the night wood.
A beat of great wings. Then silence. So the end comes
For one of the small nesters, called peaceful and good,
Who feed at least on nothing worthier than worms;
The owl has made a kill. I saw his gray solemn
Form, hooded and blinking in the late afternoon,
Sitting on an alder limb over the green shallow
Pool, and thought—here is a type of worldly wisdom;
Better be a fool and carol in the sweet sun
Though night come with the chances that follow,
Than be such a day-shunning, death-contriving drone,
Hated scourge of the powerless and poor.
But since I have heard, like a voice of my own,
That terrible last cry—no—I am not sure.

Teaching and visiting done, it was my turn to sail again from

Le Harvre. We docked, as in 1948, at Southampton. This time, of course, no Danny came aboard. I penned another "Island Greeting" (August, 1952):

> A call in passing:— hail to a great people
> In the country of parks and hedgerows. Summer blooms.
> Under moist clouds, a smooth lawn leads aslant—
> Between oaks by the harbor—folds the serenity
> Of a stone house, church, and cottages.
> One would almost stay, maugre austerities
> Of cold and ration. Sailors and landsfolk
> Come aboard, joking. Old Britain in her dearth
> Keeps dignity, expects no miracle,
> Plays the human game, smiles. The ship
> Turns. Never in all her ocean miles,
> Will she anchor at a comelier land
> Than this good island, green, in the gray wash of the sea.

So I crossed more water and land to take Danny, Carola, and our newborn Sandra from Little Pines Farm to Chicago—and the same welcoming Harper House on Woodlawn Avenue. What loomed there was the 1952 Fall election: Adlai versus Ike and the creeping Nixon. My verse record comes from a pre-election meeting with Galway Kinnell and Jim Gilbert in the latter's Dunes cabin. The foreboding we all felt about the election's result was expressed in a notebook scribble I have only lately thought to polish a bit.

PRE-ELECTION RHYMES
(To Adlai, from the Indiana Dunes)

> In a frame cabin by the shore
> Where waves break in the fall wind's roar
> And leaves go golden in that wind
> And drive to leeward, here we find
> Some flawed peace—preferring again
> A Dunes' retreat to Chicago's snarl of men.
> "Flawed? What flaw?" "Cold room." Well, stoke the fire!
> And sit to meditate on what we are,
> And where the country we would like to call
> Our own, is going this decisive fall.

> With television master, folk can judge

Of politicians how they hedge
On vital issues; but the spoiled demand
A soap opera they can understand.
The vice (say vicious) candidate,
To cover doubtful deals, tells of his Pat
And their great mortgages. "Oh, you're our boy!"
The telegrams tell thousands: "Look," they say,
"He's bared his soul to the people"
(Which may be true, for he bared nothing)
"And now the next," they say,
"Must follow him and bare his income tax."

What both should do, and that on television,
Is bare their bums for public decision:
Who has the sounder fundament
For a solid seat of government?
In any case, if the test fail,
There's one collateral good: for such a trial,
Each must wash well; so our nation shall
Enjoy clean candidates a while.

Jokes come easy, but heavy hangs the choice
On all who would guide freedom. Stevenson's voice
Has counseled boldly for the best:
"It is no time for private interest."
(Confronting old escapes and lies
With the call to higher sacrifice.)
While Ike, whom one hoped honest, if no more,
Says he will end the century's war,
Leave our boys undrafted,
Lower everybody's taxes.
Besides he'll give us back a dollar
Worth a hundred cents. The people holler,
For such a man, who's either false or shallow;
While you they call Egghead, having brain,
And talking straight—rare Stevenson;
I fear you'll pay the common price
Of honesty, in loss of place.
And yet if worse should come to worst,
And make us mourn your vision lost,
You shall have served—earth surprising—
An office of your own devising:

In beauty and truth opposing all
Corruptive powers—as this rich Fall
Casts defiance in the winter's teeth
With such extravagance of golden death.

Never have I ventured so much on politics, or been so thrown down by a shift (as I felt) from Hellenic vision to Roman hardening. No wonder, as "Prophet to the People" ("This song shall testify against them as a witness"—Deut. XXXI, 21) I addressed some hypothetical elected Republican (as published by Coleman Rosenberger in *The Poet in Washington*, 1974):

BOOBY POLITICIAN

Listen, child of the gods, listen—I will personify you—
Rich town-booby with the dill-pickled eyes,
And slobber dropping from a trap-swung jaw—
Listen (though you are deaf, I know,
Deaf as dumb, if hideously vocal,
And it is hardly a satisfaction to pretend
To address you as you are, shouting into the void;
Yet I will speak, if only to be cracking the whip of words)—
Brave booby, darling blockhead, listen:

Whatever produced you from the beasts
And set you on the crown of the world
Like the king on Fortune's wheel,
Is now urging and requiring, and the thing it requires
Is to launch this nation on the space flight of mind,
Of which you begin at the level of rockets and missiles,
To have a dim conception—as if the genes
Of a dinosaur would so far comprehend the problem
As to arm him for his own extinction, when what he needed
Was warm blood and a four-chambered heart, a nerve net
With a capacious brain, and such familial ways
As weave the texture of transmitted lore—
You are being called, most fortunate booby,
By the remorseless gods, whose prophet I am,
And if you do not answer, there are those who will.

It may be repugnant to you, but you cannot avoid it:
There are countless nations, carriers, countless worlds,

Parcels of being on which ride directional waves;
And the mystery of nature's god may be thus expressed:
That such spirit and concern, such loving fatherly care
As guides and scolds and urges to all this
(Shouting at you, booby, by his prophets, time out of mind).
Is so ruthlessly indifferent, so murderously cold
To those who will not be proved his chosen people.
And do not forget, as you face your luminous screen
Or drive your great-finned car,
Your jaw swung drooling, your pickled eyes awall.
Do not forget—Ah booby—each moment
Act and choosing, each avoidance of choosing
Proves.

At this point in our Chicago stay, Isabel Vincent Harper, sister-in-law of Samuel Harper, the outstanding Russian scholar who inhabited Harper House until his death, brought there a wonderful old Russian helped to America by the Harpers. The whole evening he sang Russian songs to the balalaika, and afterward by talk (and I think writing) gave me some insight into who he was and what he was chanting. So I stayed up most of the night and wrote it down in the improvised deca- and hendeca-syllabic lines such involvement brings from me. Looking now at the rhapsody I wrote half a century ago, it comes into focus that he was singing what he had heard in his boyhood from prisoners chained in barges headed somehow to (or from) Odessa (perhaps for the Volga—ultimately north to Siberia?). One prisoner, at any rate, has been there before, by Lake Baikal, having escaped from mine-slavery. Our singer's concern seems to range from criminals, beggars, and outcasts from Moscow and elsewhere, to his own patrician agony and flight from the violence of Communism. Between precision and mystery, here is the poem I somehow received and wrote down:

PROTROVICH SINGS

Down to Odessa on the outward stream
Into prison exile slipped the violent lost.
The prow cut waters west, east was the aim,
Past lands of freedom forty days of sail
To Vladivostok, port of lifetime jail.
Down from the broad plains wasting Russian soil
Blood red the river ran. Down from Asia's
Steppes and Europe's bowl, spilled from the Russian

Folk this blood of man, a people's wound—
Beggars of Moscow, thieves, the Kronstadt hand,
The Rostov red, the murderer from Kazan.

A boy by the bank I saw them all—hung neck
And arms with chains, the great and small. And as
They sang (like the river pouring red, song from
Their ruin rose), they clanked the iron chains,
High and low—a burst of brass and cymbals;
That iron's self, the substance of their wrong,
They changed with beating to the stuff of song;
And the savage cry and clashing noise, became
The defiant music of a broken voice.
Deep in the land's heart, deep from a people's pain,
These auguries of future:— one began:—

"By the shores of Lake Baikal we sat down
Having walked all day in the freezing wood,
The stalking wolves at the trail. We lit the fire.
Over the frosty waters rose the moon,
And at our backs the yellow beast eyes shone,
Paired under circling trees. We heaped the blaze
And sang. Chains were behind, the slave's work of
The mine. The beasts might come. Now on the creeping
River we go down, west into east,
Over the round world back into chains.
When will the night end, brothers, freedom dawn,
After the beast eyes under the winter moon?
Strike the iron links and sing the song;
The lost, in will, as in their bonds, are one."

I close my eyes. The river sweeps before me;
The peopled well-deck of the drifting barge;
Sounds with beating chains, the single voice,
The throb. Must men always be drawn by the dream
To the precipice they shun? Always the prisoner
In escape be taken and returned?
Witness a great land pulsing like a heart
In the mortal agonies of being born,
While elemental violence, in cloud,
Pours rain of terror over the world . . .

                                        Patience.

Give us, Lord, for past and future wrong.
In the end the powers know best, who made the song.

And then a performance of Beethoven's Ninth, with some
reading in the literature, touched off a poem about that marvelous
creation of a deaf composer. First, the soprano's scribbled thoughts
against Beethoven's reply. In revision, I found no way to present
Beethoven's inner rapture during the applause but to appropriate from
Goethe's *Faust* my earlier translation of the Bacchic earth passage,
which Mephistopheles' spirits sing to put Faust to sleep—the "Ein-
schläferungslied," which Beethoven partially set in the *Pastoral Sym-
phony* and which Disney (alas) vulgarized in his *Fantasia*.

BEETHOVEN'S NINTH (Chicago, May 1953?)

"The note is high, Master, beyond all compass;
Changing voices would make it accessible."
Spirit and deafness take no thought of ease,
The whole life being the wrought impossible—
"It stands where it belongs; the gods may sing."
"Well, in their name," she wrote him, "let us then
Afflict ourselves with the divine song again."
And so she sang . . .
              The voice now filled the hall:
"All men shall be brothers." He, absorbed,
Heard off and on some murmurs; by the score
Sensed the high soaring. And they broke in tears.
Music moves beyond the reach of words,
Like primal will stirred in the mingled depths;
The begotten feels in the cadences of time
The birth of light, rich in recovery.
Captive bonds are broken; what we dream
Confirms the inwardness of what we are—
Not only all men brothers, all one soul
Sensing its own god-image.
              And the last chord.
They rose, frenzied, cheering. He, self-closed,
Clung still to the page, the great head bowed,
Spirit on the waters—caught in Goethe's dream-song
As sung to Faust:
        "Let the stone-dark arches vanish above us,
Smiling reaches of blue aether crown us . . .

Suns without number, milder than ours;
Heavens plumed powers, in beauty and yearning
Bend and sway to us: how blown garments
Of gossamer cover meadows of clover,
Bowers where lovers, hushed in fervor,
Wreathe love forever, arbor on arbor,
Green leaves and tendrils; and harvest clusters
Of grapes heap panniers; crushed in presses
The red juice gushes, foams into torrents
Of blushing bright wine, streams that rush down
Crystalline channels, leave peaks and highlands
Gleaming behind them; spread into basins
Of ponds, lakes and bays; shores flanked with pastures,
Flower-slopes of pleasure; there winged creatures
Skim purple ocean, dip, sip, and rising,
Soar into sunlight; bank over islands—
Wave-borne on billows that lap the shallows;
Hear clear voices from echoing hollows,
In choirs rejoicing, as they dance and scatter;
Some air-nimble climb sheer mountains;
In must-fountains others are swimming,
While sky-flights hover on pinions of azure—
All singing, all craving life, and the far-figured
Stars of loving rapture and grace."

She touched his arm and turned him round,
To the cheering cries whose utmost sound
Could not pierce the silence where he stood.
It was not self so praised, but vision shared,
That bowed his head and spoke: "God's gifts are good."

So we approach that Fall of 1953, when the poems (since about 1944), which seemed to me revised and best (many already in journals) and submitted that spring to Indiana University Press for their poetry series, were accepted and, in fact, published—*Songs for a New America.*

"The Chestnut Trees" was the only thing of mine up to then accepted by *The New Yorker*, and even that on condition that I omit the next-to-last stanza. I gave in, assuming their problem was page-space; but now nearer study reveals, in the close of that stanza, a flaw in syntax, which also means in logic. Thus the canceled stanza:

> This saprophytic lingering and reversion
> Haunts the old place. But I have known too well
> The lost wild goodness in the spiny shell;
> I close my eyes and revive the native vision,
> Like a race of giant men and dauntless dreamers,
> On bold trunks lifting flowers above all other trees.

But surely "giant men" do not have "bold trunks lifting flowers." To bring the stanza back into this collection, I had to reshape the last three lines-thus:

> I close my eyes to quicken remembered vision—
> Like a race of giants feigned by folk-tale dreamers—
> I dream bold trunks lifting flowers above all other trees.

Still, the trimmed *New Yorker* page brought precious letters from friends: Russell Lord, Abbie Houston Evans and, best, one from our Granny Harper, which I sample here:

> I love "The Chestnuts." But how do you know about them? Either they lasted longer on your hills than on mine [so they did], or you are older than I thought. When I was a child the chestnuts were the high point in the year—we not only scrabbled in the leaves for the smooth brown nuts but climbed the trees and knocked down the burrs . . . then we split them with a rock. Those were gray rocks with white shining pebbles in them (glacial?) under the trees in Grandfather's pasture. Mother loved the chestnuts above all trees, and not so long ago found a shoot in the Greenwich woods that was large enough to bear nuts, but next year when she took me in pride to see it, it was dead. Still, someday, one will live, and your Carola's grandchildren will pick chestnuts and roast or boil them over the nursery fire . . . My Jane can't imagine how they tasted—or looked when they were in bloom! So many things my children have not known—like a world where wars seemed impossible, or where a passport and "papers" were a quaint, remote idea. Thank you for giving me back the chestnuts. I miss you, all four. Isabel V. H.

Turning from a poem already published, I can still pull out a stack of rather acceptable pieces not yet in my books. Thus a page-long Princeton poem of June 1946—first called "Ein Feuermeer" and then "Sea of Fire," with one of Goethe's greatest lines as motto; from *Faust*, Part II, Scene 1: "Am farbigen Abglanz haben wir das Leben" (In the colored refraction we have our life)—was published, *Country Poet*, 1947:

For two days there was rain. Then scudding clouds
Revealed toward evening opening slips of blue.
I left immurement and with eager bounds
Ran for the known knoll, freedom from these trees.
Here I paused panting, above the branching glooms
That arch the lower world, like one who cleaves
Through vapor to the stars. When shall we stand
On the tall granite of earth's mountain land
Over a wide sea under deepening skies?

No matter. All the world has glimpses. Here
We feel the rain-washed crispness of the air.
It is the first of June, but this might be
A breath of spring or fall. The distant hills
Rise touched with autumn, and southeast slip the clouds.
From every spray of weed and blade of grass
Hang drops of remnant rain.
                              At the day's end
Look, the expected hour: our sun somewhere,
Spilling his power down the vaulted gray,
Strikes through the rifting floor, shoots one long ray
Of sudden splendor to the rambling chain
Of hills and folded valleys. In that gleam
Tongues of rising mist spurt instant flame
As if all forests in a kindling swirl
Of steel-struck flint had fired a radiant world,
Responsive to the sun. Now the clouds drift toward me,
While the moving beam sweeps out the wide land
From the hills to here, in one great arc
Of glory. The rayed air between trembles
With rose, conquers the burning range, and up
These fields, even to my sandaled feet, billows
The wild flood, waking in each drop
Of pendant water, quick antiphonal sparks,
Until over me the great fire-sea breaks

In one wave-comb of gold divinity
That lights and bursts and leaves behind
A ghost of sun on eyes struck blind.
Always the expected vision burns the heart
That waits his coming; human kind sustain
Only the mild air distant from the flame.
Contented where I go, let me enjoy
The slow circling of powers that destroy.

No sooner had I sent off *Songs for a New America*, meant to celebrate the tragic daring of the flight west, than I took off, June 1953, to visit my mother in my hometown of Greenville, Mississippi. Here the Promethean theme shifts to the water-death-and-ebbing of the motion south and home. Unlike *Songs*, which gathered into a somewhat arbitrary three-fold grouping of poems written over nine years, *Delta Return* was conceived and delivered as a unit, the first of its three parts picking up the sights and stirred memories of my trip from Chicago down to Greenville—those twenty-five poems ending with ancient Black Lethe's coming to our columned house to greet me. The third and last twenty-five poem section leads through other original impressions of my Delta stay-from "Baptism" in a River section through a Flood section, then one called "The Living" and another "The Dead," to a final "Tomorrow," anticipating the Chicago return, with a night in the cemetery by our family graves. Between these, the Delta (Δ) required a middle section, which, for the unity of the whole, became five dialectics or linked complementarities of mind—the first about Love, the second Knowledge, the third Law, the fourth History and Philosophy, the fifth Creed. In this way the whole structure was unified, not random. I finished the book as published (1956), plus a few spillovers where Delta memories produced poems beyond the seventy-five required. For curiosity, I add one here:

TWO SWORDS

Two swords hung in our house: one nicked and brown,
A saber that had run with Northern blood;
It was a cavalry sword, praised in fable;
The second was edgeless, pointless, gilt-enamel—
A laughing-stock to draw it from the scabbard.

With the first my mother's father fought four years,
Came home, broken, to a gullied farm;

In the gaunt age that followed, my mother was born.
Once, as a girl, she took that sword unsheathed,
And said, holding it like a deadly charm:

"I bet this sword has killed many a man."
Which he, who shunned all mention of that past,
Countered: "Better it had not"; in such a voice
As burned his daughter's heart—mine in her telling.
What remains but ash where hell-fire has fallen?

My father's northern father photographed through
        that war:
("A plague on both your houses!"). Married, he came
South (with carpet bag!). It was hard to win men over.
This sign of bloodless victory he wore,
When chosen for the State's Grand Chancellor

In the Knights of Pythias, an order of friends.
The old sword rusts in the scabbard, will not be drawn;
Let its war of brothers yield to brotherhood—
That photographer loved, even by his Kentucky scold.
At the family choosing, mine be the tinsel sword.

Meanwhile, in Hutchins' college, from Humanities to the
science branch of the program, which Champ Ward, college dean, had
hoped, for my sake, I would cultivate—and I tried—but Joe Schwab,
another Mississippian, as jealously hostile as he was brilliant, opposed
me, so my teaching had gravitated to the synthesizing history of Mc-
Neill and Mackauer, fine men, and a searching course, but so dispar-
aged in that scholastic McKeon setting, that it was ominous to come to
roost there. And the stir which followed my Michelangelo slide lecture,
early garnered fruit of *Symbolic History*, attested how radically I had
come to roost.

To my wider solace, the Clearing, on the wooded limestone
bluffs over Green Bay in Wisconsin, invited me, several of those sum-
mers, to lead adult classes, for which the Clearing provided housing
and meals—for us and our five daughters. At the Door County retreat,
Chicago-slum-reared into socialism, where I met Ann Markin, daugh-
ter of a Lithuanian immigrant miner, who would give her history (life,
really) in letter-memoirs to me (as Daren Leflore in the political *Half
Gods*). From my Clearing poems, written over several visits after driv-
ing through Wisconsin in our first car, an almost unused old Chevrolet,

bought for $35, I will gather what I can. The first was penned when the whole state was cheering McCarthy (already Bronxed in this chapter) though he was soon to be punctured by a true lawyer, Joseph Welsh: "Have you no shame, sir?" That first Wisconsin poem, beside the major prose encounter of *The Half Gods* may be called a minor verse projectile:

WISCONSIN IN THE TIME OF McCARTHY

Ephemerids, and blood-sucking flies,
With crowds that praise
The elected blight
Of their green state —
All day, all day.

Now wingless night—
Oh, it is good,
After the mire of blood,
To hear the old wind
Rustle again in the bloodless wood.

On that or an earlier trip (May 1950?), a solitary dogwood west of the common range suggested another poem whose title gives it, also, political implications:

LAST LIBERAL

I have seen forests white with dogwood, down
The sloping hills, above a stream, the fluted
Image like a ghost of departed snows.

There is little to remark when beauty
Favored in its native recurrence, spreads
Gregarious splendor. And I have never found

Such rush of feeling in the reach of those
White eastern hills, as where, in this west bound
And rigor of its range-sole silhouetted

On the northern pine and drifting pollen down,
Precursor or lost heir, both time-unsuited—
One last clear tree of bloom, the dogwood blows.

On one of those earliest comings to Door County, we reached the cliff-point over the bay as the sun was sinking in a cloudy mist. The poem, then sketched, has been through many changes:

GREEN BAY: BY SUNSET

The sun over the bay sets shrouded in vapor,
So dimmed, eyes can sustain the spectre:
Red and purple spilled over blue-green water;
Occluded light, in brooding solitude
Imbues a progeny of color.

On the beach, a scramble to catch a sizable water snake and having my hand bit (harmlessly) gave me this stanza:

APPEARANCES

The shadow of a cloven stick
Makes a fanged snake on the ground;
Yes, and the snake lies like a stick
Until the fang is found.

THE CLEARING

Half-island county called the Door,
Death's Door of dangerous straits,
Be door of life for me—

I stretch out on your earth to grow.
Peace comes softly with the rise-and fall
Lapping of the waves . . .

I lie in a semicircle of limestone,
Earth-masonry, sea-bedded forms,
Over Green-Bayed Michigan.

Here cedars frame the sun;
This little house where I will ripen days
Grows from the rock, limestone and logs.

It was built by Jensen, a man I did not know,
Who kept Door County for our later loves;
His spirit haunts here smiling.

Deer mice that run the floor and rafters
And crouch all eyes and ears
Fed, I think, on his crumbs.

I have not long to breathe here as time goes.
Make it present; spin past and future
In the web of embodied soul.

Wren and thrush begin their evening song;
The great white trillium beckons from the wood.
I stretch out on the earth, root in stone.

One may note, here and below, how much the meter owes to
the variable foot of William Carlos Williams, a dearest poet-friend.

SKY AND WATER

By longleaf pine
 And plunging moon
  To the cliff I come
   Over a glowing bay.

Climb and climb
 Up resinous boughs;
  Last needles brush
   My face and are gone.

Here is only sky.
 These nights of June
  Stars kindle late;
   They are flaming now:

Shielded Scorpion,
 Fire-fronted figurant,
  And the far tail curls
   Washed in the waves.

Eastward the Archer,
 Trellis and vine
  To the cloudy clusters
   Of the Milky Way.

There a new flare reigns,
 Red as Antares,
  Bright as Jupiter:
   It is the year of Mars.

No more god of war,
 But arid world
  Of wished canals and air,
   Ah, those youthful dreams.

So I climbed as a boy
 And fixed on the red eye,
  Half hoping to win free,
   Cross the void and wake there.

I will no longer seek you
 From the height, climbing
  Space and time; beneath me
   Now, where long waves

Are sliding: the same
 Fire, orange reflection
  Gleams; I am old,
   I will take you there.

Down cliffs I cling,
 Shed clothes on the stones;
  Clear lake water
   Spilled with light,

In liquid troughs and planes,
 Stirs round me, fondling.
 I swim from the land.
  They are all about me now—

Above, below,
 Known stars of night,
  And planet-wanderers
   Of the old sky-dreams—

Close crimson Mars
 Sluicing waves with blood.
  I dive down and down . . .
   Youth is nothing to age.

Here a love-poem seems to intervene:

THE WORLD BETRAYS

The solitary makes his soul a god
To whom beholders render on their knees
Love or envy of that solitude,
Calling him out. Charmed by transiencies
He lays his loneliness upon their pyre,
And stands incarnate—but incarnate fire.

Four moon-gray nights up to the Northern Dawn
He walked the woods and swam the lake alone.
She then in youth and beauty caught his hand.
They went in silence down the cedar trail
To the cliff house by the water, meeting place
Of gods and mortals, time and timelessness—

There merge love-silent. If any sound
Joined the sounds of nature, it like those
Was not of word or reason: lapping of waves,
Murmurs or sighs, now and then, chortled soft
Responses, as birds and squirrels make:
"Good year and good luck, with chuck chuck, chuck chuck."

What one tongue asked the other tongue revealed
In an older language than the school-taught signs.
They left late, still silent. But the soul of man
Depends on meaning; its doubts rose in a cry;
To which she answered: "No one plucks a flower
Of such a kind, and goes away unchanged."

They say the modern young make casual love,
Drift in and out like shades. Is silence the key?
For words arrest the flow-seeds of the soul
That raise impermanence to a deathless claim,
Fixing that night forever, where the lonely god,
Plucks the flower that is fire, and flowers in flame.

THE CLOSE

Down the rock stair
For the last time
I climb to the cliff room
After the storm.

The waters gray
With engorged earth
Break in foam
At the crumbling base.

This crack in the floor
Where the whole cliff settles
Is no wider
But more sure.

The cedar that leans
Far out and hangs
While last roots cling—
When it goes, all will go.

Below on the beach
Three rocks are cast:
Red sandstone of the eastern flats,
Black lava from the Canadian flow,

White limestone of the Niagara sea—
Earth, fire and water,
Familiar wrecks
Of other vanished worlds.

I climb the rock
And go out through the wood,
Turning my back
On the booming shore.

As we drove south toward far-off Chicago, near the growing town of Green Bay, we saw flowers, the local Foolscap more likely being Turkscap:

TWO FLOWERS

Two flowers, by the superhighway, fill the field:
Foolscap lilies, orange and gold,
Four or more to the stalk by marshy pools;

And lost in lilies, here and there,
Red iron shoots, intrusive toadstools,
Whose sap is water meant for future fires.

Harbingers of the city, they wait yearlong
The slow coming they are planted for—
To bring urban water to this wild.

The planners, surely, do not plan to fail.
Meanwhile lilies that toil not, neither spin,
Crowd swamp and hydrants mile on mile

With transient bloom. Two flowers are in the field:
Metal stems of the city, and brief as dawn,
Foolscap lilies, to crown what fools?

One of those summers, when we had returned from the Clearing—our two joined by my older three, while two young Overtons, and a friend, had come from upstairs—as all were contending for toys from a chest and for the furnishings of a doll house from Danny's early times—the shrill claims of our youngest called forth this poem:

OUT OF THE MOUTHS OF BABES
(Chicago, c. 1955)

The little one snatching the others' toys—
"Sandra, why do you call them yours?"
"Cause I want to," sounds the voice.

Three years ago she was nothing;
She has come like a bubble;
She can hardly talk, and her first utterance

Is Lucifer's defiant "I."
Time is, time was; I write, they play.
But who am I, and what are they?

Surely my saddling Sandra with Lucifer's voice—that assertion which every being who can say "I AM" may fall into—was playful; but around the same time, at one of many heightenings of Cold War risk, I waked from a dream more fatally tied to the Archangel's fall—waked and wrote (compare the maniac in Johnson's *Rasselas*):

MAN; TRAIN; MOON

The mile-long freight rounds the great plateau;
The heavy climbing stretches into speed.
Headlights glint along tracks of steel.
A dark plain sweeps by; the piston thud
Fills tall night, the quickening beat of steam.
A man swings the throttle. Well he knows
The thrust of what he masters. It is routine.
Always he has climbed the slopes and across these miles
Of earth's upland, given it all he could.

Yet now behind his back from the low east
Rises a gibbous moon and drives wan light
With him down the rails. In a rush of wind
He leans out and around. A strange dream
Takes his mortal body and coiled brain:—
He sits as God upon His world-throne,
Hands on levers of power, and as he pulls
The pounding throttle, earth's moon mounts at his will.
He roars into the night, mad with all-rule.

One of those winters, maybe earlier (December '51?), a snow-devil advancing like a cyclone, gave me—opposing Man-Train-Moon nightmares—the clue to a creative and constructive pact with nature:

THE FOUNTAIN

A winter whirl of snow
Blows from the flat land;
It goes as winds go,
A course unplanned.

Meeting an adverse wind
It does not bend
The vortex holds its own,
Like ours of flesh, breath, bone.

If all act is kin:
Whether random or planned
Must vary with your stand;
The cosmic way (clear as day)
Is: harness chance to form, without and within.

On another summer trip we took the kids to see Niagara.
Looking down on the great whirling pool between fall and rapids
brought back my adventure at sixteen, when the family drove me
by Chicago and Niagara down to the University of Virginia to begin
college. At Niagara, while they were resting, I wore my shorts to the
American shore beneath the falls. Here is the poetic narrative:

MAID OF THE MIST

A man in middle age, with wife and children,
I stand, this troubled time, again at the fall:
Watch the flood of Niagara crash to the pool
That far below contains it, circling cauldron.
Am I the man who once defied that current?

It was when I left for school. All that summer
I had swum the Mississippi across and return,
Warm brown water. Then we went north, and I swam
In the Great Lakes as we passed. That clear shimmer
Of waves cold on sand was a calling vision.

So we reached this gorge where lakes compounded
Plunge off the rock ledge, and wild with a dream urge,
I leapt to the pool, swam for the mile—far verge—

The width of our Mississippi, but blue cold, and blended
With streak on streak of foam where whirls contended.

More than half way across, the stream sets in
Beyond the backwash, racing to descend
The terrible rapids where no man can swim.
There my strength went from me; arm to arm,
I feebly raised and splashed them, ready to drown . . .

No children, I did not; you see me here.
Romantic fool in a Promethean hour,
At the Fall's call I had pushed off from the shore.
Now the current tugged my feet; I had no power.
The Maid of the Mist came, and took me aboard.

With age more cautious, I stand and review
That past which looms again: I sense appalled
The old mad urge, not mine alone, but of all
That I am part of—earth, planet of our hope,
How whelmed. And Maid of the Mist, where are you now?

To get back to University of Chicago events—at the same time
recalling parties at Berryman's Princeton flat, where his whole clutch of
poet friends would meet and overflow mostly lachrymose verses, none
with the controlled energy of Berryman himself—I risk my response to a
reading by Delmore Schwartz, whom I had met before (guess where?):

AT A POET'S READING

Come back, my heart,
Wall up, revert
To stone, be stoic—
Headland rock
Where waves break,
And subside to quiet.

Would you ply this trade?
Exhibit and bleed
In the market place
For smart applause
Of the like diseased?
Heart, be firm.

Quit that effete
Cult of the hurt.
What is whole and clean,
Speak it; and then
Revert to stone;
As proud, as mute.

Later, when younger such poetasters had worried my first two collections, I ridiculed the lot under the Bosch image of a landscape where a brown flux gushes from a rump-like hummocked hill:

WORLD PURGE

Some rack-words of our current muse-abuse
Are so greedy to flow with something
They strain on any terms to be made conduits. OM! OM!

When the spring from the rock slows to a trickle
How they let go, sluices of diarrhetic water. OM!

Look! Theirs, the Bosch horizon, earth's cloven buttocked
      hill . . .
Hold your nose! OM! OM!
That brown flood gushes from art's widened sphincter.
OM! OM!   OM! OM!

Now poets have mounted the stage, I will touch on Pound and Eliot. As for Pound, my *Symbolic History* had taught me long ago that my personal leanings must be transcended in a fair attempt to absorb and participate in everything that has shaped history. So the modern shows have variously used Expressionist Pound—even to the *Cantos*. But when these were honored in an annual award at the very time when the man himself had behaved in Fascist Italy and through the war with such mad irresponsibility, I did overflow in a rather vitriolic diatribe:

ON THE MAKING OF THE *CANTOS* (1950)

I suppose there is a kind of honesty
In speaking confusion when one is confused,
And some sophistication in doing it well;
But I think an award were better forgotten
Than granted such juggling at our turn of time.

What political responsibility
Can we expect of leaders, what unabused
Birthright of franchise, when sons are of sibyl
And prophet so fallen, that of poets, begotten
Heirs of Delphi, we garland nihilist rime?

There was a time when irrationality
Expressed the rupture with reason late abused;
Then this man with others thought to bear the bell.
But that has all turned now to an easy fashion,
Where senescence tutors youth in the smart crime.

There is no more place for heart and sanity
In their aesthetic than in the most diseased
Body of state for a true man counseling well.
Are not liberals near enough annihilation,
Without themselves whetting the blade of the time?

Eliot was another matter. I had long read, taught, and even, in a
sense, admired his work; though the organic humanism I was celebrating
in my essays ("Turning and Turning in the Widening Gyre") could not
fail to oppose the skeptic neo-Christian surrender of Eliot's "Gerontion"
or "Ash Wednesday": "Teach us to care and not to care / Teach us to sit
still"; though, as "The Brief I Am" records, I made an effort:

> Our second year, when T. S. Eliot came to
> lecture on "Runcible Spoons," it was from my
> Oxford tutor Coghill that he brought greetings. At
> the thronged reception, I thought to persuade him that
> the crown of his poetic career should be a translation
> of *The Divine Comedy*. Had he not given the best
> English sample of the mood and meter in his fourth
> Quartet? And unbelievably no translator has had a
> clue to Dante's shifting from what we would call
> pentameter to the Gothic lilt of his four-stress
> hendecasyllable: (for a Gothic smile: "Con angelica
> voce in sua favella . . ." or for violence, "Galeotto fu
> 'l libro e chi lo scrisse.")
> Eliot answered: he did not think he should
> do it, and for two reasons, one of humility and the
> other of pride. "Yes?" I said.—"Of humility: I don't
> know enough Italian." I doubted that: "You know as

much as Pound!"—"And of pride," he pursued—
"Yes?"—"I think I might have better things to
do."—"If you mean writing original poetry, I agree;
if giving lectures on runcible spoons, I strongly
dissent." Then I asked him for lunch with the
Borgeses and other colleagues, in the oak-paneled
Harper hall. He came; but I got nowhere with luring
him to compare "Christ the Tiger" in "Gerontion"
with Yeats' "what rough beast." He answered as if I
had not even mentioned his own poem. "As for the
Yeats," he said, "I think the rough beast is Anti-
Christ." I could hardly tell him at a party that he
should know from Yeats' *Vision* how wrong he was.

My poetic offshoot, however, was a somewhat negative ap-
praisal:

NOT TO SIT STILL (November, 1950)

Eliot, a retiring and beautiful man,
Sows lectures drier than Sahara sand,
Bites off his paradox with a smile
Of Neo-Christian-skeptical denial.

We who turn not East but urge our blood
Of Promethean passion through the darkening wood
And rock-hung cedar, to this cliff for the last
Great burst of fire from the ultimate West—

Here by the round sea and setting sun,
The void of space, its stars and moon—
Assuming all names of black and red
That force must bear in the cult of the dead,

Regretting the act, and the punished charm
With regret that builds one part of the storm—
To the beauty we seek and are told we should not—
The vision Bruno and Leibnitz wrought—
Here immolate the resigned, the gentle Eliot.

A relief: for that polemic of poetry to give way to poems of
Nature, Spring and Fall. First, "Dusk of May":

Now every willow leaf
Like a new moon braids
The nascent twilight
Where a new moon rides.
Let us sit in the dusk,
Dream-garnering.
All things are crescent, Love,
In love's quickening Spring.

The next is a Dunes poem (Fall, '52), once called "Ruined Choirs" after Shakespeare's sonnet, called now "Earth Dreams," suggesting idealists who hope beyond autumnal possibility:

We lie in the sun
Pillowed on sand.
Winds are shifting;
Tomorrow from wide lands
Of the west and north
A change will come
And the waters warp.
In this drifting
Island of November
We cull the last
Warmth of summer.

There is no horizon;
The blue lake runs
To the sky's haze.
We have slept on the Dunes
While yellow blades
Of grass were swaying
In the southeast wind.
The little pines
Green as Spring
Unfold and expand
To the declining sun.

But the spice bushes are brown,
Relinquishing
Our threatened world.
Withered staves
Of heart' s withdrawal,

They shed their leaves.
This lingering present
They have forgone,
Bared for the utopian
Dream of Spring.

These two gentle poems of Chicago Spring and Fall may be
complemented by a sterner confrontation: the February-March divide
between Winter and Spring (more cruel than Eliot's "April is the cruel-
est month"). My poem is called (after Heraclitus) "Not Twice in the
Same River." In three stanzas of six lines each, sharing rhymes and
repetitions, it voices the bafflement of one attempting to summon up a
seasonal contrast when involved in the reality of its opposite—as if our
Being were mere Becoming, swept on the flux of now.

NOT TWICE IN THE SAME RIVER

Again the withered earth, brown grass, bare trees;
Mud refreezes after melting snows,
Down to the zero hour . . . And many a season,
Bright spring or height of summer, when but reworked
        hope renews
Its costly green in poignancy of leaves,
I have looked and thought: it is the year's recurrence;
This strange sweetness a time; and again the dead season.

So, tried to remember, with closed eyes—
Blank to the dance of everything that grows—
To revive in thought that other season,
Of deprivation under winter snows
But could never call it back:— always the birds
Were singing in the covert; the lean recurrence
Could only be re-lived, suffered in its season.

Be it so, I said: Nature puts barriers
Between past and present; the things we know
Are of the moment, migrants of a season—
Time's code is set against too sharp a gaze
Looking before or after. Its absolutes,
Mild or terrible, wear veils of recurrence,
Abated by us to the relatives of a season.

There is one more Dunes poem I had thought to omit—it had four stanzas, each of six plodding pentameter lines—but the title and closing question moved me to a salvage and renewal, trimmed to seven lines:

SPRING IN THE BARRENS

Today we walk the sand-dunes where a fire,
By campers' neglect or storm-rage of the sky,
Has swept through. Look, already grass is returning.
Leaves even, over trunks scorched or smoldering—
In a sun-warmed wind tossing and swaying—
Pose the green question:
"What is life but a bridled burning?"

Here a mysterious poem pops up requiring a brief account. It was in Ames, Iowa (1943), when I was searching great books, especially of thought, that I ordered Nahm's *Selections from Early Greek Philosophy*, copied passages for classes, adding the Greek as I could find it. Empedocles' anticipation of Plato's "Recollection," as of a higher life, deeply stirred me (Empedocles: "From what honor and blessedness have I fallen here to consort with mortal beings?"—reaching, as it did, all the way to Shakespeare's Titania: "Come my lord, and in our flight, / Tell me how it came this night, / That I sleeping here was found, / With these mortals on the ground?"). But it was at Chicago that the ferment of such "Intimations" waked me to the role of charmed prince, as in a fable from the Brothers Grimm:

PLATONIC GRIMM

Under earth and water the first "I" swirled to dream,
Loved and dissolved by the Nix of lake and stream.
Strange music called me to the air:
I rose a fish and climbed the stair
Of newt and lizard, until I took on man,
And here I graze my sheep upon this dark hill span.

Another time there was, another form and face,
Before the waters brought me to this place;
But here lives one, a shepherdess,
With whom I drive afield in peace,
Though I dream of the realm that was mine before
I dipped cupped hands, bending at the fatal shore.

It must have been the summer of 1954 that I drove with Jim Gilbert, our last Old Master painter in oil and watercolor and inspiring mentor to the Spanish-born Esteban Vicente (1903-2001), to visit his retreat on Martha's Vineyard, seeing on the way, in Princeton, my intellectual father-figure, Erich Kahler. I resurrect two poems from that trip: the first, of the night drive to Princeton and then New York:

IN CENTRAL PARK

Last night I drove through Pennsylvania hills
Wind-brushed with snow, gray foldings under the moon,
Bridge-leapt the valleys, tunneled the ridge stone,
At seventy miles an hour. When dawn rose

Between me and the stars, I was east again
On the spoiled plain by the sea; like coming home,
Drove to Princeton, and through that hollow shell,
Returned to the true—old Kahler in his room.

Tonight I reach New York, still driving on—
Chicago yesterday: the country recalled
Is a rush of long hills lighted by the moon
Between great cities, a sage in his loft, alone.

II
Here in the park I have walked and seen these towers
Wreathed in sunset, breathe and expire,
To revive from the dusk, slim shapes returning,
Transfigured into light, electric shafts of burning.

And the boughs of winter silhouetted
On that boldness beyond, frame the city.
I thought: here is the town of a daring people
Who rocketing, leave earth a pricked balloon behind them.

And I remember Kahler, pacing and grieving
For the crucified hope of his peaceable vision,
Tugging shreds of hair, and the voice of his brooding:
"We are foreclosed; I no longer write or lecture."

III

Prophetic Jew, old man, abandoned now
By temporal power, weaving noble dreams
On looms of solitude, I hear your words:
"The law of history for all who would rule,

Is to ride the wave of fire, the force that drives;
These fools forsake the cause from which we spring . . ."
"But who are the fools?" I ask; "Leaders, you mean?"
"Not they, not they alone." "Who then?" And he groans:

"It is the trusted people, the election down,
This blind pride of the worst, the course we have run . . ."
(Ah, but the city on the black wind blows a flag
Of light—freedom always in weak hands.)

IV

And to deal a little whimsically with you, loved sage,
As you pace the floor, tearing your tatters of paleo-
Anthropus fur, what was that world-state but a wilder
Venture of pride, now stranding on these beaches?

And therefore nature, of her tragic pity,
Plants on the luckless mast this starred banner,
High in the wind over whirls of the sea-drowning . . .
Seer, you are right: we are a spendthrift people,

And humility were better and a little wisdom;
But I stand in Central Park and take before me
This moment, on the wing, spire-plumes glowing;
And the lost heart leaps with pride to affirm that glory.

The second poem is of driving on Vineyard Island through
woods of gum ("bettlebung") and of picking up an Indian girl of the tribe
still resident there. The poem, "Martha's Vineyard," was finished soon
enough to be sent to Henry Rago and published in *Poetry*, October 1954:

We drove through Bettlebung Wood by Glimmerglass Pool.
Indians cling to the island; squaws in summer
Serve the seasonal rich; the old braves indulge
As they loaf and fish, in tales of past danger.
When they put out over the sea for porpoise and whale.

We were bound for Gay Head. A dark-skinned girl
With ebon braids flagged us for a ride.
As we drove east past Glimmerglass Pool,
"Wait," she asked, "while I put a stone on the cairn."
They call it the oldest custom of the New World,

That Mahew, their missionary, should have from all
The tribe who pass this tribute of a stone.
One looks for a pyramid, a mountainous mole;
But the cairn is small and dwindling, the Indians few,
And the rocks make souvenirs of the shrine by the pool.

I thought how face and form, custom, school,
All gathered things, unraveling in the void,
Hold while myth remakes them. Straightway the girl
Came back to the car. We drove under Beetlebung Wood
Along the sliding surface of Glimmerglass Pool.

The tie of Jim and Cecil Gilbert in their summer house and art
studio on Martha's Vineyard, an island washed by cold sea, draws me
forward two years to a summer visit Danny and I, with our two chil-
dren, were to make after returning from our Puerto Rican year. I would
write a poem called "Sea Love" (or "Gay Head," actually, 1956):

The bluffs are painted—
Kaolin and clay—
Granite of old glaciers
Breaks the blue bay
Dark with mussels
And fruit of the sea.

From the rust shadow
I watch at their play
God's naked children—
One flesh with me—
Give their white beauty
To the fierce dark of the sea.

After which I also add three neglected Chicago poems: first,
"Thanksgiving" (November 1953, *Country Poet*)—the scene, our
Harper House library:

It was Thanksgiving in the bad time of Korea—
A cold season, bare trees, the snows came early.
Roasting the fowl had sent a warm vapor
Through the house; the windows were deep frosted.
We sat down to eat, having read the papers:
Our past losses and present danger,
Threats of the bomb, forecasts of disaster.

There was nothing to be seen: gray cloud the window.
Outside too was all under cloud-shadow—
Not a good season to give thanks to the Maker.
As we ate, the vapor cleared, dissolving slowly;
The clouds too, on the wind's shifting.
Our sky broke blue; the trees cut calligraphic
On the low sun of winter, gold with setting.

So we found ourselves alive. These leaps and rushes
Come despite us—the texture of our joy,
Always surprising; since the once conquered terror
Returns so masked, that we quake like children,
And cannot see it is what it always was,
The same shade and denial, spirit the same protagonist—
Covenant, fall and winter, to the life—renewal of spring.

Second, of a desperately damp summer:

RAIN

Leaden clouds—
The cottonwoods
Melt in mist
As rain pours;
Slime trails cross
Where slugs pass
On the stone threshold;
Melons mould
In the melon bed—
A double curse
When blessings overbless.

Third: from Chicago, after glancing at a newspaper:

EPITHALAMION

Another man-wife-killing case;
Married murder mounts apace.
When I consider the couples I know,
I marvel the killing rate's so low.

Our seventh Chicago year (1955-56) was spent, in fact, on
loan to Puerto Rico. The chancellor of the university at Rio Piedras,
was, like many of us, a fan of Hutchins; he wanted to found a Chicago
program on an island where language skills (English or Spanish) were
not up to the level of those books. So every year we were sending them
a helper from Chicago. The last had been Jim Gilbert. His conspiring to
be neglected has been treated in *The Half Gods*; what is relevant here is
that he preferred me as his Puerto Rican successor. He knew Spanish; I
had to rape my Italian (*non voglio; quiero*, etc.); it worked well enough,
but Italian hardly forgives. I went down, took the blaze of sunlight
on the palms, ate wild mangoes (akin to poison ivy) until my mouth
swelled, while I searched out a place for my family.

My job was to build a Chicago honors program in Mayaguez,
where the former College of Agriculture and Mechanical Arts was be-
ing upgraded. Besides classes, I taught teachers how to stir up semi-
nars on Great Books. With a few others I worked pretty hard; though
everybody partied at beach joints on blood sausage and land crabs,
drank beer or rum, and danced the *chachacha* with the secretaries. I had
grown up where Blacks danced with abandon, but Delta Whites had
not yet broken from ballroom formality. It came easy in Puerto Rico, as
indeed, thereafter. I also invested loads of time, with flippers, mask and
snorkel, on near and far reefs—becoming to all intents and purposes a
sea-beast: one of life's great experiences. In spare moments I tried to
seduce the tropics into short stories (a couple later published).

For one of the native stenographers who would dance around
the office, I also wrote two quatrains called "Island Secretary," though I
should have punned in Spanish: "Muchacha Sexetaria":

Ease off, brown muchacha,
Control those undulations!
How can we mind state affairs
And your hips quaking?
If this is a sample

Of secretarial office,
No wonder business
Goes neglected in the tropics.

We were having a fine time, and were asked to stay, but the few books I had brought down were being tunneled by termites, and to move my library from the States seemed appalling. Moreover the little dive-bomber mosquitoes that carry elephantiasis were always active in the screenless houses; and when they zoomed under the table where I was trying to work, I dropped everything to swat them. To Erich Kahler in Princeton I wrote it all, with my doubts about returning to Chicago, where the independents had lost ground.

At this juncture, Erich sent my Puerto Rican letter—termites, mosquitoes, and all—to his friend Victor Zuckerkandl, author of *The Sense of Music* and other books, at St John's in Annapolis, a place to which Barr and Buchanan had invited me, before they bailed out. Zuckerkandl took it to Jascha Klein, new dean, another of the great Europeans and a shrewd administrator. He read it and is reported to have said: "We've got to get that boy out of there." So I would wind up in Annapolis.

Meanwhile, various of my tropical poems were first published in the 1957 Humphries *New Poems #2* (Ballantine). Of the four Rolfe printed, I worked three into my *Five Chambered Heart*: "Termites" "Banana," "Girl Walking." His fourth, not in my books, I offer here, though far from cheerful:

ISLAND DOGS

The island crawls with dogs; scrawny couples
Make bookends in the streets and the swagged
                bitches
With bone-bare ribs drop brown litters,
Give suck a while from dugs like tumors,

Then stagger off with prolapsed parts;
The pups beg from house to house,
Till garbage grown, with a mate as lean,
They make bookends. And nobody minds

(Tender-hearted!), except the impersonal law,
Having some modern crotchets half-digested,
From time to time gives obvious strays
A pellet of beef with a heart of poison.

In the name of health the poisoned wander.
But O the dog days of stinking heat
On the heels of the law, when the blown corpses
Lie in the street and flies quicken.

So health is guarded. But there remain
Chosen remnants, drab as the dead,
To beg and steal, make bookends—
The old succession; run it again . . .

This is the character of returning dawn,
The way of planet earth, our consumptive star,

Islands in space and sea and air,
All hatching places of the flesh we are.

A more pleasing poem appeared only in my *Heart* volume,
"Dancing Mother." Two others, never before printed, I add here.

TROPIC POOL

Forest water,
Shattered rocks:
The tragic mirror
Where earth looks.

Where all the sunlit
Leaves are blurred
In the deep and dark—
And brown as blood.

TROPIC ROUND

On night and day
Fall sun and rain:
The sun burning
Fires the morning;
Over mangos
Rise the mountains;
Out of the ocean
Clouds fountain,
Shade the breadfruit,

Shade the almond;
Then thunder, thunder:
Dark mahoganies
Sway green waves
On pale boughs under
Gray rivers of rain;
Then a silver calm
Drops on fronds
Of banana and palm
Until evening kindles
Fruit in the leaves;
And night returns
With its strange stars
Sweeping the hills
Where tree frogs call:
Coquí, coquí—
Until the bright dawn.

To close the seventh and last year of our Chicago employment, I add to the Puerto Rican poems a five-page adventure of my own (though told in the third person). It may have started out as a short story, but it became a factual prose poem: marveling at the beauty and vengeful danger of that Caribbean:

THE ROMANTIC SEA

The first time he had bought a mask and fins and come to this beach with its crescent of white sand closed by coconut groves and hedged with seagrape—and beyond in the calm blue-green of the transparent reef-sheltered bay, purple patches showing where coral from the bottom thrust in curves and ridges on which, if storm waves reached these stillnesses, a slight surf broke in foam and milky stirrings of a water otherwise clear—he had hardly known where to begin, to enter the mysteries at their nearest, and with least exposure to the rumored dangers of the open sea.

He had walked to the south horn of the beach, where the reefs joined the sand; had stumbled out in his flippered feet over the coral which was first dry rock, then living substance, grown with seaweed and washed an inch or so deep by the slow pulse of the swell. There were urchins, but only the small red ones, not too sharp, mostly tucked in the rock, and besides he could watch his step. A little way, and the pools and alleys began, a foot deep at first, but winding out and down to the ultramarine.

It seemed strange for a grown man and something of a swimmer to wade like a child, stranger still for him to go down, as he did at the first suspicion of colored small minnows, onto his knees, then belly, flat in the bathtub water, his head barely under, the glass mask bringing him with the suddenness of hallucination into the diminutive realm of coral, anemone, waving weed, bronze and russet in the blue, that crystalline blue, through which now bright small fish darted, turned and delayed. There was one of blue and gold, one red on silver, and one brightest and darkest of all, blue-black, sparkled like a starry night.

So he became a worshipper, neglecting his business and his family to be prying under that luminous interface, drawn always farther out, deeper, more afield.

Even that first time he had not stayed in the knee-deep tide aquarium. Flat, under the surface that glistened like a reflecting wall, making emergence a fable and all other worlds unreal, he had seen the alleys between coral rocks, winding out and down to always deeper pools. He had pursued them, drawing forward with his hands, then kicking with those rubber fins. He scraped a bank of flame-fingered horns, scraped his belly and it burned like fire, seared red streaks which later blistered and peeled. So as always, with strange beauty, it was hostile too—which could only heighten what compellingly lured.

Here the big urchins began, the black ones like radiating long needles, shifting their spines as they crawled over indentations of coral ledges and the rocky floor. He put out a finger and touched one, feather-light; he could hardly have affirmed the touch: the affirmation was an inoculating small pain, and as he drew back, the thinnest thread of blood, spreading in the blue until it disappeared.

Yellow striped grunts slipped by him, from a side rift, toward the open. He followed, past brain coral, spheres wider than tables; then rising into the waterways, the slow swinging spread of lavender fans. With a suddenness that caught his breath, from an open cave behind him, a school of parrotfish, up to a foot long, purple, blue and green, with their horny blunt mouths for crunching coral, swept by him.

It was over six feet deep in the hollows now, though

the sides of the coral gorge still rose almost to the gleaming surface. Then the formation broke, the ridges withdrew, there was the open water shelving down to deeper and darker blue, and in that blue, staring at him as he stared, was a barracuda, its lean body drooped like a bow, pike-mouth crowded with teeth, lounging lazy; it must have been five feet long.

The man began to move back into the sheltering alley. The fish followed slowly, only the pectoral fins working, curious, like a sniffing hound. One had grown up on tales of this tiger of the seas. Panic seized him. He flung out paddling hands to back faster toward the reef. As if the man had threatened, the barracuda became the timid one. That restless first sign of retreat changed the balance of power. Scissoring with his legs, the man sped through the water to where the fish had been. It had vanished, like an imagined fear. So he learned the lesson of the hunter: when threatened, charge. But he had not yet tangled with a shark.

The first time, luckily, he was on the shore. He had a spear gun now. They had driven north from the town, past the cinderblock slum clearance on a clay-flat, over the first rain-caving hills, shadowed with mango and mamey, across the sugar cane valley, the refinery spilling smoke into the air by the liver-fluke river silting into the sea; up again over the dry sierra, where waves once had carved its serpentine into a canyon of royal palms, trunks like white cement and fronds of metallic green; off on the side road, a bed of gullied rock, around the point, to park under pungent tamarind—and there was the other cove, the reef-diminished waves hissing up the sand. His wife fired the charcoal, the children played; he swam with spear gun, past the chalky surf to the last and deepest reef, fish of all kinds lurking among coral caves and fans. As deep as he could dive he got a thigh-long grouper, swam it back bleeding, cleaned it on a board by the water, left the guts and head, took the fish to the palm tree to help with the broiling.

The kids began to yell: "Shark!" The man scanned the lagoon for the dorsal cutting fin. It was not out there. They were pointing at the beach. It must have followed the blood; now like an amphibian, it was wallowing, half out of water, snapping for the guts on the board.

He grabbed his gun again and started for the place, cocking the arbolette as he went. He had fitted it, stronger than rubber bands, with laboratory hose. He had to stop twice, putting his foot on the bow, setting the spear in the notch at his chin—hard to manage out of water.

On a shell-littered rise he stood over the leathery gray shape, floundering, instinctive for blood. It was a big shark. As he pulled the trigger he assessed the enormity of what the blue sea had spawned.

Point blank, in the air, the gun would have pierced a whale. The shark was on its side. The steel shaft went through him below the dorsal fin. Just the place for a deathblow. The shark heaved into the air, freeing the spear from the sand, churned into the water, foaming it with his tail. The man braced for the battle, not to be tugged out by seven feet of fish.

As wire and cord went taut, the cable broke from the clip at the end of the gun. A twang. Harpoon, line, farewell. But it was not the end. The black fin cut the surface: a hundred yards out, almost to the reefs, deep water. The gray torpedo rose from ocean to air, shook. The earth-watchers felt the torsion of that shake. The spear was flung out, as if fired from the gun, but twisted; it plunged down, where the fish also plunged.

The man stood in the surf, looking. "He's coming back," they screamed. The black fin had circled, was heading for the shore like the strut of an airplane. Was it Melville's Moby Dick that took bearings, wavered, straightened, toward the spot where the man had stood? The hunter did not attack this time. Before the fish reached the beach, man had put certain yards of assuring earth between himself and the sea. Shark did not pause. Like a volplaning boat it rose from water to air, and from air fell to the strand with the impact of weight and rage. How could it see outside the water, much less smell? It didn't stride on hind flippers to avenge, on the man-thing, that passage of barbed steel through cartilaginous guts. But what obscure and perhaps dying urge had driven him back to tear whatever had struck him? In any case, he reared, flounced, cavorted, the double rows of intermeshed razor- and saw-edged teeth dovetailing time and again like the blades of a mowing machine. Until, by chance or design, he lurched back to his element. Wounded or whole, alive or dead, they never knew—he disappeared.

All the man knew was that, as he returned to the shore, looking over the lagoon for that swerving devil's sign, he saw, stamped and scratched into the sand like the warning hieroglyphics on Belshazzar's wall, the crisscrossed imprint of the great threshing body and snapping jaws. He saw in amazement that the footprints where he had stood to fire the gun were smeared and almost obliterated from the recording sand.

Yet he went on exploring: great sea turtles, a wingspread sting ray, once another shark, pursuing a school of carite (mackerel) and happily ignoring him. He went on spear fishing, even off the slaughterhouse past Cabo Rojo.

Here, let William Carlos Williams, with his plucky wife, Floss, bridge the span from Chicago to the future we were anxiously debating. We had met them there, late in our stay. He was recovering from one of his speech-and-motion-impairing strokes, and had come to read in the Rockefeller Chapel—where he sat, looking up, unaware of the microphone. We heard his musing voice, "Well, it's an awful impressive place and not to my liking, but if He can stand it, I reckon I can." Then he rose and battled his handicap to a cheering ovation. At a crowded lunch in his honor we were somehow seated at a table where he was being harassed (fruit of that Carlos heritage) by a Jesuit whom Williams' halting enunciation could not exorcise. For quite a time I had been reading and teaching theology from the Fathers down (with Dante besides), especially at Thomistic Chicago; so I pitched in like Socrates, and before long had that priest as tangled in contradiction as a bluebottle meshed in an orb spider's web—a rescue for which Williams proclaimed himself my friend for life, and indeed we wrote, visited, and were fond of each other until his death.

The next meeting was in Puerto Rico. Casals had been invited for a memorial playing in the Mayaguez house where his mother had been born, though instead of the Bach last cello suite I was wild for, the master gave a tearful rendition of "Songs My Mother Taught Me." Having learned that Bill Williams' mother also came from Mayaguez, in fact from the same street, we contrived that he and Floss should be brought down for readings—and, as it happened, splashings off coral beaches in cerulean seas.

Later, he would come to Annapolis, and whenever I passed New York, headed anywhere, I would take a bus to East Rutherford, spend the night, with an evening and morning of food, reading, and talk. Floss steered him through my *Delta Return*, on which he wrote helpful reviews; then through carbons of *The Married Land,* for which he provided a jacket blurb. Finally he took up mythic residence in *The Half Gods*; as Richard Ramon Richards, he lived, wrote, and died there.

For the *Delta*, Bill wrote in *The New Republic* (January 21,1957) a review called "Five to the Fifth Power":

> That is form with a vengeance . . . though for some reason, appealing to me . . . . An amazing freedom of name-calling, colloquial diction and particularly descriptive passages relating to the very trees and beasts and rivers of his chosen locale, which he has been lovingly familiar with since boyhood, enriches the recital. . . . When he climbs as a boy about the branches of a tree, glimpsing the sky above, few passages in recent verse can give me that feeling of soaring into the unknown. . . . This is a book of poems that strikes a high mark among writers in America. It is a book that will appeal to many readers of orderly habits. Don't be surprised at the vigor of the feelings and gentleness of touch you will find here.

As for *The Married Land*, which Floss also read him, this text appears on the dust jacket in color: "Overwhelmed with the story and the magnificence of the writing. A great book . . . How those people live!"

Perhaps I have given the impression in this Chicago chapter that the younger avant-garde smart poets gave my *Songs* and *Delta* a rough time. It might be better to say my poetry became controversial; and if the Dickey-birds or whatever we are to call some reviewers for *Poetry* Magazine were snide, Galway Kinnell, an emergent poetic power, championed the *Songs* from the first:

> No other poet of our time, I believe, has written of the American country and of the tragic ground by which our dignity is renewed, this resilience of spirit, with an equal combination of philosophic intelligence, responsible faith, compassion, and honesty. (*Beloit Poetry Journal*, 1955).

Charles Bell and Erich Kahler in the Tower Room at
St. John's Annapolis; Jim Gilbert's paintings in
the background.
Right: James I. Gibert.

Galway Kinnell (at top) with five Bells (Danny, seated left of Charles).
Bottom: Charles Bell, St. John's College Annapolis.

5. ANNAPOLIS (1956-66)

Having exhibited some Puerto Rican verse and prose from my Chicago-extended island employment, I take up the Annapolis move as a fresh departure, though the following poem may seem to deny that.

    The poem was begun in Mayaguez as we looked west from our cottage, after reading fairy tales to the children, when we saw low in the sunset, Venus, under a slim crescent moon. The verse, however, did not take form until we had settled into our new Annapolis house on Spa Creek, also with a western view. When I had finished the usual evening readings, I looked up and beheld Venus, both brighter and higher in the sky. Then the poem delivered itself:

VESPERS

The children, told
Of Cinderella,
At that dream window
Close their eyes.
While we, lifetimes older,
Almost wonder
What magic may answer
(As twilight fades)
Hearts' fond sighs . . .
When look: like a prince's jewel,
A crystal slipper,
Venus returning,
Blooms, in our dooryard skies.

    That was the Fall of '56. Now, some fifty years later, in one of my notebooks I find the following poem, which I scarcely recall writing. It should be from the same time—spilling over from Hutchins' Chicago—"that Baptist University where atheistic professors teach Catholicism to Jews"—into the Annapolis St. John's of Great Books (some theological). Anyway, it complements, at the close of Dante's *Paradiso*, that pure circle "which bears our human image ("pinta della nostra effige"):

REDEMPTION (1956-57)

When the abstract one
Took root in time
Who was it then
Was saved by whom?
Were time and process

Changed by the changeless,
Or timelessness
By these and flesh?

O when the silence
Praised as God
Was deified
In word and tone,

It was the torchlight
Law of the members
Led through dark
To the Bridegroom's chambers.

From my stretch of notebook files I have just retrieved a carbon more daringly radical than the above:

GLORIA

The angels were singing;
The light of a star
Brightened the pastures
Where shepherds were.

Had earth or heaven
More to gain
By God's assuming
Flesh of pain?—

When drunk with gladness
The angel of guile
Brought from the changeless
Mary's burning child?

Reason staggered;
But the snake of love,
Down from the Garden,
Came winged, like a dove.

     Here (perhaps for so heretical a poem) what might have been a
life catastrophe fell on me. We were living in a cottage Danny's parents
had helped us buy, right on Spa Creek, looking over the water. But it
was small, one floor with an attic accessed by one of those pull-down
stairs with a trap door covering. Evenings I had to build shelves for
my books and records, and I could keep my tools only in the attic.
One night, running full speed up the stairs for a saw, I encountered the
trap door closed. My already thrown-back head whiplashed, cracking
my neck like peanuts. After a week of pain, I went to a fine joint-man,
whose x-rays showed crushed disks and a cracked vertebra, for which,
in motion, I wore a wracking frame or, at my typing table, had my head
hoisted like a hanged man's by a cord over pulleys to a weight. This the
doctor had come to the house to devise for me, and when I sat down,
as to type, it lifted the whole weight of gray matter from my neck and
shoulders. For the first time—as if I had gone through death—I got
outside myself. At last my Wolfian fiction could be cleaned up. I was as
conscious an egoist as ever, my subject the experienced life and cosmos
of protagonist Bell; but like the masks the Greeks donned for tragedy,
my halter gave me a distance. I published some Puerto Rican stories,
then took the forceps to my first novel, as in its throes of birth—the
celebration of a marriage.
     The novel asked for more deaths than my own symbolic one.
Danny's rebel Quaker father would leave marvelous journals from his
1918 pacifist protest, through reconstruction in northern France, to his
bringing Carola Middlemore, a baronet's daughter, to farm with him
in Maryland. At her death she also was to leave invaluable memoirs.
Likewise, from my dead father had come *A Child of the Delta*; from
my failing mother, poems and letters. "Gainst death and all oblivious
enmity" these assumed the searching suspension of a union bridging
opposite shores—from the dry rot and fire of the broken South to the
stable order of the Quaker (and British) East—for which *The Mar-
ried Land* took its title-page motto from Augustine: "The beauty of
the course of this world is achieved by the opposition of contraries,
arranged as it were by an eloquence not of words but of things."
     With so much time going both to *Symbolic History* and to that
novel, it's lucky I had two books of poetry published and, as it were,
laid by; though poems would still wake me from sleep and be written

down. Here is one defying the months' pain of that cracked neck:

AUTUMN: WITH A CRACKED NECK (1956)

I had not thought that broken flesh
Could be so charmed by nature's voice.

These last colors melting into brown
Along the wind-blown water, leaves blown down
In their fierce dying, the rush of air,
Shake me with the fall-spring of desire.

How hurt a body still sustains the love,
Threatened by fate's blow; what windlass moves
The dead weight of a world; under what pain
The seed of hope puts up its flag of green.

So with a cracked neck, and for classes, that brace which could only lift my head at the cost of the shoulders (though it helped me sleep at lectures without nodding my head), I tackled the most challenging program of my career, with more class-hours than even at Chicago. To be sure, it was what *Symbolic History* had demanded: I could teach (by turns) all the courses from all four years. I quote a St John's experience:

> Early in my career at our Platonic Academe, I was teaching at once Greek mathematics and modern chemistry. As we were working in the laboratory exploring combinations of sulphur (while I had fled to the window to catch a breath of air), one of my brightest students came coughing through the fog to put a question to me which Plato also might have proposed: "Why at this college, where we are expected to give our souls to philosophical inquiry, must we waste our time on these stinking experiments?"
>
> I had come from the pure forms of Euclid; here I stood like Faust in the witches' kitchen, or a medieval alchemist in his den, the very smoke flaunting some satanic relation. We were working with the stuff of probability, and I was supposed to give an answer to such an imperative why. In my poetry group we had just read Yeats. I quoted:

A woman can be proud and stiff
When on love intent;
But Love has pitched his mansion in
The place of excrement;
For nothing can be sole or whole
That has not been rent.

The answer baffled him: "Why?" I
answered. "Because the changeless One took flesh in
a stall, to become among beasts a pattern for the
Western world." The student, muttering his protest,
went back to the crucible and flame.

No doubt I was at St. John's as disturbing as elsewhere; but
they gave me tenure, gave me a community, almost a family (both
loving and hostile) of ancient reason. I never thought I would profit by
going back to departmental belles-lettres.

At this point, before the web of Annapolis gets going, let me
specify (besides Dean Jascha Klein and the thrilling musician, Douglas
Allanbrook, composer, harpsichordist, etc.) two other stars of the St.
John's family, the Zuckerkandls. Victor (Vicki), already mentioned as
Princeton Kahler's friend and my Annapolis contact, was forging a col-
lege music program from the materials of his first book, a philosophy of
tone called *The Sense of Music*, and even more powerful, the Leibnit-
zian sequel, *Sound and Symbol*, from which I should quote a crucial
passage:

A system in which the whole is present and operative
in each individual locus, in which each individual
locus knows, so to speak, its position in the whole,
its relation to a center, must be called a dynamic
system. The dynamic qualities of tone can only be
understood as manifestations of an orderly action of
forces within a given system. The tones of our tonal
system are events in a dynamic field, and each tone,
as it sounds, gives expression to the exact
constellation of force present at the point in the field
at which the tone is situated. Musical tones are
conveyors of forces. Hearing music means hearing
an action of forces.

Then Mimi Zuckerkandl, an astonishing character of subtle and always surprising insights, who helped me with the revision of my Princeton translation of Goethe's great novel, *Die Wahlverwandtschaften*, or *Elective Affinities* (which I call "The Chemistry of Love"). Here is a free verse "Birthday Greeting" (August 6, 1962) which I wrote on her eightieth birthday in whimsical admiration:

> They tell me that child is eighty.
> A left to the jaw. I stop, staggered.
> What! Little Mimi? Old Vicki's wife?
> You mean the time I saw her first
> She was twice as old—and me gray haired?
> Yes, twice as old, and that ain't all:
> That little child
> Was twice as naughty and three times as good,
> Had lived four times as much, and her zest for life
> Was five times yours; yes, and in love
> She made six of you, and seven in hate;
> And was eleven times subtler than you'll ever be
> At loosing death's nooses—Houdini himself,
> In his very prime, was nothing to her.
>
> Come on now!
> Give the girl a hand.
> It's her encore. She's going to keep on!

Still, as that teaching load bore down (at the same time temptingly enjoyable), it wrenched a poem from me—a long Chicago sketch, compressed to a sort of sonnet:

POET-TEACHER JUDGED

> Having taught three classes the first day of school,
> Spilling my life to quicken young eyes;
> The excitement of this art, whose stuff is soul,
> Always changing like water and cloud,
> Sets the heart racing, then subsides.
> I see myself with the late or early dead
> On the bier of the world under a storm-sky
> That boils the eternal face, thunders his cry:
>
> "Wastrel of my grace, on whom I poised
> The secret and sole charge of deathless praise,

You flashed quick words at eager girls and boys;
Now time runs out: what pleads your case?"
Dead and lost I lie, while in my need,
None but the bright-eyed youngsters intercede.

Surely the teaching (so cracked and braced) with night prepa-
ration of assignments, and trying to keep up my own writing, hardly
helped my temper that year, or made it easy for Danny, who had the
charge of house and children, with worries about her aging parents.
One poem from our first winter reflects her cares; though its stress
somehow appealed to *The Ladies' Home Journal*, who published it in
March 1957 under the title "Aubade" (Awake):

> Two days we quarreled
> While the gray wrath
> Of tedious winter spent itself.
>
> Awake: for the leaf-wooing wind of the south
> Lays a limb of love on the folded earth;
> Awake, my blessing, smile, come forth.

Though for all my slow-healing neck, I was surer all the time
what a treasure I had in Danny. A spring poem comparing her to the
May Apple (blossom of the eastern woods) would be picked up by *The
New York Times*:

> May Apple is your flower,
> Cream-white, withdrawing,
> Hardly noticed under its leaves—
>
> Until we bend down
> And see the green tent
> Filled with glowing,
>
> And sense reels,
> As breathing the wine—
> Ripeness of fruit.

A more rugged fruit of the first year's Greek concentration
was a poem to the comedian Aristophanes—first, blaming, and then
invoking him, as if needed by our age, more corrupt than his (this, too,
published by *The New York Times*, April 5, 1962):

Something reeks of carrion; what is dead?
Watchdog of the Polis, is it you?
Or the Athens you kept watch on? Can you show
An impartial court you did not foul the bed
Of your proud mother Polis? Those plays, such mockeries,
Did they defend or assail her? Surely you betrayed
Her sacred image, scorned a noble speech by Pericles?
What if you burned the Sophist cloud-house, confess it true,
The blade you honed out-flayed that of Socrates.
Do not claim ignorance, clown. We say you knew.

Knew yourself a part of the crime you scourged.
Living, sick, and dead, you reviled the laws,
And fed your comedies on their decay,
Mocking men and gods, commons, lords,
Making new gods of laughter, wingéd words—
To quicken in the unborn.
                              Why not in us today?
We offer total pardon. Our demos of lies
Stinks worse than ever yours. Revive the wit that brings,
As to our maggots of decay, punitive wings;
Let them rise and laugh around us like a swarm of flies!

An inner voice tells me I should go from politics and the
Greek scoffer to a love poem, "The Fire" from *Five Chambered Heart*,
which transforms the autumnal chill of our Annapolis house. Indeed,
my note on an early sketch says it was written by the fireplace in our
living room, probably coaxing some damp wood to burn. Against the
flat fireside interior, that poem invokes a wonder both Danny and I
grew up with: camping out under the trees and sky—she with her na-
ture-sage father (and family), I from early scouting and Ozark camping,
down to a Black Mountain climax, whether walking with Galway, or
with the beautiful Trude Guermonprez, veteran of fearless underground
war-work against the Nazi occupation. That change of scene, however,
lifts the factual on a creative leap of the imagination, so the friendly
Ladies' published it, May 1960, and Doubleday chose it for their
Anthology of Modern Love Poems. Best of all, my mother, to whom I
had sent, for her perceptive judgment (as I often did), a packet of my
writing, answered: "I have enjoyed all the poems sent, but my greatest
delight has been from 'The Fire.' To me it seems one of the finest you
have ever written. I cannot express my joy in its beauty and originality
and purity—Love to all—etc. M." That letter increased the joy of hav-

ing written what raised our fireside love to the night-rapture of a blaze sending sparks across a starry sky. In the context of this background I think to quote here three five-lined stanzas:

THE FIRE (September 15, 1956, Annapolis)

The fire was slow kindling; it was damp wood.
Twice I rose, to mend it, from your side;
Stirred the wet sticks and blew the smoldering ends.
Then in the cold night-clearing of the wood,
We two, not young, wet with time's worse rains,

Forgot the fire; until suddenly it was there,
Point kindling point to take us by surprise;
A majesty of light, a living blaze,
That sent up sparks to coil across the sky,
Earth's poor matter assaulting the dark.

On this ground, the shore where we are bred,
We watched the lattice of transfigured wood
Slough films of gray ash and renew its glowing,
And in the clear space of the dew-cold forest,
Saw the last sparks waver among the stars.

In Shipwright Harbor on Spa Creek, an Annapolis inlet of the Severn and the bay, our two closest neighbors had sailboats; besides which, as a new St John's tutor, I was invited by an alumnus who enjoyed the use of navy yawls. So we had exciting times as long as we contended only with natural wind and waves. But the super-speed motorboats passing and even cutting across our bows did wrench a poem from me:

SAILING SONG

Effortlessly given to the spirits of air,
Under the white sail gently we wing,
Gently, between shores of green;
Gods of the sky granting such favor.

When, with the roar of a rocket,
Tearing waves and leaping,
Like an unfledged aeroplane, something
Wounds the water in a passage of speed.

The wind fails a breath, disturbed
By a power for the moment stronger;
It is the lord of flame, whom man
From earlier was importunate to serve.

But stay, my heart, await the end:
They speed a while who ride the fiend.

Now I began writing the poems necessary to enlarge the
design of *Delta Return*. My boyhood memory brought me one—tell-
ing of my grandfather's friend, the woodcarver Grimm, from the Black
Forest, who taught me chess, made his own chessmen, carved bowls,
a violin; but for his practical support turned tops, supreme in competi-
tion. My poem about him overflowed the *Delta Return* twenty-five line
measure. Still, it lurked in my files, and as more and more varied lyrics
accumulated, from Princeton, Chicago, and then Annapolis, I began to
consider making that elegiac ode the title of a volume in which phrases
appropriate to what Grimm had carved might form categories for my
next poetic ingathering (though my plan would be changed later to that
of *Five Chambered Heart*). Here, however, let me revive the neglected
"Woodcarver," with a list of thematic passages, each introducing poems
not so far published here or in my other books.

THE WOODCARVER

When I was a boy there was an old man
Who taught me chess; he had been my grandfather's friend:
A craftsman in wood: he carved his own chessmen;
And once he had made a sweet-toned violin
Which he played for us sometimes, in the evening.

Born in the Black Forest, his name was Grimm;
An impractical man; his art had no sale.
It was factory stuff they brought him to mend.
He went on at his musing and his lathe,
Turning out bowls and curios, unpaid.

Tops were the only sellouts of his trade:
Shapely spinners of hard yellow wood,
Slim as a hornet and spiked with steel;
They would split a dime store top at a fall,
As a fighting cock might spur a barnyard fowl.

I have not his white beard or wrinkled skin,
But I like the notion of that old man.
I like that honest way of the neglected crafts.
I am told Surrealism is the door
To make a man modern like René Char.

I say I have bowls to make, or a violin;
I will even turn out tops now and then,
Small things for child-hearts to spin.
If such they please, of such we have heard:
"Forbid them not, for the kingdom is theirs."

Suppose I have kingdoms they do not share;
They are closer at least than the smart fellows are.
Why should I sing in the falsetto choir?
I will go back to the dark shop where I went as a boy,
Among strange treasures: ostrich eggs, a crocodile,

Carved clocks and pipes and puppets; there I will stand
By the white-haired companion of one for whom I
          was named,
Watch him choose from seasoned wood something
          with a tough grain,
And turn it slowly to a polished form,
As he leans in the cave of light by his whirring lathe.

In an old notebook, six file-dividers labeled "Polished Bowls,"
"Little Tops," "Tough Grain," "Strange Treasures." "Kingdoms Not
Shared," and "In the Evening" comprise a fat volume of my Woodcarv-
er verse. Below, for each division, I offer sample poems.

For "Polished Bowls," "The Mocking Bird" seems natural.
The song itself, all night from the garden that first Annapolis spring (as
through my Delta youth), was musical enough for any polished-bowl
comparison. Published by *The New York Times,* the poem, of course,
could begin otherwise: "plain gray . . . quarrelsome bird" so long as
it found a way, by the close, to invoke, somehow, night-murmuring
waters of the archetypal Paradise Garden:

THE MOCKING BIRD (August 16, 1962)

That plain gray bird with the blur of white on the
        wings—
Call him an artist in the modern sense:
A mountebank, a charlatan, a mimic,
The most quarrelsome bird,
Fighting all day with the robins;
Well, he makes amends.

It is spring; the nights are warm, full
Of blossoming. Roses distill themselves,
Contending with honeysuckle.
Through dark foliage, magnolias are white in the moon.
I wake as the leaf-fringed hollow,
Already filled with fragrance, overflows with song.

Let him be as cursed all day as he pleases,
If only the midnight reaches of the soul
He quicken with the transport of such sound—
As of the stream, to the pool, by the rock,
Under the Tree of Life, in the Garden.

For a second so polished, "Love in Age" seemed smooth
enough for Rolfe Humphries to have put it in his New Poems II, of 1957:

We shall have music
In the songless land:
All brown October
Hand in hand

Two go walking
The scrubby wood;
Idle talk
Common mood

Break in silence—
Have you heard?
Not a song, not a word,
With the ear, nothing;

But hand in hand
All fall we go
In music through
The songless land.

For a third to close "Polished Bowls," this, of about 1961,
which was then called "Atomic Fall," loads a gold-leafed Autumn with
the threat of rumored wars; yet as a poem it may still be sufficiently
smooth—a polished death's-head!

FALL—UNDER GLOBAL THREAT

Never such a fall,
Such flawless lingering
of gold through gold . . .

To wake startled with it,
As if for the first time
After night came dawn . . .

And know: of all falls,
Never one so longed
To be time's last, and end all.

For "Little Tops" (those pointed spinners, woodcarver
Grimm's only sell-outs), I will draw from the file some poems the
blessed ladies of the *Home Journal* bought for $10 a line—this first
published there in July 1962:

DIVINERS

By all these things
That hold and retain
Something
Until spring—

By winter dry tulips
On the tulip tree,
By brown leaves
The oak braves,

By golden grasses
That cling to summer
In sun-warmed places
Of the hill's hollow—

I swear,
And call them all
Diviners
Of my soul.

Those Tops would often turn out to be of love. Here, one that
went about as far as the *Ladies* could go, but its charm brought it through:

A CHARM

Meet me tonight
Where elms tower
Over the stream

Where willows stir
Leaves in the water
Meet me tonight

Where day's fire
Bewildered in eddies
Rocks and blurs

Come when stars
As they sweep the dark
Sweep strings of desire

Come, meet me tonight

And the saunterers
Let them saunter your valleys
And your hills of myrrh.

For the last small Top, I choose a nature poem also published
by *The New York Times* (January 11, 1962?)

TANGLED WILLOW

All night the dying winter
Has troubled the dark air.
By dawn strands of the willow
Are tangled as a woman's hair.

The storm abates
On a bright morning;
Long rays dilate
With the world's turning.

It is time . . . Let the willow awake
And the dove-bearing Spring comb and dress
And prepare her again for Summer's love.

Something now with a "Tough Grain": cut your teeth on this
Chicago-to-Annapolis discourse. Though tough in form and thought, it
is a serious poem, published 1955 by the quarterly *Flame*:

RUDE AWAKENING

When I hear the old Romantics were in love with life, I laugh;
   They loved a veiled mistress, a dream of their own devising.
      It was easy in the shadows of self-deceiving
         Illusion to whisper "I love you" to a shape
            Of moonlight, and strangely neglect the serpent,
               Who even in England and the temperate
                  Zone crawled under the fostered foliage
                     Of innocent man and nature
                        To reward our century
                           With the disheartening
                              Revelation of
                                 His virulence.

No, it is only we who can love life, we who have learned that
  Living and dying are one and that love is the solvent,
    We who know, schooled to know, that we love the dissolving—
      Not wild nor in defiance, no more demi-gods
        Of ocean-perishing crying that madness,
          But calm, aware—not to say stoical,
            Although the word has relevance—
              But of Christian calling, if not
                Investiture, burning love's
                  Sweetness in the gray dawn
                    Of our terrible
                      Awakening.

Second "Tough Grain," Vietnam, about 1970:

                    Comes the daily witness and deposes
                    We have dropped more bombs on Asiatics
                    Whom poverty and oppression had alienated from us
                    Than on all of Europe in the last war:
                    Thus, evincing the power of freedom,
                    We leave them in worse shape than they ever were.

                    He grins headlines at the world-court
                    And bobs for applause. And am I to blush
                    That he and I are of one people,
                    Or marvel that he has not yet learned
                    That martyrs' blood may spread the seed of faith?

While we are displaying "Tough Grain," what about something from
the Spanish Civil War?

                    RINTRAH ROARS (Blake) and OLAF (cummings)
                      Who restrain desire . . . theirs . . . weak
                      enough to be restrained.
                      I will not kiss your fucking flag.

                    Leaders, teachers,
                    Most of all, poets,
                    Quickly forgetting,
                    Do not forget:
                    No poet made peace
                    With Franco in Spain.

Hernández in prison,
Lorca in war,
Starved, killed;
Jiménez exiled
Sought roosts of song.
Tyrants, pedagogues,
Poets, most of all:
Lured to forgetting,
Do not forget.

It is not reason fights;
But reasoning reminds you
What you have to gain
By reasonable surrender.
It is only the heart
Cries in its madness:
"Bugger your mother,
You and your 20 thousand;
Some shit I will not eat."

Poets, reasoners of passion,
Prone to forgetting,
Do not forget:
No singer sings of his chains.

On a dim carbon just slipped from a file, another "Tough Grain" piece comes closer to home—no sign of a date:

ON THE HIGHWAY

Sleep, death's image, took him
Driving, and became the thing
Itself. The truck from the shoulders

Veered; trunks of trees
Came crashing in upon him;
A cage of splintered glass.

If now he looks with the cold
Impartial eye of what
He comes to, he takes the gathering

Cars, the turret red
With warning, sees round the wheel—
Up monster van; the always

Beggared crowds, rattling
The tin cups of their eyes
To catch his coin of dying.

And for a closing fifth, what about NYC as "Corporate Nero"?

In a city hotel I wake without a clock,
Flick on the radio to get the time,
Take the blast of America
Kicking its dawn heels still in the night of jive.
Will its greedy desire never rest?

Then speech, frenzied as a drum
Shrills the pitch of "flying
Eating, living American."
All night sirens blew: looting and fire—
The napalm-beast home-turning—let Rome burn!

In "Strange Treasures," the first poem, which might apply
either in Annapolis or Santa Fe to the musical pursuits of *Symbolic His-
tory,* is entitled "Cave of Sound":

There is a new place of concentration in the American home.
We pitch above ourselves a shelter of densely vaulted
        sound—
Put on a record of Bach, advance the dial,
Boost the vocal and orchestral noise . . .
The study where I sit in the child-crowded house
Becomes a plenum of tone:
"Cum Sancto Spiritu in Gloria Dei Patris, Amen."
Cries of children, desperate pleas of wives,
All loves, all obligations, go down for the third time.
Who am I to turn lifesaver for any but my own
        thought's child?
One voice requires my attention—
You call it self, I call it God—
In either case, space charged with music,
It heaps and furrows under the roof of sound

A cave of mind, Urthona's or the Cyclops' forge:
"Bongo, bongo, bongo, I don' wanna leave the
            Congo."
Dishes crash in the distance.
How should I wake but for the coming of the Lord?

For a second "Strange Treasure," I suggest "Charm for a Modest Couple." We've had one "Charm" already—a boldly amorous Little Top (with its closing "saunterers"). This modest "charm" is certainly strange, though more a grotesque doggerel than a treasure:

ZIPPER CHARM—FOR A MODEST COUPLE

Powers of earth and air, wizards, witches:
Sun, Moon, and heavenly Dipper—,
Defend our plackets and our britches
From the slipping or the gripping Zipper.

When I declaimed that once at a poetry reading, a lively discourse arose: which is worse, the slipping or the gripping zipper? To which a bold male made answer: "That depends on what it grips."

Continuing "Strange Treasures," the third and last may best fit that Woodcarver phrase. The phenomenon of *gossamer*, a word grossly traced, even by Partridge, to "goose summer" but which Thoreau perceptively drew from the French *gauze á Marie*, I have witnessed by a stream in northern France; but the timing of this poem links it to Mayaguez or even our later residence in Chiapas. Yet here its symbolic tie to post-War jet flights, and perhaps space stations, may lend a global menace:

AERONAUTS

Here by the river we enter a shady grove;
Through the low shelter of haws a slow dusk filters;
Woven above us the green covert of trees
Is close and comforting; the ground is of ginger

And phlox—the heart-round leaves and purple flowers—
That we might lose us in that scented peace.
Beyond, far-soaring jets, invisible powers,
Lace the blue vault with a restless fleece.

Protect us from that yearning, buttressed green
Of the heart's remnant arches, and let searching
Eyes be trained along the quiet lanes of the stream.
But there, by the sun-webbed water, what shimmering?

Flights and strands of iridescent gossamer-
"Gauze of Mary" they call it, as if the mantle
Of some sky-mounting blessed this lower air:—
A thousand spiders launch from blades and petals.

Who can cling to the grove? Earth takes wings.
A bright gauze fills the air. All venturers
Of the sky's peril, we are drawn, poor living things,
From the sweet earth we have known—blown gossamer.

As for the fifth Woodcarver division, "Kingdoms Not Shared,"
the following vision of our wasted globe as a haunted house is mad
enough to be unshared—or perhaps shared by Nietzsche ("Who stares
into the void long enough, the void will stare back at him"):

HAUNTED HOUSE

The sun setting at his back, he looked in the window
And saw a face in a blaze of red.
"The place," he cried, "is haunted;
Let the ridgepole fall and the walls crumble."

We have seen our own face, in a fiery nimbus,
Stare upon us from voids of space:
"The great house is haunted; let it fall; let it burn!"
Alas: the sacred earth, our fathers' home.

For that same fifth division, one other and longer poem (pub-
lished in *New Ventures*, Summer 1954) may be enough:

PARABLE OF WATER
Seele . . . gleicht dem wasser, Goethe

Consider the round of mountain-furrowed earth,
The widening valleys down from sky-peaks
To the plain, the incredible basins of cloud—
Shadowed shifting oceans; and think as if streams

Of light were threading darkness, the spring and motion
Of waters—(Harvey's image: circulation,
Pumped by the sun, of gravitating earth's
Life-blood). From the highest bare fissure
Of rock, drops in liquid pearl, or breaks
Under granite crags in the formed hollow
Of sweet-scented balsam, red-berried star-leaf,
Long grass and ground-pine, the light-refracting pool;
Or flows from the cave mouth under limestone mountains
A river drenched with morning—from all the wrinkled
Round of earth issuing and pouring, the course
Down forever, falling from swift clarity,
Down the slant rocks drifting, sunrise-tinted
Veils, sparks of beauty melting to osier-
Shadowed streams, silting broad diffusion
Across alluvial plains; down to the patient
Glowing of the globe-encircling ocean.

Perhaps material vision presents no more
Than everywhere a luminance of birth
Falling to its quietness; the other motion
Is not of water but air-the invisible
Subliming and translation skyward, a subtle
Alchemy giving life to the globe.

Down, down, the entropic path on the land's
Surface. Above, inscrutable return
Summons from its sea-ebb what runs again
In the high wells of nativity . . .

Atoms of Lucretius, like the forms
They build, are prints of working power. Our angels
Sing from the treetops: Matter is deposed;
What bore that name is spirit, golden sun,
Feeding the leaves it lingers on. All things
Are living waters spent and restored—lights besouled—
Metempsychosis nourishing the world.

Taken as a meditation or organic world-view, this poem sug-
gests the defect of the Woodcarver ordering: I hardly knew whether to
group it with "Tough Grain," "Strange Treasures," or "Kingdoms Not
Shared." The last won out as having more space.

For phrase six, "In the Evening," a strange poem about waking, though not appearing in my books, seems to have been taken more than twenty years ago by *Southern Poetry Review*. Curious, that the word most searched for, "memory," never appears in the poem.

NIGHT WAKING (c. 1960-70)

It tunes in, my soul.
At first it does not know where it is.
Working late, otherwise possessed,
Mind had fallen asleep.
In the still hours, something wakes,
Troubled, as it seats itself:
Who am I, what and how?—a lost self, tuning in.

Secret behest lies on it, loath
To give a clue; little in its stirring
To inform oceanic oneness;
Every stage, puzzle, recovery, what mere
Cells, rallying, might substantiate—
Flicker of consciousness in chance material;

But for the haunted recognition,
While inwardness wells back, aroused;
And questioning the gray space-time of dawn—
As hand takes up the pen: "Let be.
Mine is the void in all that wakes and sighs, I AM."

For another "In the Evening" sample, take a short-lined love lyric; I may not have sent it off to the *Ladies*. It must date from the Annapolis 60s, when the hippie liberation was getting under way.

NOCTURNE

The night is quiet
The stars' vault
Yields to the heart;

Now flesh on grass
As soft as quiet
Yields like night.

Thinking "flesh on grass" might be a *Ladies'* liability, I made another version (published, in fact, by *The New York Times*):

> The night
> Is quiet
> The stars'
> Vault
> Yields to the heart.
>
> On flowers
> On grass
> As soft
> As quiet
> Love yields like night.

The next poem must have come to me when I was deliberating the loves of *The Half Gods*—as if inspired by a fictional lady, say from about 1964 to 1968. I bring it in here to emphasize what I have already mentioned about the Woodcarver phrase-sequence: how it lacks specificity as an organizing principle. One might ask: which poem goes where; or where do Little Tops slide over into Strange Treasures? Thus the present poem points that question: a "Strange Treasure," perhaps "Kingdoms Not Shared," but with its denouement, hopefully, to be enjoyed some late "Evening." In any case, "The Woodcarver" as title-poem and organizer here gives way to later possibilities.

PROUD BEAUTY
Why a little curtain of flesh? Blake

> When the mantle of chastity is torn,
> Bodies (by an ancient compact of love)
> No longer resist communion;
> The smooth and desirable complement
> Becomes ours without exclusion—
> Its covert arts of separation ended.
>
> Lady, whose burnished hair and conscious laughter
> Lightly clothe voluptuous curves of sadness—
> A discretely curtained actualness of person—
> There is an integument of you I would like to break,
> That our speaking souls might flow into their union,
> Each breathing and sighing to the penetrated other.

I would welcome any road to that meeting,
Even the dark and fateful way of body.
Surgeons have equipped whores with virginity:
You have married, loved, and borne children;
Let me take again the "maidenhead"
Proud beauty has rebuilt on your loneliness.

Summer visits to Danny's parents at Little Pines Farm were
a custom of the Chicago year. Like a backdrop to Annapolis, the same
farm lay only about sixty miles north, in the river-hills of the Susque-
hanna. The poems of its celebration merge with those to Danny. I have
variously suggested that the reader go back to the poem of my first visit
there, from Princeton, the Fall of 1948: "Woodbird" in *Songs*. Here
is another Fall poem, from about ten years later and from the same
setting, entitled "To Danny," though it invokes the German rhapsode
Hölderlin: "Nur einen Sommer gönnt, Ihr Gewaltigen" (One summer
only, grant, Ye Powers):

TO DANNY

Now last gold
Has touched the trees
Whose tallest plumes
Night sways.

More gold with dawn—
As leaf-plumes fall—
Let song's ripe sunset
Love's bright morning
Consecrate
Our time's turning.

You might even anticipate a couple more: one contrasting
Victor Hugo's "Autumn" with ours on those Susquehanna hills, "Less
Miserable"—pardon the pun—than the Fall of Hugo's poem, from
which I quote:

TWO FALLS

"Triste, triste, is the fall, the sad fall
With wind and mist and leaves that fall."

(Victor Hugo, who was, alas,
"The foremost poet produced in France.")

While we in a culminance of gold—
Tulip-poplar, maple, sassafras, ash,
With the scarlet of dogwood, red oak, gum,
And filigrees of creeper and thorn—

We stripped to the skin, up rivers of sun,
On the hilltop stand—and cry the love
Of our twined selves on an earth that goes
Toward the waste of winter by a burning road;

And swear the rapture of this new world
Is the sun's seizure on the earth-flesh of fall.

Finally, there is a poem called "Two Times," which dates itself
as ten years from my first visit to the farm—as with all life's blessings,
too transient. My notes tell me that Danny's father, Sam Mason, died
in April 18, 1957, her mother—grief and cancer-stricken—died with
us on May 11, 1958. What sorrow and love as I sat by that high-born
lady the last day, and she spoke through drugged pain: "I am waiting,
son, waiting. Am I behaving well?" "Lord," I said, "you're a lesson to
the heathen." "Well," her failing voice: "that's some consolation." The
nurse came in. It was time for me to leave. The following poem marks
my last farm return before the property was sold. The more remarkable,
that coincidences of nature should become a gratulation and thanks for
the gift of those ten years; though memory now can hardly credit that
so rich an experience could have lasted but a single decade.

TWO TIMES

The sun goes under the dark wood;
Walnut Hill lifts lighted plumes
Toward a brighter plume of cloud,
And up that light a swallow flies.

Ten years ago on the same hill
I saw such wings mount such a sky;
And then the wood thrush sang, as now—
Ten years ago, the same song.

Shall I not praise the high great good
By which two times world chance and soul
Touched my passing on this hill
And brought the darkness down with song?

There the Little Pines sequence might end; but I have hit on
three lighter treatments of the theme: the first, published by the *Ladies*:

SONG OF OUR SEASON

When russet apples
Fall from the trees,
The cider sweetness
Calls last bees.

Love, the bitter nights and days
End harvest pleasure;
To the woodland, come again, my dove,
Before the white seizure.

The pumpkin vine
The walnut tree
Employ the time;
And shall not we?

The second is surely Little Pines vintage:

EARTH VOICES

A song sparrow,
A dove, bobwhite,
And with the sun
A cardinal crying
"Dawn, dawn."

Still from the pond
The bullfrog belches;
The crow on the hill
Takes it up, and
"Caw, caw"—curses.

The third was a kind of legend of the farm, told at butchering time, with reference to a peach tree, growing from the cracked base of what was once a hog's pen:

THE SEED

We revel in a flood of fruit,
Peaches golden ripe, and sweet;
And this we owe,
Great-jowled hog, to you,
Your careless haste.

The stone uncrushed
Fell in the crevice wedged by frost
In the floor of the pen;
You are bacon now, old hog—

Past bacon, eaten and cast;
Dung, rather, and from your waste
These peaches come, a golden burst,
Distilled from slops and turds.

We gulp them down
As you gulped once, and in your greed
Spared (O may the devouring lord
Of our fruit so spare)
The seed.

As I sort my memories and writings through those Annapo-
lis years, I find as many crossing threads as in a chivalric romance
of the Renaissance—Ariosto in Italy, say, or, in England, Spenser.
For instance, I have mentioned Danny's father, Sam Mason, and her
English mother, Carola Middlemore, whom Danny called Cratchet; but
I despaired of doing them poetic justice. Early in this chapter, I hinted
at their tie to *The Married Land* in which those astonishing parents
became Adam Woodruff and Meryl Grafton. For more about the father,
the reader has at least one stanza, the second, from the title-poem
of *Songs for a New America*, as a plane from New York southbound
passed somewhere over Little Pines:

We are crossing the Susquehanna. Just about here,
In a farmhouse by the woods I know a man
Who lives as his fathers did. As far as he can

He keeps away from the city. He dips the clear
Water from his own spring. There is virgin timber—
Oaks and enormous hemlocks—in his ravine;
And he has planted all his hills with pine.
He gathers maple sap in the snows of winter,
Makes beautiful furniture, carves and weaves,
And fashions with wrought iron at his forge.
He is a Quaker—honest as his streams.
He has no radio, and when new roads
Appear in the forest, and drab frames
Spread from the city, he returns to his hearth and grieves.

I could also risk one from July 1950: how that inveterate
spiritual seeker would lie down, cover his face and his open eyes with
his old handkerchief ("Enough," Cratchet would say, "to put him
into a swoon right there") and see visions of which he told me in this
more-or-less dictated account of "Inner Sight: And behind the retina is
another eye, the reflection of the outer, but which sees the inner forms":

I open my eyes in dark and dwell on darkness,
Not the vague obscure but that last wall,
Termination of the temporal vision.
It assumes color and begins to swirl.
The first appearance is motion undefined,

Then paths and passages encircling a point,
Until the whole field is absorbed in blue,
An oceanic transparency of blue,
With waves converging to an iris of light,
A well and spring of complementary yellow.
It is here I fix, or more subtly, draw
Abstract attention, as if raising myself
To the casement of space, through which appear
Prints of the transcendental I.
                                    I have seen
Forests inverted in air and plunging streams;
And a white Spitz dog who stood at the rim
And gazed into time and as quietly withdrew.
These are preludes. Then the known face never seen
By eyes, the still-abiding ghost-remembered
Smile. How is this more than memory
Or dream? Not only that my eyes are wide,

While practiced shifting of the head, in no
Way shifts the forms from their own center.
Not this alone, nor any shape or meaning,
Only the still pervasion of what spirit
Prefigures by returning symbol—under
Purple lids, the smile and eyes of gold.

On the other hand, my two-page poem just after his death
("The farm is your praise, your art, your work; your great poem . . . is
Being") hardly became the swan song it should have been.

For my celebration of the Masons, Sam and Carola, one
should turn to the novel—a book, alas, out of print for many years,
though I can still outline how fortune gave it to me.

At Ames, Fall 1940 to Spring 1945, I had attempted to turn
my Oxford diary notes into a semi-fiction, submitting it without success
for the Houghton-Mifflin yearly award. Later, I dared not use it for the
"Dark Love" and first union of *The Married Land*, since Houghton-
Mifflin feared such a seal of reality might open us to a first-wife suit.
Besides the diary, I wrote sections of a projected "War and Peace"
of our time (but too Wolfian in its "lost and by the wind grieved,
ghost")—a fault which in Princeton, 1945-49, continually darkened,
until the marriage break-up left that plot hanging.

The contemporary ship-board meeting with Danny planted
in our love the possibility of a New Life sprouting from the Old and
bringing her benign Quaker and high-born English families to counter
the pathos and hard times of my South, which the reader may partly ex-
perience in the manifold fives of *Delta Return*. But for my transformed
first fiction, *The Married Land*, there were painful guiding events. I
have mentioned the invaluable journals brought by the 1957 and '58
deaths of Danny's parents (the novel's Adam Woodruff IV and Meryl
Grafton). Other Quaker materials followed, good for that phase of the
romance.

In about the same period, my Aunt Bets (the fictional Betsy
Byrne), who had wrecked and been thrown from her car, was being
held for fees in the hospital. I flew south to her rescue, comforting her
until she could be released; meanwhile, I relived my father's grim death
in that same hospital (which became the "Let There Be Light" chapter
of *The Married Land*, the tragic climax of my now interrupted novel).
Next I took Aunt Bets to her run-down and ill-kept house until I could
find dependent po-whites who had worked on her rental properties and
who could be paid to take care of her.

All that time, wonderful to say, I was scribbling in a notebook

what would become the core of *The Married Land's* setting: that Delta
landscape of flood, dry rot, and trial set against my remembered op-
posite of Quaker and British order with Diana (called Lucy, for Light,
in the novel) and the moderate security of her inheritance.

My first-hand notes on all this (Bessie's broken South: "That
house, that desk, that drawer" as against my mother's mystical tran-
scendence, matched by Mason family gleanings from North and East)
formed the potential core of the novel on which I was scheduled to
work that summer of 1958 at Yaddo. But I'd hardly begun when a
telegram from a Delta lawyer, my father's friend, announced that the
Jones-Coleson dependents were suing the estate for $12,000 for ser-
vices rendered.

Here I switch almost automatically to my surrogate, Dan,
the novel's protagonist: "what a trick fate had played on him; though
it would pay off in the furious outburst of a final chapter. Three days
before hearing of the suit, Dan had leafed through the Colesons' let-
ters from those months of Betsy care, chosen a few of the tenderest as
mementos, and thrown the rest in his Yaddo trash basket (daily emp-
tied). So he was fated to rush around crying "Where?" To learn that
the week's trash of the colony had gone yesterday by truck to the huge
north dump under the last hill at the estate's edge. So he had to go out
and plunge down into the fly-harried dump and grub with his hands in
the muck, to find here and there a stained page of blue paper scribbled
'Sincerely, a friend . . . ' as he spat what, that night, he would type into
the novel: 'garbage, trash, po-white trash!' If he had had all the letters,
he might have thrown the case out of court; but he had enough to make
the suing shyster lawyer settle for a thousand dollars—fair enough for
the services rendered, if commercial."

In the late Summer of 1958 Danny and I embarked for a
blessed year abroad. Another of the Princeton circle, Max Knoll, who
had come with my best man, Erich Kahler, to our wedding at Little
Pines Farm, and was, with Ernst Ruska, the creator of a prototype
electron microscope in 1931 and now director of the Munich Institute
for Electronics, had gotten me a Fulbright for 1958-59 to broaden his
graduate students with my slide-music-word lectures and a seminar on
ambivalence. Besides the slides and records for the Munich shows, I
carried all my first novel's sketches with me, though photographing,
and composing Teutonic texts for *Symbolic History*, took most of my
time. Indeed, I thought I had lost the novel altogether.

Driving back through France, we went to Versailles and
parked while I took thrilling shots with my new Exacta. When we
returned to our station wagon, we discovered that the tailgate had

been prized open and a satchel containing those irreplaceable sketches stolen. I have not been gloomier in all my life. Here, it was Chicago friends who came to the rescue. We were visiting Lulix and Otto (von) Simson, he then working for UNESCO. With horror Lulix heard of the loss. It turned out she knew a composer who gave the best musical program on the French radio. "Everybody listens to him," she said. "We'll go tomorrow and he'll announce it on the air." He greeted us at the Radio Diffusion Française. The devastating story was told. "I lost my first symphony the same way," he cried. "Gone, forever! I'll be on the air again this afternoon. I'll spread the news."

Our schedule took us to London. We were staying with Danny's relatives when Lulix phoned us there. The "grief-case," rifled of a little money, had been tossed over a Versailles wall into the garden of people who heard the program. I had almost despaired of taking up an intended residence at Yaddo. What could I do with nothing to write? Now the scribbled bulk would be there waiting for me. Though even with such favor from the gods, the through-writing was to take from 1959-61.

I would finish at Yaddo during the cold January of Kennedy's inauguration, when Galway and I, in next-door rooms, would work until midnight, and then go for a run round the forest road, the forty-below air at each breath piercing the chest like a knife. Pati Hill, sensitive stylist, was also there. She had been dumbfounded by the tangle of my Delta chapters (as in fishing, when you snag a line and drag up the whole bottom of the lake). The night I typed the close she phoned her agent, protesting scion of the Yeats circle, Diarmuid Russell, universally and rightly admired. Next day, going home to Annapolis, I took the manuscript by his office in New York. He promised to read it that night. How he did it I don't know; but by dawn, he phoned that he was sending *The Married Land* to his friend, Craig Wylie, at Houghton Mifflin, who was sure to like it. Indeed, it seemed not long before Craig came to spend the night and discuss publication.

Walker Percy and Shelby Foote, my old schoolmates, with others, being then ascendant, Craig was staggered by the phenomenon of Greenville, and asked if I knew of any other writers down there. I happened to have by my bedside the typescript of a first novel just sent me by Josephine Haxton, wife of my brother's best friend, Kenneth (1919-2002), himself a writer and the town composer, with an amazing body of work which includes the large-scale *The Sound and the Fury*, in five movements with a contralto solo, and *Moses*, for narrator, soprano, tenor, chorus and orchestra. Craig grabbed Josephine's *A Family's Affairs* like manna from heaven. By morning he had read it and decided not only to publish it but also to give it the Houghton Mifflin fellowship award. (He might have been considering me before, but I would joyfully have given it to Josephine—her pen name, Ellen Douglas.)[1]

My first novel took time which might otherwise have gone to poetry, but perhaps the fiction itself is a narrative prose poem. "The Last Night," near the end of the book, is built around three dreams, which, as the symbolic structure required, would represent in some way: Earth, then Water, third Air and Fire. Through those years I had been waking up to catch and write down significant dreams, and it happened I had on file two grim nightmares: number one, of Earth, involves the three children of my first marriage:

> Under the caving clay embankment of a river
> somewhere up east, though the brown glimpsed
> dread of water could be nothing but the
> Mississippi—to slip and crawl under the belly of
> it, and arrive at a place so far overhung and gaping,
> it pays to slough it off; so the hand and whole arm
> inserted in the moist earth-fold—to heave and then
> duck, as small chunks clobber the neck and
> shoulders; but ahead there to watch the main mass
> come rumping down, and be reminded: the voices
> smothered now—the children—and nothing, not a
> cry or finger, but absence to mock the buried struggle.
> Clawing through amorphous thudding dark, he tears
> sleep, treading the muck, crying: "Mardie, Hester,
> Octavia!"

---

1. *A Family's Affairs* was cited as one of 1961's five best novels by the *New York Times*; the paper also named Haxton's *Black Cloud, White Cloud* one of the five best works of fiction in 1963. In 1973 *Apostles of Light*, another novel, was nominated for the National Book Award. Her most recent book is *Witnessing* (2004), which was prededed by *Truth: Four Stories I'm Finally Old Enough to Tell* (1998).

In her essay-memoir, "Blessings" from *Witnessing*, Josephine (Ellen Douglas) wrote: "During those years and later, Charles Bell, who had been a high school classmate of Walker's and Shelby's, two years ahead of Kenneth, often came through Greenville with his wife, Danny, visiting his mother and sister. He was at work on novels and poetry to begin with, and later on his huge erudite, fascinating (but little known) *Symbolic History*. I remember picnics with Charles and Danny by the barrow pits below the levee and evenings listening to music from the Anthologie Sonore, the multi-volume collection of medieval and early Renaissance music which Kenneth was acquiring volume by volume . . . . I remember drinking wine and whisky and staying up late and talking foolishness. It was Charles who gave the manuscript of my first novel to Craig Wylie, his editor at Houghton Mifflin, and so it was through Charles that my first book was published."

The second, of water, begins off a Mississippi bank of cotton-mouths, then shifts to a sandy cove of the sea:

> The whole bank peppered with moccasins. Swim
> back. Better the open water, the devouring river. To
> float out under the Milky Way, stars bunched like
> grapes. Antares red, and below it, Mars, in the tail of
> the Scorpion, sluicing the waves with blood. To dive
> down and down, water rustling in his ears.
>   And come up in a bright cove, red rocks,
> the ocean violet, a floor of white sand. A retreat of
> land by the sea. Lucy by his side, the combers
> breaking in foam. He thinks: no menace. And then, as
> if the word had summoned an avenging sinusoid of
> tide, to see the wall of water coming in, cresting to
> a blue broken claw that hangs above, a moment of
> live suspension, everywhere shattering in spires and
> drops, the sunlight refracted orange through green;
> and falls. Choked. Fighting the backwash, to glimpse
> Lucy drifting out, crying. And dive. Breaststroke
> through the sand-settling water, eyes and hands
> groping . . . Found . . . But he cannot swim her to the
> surface. Planting his feet on the firm sand and her
> feet on his shoulders, he takes the traction of the
> weight and walks, as children play at doing, step by
> step, to walk her out. Until with a gurgling wail, her
> lips go under. On the roll of the wave he has lost his
> bearings; he is not walking back to land but deeper
> into the ocean. The want of air at the same instant
> stabbing his chest with pain, he springs up, thrusting
> her with him, kicking in the frenzy of suffocation.
> Air!
>   (He surfaces from sleep, having actually
> held his breath; he gasps, his heart racing . . .
> Tomorrow he will be with his Lucy . . .)

The closing dream joining fire and air I had never really experienced. I had to make it up. The only simulation available to me was Joycean, to play with the blending and punning of words. Lucy has phoned that evening, her voice joyful. Now sleep brings Daniel a glad symbolic anticipation of the actual meeting in the airport the next day; though at first Lucy seems confined in the dark of her Great Uncle

Stewart's Mill:

> Daniel drifts out under the ripple of the voice, lucent,
> evocative, as it takes up residence in the raftered
> dark room of the mill, voluminously enfolded,
> Gretchen at the spinwhorl in a shaft of sunlust
> singing: "The male is a furnace of beryl, the female is
> a golden loom." In moony night singing, noumena.
> Closed in the walls, the whirring dark, spinning with
> wheels, cogs turning and creaking, in the dry
> webwork she hangs, a lobe of luminous water.
> He outside, by the wall and roof cut from
> her, mounts spirantly, a fire-drake, a pyrrhous ram,
> roots at the woundruff, shattering mullions, glass and
> bars—comet through crystal, beast onto beauty,
> comose in glaphyrous, combs the vaultings, cunous
> gynous. Hair of flame pubescent runs in the branches;
> in gouts of light, wood and stone flower, wax into
> radiance. She leafs up, crying, wavers, and becomes
> a vapor, a wraithing. They are clouds, nymphalids,
> over sea and island, nubes nubiles, jubilant in marriage.
> From dark bellies below lightnings lunge
> into each, zygous conjunctive, sluice rivers of rain,
> infundate earth-furrows, cundle Gaie kyme: vines,
> fructuant, melons, mangoes, nuccioles, glandes, corn
> copious, and gorbeilles of ficos in overy geardon.
> And again subliming, leaves into vapor, and her voice
> through the vapors: "Prince of fire and storms, tell
> me of your learning: Are we clouds of thunder,
> tumulous?" And his tongue's lightning: "Queen of
> waves and islands, and quell of burning: In cumular
> tumescence earth and cloud wreathe fructifying
> favors, such gods as we."
> They fold long limbs to the twilight,
> gleaming devotive arms.

So much for the novel's imaginative close.

I find only five or so poems from our Munich year—otherwise taken up with composing, for the first time, a volume of scripts, at first in German, for the cultural epic I was presenting, with slides, recorded music, and voiced text.

ITALIAN DAWN

In the dark
And silence
Before the dawn

As the night-
ingale sings
A dream falls:

Peacocks and
Dancers tread
A closed lawn.

The poignance of
Vision breaks
Down the wall.

As the last
Warblings
Die away.

Night and
Silence
Roar into day.

BAVARIAN DAWN

Lying abed in the gray morning
I hear a first bird; the low calling
Is a blue shell of light.

It is met by another whose trilled turning
Is a crimson snake that strikes and lances
The round wall of the shell.

An act of generation, from which day
Is born—with cowbells and birds all crying:
"Halleluia," and "Dawn! Dawn!"

OVER BERCHTESGADEN
(at the site of Hitler's Mountain Retreat)

Seeing with my own eyes what years ago
In *Life* magazine, and through a picture window
(Folded fir-dark-ridges, rock and snow,
Over Berchtesgarden cleaving Bavarian blue—
At that remove, and before the war) I saw;
"Where is the house?" I ask. Sprung stone from stone—
An absence in the forest. Except four cairns,
Heaped again at the corners, betray a ghost
Haunting the place, inveterate for that past.
Which now a British schoolmarm counters, shocked:
"His curse is on the land." While the cuckoo shouts
From the larch and clouds melt and reform, both
Sound and silence answer: "Child! Had you thought
A mustached corporal, for all his strut,
Could lay a curse on mountains and not be mocked?"

In Florence, 1958, a parade of the Old City brought back one
of 1948, from my Rockefeller time, when I climbed the war ruins by
the spared Ponte Vecchio to watch the postwar celebration of the city.
The memory, with the fresh experience, produced this sonnet:

PARADES OF THE OLD FLORENCE (1948-58)

The city crowned with banners. Drowned in cries.
I watch another city shake the years—
As Farinata hell's indignities—
Vaunt to the sky sennets from trumpeters.
Those streets once rang with battle, and by night
Some kiss of rival families lit a flare
Of sweetness dipped in poison. Past the gate
A poet climbs the heaven-spiraling stair.

And wars, the wars of Guelph and Ghibeline
Hawked now for tourists, were live Dante's food.
If yet the houses of that hate and spleen
Parade before the garlicked multitude,

They're tame as circus donkeys, who were once
Portents of the heart's magnificence.

In Rome, Giuliano Bonfante, my retired Italian leader of the weekly Princeton Dante readings, told me a funny story of American diplomacy, which I have loosely versified:

ROMAN SNAPSHOT

And there was the wife of the American ambassador
A woman too precious in her culture, whose Italian,
However, suffered slight lapses. Like that
Which brought her a whispered notoriety
For her repeated lectures about America—
Until the King of Italy came—in well-groomed person
(She proud of success, such crowds attending)—
To honor, with the concealment of a royal smile,
Her favorite phrase—as she spoke, lengthening the vowel:
"Siamo uno popule giovane. Abiamo âni."

She should have hit a short "a" with the double "n" (*anni,* "years"), though her pronunciation, as with one "n," means something else: "We are a young people; we have anuses." No wonder the king himself came to hear her.

In another notebook I discover not only the train-scribbled sketch of "The Berlin Titian," but also a couple of bold off-shoots, flint-struck sparks from translating such shows as my "Early Christianity" into German—one, an Augustinian "Confession":

Great Augustine turned from the world
With one consuming thought:
"The transitory must be spurned,
The eternal sought."

But since eternals tend to nest
On the flowering branch of time,
He harvested much love of flesh
For his eternal shrine.

A second is called "Number Play":

Man has two homes
And both are one:
A home of spirit,
Another: flesh and bone.

These united
Clasp heaven and hell,
With earth, a three
Of One alone.

Who lives this
And lives it well
At rest in flux,
At peace with storm—

Joins a vaster
Trinity:
Man, World and God—
Mind's cosmic home.

At the other extreme, the pleasure of boating would take the helm—those old universities, English, yes, and German, with their stream or lake amenities—how many couples meeting: "Madam, I'm Adam—up and at 'em". And she: "At 'em, then Adam; I'm spread like macadam." So they push off. One night such a dream waked me with a rhyme I hardly needed to write down: "Bouncing Canoe":

Buxom Jane and lusty Jake
Go canoeing on the lake;
She goes down, he comes up.
And the boat bobbles as they tup.

We could not have traveled though, or I have written those poems, had we not found in Munich a British baby-sitter, very large and very haughty, of whom, as we left, I hatched a song with a stomp-dance tune:

She's a great big woman with a great big tail,
And she sits on the sofa and the springs all fail;
She sits on the babies and the babies give a "Yip!"
While the mommy and the daddy go off for a trip.

On our return to the United States, I began the poem "Cold War" about June 1946 but recast it after the Fulbright year and during our Annapolis stay, when our daughters, with the Cuban missile crisis, were most shaken by fears of Cold War and nuclear attack—especially as the Black quarters of the old frame town, heated by faulty stoves and chimneys, were subject to night fires, with alarms of the volunteer

fire department and sirens of racing engines down our narrow streets—
waking the girls to a terror of Russian bombs.

COLD WAR

In the quaking bog between world-floods,
Ague parting fevers,
Palsied pause,
Holding the first strokes from a worse to come;

Here we waste the interval of pause
Deny our fever, defy the stroke foretold—
Cumuli, mushroom-formed,
Missiled upon us in atomic storm.

Having borne two, we shall bear no further floods;
No sequent fevers will have sequent pause;
And yet we foment fate, in rival rooms,
Twisting, each, a noose plaited for paired dooms.

Fearful, to read the suicide of one
In his eyes' madness; worse in the lunge
Of mass delirium, to find the whole race
At the cliff's cornice, leaning into space—

Hypnotized:
"We have read our destiny of wars
In the death-cycle of the giant stars."

I was prompt about taking up my second Yaddo residence in
the summer of 1959, and the briefcase with the sketches for the novel
had arrived, though with pages somewhat shuffled. In the first days
of fictional search and delay, the muse of poetry came to the rescue,
dictating, as it seemed, the most ambitious and even most modern love
poem of my life, "The Number of My Loves," in Section IV of *Five
Chambered Heart*. The title of course does not betray how many loves I
have been blessed withal. The symbology refers to the stanza structures
of the four (or five) divisions of the whole. I even wrote a lesser poem,
printed in front of the main one, called "Love of Number," designed to
clear up the Pythagorean secrets of the other, though it hardly explained
itself. We can let that one go, while I briefly clarify what came to me
spontaneously: the structural underlay of "The Number of My Loves."

The first love—sublimated, Platonic, or whatever such a balanced life-affection should be called—is for Gabriella in Florence, and as a sign of that quadrate stability, section one was given to me in four-line stanzas—as it happened, six of them, which adds to twenty-four lines. The second section, of destructive passion, assumes the Pythagorean three, or triangle of flame; and, by chance, the eight stanzas bring the whole to the same twenty-four. The third section had to be of free love, so it pursued two-line couplings, though these came grouped in couplets of threes, making four multiple stanzas of six lines each. I knew at once what that fire-three and ice-six must signify: that if free love can't keep cool, it runs the danger of turning to fire. Last, married or generative love must take the water and flower life-geometry of five. But five fives exceed the total of twenty-four. Good. Let a line spill over as a Pythagorean basic One, which also raises the section count to five. Having heard that, the clever reader can surely grasp and fathom the introductory "Love of Number" symbology.

With the long poem finished, the remaining Yaddo weeks got the novel moving ahead. I would have wished to go on leave from St. John's without pay, but so soon after the Fulbright, I was needed. The next year, however, 1960-61, I could take off.

Meanwhile, they found me an office in a colonial building lately moved to the campus. Mine was an insulated garret room with a window looking to the street. One poem, "The White Room," about that chamber would be published twenty-five years later in *Five Chambered Heart*. The discouragement of trying to complete a novel, short stories, body of poems, and get them to the public, so burdened that poem that it sank to the fourth or Waste position in the book. Consider the last stanza:

> Is the vigil of the word
> At a cradle or a tomb?
> And how to work the will of God
> With God alone, in the white room?

Another testimony, perhaps more moving, I have lately found: a double message—first, prose, from 1961, looking back to 1960 as a creative time of blessing; but followed by a small poem from that year expressing the dark trial of the white room—"Return to The White Room"; here it is, prose, then verse:

> Looking back on the school year before this
> (after Munich) when I took off and tackled my novel, as
> being such a blessed time, I am startled to recover this

scratched reminder of the trials of that beginning, when
a work half done and gone cold had to be brought back
to the heat of fusion:

JUNE 4, 1960

School is over,
The yearlong grind,
Tempting hourly from the call,
Ends; the time
Expected dawns,
Under cloud, and vision cold.

The letter bins,
Unfilled, provide
No pastime papers, no small chores.

I climb the stairs
To the white room—
The book begun and half abandoned

Opens
Like God's tomb.
Day brings on the dark night of the soul.

A third such poem just discovered extends the crisis—through
the image of a squirrel in a blighted oak—to our rather scurvy age:

IN A BLIGHTED TREE

I stand at a high window in a white room.
Out there, by the street, is a dying oak.
The rot spreads. Ribbons of dark bark
Peel from the sick alburnum. It goes on
Making leaves a few years. A small red squirrel
Runs all day in the branches, excites himself
With something. Gathering acorns? His task he knows.
But does he know the prospects of that tree?
What if he was born there, as I in a nation
Where the poet-seer has no calling—
All tele-belly shows for couch-potatoes—
I, wondering: "Is the squirrel enviable,

To be so chipper? So blessed with ignorance—
Leaping the skyways of a blighted tree?"

A fourth seems to right everything by the inverted ceiling of
the room:

THE GARRET STUDY

This garret, where for three years I
Have held the tiller of mind, is groined
Like a ship, but upside down.
Good, the keel of my voyage
Is aimed at the sky.

In the college year of 1961-62, the *Encyclopedia Britannica*
photographer, John Barnes, came to make a St. John's promotional; I
helped, by leading seminars, and also showed him my *Symbolic History* Rome show, upon which he got the Britannica people to appoint me
author of their *Heritage of Rome*. We were to meet abroad the next year
and plan the shots, I meanwhile writing the script. I projected an opening
poem that might have made a visionary film sequence, but the educational board said it was beyond the kiddies, so it was never used:

THE MEDITERRANEAN

This is the water that bathes three continents,
This pocket of ocean, breeder and consumer,
Homer's wine-dark sea; this is the Mediterranean.
Ulysses was storm-tossed here; here rode the galleys—
Crash of armored prows, cries of drowning—
Here trireme merchants sailed bearing spice and wine.
Out of this liquid loomed the promontories,
That earth of Greece and Rome, their gods, their laws—
Islands brought from water, peninsulas in time,
Vineyards on terraced mountains above these sounds.

Go down into that water,
Pool of clouds and rain,
Source and garner of all sacred springs . . .
This blue-green ambiance rippling into depths
Stands well for an image of time.
Think Love came from this element

And set her templed traces on the land
And went down into the sea—
Where now we dive,
To recover millennial treasures:
Amphora of gods and kings,
Ships and sunken cities,
Porches and columns of Rome . . .

That would not be the last of the cautious "guidance" of the Encyclopedia Film Board, consisting mostly of principals and teachers, from high and even grade-school levels, where the main market was hoped to lie. Still, I took to photographer Barnes, and had a fine time casing Rome for his movie shots; though even he shied away from the subtleties of my *Symbolic History*, so that when I had finished I felt I had compromised—perhaps even prostituted—my vision. Thereafter, when sales began, and terrific royalties rolled in year after year, my satisfaction was shadowed by the question of whether, for an artist or thinker in these United Snakes of America, perhaps only prostitution pays. Yet how could I complain, since a side advantage of the Roman trip was to give a life-boost to Deedie, youngest daughter of what I fondly refer to as my first litter of three.

She had begun college in Bloomington, Indiana, where, since the divorce, she had lived with her mother and a fine step-father; but twelve public school years in the same place had left her, a brilliant and creative girl, so bored that, as she wrote, she was making C's in everything. I contacted Elizabeth Mann Borgese, partial to Deedie since our Chicago years, and moved now, after Antonio's death, to a cheerful Fiesole house overlooking Florence. Elizabeth said: send her over, she can live here and study at the university. So when Barnes and I had knocked Rome into shape, I met Deedie's boat in Naples and took her for a guided tour over Rome, then Orvieto, Assisi, Arezzo, and Siena to Florence—though only to leave some baggage and to greet Elizabeth. So we trained north over Switzerland, and by Rhine steamer to Belgium, then across to visit admired English relatives. A return tour through Cathedral France got us back to the perch of Fiesole. There I met Arli, Elizabeth's typing dog—a young setter she called her typesetter.[2]

---

2. Joseph Cornell was so impressed by Arli's typing "Bad Dog" whenever he made a mistake that the artist considered this feat one of the great events of his century; but Elizabeth Mann Borgese (1918-2002) was a considerable and effective force in her time. Author of some fifteen books, such as *The Ascent of Woman, The New International Economic Order, The Law of the Sea*, as well as poetry, plays, and fiction, she titled one of her stories "The Intelligence of Elephants," which reflects her love of animals and mode

That Mann daughter was making a remarkable study of the intelligence of animals, and since their tongues were not fit for speech, she had got her friend Olivetti to design a typewriter where the keys rose and spread on stems to a comparable array of slobber cups. With these, by calling the letter and putting a morsel into the appropriate concave, she had already taught Arli his alphabet. Now Deedie (more crucially than tackling the University of Florence) was to help Elizabeth get Arli, by a voiced spelling of brief words, to the recognition and typing of spoken phrases. I left the two there together and found my readiest way back to America and Annapolis.

Though that was not the end of the story. Somewhere in my files is a packet of correspondence from Arli. His favorite letter, of course, was the "r" of his name, and his holding his nose on it would scoot the electric typewriter through a duplication which could only be called a rolled "r". His favorite statement was "Arrrli go carrr." But when the London *Times Literary Supplement* published a series of what they called Arli's poems, the most literary was "Arrli hate warrr." I had experienced how real to Arli (as to any dog) the query "Want to go in the car?" could be; but I never understood how Arli had conceived a hatred for war. And still the tale does not end. That same year, Elizabeth managed a trip to India to test the intelligence of elephants. Olivetti failed to produce a typewriter. But she and Deedie, with a helping driver, took a Landrover, that could swim the rivers, from Florence clear to India. There they rode tame elephants among wild herds—secure, since people seemed hardly noticed, if mounted on elephants. Deedie said the sight of those huge beasts, so powerful, peaceful, and intelligent had changed her life.

Still, the change did not immediately operate. I next saw Elizabeth and Deedie, with Arli, in Santa Barbara, California, when I went to Hutchins' think-tank for conferences with my old Virginia teachers,

---

of assisting my daughter, Deedie. Before her husband's death in 1952, Elizabeth worked with Borgese on The Committee to Frame a World Constitution and edited its publication, *Common Cause*. She held various international editorships and served as Executive Secretary to the Board of Editors of the *Encyclopedia Britannica*. She wrote an introduction for the Constitution of the World, reissued by the Center for the Study of Democratic Institutions, where she was a Senior Fellow, 1964-1978. Her work there with Malta's ambassador, Arvid Pardo, first led to The Ocean Regime, a "constitution for the world's oceans," urging world leaders to examine the laws of the oceans, and eventually to her founding Pacem in Maribus, 1970, a recurrent international conference that prepared the way for the 1982 UN Convention of the Law of the Sea, whose subsequent adoption she guided. After 1978, she held Canadian citizenship and became a professor at Dalhousie University, where she taught political science and worked on disarmament, international development, and issues of the seas' resources.

Barr and Buchanan. Elizabeth had rented a large residence near by. There various of us visited. As we sat in the combined bar and living room, Elizabeth asked Arli if he wanted to type. By this time, his frenzy for typing had put him where (like Berryman in my Princeton days) he could hardly distinguish the poetic drive from the sexual. Arli sprang up and made the round of seated guests, humping each one's knees as he passed. Elizabeth opened a door behind the bar and he rushed into a room of his own—his typewriter spraddled on a table, and before it a chair into which he leapt and went to work, typing out his loved phrases: "Arrrli go carrr," and the rest.

   Though what Elizabeth had advanced to was apes. She had a big cage-habitat for several chimpanzees, and Deedie now was supposed to be teaching them. But they conspired in a blackboard jungle— saving their dung all night, to throw at her when she appeared in the morning. It did not take her long to decide, if that was monkey education, she had better go back to the University of Indiana. This she did, and made all A's. Indeed, she did so well in graduate nursing that she was put in charge of the emergency room of the hospital—all of which life-power she attributed to having experienced the intelligence and social gentleness of those Indian elephants. Since, married to a doctor, she transferred nursing to her own children, at the same time becoming an artist—first making whistles with inventive figures shaped in clay and fired, now oil paintings which sell faster than she would wish, she reluctant to part with them.

   As so often, this Life has led from event to event and from poem to poem, and has skipped something, a death in a house upslope from ours—a grief overshadowed about the same time by the loss of Danny's parents. Yet it stirred me to a ballad called "Child Bride" (Annapolis, November 1957). Some might say the tie to us was hardly close enough to justify the poem here. I reply: "I have no other like it, and the feelings described were real."

CHILD BRIDE

   Through my study window
   Past the privet and the rose,
   The neighbor's lights are burning
   As they burned a week ago.

   Then, it was a wedding
   And the lights let me recall

I also was invited
To the festival.

Some niece of the family
Was a cadet's bride;
As I came, she cut the cake
With his gleaming sword.

But the brightest life-feature
Of that bridal world
Was the twelve-year-old daughter
As a flower girl.

She was the beauty of our valley:
Why not joke with her?
My old hand on her shoulder
Like the specter from allegory:

"Claire," I said, "My charmer,
I'm going to ask God
To let me be born again,
And have you for my bride."

She ran, laughing, blushing;
That blush, too great,
By morning was a fever
Penicillin failed to treat.

The lights now
Are burning,
Not for feast
But mourning.

Shall I go up to my bride?
Poor breathless one—
I told you it was I
Who should have been reborn.

With Kennedy in, and our friend, Harris Wofford, his adviser
on race relations; with Galway clubbed, peace-marching in Louisi-
ana (as in the poem revised from "Weed Farm" to "Burdock" in *Five
Chambered Heart*; or with myself in *The Half Gods*, where the protago-

nist receives my neck injury but from Bull Connor's hoses in Birmingham); so with Black friends, we protested in Annapolis, together frequenting WHITE ONLY restaurants. Thus the poem "Pickets," negative; before the affirming breakthrough of "Threshold"— inscribed to Martin Luther King, whose Dream cheered our marches.

PICKETS

No life stirs at the center of negation,
Fear-impacted pit of Southern hell;
But fierce thaw begins in the peripheries.
Streets of a border city. Come from a pall

Of Delta dyings, I mount, seeking what springtide?
And look: a black man and a drugstore white,
Sandwiched in these signs—GIVE US FREE MEN'S RIGHTS,
And: NIGGER GO HOME—picket side by side.

The rights one seeks have washed the other out:
Black man, beware of that. And set your hopes
Above what the chromium car and suburb flat
Lend this scarecrow for his stubborn hate.

He wheels to face you, jeering. Eyes ahead,
Your polished ebony assumes the mask
Of gathered purpose, will and conscious right,
Features always of the temporal great.

Go where outrage takes you. Time gives you leave.
But remember time quits all who ride a tide
Of partial winning—as I, soul-surfeited
With the wrong they hold to, quit these niggard whites.

THRESHOLD
To Martin Luther King, Jr.

Gray March, gray April, under the gray,
Still leafless at the heart of things,

In the aching and the void,
Could the brooding darkness sing?

Some morning of our nothingness—
Nothing threshold everything?

Yes—as the sungates of our power
Break, and crown lost hopes with spring.

Over the long course of searching out and choosing poems for
this Life, I am bound to hit (as with the pieces of a jig-saw puzzle) on
other neglected things. Thus from 1944, nature-search year of "Pat-
terned Evening," a poem then prescient of insights to come, but so long
that I cut to its closing lines, first garnered and typed for an Annapolis
reading about 1960:

THE SPOOR

Strange world, labyrinth where thought—lost—swoons;
What glimmering is this that pools your spaces:
Phosphorescent waves, gray limbs of trees,
Merging under the moon?

Another poem, originally from my Annapolis teaching of
Plato and attempt to transcend his cave, has a metamorphic history:
the original of seven three-line stanzas having spawned two comple-
mentary poems, each of two stanzas—together a related pair. I begin
with the only off-shoot so far published (or seen)—a concentrate I put
into "The Brief I Am," where I introduce it thus: "For years, I have
treasured a dream (used in poetry, in my novels, and in *Symbolic His-
tory*, 38: "NOW, Alpha,") where Plato's Cave—imaged in the vault of
the planet we have smogged and soiled—expands from torch-lighted
calcite glints, through Byzantine mosaics, to a summer sky, starred with
constellations of a symbolic destiny. Though the poem there quoted,
"World-Cave" (also to be found in *Five Chambered Heart*), is a fraction
of that dream:

I light the torch
And lift it to inscribe in smoke
My curse, my warning on the wall.

Is it rock crystal
Shining? Gold mosaics? Shapes
I have known: Cross, Lyre, Crown!

Curious: nothing about Plato's cave remains in the excerpt. Contrast, from my file, the seven-stanzaed original: "Transformation of the Cave":

> I had talked of living in a cave,
> Spending the later years withdrawn,
> Writing disaster on the wall.
>
> As if the vault of the world
> Were such a dark commitment, and I shared
> Plato's somber duty of return.
>
> Forgetting how the incarnate one
> Had melted opposites in flame
> And made retreat his battle cry;
>
> How obligation to the Forms
> Became a birth under wings and song,
> And how the blessing was the trial.
>
> And so I light the torch
> And lift it to inscribe in smoke
> My word of warning on the wall.
>
> Is it rock crystal shining?
> Gold of mosaics? Shapes I have known:
> Cross, Lyre, Crown.

That seemed loose enough to have prompted my "World Cave" extract. Yet the loss of meaning also triggered another poetic complement:

WORLD SKY

> Lift up your arms! In winds of space
> The vault unbinds:
> This tomb of flesh, Plato's shadow-cave,
> Are earth, besouled, and cosmic sky.

The pair seems stronger than either alone, and stronger yet than the germinal poem.

Note: When I would send this, or "The Spoor," or other such

assertions to Henry Rago, editor of *Poetry* (or to the quarterlies), they would reject with cautions about overblown rhetoric. It was then I wrote (but never sent) a sharper reply, called "Kibitzers":

> When style kibitzers
> Betwixt God and me
> Called infinity
> A dirty word—
>
> Thunder roared:
>
> Blast such prissy
> Truth-inhibiters.
> Speak that word:
> I am the Lord!

Before and during our Fulbright year, St. John's was constructing new quarters for the laboratory, with Foucault pendulum, plus a grand hall for lectures and concerts. For the dedication an imported period performance of Monteverdi's *Orfeo* was planned. Before I left, I wrote, for recitation, an accompanying poem of text and comment; but with me in Munich, my narrative was not performed with the opera:

FOR MONTEVERDI'S *ORFEO*

> Prologue.
> (Let the triple toccato of brass be played with the curtains closed. Then in a box, right front, the NARRATOR appears, and as he speaks, LA MUSICA, left, with her lute. NARRATOR:)
>
> The blaze of trumpets ends. And Music now
> Sings to her golden lute in poignant rounds
> Under the dulcet dyings of the viols.
> She celebrates her power, the power of tone,
> With Orpheus, who made the wild things tame,
> Whose song like water from Apollo's well
> Shimmered through the dark and took death thrall.
>
> (The curtain opens on a Renaissance Arcady.)
>
> But look, the lures: woods and fields,

All hushed with music; no breath stirs the waves;
The birds are silent in the silent trees.
Be silent you, while Music sings.

(LA MUSICA sings her prologue. Between the verses, nymphs
and shepherds enter dancing to the ritornelli. When the
prologue is done and the chorus is on stage, the NARRATOR
speaks:)

These are nymphs and shepherds who have found
A garden of the heart, this Arcady.
They have no life but song; and song this day—
Bountiful day that matches youth with love—
Must be as joyful as the earth it charms.
For Orpheus, who made our grottoes grieve
With unrequited love, requited folds
Euridice, his blessing, in his arms—
Immortal transience of embodied souls,
Immortal happiness-until grief falls . . .

(Recitatives, choruses, dances, down through the Second
Shepherd's invitation to prayer. The chorus files across stage
toward the altar. NARRATOR:)

But one remembers, one shepherd young or old
Who has known loss, remembers and gives counsel:
"Since in the garden of god all fortunes grow,
Sweet herbs and killing potions, and we receive
Out of his hand the inscrutable dispose
Of benefits or harms, let dancing cease,
And in his temple kneeling make our prayer:
This island good he gives us may endure."
(Yet even the prayer is hopeful, speaks a power
Conforming to our wish and ruled by measure:
"Let no one give himself a prey to sorrow
Because sometimes dreaded fate is stronger;
For even if tempest laid the whole world waste,
Always the sun would return, and light, and peace.")
And so they pray and having prayed they dance . . .

Act II
(A shadowed wood. The meadows of Act I show far off

through the trees. Everything has a sinister cast, though the
opening music seems glad. NARRATOR:)

> What shade has fallen on the sunlit fields?
> What rocks, what woods, what stream-worn
>   limestone caves?
> This is the forest of Thrace; to these dim groves
> Comes Orpheus and brings the brightness of song.
> You see the sunlight filter through the trees,
> And through their arches glimpse the open ways
> Where nymphs and shepherds wanton in the sun.
> But it is sweet to return to these oak glooms
> Where the singer once, in loneliness, would brood . . .

(Act II continues through Orpheus' solo: "Vi ricordi o boschi
ombrosi." Then NARRATOR:)

> So Orpheus fills the forest with the vaunt
> Of love's possession and his soul's content
> While she, his promise, strays through sunlit fields.
> And as the friendly shepherd in a voice
> Half-tuned to poignance, as if cognizant
> Of what must come—the nectar of all wish
> Turning to poison at the flower's heart—
> Cries the bright air and comfort of the day,
> The Messenger, who has walked with Euridice,
> Returns alone, and with such face of sorrow
> As dims the light and mutes the laughing strings
> To the deep moaning of pipe-organ pain,
> With the great arch-lute that plucks the heart's own chords.
> She curses fortune, destiny, the stars,
> The gods themselves, this earth, the greedy sky.
> And the joyful ones, the shepherds, trembling say:
> "What sound of sadness shakes the eternal spring?
> Let it be nothing. Though this is the boon companion
> Of the lovely bride, and wears that mask of sorrow,
> Gods, do not change your bounty into horror."
> "Speak," says Orpheus, "speak, what is your burden?"
> And she: "The girl you wooed and won Death now
>   has married."
> And he: "Ay me." No language, but a cry . . .

(The music, from "Mira, deh mira, Orfeo," through the
"Ohime." Then the NARRATOR:)

"In a field of flowers, happy field,
A dream of pleasure from this blighted soil"
(So sings the messenger) "she gathering flowers—
Herself the fairer-wandered with her girls
Weaving a garland for her bridal crown.
Yet even in Arcady among wild bloom
It is the snake that harbors. He struck her heel.
And now how fast the orient face discolored
And the lamps went out in those sun-scorning eyes;
While all her maidens running, pale, distraught,
And clustering round her, tried to bring back life
With clear spring water and with potent charms.
In vain, all vain. Her languid eyes upraised,
She called on Orpheus, Orpheus. Then in these arms"
(And the singer's sorrow bleeds in half-tone pangs)
"She breathed her breath away. So I remained,
My heart a lake of waves, and the waves, pain."

What can the shepherd or the chorus do
In such a case but join the human cry
Against the murderous stars and bitter sky?
Ah, but the hero, he is more than man.
He does not know, he cannot feel
The limits of the possible.
He takes the inspiration of despair:
"I will go down into the lifeless land
And lose myself, or bring my love again."
Music's child
Bids farewell to the earth and the sky's wheel.

The chorus still laments, still lifts the cry
Against the brittle world and remorseless sky.
The Messenger, who has seen beauty fail
Like some frosted daffodil
Hating herself and light, withdraws to grieve
Her time away in some dark lonely cave.
Earth is returned to earth. What man or god
Enters the grave, and like the incarnate Word
Back to the buried ash invokes the Form?

Is that the grave where Orphic act is born? . . .

Act III & IV
(The Entrance of Hell. Orpheus enters with Hope to the
sinfonia of horns and regal; he walks to the portal. NARRATOR:)

> To the trombone's hollow march the hero comes,
> With Hope his only guide. The portal stands
> As another wanderer told us, fire-inscribed:
> "Abandon all hope you who enter here,"
> And so Hope leaves him. But he steps within,
> Stripped of all goods but song. And he will sing,
> To the paired accompaniment of the violins,
> And then the horns, and then the delicious harp,
> Melting the shadows: "Powers of the underworld,
> Night-guarding spirits: Charon, Furies, Hounds—
> You dark inhabitants of God's dark dream—
> I am not living, for my life is dead;
> Give her life or me death, let us be wed.
> Where she keeps court she makes a heaven of hell;
> Give me her heaven or let her leave this hell.
> Else I will sing forever, consume to song:—
> Render back life its good, great powers of the gloom."

(When Orpheus enters the bark to cross the stream, let the
outer Hell of Act III be on the left stage, and the inner Hell of
Act IV on the right, and as the boat moves slowly across,
bridging the acts, let the NARRATOR speak:)

> The sound of music ripples through the hollow
> Abyss, melting the remorseless laws:—
> "Render back life its good, Tartarean powers."
>
> The threshold monster slumbers. From those caves
> Of the vaulted underworld, the undying dead
> Of Greece and Rome—pawns of lifelessness
> Yearning for life—sing the brave madrigal,
> While the hero steers the boat across the stream.
> You will hear the voices of those noble dead,
> Ulysses, Virgil, Dante, seekers of Fame:
> "Man does not vainly dare, nor nature raise
> Its spite too high against his spirit's claim.

From that sparse seed a golden harvest gleams;
And memory will always chant his name
Who reins the sea and makes the storm his slave."

And now Orpheus' voice breaks on the shore
Of inner dark, to which his longing moves.
While still the monster slumbers. With dewed eyes,
Proserpina, remembering the lark's song
Over the flowers of Enna drenched in sun,
Kneels to the shadowed King. He grants with a nod
The inscrutable allowance Hell holds good—
The gift, but with proviso: Their eyebeams shall not cross
Within the purlieus of the dead abyss.
The caverns echo; through the stygian reeds
An unaccustomed voice of beauty breathes—
"Now love and mercy wake in the rock caves."
Death yields to life, night opens to the sun;
The road is upward, but where does it wind on?
What have you granted, Gods; and for how long, how long?

Act V
(The forest of Thrace, as in Act III, but darker, until Apollo's
coming sheds light. Orpheus alone. THE NARATOR:")

Once more to the woods of Thrace, the shadowed glooms
Where first he learned his loss, the singer comes.
No nymphs and shepherds now—he is alone.
Not even Hope is with him; but Echo sighs
The hollow closes of each mournful phrase.
And here the Thracian women, the violence
That shatters earthly things, should drown his voice
With their harsh cries and tear him with their nails,
And send his bleeding head down Hebrus' flood.
And the only miracle should be of tone,
That voice and lyre still sound. Have we not heard
Of old: dead tongues will speak such prophecies
As change oppressors into hierophants?
And thus the tragic tale let Orpheus' lips
Breathe dulcet airs, in watery death.
Though transcendence finds another way:
This music lightens and is almost gay.
Apollo comes, who holds art in his care,

And takes his favorite to a shore
Where shepherds dance through amaranth and myrrh,
A dance of spirits freed from flesh and bone.
This is the realm of all myth has redeemed,
And every comer here becomes a god
To whom the living pray, avoiding harm.
For music can do much. Only it fails
To bring back earthly joy. Orpheus will find
Euridice in heaven always young,
But the mere semblance of that flesh and blood
He held once in his arms, a shadowy form,
Although undying as this art of song.

For relief now: a love poem for flesh-and-blood wife Danny,
by the wooded creek shores near Annapolis,

LOVE'S IDYLL (c. 1963)

Beech leaves above,
    first green
        against
            the blue;

Below, in such a blue,
    green glints
        bestrew
            your eyes—
So laughing
    at that
        sky.

In years of commuting on the roads and through the cities of
the East—first to Little Pines and after to our Vermont summer house—
I was moved to write the following; but note: although I still read,
admire, and enjoy Jane Austen, I cannot share in her neglect of passion
and sex in marriage, thus this poem (about 1959) of "Commuter Love"
once subtitled "Cult of Nature":

Commuters who drive to work down concrete speedways,
Past houses rowed and boxed monotonously the same
As that aseptic one they call their own,
Even commuters must catch at nature somewhere.

Is it any wonder they go for sex?
In a pair of mirroring eyes they may forget
Rock pools where soul's deep longing almost drowns;
A brace of cupped breasts serve for green hill-paps
They did not wander young or ponder old;
For beech-grove stream-bank paths they did not roam,
Or limestone steeps over which they never climbed,
They dote on the smooth slopes of a lady's thighs;
And I who drive much now down turnpike roads,
Who am I, not to worship the gods of my kind?
Twenty years my bride, and prone to jousts of love—
Bare the spread altar of your lips, tits, loins.

Indeed, even in the ideal love of *The Married Land*, faithful
Dan Byrne may break into a barely publishable ditty, sung and enacted
as he fondles his beloved Lucy. Two samples: "Kneading Rear" ("I
need you"):

Oh the ladies have their asses where they set;
We call them little assets
Le mot Français è fesse;
So when we get aggressive
And we want to tup
We catch them by their dresses
And we say: "Fess up, fess up, fess up!"

Likewise (Patter Song Pantomime):

When we would make love to ladies
We must catch them by the titties
If they strike or do disdain us
Fondly poke them in the anus,
Till they spread themselves like Venus
To receive the manly penis
Then we labor like a miner
In the cave of the vagina
Till we demonstrate in semen
Our entire regard for women.

(Suspend bawdy verse.)

However, as the toils of St. John's moved toward 1965 with all the cares detailed in the following poem, a backlash was bound to trouble the surface of my consciousness:

TO ONE WHO ASKED

One of our martyr-students, stretched three ways
By Christ, world-soul, and woman—a face as plump
As my dead brother's, soul as resonant—
Tries what the first finished. I find him almost gone,
Quoting from that Sibyl in a cage,
Who said: "I want to die." After an hour,
He takes the chlorined water I tell him is life.

Then to the girl on whose rack he was torn,
Another sleepwalker, wringing her hands.
"I have five daughters," I say, "and every one
Could be as crazy as you. Take time; take time."

That night back at home, long-distance calls:
The saddest of my five, all allergies
And adolescent moods. She is heading west
For the desert, as if a desert could help—
Parched to her own desert—of the heart.
I get off letters to friends, banks, schools.

Today my niece comes in a failing gloom.
I drive her north to cities where the young
Learn trades—(for her) to nurse the sick—
They sick themselves, and I, her soul-sick nurse,
Speed the trafficked road, talking of the Good Life.

Tonight, at a seminar, a woman brings
A friend—a bozo from Paris, Left Bank guy—
No students, no family, he lives to paint.
Asked what he thinks of me, he condescends:
"Seems a bright enough fellow; but why so cold?"
And the babe puts it to me: "Am I so?"
How can I answer but to rave:
"Cold, cold, my girl? Luxury! To write:
'Solitude' on the cold vault of some cave."

Here the piled negations of this poem summoned, for my own sanity, an "Envoi":

> Life spent in love, works, causes—
> What comfort in sage Goethe's phrases:
> The man gains what the poet loses?
>
> Back to the study and the pen:
> The Poem of Earth . . .Yet to what gain,
> In a void where earth and poems end?
> And still the Uncreated Word
> Lives, and pours into that void
> The poems, the loves of gods to God.

But we are again in Annapolis, where after a visit to my mother in the rather segregated South and a home-night with Danny, I took off once more for Yaddo, to advance my second novel; though stopping, as often, at Newark, to take the crowded bus to visit Bill Williams and Floss. That integrated ride gave me a poem, "Renegade":

> Having flown to Newark after weeks of Mississippi,
> And running with all bags across the road for a transit
> Bus, the cheapest ride to William Carlos Williams',
> I sit in a Number Four full of smoke and laughter:
> A mechanic haranguing the driver about nuts and bolts,
> Then off to his grape arbor and how he makes wine;
> Voices, scrambled, converging from all sides:
> "Well fer cryin out loud, ya can't do it that way . . ."
> "I must have fleas. Soon as the double-crossin cur
> Begins to scratch I feel things crawlin on me . . ."
> "Didn't rain hard? Are ya kiddin? It flooded the place."
> "Christ, did she think she could break it up and not pay?"
> By my side a black woman, having, whatever else,
> Her right to be there, and damned well knowing it—
> And not a drawling planter or wife-and-slave-holding
> Caucasian toting his coon gun—
> It was home down there I stayed at, thought I enjoyed it.
> Now I heave the rib cage and gulp air, snuff up
> The Northern city, slums and all, one little purchase
> Against enormity. "By God," I catch myself mouthing:
> "It's good to be in a free country again."

Here is a poem dedicated to Dr. Harry Slack, of Johns Hopkins, old friend of Danny's family, who had taken out her tonsils, neglected till she was twenty-three. He narrated this dream to her; she told it to me, and I recorded it in a kind of triple-free-verse. Quite a dream!

A DESERT DREAM
For Doctor Harry

I dreamed I was in a desert, the waste
In which, symbolically, we are,
And before me, paint and canvas.

I who cannot paint or even draw
Was required to make a picture,
At no insistence but this of inner law.

Nothing was alive, it was utterly dry,
Yellow and brown, the palette splotched the same,
With other pigments of the sun and sky.

I sat, delaying the encounter with form,
And saw southeast a cloud, a patch the size
Of a man's hand, writhing like a worm.

It neared and grew, resolved into spots like bees;
Locusts to the palette descended in loud swarms,
Threshing in the colors, the purples, browns and greens;

They flowed in arcs to the canvas, a vortex like flame,
Struck their wings and returned—it was pointillism assumed
By the Nile pests of Biblical fame.

So the landscape was made, but bright, a flowered world;
And as I saw it in wonder signed with my name,
And in wonder saw those locusts whirled

Again into space, their vacant home;
Cumulus darkened around me, rain fell; then
I beheld in wonder how the desert broke into bloom—

Colors of the picture; that gift of the sky
Became time's prophecy, and the locusts withdrew,
Down rivers of light; where I descried:

How, stained in their colors still, they arched a
      rainbow, sign
To the desert dreamer of our desert to be reclaimed;
And I awoke to the poem out of the dream.

The next story climaxes in Annapolis, though it began in Chicago. My loving tie to the Borgeses occasioned another curious contact—with Mortimer Adler, like Hutchins, a sometime guest at their dwelling. In fact, I had gone to a lecture of his when I arrived in Chicago. My Virginia pursuit of Barr and Buchanan made that one seem ordinary, but I was amazed in the following question period how he responded to raised hands. If the input seemed anti-Mortimer, he put it down with an ironic quip that Groucho Marx could hardly have sharpened. If pro, or friendly, with what encouragement he dwelt on the speaker's agreement!

Some years after, when Antonio and Elizabeth had agreed on christening their first daughter into the church, we Delta louts used to call "Piss-over-the-Pailean," I agreed, for all my Blakean protest, to be godfather, while Mortimer's then-wife joined us as godmother. So Mortimer and I became god-sib, that earlier English "sib" meaning "kin." (Over the years godparents, perhaps given to small talk, as I may be now, and the hyphenated "god-sib" became "gossip.") Anyway, Mortimer and I, though god-kin, would argue—as when he condemned all memorization (calling it "by rote" to which I countered "by heart"); he claiming "Greek reason," though the Greeks (as in Plato) had a memorized devotion to their poets, Homer and the rest. Still, we kept the peace, and I had to admire how the old codger spread his Great Books seminars, which I was glad enough to teach; how he held to his guns, even in his drive to invade the public schools.

Well now, it turned out that St. John's—honoring the old Great Text revolution which spawned Hutchins' Chicago College, our program, and Mortimer's seminars—would bring Mortimer to lecture in Annapolis. Late in my time there, having dumped his first wife (my god-sib) and married his young secretary, he came to give a lecture on Love. As so often, he hit on a neo-Platonic absolute: that love has to be purely self-sacrificing; as soon as interest (money or other advantage) enters, the relation ceases to be love. In the question period, Dean Klein having told the faculty we should first let the students have a chance, I sat while they fumbled and Mortimer mauled them. At last, when I felt it was high time, I said, calling his full name, "I don't understand this notion of disinterested love, according to which no nursing child could love its mother or the mother her child, since one needs the milk and the other needs the sucking." What I meant to show was that need, or interest, is probably ingredient in most loves; but the room shook with such a roar of laughter that poor Mortimer was furious and never spoke to me again. Yet still, I praise the man for his indefatigable pushing of a good idea, in which he almost desperately believed.

Here is a poem sketched in Munich from notes made in Maryland before the fellowship year, as we picnicked in the woods and by a waterfall on a Susquehanna Hills stream, called, as in the title of the poem, "Falling Branch." The body of the poem, four and one half stanzas, shows how swayed I was, or thought I was, by Thoreau's *Walden*, then and still a favorite book. But here I was fancying some such escape from the college-teaching grind, which would, nonetheless, remain my livelihood and the cultural arena of my *Symbolic History*. Hence, the last (altered) stanza goes quite the other way.

FALLING BRANCH

Having hunted home through reaches of space,
One might settle at last for homelessness:
A scrawny valley by a clouded stream,
A ruined house, a blackberry vine;
Pitch camp there, saw up windfalls;
Patch a roof over old crumbling walls;
Destitution defies the profaner.

If you conceived a state of another kind,
Think all states are states of the mind.
Europe lies here in the shade of this rock;
Florence, Solesmes, the vines of Medoc;
The Danube and Mosel in that falling water;
All times and places attend eyes' closure:
Are not stars thus brighter, meadows greener?

Once hope led to the open: a lake, a grove
Could lure dreamers from resignation's cave.
Our ravaged nature is almost a tomb,
For flight of the alone to the Alone.
Why not this blackberry valley for my land,

This rock my tower, this mangled wood my stand?
Poor and content maims truth's disdainers.

While forests fall whose wood is brayed
To paper pulp for the worthless word;
While fools rule and sold media please,
So long dies this, and dying utters praise . . .

So far this poem is a mad nightmare—
Mind says resume
Your skilled teaching and writing endeavor;
What if your five-times-great-uncle was Dan Boone,
It is hardly your proper life-share
To be a backward, backwoods squatter.

In that Hippie time, everything loosening up—so many temptations to clandestine romance. Here one little hippie piece of observational possibility:

BIRD OF PREY

Her slacks loose at the waist,
His hand, swift hawk,
Down smooth belly swoops;
Beak of middle finger
Plunging to the secrets of her life.

Mere thinking about the new mores supplied a quatrain on the paradox of such infidelities, how many of which would lead to divorce and remarriage:

ADULTERY

I want you loyal, but to me;
I pit my breath
Against the grain of loyalty
Squaring false faith.

During one of our travels the St. John's Admission Office overflowed from downstairs into my garret; but I was given a bolder space: the great windowed octagon of the bell tower, over the college and tree-banked town between creeks and bay. Tower poems sprinkle my later published *Five Chambered Heart*: on love: "March Snow," and "From Height and Silence," the realistic "November Tower" confronts the cold up there; another, "Resonance of Towers", claims with Dante, Yeats, and Jeffers that all-night legacy (why not Milton?). For comic actuality, a rather plump senior, whose thesis on *Moby Dick* I was advising, was loath to climb all that way, if I might perhaps be elsewhere. He persuaded me to keep a window open, so that I could hear him bellowing from below: "Ship ahoy! Have you seen the White Whale?" If I called back, he would pant up the steep stairs.

It was through several tower years that I scribbled and typed at my monstrous second fiction, *The Half Gods*. Sometimes our painter, Jim Gilbert, retired from Chicago, who had joined us in Annapolis as St. John's artist-in-residence, would take advantage of my power to compose at the typewriter without the need of glasses, and thus use me as model for anything from side to front view—as when my recapturing that first Florentine visit and fondness for Gabriella gave me a smiling glow. Many of those evenings he would come to the house for his "mother's milk" (a gin with vermouth), while I would read a chapter. It did not discourage me that he would say afterward: "You're not writing a novel; you're trying to revive the tradition of Greek rhapsode, and you can't do it."

Anyway, several tower years produced such a swollen briefcase of sketches as would take me another year living on a Worcestershire farm near Danny's Married-Land cousins (again on leave, and on funds gleaned from such forebears) to melt it down and through—write it as *The Half Gods*. Though for the reading public that made little difference; since the challenge of the book, with the voiced Communism of Leflore's first wife (however debated and answered all the way) had the book dropped from the shelves as if it had never been there. To revive it as politics turned almost to poetry, I quote from the close:

> When the Sunday school was dynamited in Reading (after Daren hurt his neck, at the end of that smoldering summer) and the news fanned out over the nation, the mother holding a shoe, the father telling his wife, "She's dead, baby; she's dead," touching even the South almost to Biblical strains (oratory easier than reform): "We created the day; we bear the judgment. In bitter ruins we stand with a Negro mother, weeping, holding a shoe"—at that outrage horror had gripped America.
>
> And now, for reasons not much clearer, we were

inundating a people 6000 miles away, who had not attacked us and on whom we had never declared war, with more explosive and fire than the Nazis had poured over the whole of Europe, destroying and mutilating enough children, mothers, fathers, to stock the Sunday schools of the South, and the papers were writing it up as an operation to be condoned, one might almost think, applauded.

In the resolve, even in dream, not to go callous, not to be shrugged down, to preserve at all costs the one poor assurance of humanity, the power to be appalled, Daren tore at the veils of distance; and it was there, inescapable as Dürer's nude study of himself: the archetypal Son of Man, an Asian peasant, standing in a Delta of rice paddies across a little pool. His image in the water was Daren's naked form.

"To us in the past, America meant Beautiful. But now . . ." The voice trailed off. The body decomposed in the shaking of the water. A deafening noise of planes . . . Unbelievable, the blinding flash, the thunder crack and deep off-going roar.

Leflore had loved storms since he was a boy. But living in a country where commerce has fastened on the fact of fear, so many people, journalists, manufacturers, politicians, psychiatrists, cashing in on mass hysteria, until every fire siren in the night goes through the unconscious like the last trumpet—the jolt and unseasonable surprise, on Christmas night, of so much lightning and explosive sound, had Daren up and standing at the window while he was still half wrapped in dream.

The dark came to focus in another flash, an instant, ear-splitting roar. It was brighter than summer lightning, incredibly, weirdly bright. His eyes widened.

On the cold front that had brought the storm, the rain was changing through hail into snow, great driving flakes of snow, which suddenly whitened the whole earth and air; and at the heart of that winter-white cold, the summer-fierce lightning seared again, a blinding consummation of ice and fire.

At dead center, the inversion and intersection of cones where the moment opens to a timeless and spaceless sphere, the blaze of opposites. Reinentsprungenes. All time gaping, panting for that seizure.

When would it be? The mystical year 2000? At the turning of a hair?

Everywhere and always?

Was it Now?

Had He made this, or was this the fury where He was being made?

My novels, as extensions of world history, have to forge the actual into symbolic paradigm. In the first, the love-union to be celebrated fictionalizes my own second marriage: as that of Daniel Byrne (from the almost Faulkner dry-rot, flood, and fire of Mississippi) to Lucy Woodruff (my own Danny—or Diana Mason—she, from the almost Austen well-being and order of Quaker East and aristocratic England). Even the protagonist, though not me, stands in my shoes. But for the political allegory of *The Half Gods*, I had to seat my alter ego in another family, assembled from Greenville memories (suggesting the Percys)—shaping other characters from the oral and written contributions of willing donors. Thus for my Welsh poet mother, I persuaded that fine nature poet, Abbie Houston Evans, to play the role, for which she gave me choice ancestral material. I have already mentioned the generous contribution of Ann Markin, met at the Clearing, whose slum childhood and socialist conversion had to be somehow spliced into the record of my Oxford journals, thereafter replacing the actual Mildred as first wife. Let me quote here from "The Brief I Am":

> Nor was that all; I hit on a real house a separating wife was renting in Ellicott City on the Patapsco; there I went through all seasons to observe and record. As if living and writing were one, I called my novel participants to join me in our book-haunts and to send details of theirs. Thus Cecil Roberts, British charmer, fighting for liberal causes in the Deep South—having read my first novel, and wishing to contribute to its sequel—gave me her memories for the second-love fiction which some Birmingham fools took for fact and turned to scandal. A clumsy way to compose a novel, but my larger aim did not admit of easier composition.

That single case might illustrate how the threads of invention formed a fabric. I had never known Cecil Roberts (in the fiction, Jeffrey Strange, married to fictional Tom Lawless) until she invited me, as guest writer to a yearly culture-fair she seemed to direct. When she met the plane, she seized on a briefcase I called "the womb", which had already been stretched by several almost caesarean book-deliveries. At the moment it was large with the future *Half Gods*. As the novel quotes Jeffrey: "It was the womb which captured me." To use her rich material for the essential formation of Daren's final love, I had to plant her in my Oxford youth, where she fused with the now nameless child-niece of my Oxford tutor Neville Coghill, like Neville of Irish descent but living with her parents on a Cotswold farm. My cycle-visits there with Lou Palmer, another of Neville's English students at Exeter College, are humorously recorded in my Oxford journals—especially the mischievously lovable doings of that daughter, ten to twelve years old—all of which was seized on as an imagined background for the imagined Jeffrey Lawless.

The next problem was how to get her to America. The Bromleys, our Vermont summer neighbors through those years (near Danby Four Corners), supplied their story: how she, British, and he, a U.S. airman, during the Second World War, met in London, with all remembered details of their love and marriage—another fictional thread. Change him to a Birmingham, Alabama, banker's son, later to take over his father's business. But not before I could contrive for her a first love-meeting with my alter-ego, Daren. Where else but at the Wisconsin Clearing?

These facts not only explode any Birmingham crazy gossip, they also give a clue to the nature and needs of fictional creation. In this regard, I append an example from Thomas Mann, whose youngest daughter, Elizabeth, he fondly called Elsbeth. Hers were the lovely pendent ear lobes the father would stroke in Mann's short story of between-war troubles, "Disorder and Early Sorrow." Mann, in Chicago for some dire illness, having been, as they said, taken completely apart and put back together at the University Hospital was recovering with Elizabeth and Antonio Borgese. When he could be active again, he had been driven (by Elizabeth, with me) to the Museum of Natural History, where we rolled him in a wheelchair, especially to the thrilling dioramas of the stages of prehistoric man (including the always doubtful and later discredited Piltdown group); here Mann took notes the whole time we lingered on those realistic scenes. Later, when he resumed the broken-off story of "Felix Krull, Confidence Man," I found that after the youth meets the director of such a museum in Lisbon, he is guided (conceive my delight!) to the same dioramas of Early Man accurately described.

By now it was clear that the creative stages of my novels had yielded to the Kingdoms of Joachim de Flores: the first of the Father (thus the ancestral focus and stability of *The Married Land*); the second of the Son (the institutional quest of *The Half Gods*); then the intended Third Kingdom, of Spirit (the Beat and Hippy dreamers of the next generation, talking in tongues, the fire burning on their foreheads). So far, the third, interrupted by *Symbolic History*, is yet to be completed, though portions were sketched and a story, "Prodigal Father," pulled out and published. Most of my time has gone into the Winkie Barr project, *Symbolic History: Through Sight and Sound*—forty recorded slide-tape programs, now on video and CD; as if I had conceived a stage for the actual voices of time (art, music, poetry, and thought) to enact the tragedy of consciousness, the only great tragic action left: of man and world.

Meanwhile, St. John's College had planted a colony in Santa Fe. I spent a last eastern spring protesting Vietnam, and as guest teacher and writer at the University of Rochester, much with Norman O. Brown or Nobbie—he proofing *Love's Body* (a book that would become a sort of Hippie Bible), while I revised *The Half Gods*, he demanding as we read to each other: "Why do you try to hold so much? Why don't you let go?" (Though later, in California, he would persuade his new university to buy a set of my *Symbolic History* videos.)

Then in 1967 Danny and I went west, as if for a year, climbed the fall mountains, looked over the wilderness and said: "We'd be fools to go back East, just for the smell of dead languages." So we bought, on a ridge above Canyon Road, the ugliest house in seven states, tore it to pieces and rebuilt it with luck and the genius-architect Bill Lumpkins into a luminous space, fit for life and work. Here, with intervals in San Cristobal, Chiapas—plus photographic outings to the vanishing Lacandon rain forest with Trude Blom—thirty-four years have passed.

But before shifting to Santa Fe, I should pick up some life-and-literary ties going back to my Greenville youth, especially as referred to in "The Brief I Am"—Shelby Foote and Walker Percy. Shelby and I were born there within a month of each other; but where I started two years ahead in the grades, Shelby, by frequent truancy, fell back a grade and finished high school in my younger brother's class. Walker, on the other hand, lived in Birmingham, Alabama until his father's suicide (or murder, staged by the Klan to look like a suicide) brought him and his siblings to the care of Greenville's William Alexander Percy, their cousin once removed, whom they called Uncle Will. So Walker, a bit older than I, joined my grade in junior high, when I was studying the heavens nightly with my 2 1/2 inch refractor—a pursuit into which I initiated him. Later he found in the vast storage rooms of the Percy house, a costlier 3-inch refractor, but with a mounting so clumsy it could not be used for astronomy. We continued with mine, helped by my books and star maps. When I came home from Oxford in '39 I played my medieval records for him to his 19th-century puzzlement. Then I would send him my poems and essays from Chicago, while he returned his excellent "The Message in the Bottle" with other pieces to be gathered into a volume so named in 1975. His first novels and my two overlapped, and he told me of his second, *The Last Gentlemen*, that our telescopy was the germ of the reality-altering glass invented for that novel. I remember he added that I was the model for his dismal Dr. Sutter character, because where he (Walker) had gone Catholic, I continued "in the orbit of transcendence." That much, I told him, might be true; but why grim Sutter?

About his third novel, *Lancelot*, of a man who blew up his house and all because of a wife's love-affair, I wrote or told him—for Danny and I used to drive from Annapolis, the Skyline, then Gulf route to Greenville, visiting Walker near New Orleans—anyway, I, with hippie daughters and some taint of a freedom beyond Victorian marriage, said he should be ashamed of blowing up his world for that old punitive morality. He answered, he didn't do that; it was only the character; and I: "Aren't the plot and character yours?"

Meanwhile, I had got N. O. Brown to send Walker a signed copy of *Love's Body*, just as a Blakean jolt. It was March '67 that a reply reached me at the University of Rochester: "A princely gift, Brown's book with his writing, since I've been aiming to get to him. Best and Thanks." It became clear he was toying with a new fiction based on such freedoms—to be my favorite: *The Second Coming* of 1980, with its saving greenhouse, which Walker said he had borrowed from the one near the close of my *Married Land* of 1962, which I had fictionally bestowed upon my mother—hers in a columned ruin by Lake Austramere.

For the central theme of *The Half Gods*, I had made free with known facts and legends of the Percy family. Not only that; I named Walker in a Guggenheim application as one of my literary sponsors. That foundation, as usual, sent him a copy of my outline and excerpts. To discover, in that way, my "Percy" appropriation upset him. He wrote me a letter which I would not quote if I could find it, though all he asked was that any prefatory detail of sources, as published in *The Married Land*, should make no mention of his family. Of course I agreed. But when the novel was accepted, I strained my wits how the obligation could be privately expressed. Remembering that I had heard of one François Huber of the late 18th century who invented a hinged and glazed hive to study the social ways of bees—remembering also that Huber, blind, trained a servant to make his observations—I composed the following dedication:

Huber was a blind man, but his servant could see.
To those who saw.

And may they remember what Telemachus says of the bard: "We have no cause against Phemius that he draws a music from the hard fate of the Danaans."

When Walker received his copy, he "made up" with me in a fine, generous note: "Telemachus was right: 'no cause against Phemius'—a strong and original novel."

Shelby needs his own account. When Random House had brought out his massive three-volume *Civil War: A Narrative* (1963-74), we all knew it was and should remain the greatest treatment of that tragic history. But his opening literary contact with me had been when the New American Library's First Mentor Selection of *New World Writing* came out in 1952, with a curious convergence of two pieces by writers from Greenville, Mississippi: a chapter from Shelby's then unpublished *Civil War* and a 1946 poem of mine, "Fall of Troy," from my Princeton years (though Yeatsian)—destined for inclusion in *Songs for a New America*, also of 1952. Shelby wrote: how striking, that two Delta boys should peak the prose and poetry of that anthology.

Next, when we were in Greenville together for a reunion, he gave me the weighty pile of his history signed, which I tried to repay with my *Delta Return* and, as soon as they were available, samples of my videos. Several times on showing-trips, Danny and I would stop to see him in Memphis; but most memorable was in the late 1980's, when Shelby had just heard from Ken Burns about making a Civil War tele-series. We stayed a night or two with him and Gwen, while I showed him the 90-minute version (audio-tape with two-carousels) of my 30th of 40 shows: "Whitman's America." Like all of them, it shapes its epic drama from still photography; and at the heart of this one is a Civil War sequence of such historical photos. Shelby was excited. He and Ken Burns had been debating, he said, whether to work with a dramatization made for actors, and if so, how to engage such players. My show, he told me, had convinced him that they should project the history from existing photographs. I encouraged him in that; and surely their fine pursuit of that method captured the audiences of America.

To bring Annapolis to a close, let me append some last poems written there, advancing from light, to deeper and darker.

TO A YOUNG GIRL (MESSAGE NOT SENT)

I could not miss you more tonight

If, the days you were here,
We had loved in fact,
As in fact we might.

LOVE IN AGE

Strange in my sixties to feel
Always more loving
And so blind I can hardly tell
If the woman smiles or is frowning.

FALL OF OUR BIRTH

Muted horns . . .
Fall days come:
Cold dews in the morning
And the leaves brown;
Born in the fall
We sing the season,
Hallway of winter
Song-forsaken.

Sing loves of age,
Sing time's last turn
To the wooded valley
In the worn land,
Trees stained
With blood of the fall,
Fall of our birth
And October of love.

Still dream in the leaves
Of the sun-warmed world,
How we took brown days
In a rush of song,
Song beguiling
Its birth season,
Fall of our birth,
This lonely fall.

(*New York Times*, October 5, 1964)

Organic antinomy, as in evolving nature, or human history, takes Western form in the vaultings of Gothic: an upward raising of stone by downward gravity, of which Hegel makes a symbol in his *Philosophie der Geschichte*: "Thus the passions . . . fortify a position for right and order against themselves." Here is a poem related to such St. John's studies:

GOTHIC SPIRE

Time and matter hatched a plan
To compromise the soul of man:
Though we with fire are called to soar,
Time bound us to earth, water, air.

How could soul counter-scheme,
But by a buttressed Gothic dream:
As gravity vaults stone to spire—
Beatricë-Dante to Love's fire prayer.

SEED TIME

The Patapsco scummed
with wind-blown seed—

The egocentricity
Of earth's creatures

Spawning as if
To possess the globe.

Let me also be
Ruthlessly prodigal,

Cosmic hope's
Seed-bearing soul.

This poem and the next, "Phanes," are no doubt related, but unconsciously. I wrote this first perhaps a year before the other, but somehow it went under in my paper Sargasso. Though another year the second took subliminal form. With packing for the western move, they wound up in different notebooks. This search of 2000 brought both to light. Since they resist fusion, I treat them as complementary.

SCHOOL OF THE SEED

If the school of the ant teaches there's no laboring
In winter, better go to school of the seed,
Like hierophants for whom grain was central:
Except wheat fall to the earth and die—
That oval door into a saving kingdom:
Halls of Demeter, the season's dying . . .

Surely you can read the signs of the seasons?
There is a snake also in the stars, the largest
Constellation, coiled, almost encircling the pole,
And he holds in his folds the round of our world.
If the wanderer must go into its caverns,
Let him go, like Orpheus, singing.

Water shines in the sun; low sun on the waves
Sows the whole surface with light—
Pale winter light down leafless trees, cold
On the leaf-brown floor where dark lies working.
Close your eyes and turn your back to the sun;
Night requires your presence in her caves.

PHANES
A me consegnárono il tempo bruno

The earth in April opens to the sun,
But in the furrow of its dark, and sealed
By the blue torch of the plow and bedded down

And vaulted in that dark, and from the hold
Of earth and winter, radicals of sweets,
Tearing the calyx of their buds, unfold

In leaves, bright leaves, but of dark, and to the night
Returning—Night, first born of things, or unborn womb
Of childing opposites: tendrils of day—with Time

Timeless itself and quiet, pillared home
Where our desires return, loved sepulcher
In which we plant our seed. To the curtained room

Of hope and time's begetting we must come, to work
Again the mysteries that rehearse this truth:—
Let the great brass gong, beat by the hierophant, speak,

And the rind of earth be split, and halcyon wheat
Spring in the fields, and old women and old men wake,
And sloughing years like bark, in leaves and shoots,
Unfold to the light, at the sunbreak world's dark heart.

OVERPOPULATIONS—A RIDDLE OF TWO
AND ONE

Dream out the dream—no, it will be the same:
Two eyes for depth of binocular vision,
Two ears for stereo hearing, two lobes to the brain
For sorting ambivalences of meaning—
One prick, one hole, one global whelm
Of bisexual generation.

PUBLICITY, A RIGGED SHOW
      (As foreseeing our evil Starr's worse
           invasion of privacy)

Put case that two
Elsewhere plighted persons screw—
Who is seduced? Seduces? Who?

Now the public and the press
Pander to each other's vice,
Is there blame in such a case?

The demos and its demons cleave
Like coupling dogs. We disapprove?
What could we expect of most
But to run the cycle of shared lust?

Or who would forbid a free people
The peculiar pleasure
Of being, as they have always sought,
In body, mind, and heart debauched.

And now, since *Symbolic History* gobbled up time, both in

Annapolis and Santa Fe, I close this section with the last page-long sequence of the almost frightening climax of my "Atomic Age" show. I introduce the text thus: In Chicago, 1950, I waked from a dream, not unlike the "Atomic Age" show and wrote:

> To perceive in the scope of its profligacy the history—that is, the self-destruction of the West—is to glimpse no mere human folly, but one of those terrifying openings out of the organically wild and wasteful, the more dire for its satanic sense of direction.
>
> To see a group of living Christian nations, fostering within their contradictory self-seeking and Machiavellian policy, a cradled bourgeoisie of idealistic hope and criticism, bringing to bear on the faith that sustained them, acids of the liberated mind—to see those nations, as birds crack the shell, break through the medium of protective tradition, the inheritance of paradox unrecognized, into the vast of a valueless freedom; to see that well-born folly change its nature in the face of all it confronted and meeting became, to the temporizing waste of violence—the technically giant and spiritually withering nationalities, as pettily suspicious as each business and free-enterprise man (though all were culturally one), undermining the other and debilitating the other, as if by mutual murder to clear a space for the alien regimen that would feed upon their ruin: this is the phenomenon we have observed and lived through and been part of, the whirl in which all values have changed; it is the turning of liberation upon itself. The compelling question remains, was this our avoidable, even now correctable folly, or is it the jealous law of every-time birth? We must assume the first to act at all, even as we read the second in the cards.

The original Chicago dream was penned, then typed, as if in verse lines; but so irregular (mixing tetrameter, pentameter, hexameter) as to be in fact liberated into the above prose, which—with slides ranging from astronomy over Christo's earth alterations to the Aztec carved goddess of birth, and all this to music selected from the score Philip Glass composed for Godfrey Reggio's extraordinary film *Koyaanisquatsi*—creates a new multimedia symphonic crisis for the power and danger of modernity.

Charles and Danny Bell.
Right: Charles pruning trees.
Bottom right: Charles working in his
Santa Fe study.

6. SANTA FE (1966-06)

When Danny and I came west in August 1967 for the St. John's College launching of a Santa Fe colony, thinking to try it out for a year, we first rented a cottage built by the Canadian naturalist, Ernest Thompson Seton, in the hills south of town. But (as I have described) the mountains and new life of the college persuaded us to buy what we could find. (Luck gave us Upper Canyon Road, with the renowned architect Bill Lumkins to rebuild, adding a master bedroom, library, and work den—as for a paired life.) Once more my time, aside from family and teaching, had been stretched between the creative word and the multimedia aspirations of *Symbolic History*. For the word, I was still placing poems in magazines and seeking a publisher for the swelling notebook of post-*Delta* verse,

It would take almost fifteen years to hit on the transformations of *Five Chambered Heart*; meanwhile, for *Symbolic History*, I had begun recording on cassettes the sound track of the slide-audio shows, some of which I presented when Harris Wofford came to visit from the East. In 1966 he had been appointed president of the College of Old Westbury, where, in undertaking an educational experiment, he persuaded St. John's to let me join him for the 1969 Spring semester.[1] It was then that I made a side trip to visit Resurrection City—my Delta origin bound to involve me in the Black struggle for rights (indeed, while gathering material for *The Half Gods*, I had marched once with the Reverend King himself).

But when I climbed up now from the Washington Mall to that pilgrim campsite, and announced—at the gate of its barbed-wire enclosure—that I was a writer from Mississippi, teaching in Santa Fe and for a guest term on Long Island, and that I was hoping to celebrate their crusade in my third novel, they held the gate shut, saying they didn't want any writers, that they had let newsmen in and had got a bad and hostile press.

I had heard rumors of northern preachers, theoretically for

---

1. Harris Wofford, author of *Of Kennedy and Kings* (1980), was born in New York City in 1926 and graduated from the University of Chicago and the Howard University Law School. He served on the U.S. Commission on Civil Rights (1954-58) before being appointed a professor of law at Notre Dame in 1959. As a special assistant to President Kennedy, he helped to form the Peace Corps and later held the agency's office of Associate Director. From 1987 to 1991, Wofford was Pennsylvania secretary of labor and industry, and succeeded to the U.S. Senate (1987-1991), after the death of Henry John Heinz III. He later served as Chief Executive Officer of the Corporation for National and Community Service, 1995-2001.

integration, who had come down with their families and settled among those powerful Blacks; but when one of the daughters had fallen for a Black youth, the outcry had made the news. Still, I didn't tell them that; I only looked over the gate at the yard or open space below their buildings and saw that it was a dump for trash, newspapers, garbage—what the whole community had brought down and thrown there.

"See here," I told them, "no wonder you get a bad press. Look at that front yard; it's a mess. I said before, I want to help you. Forget about my seeing the camp. Just call one of those strong men you've got loungin' around. Get us two rakes or rake-brooms (you've surely got something of the kind), and he and I will clean this place up; then maybe you'll get a better press."

"That's not a bad idea," one said, and called a near-by Black. Up to that time I'd been talking the international stage diction in which I teach and record my shows. That stalwart fellow got two rake-brooms; they let me in, and I joined him, still speaking the kind of cultivated English that Franklin Delano Roosevelt had used on the radio. But as we worked and talked, I let that accent slide, through my parents' polite drawl, then Huck Finn, then Nigger Jim, and so to absolute Uncle Remus. All of a sudden my helper threw down his rake and caught me by the shoulders, saying: "Where you come from, White Niggah?" "I'm from Greenville, Mississippi," I said. And he: "Well, I'm from Clarksdale."—Tennessee Williams' town, where we had the Delta Field Meets, just sixty miles to the north. So we gave the friendly hug and finished the cleaning. Then he showed me around, as far as I thought I should go—talking especially to the older Blacks. That was one time I was glad I could speak natural Delta palaver.

While I was in the East I also went, of course, to Princeton, and though my best man, Erich Kahler, had died, I stayed with his widow, Alice "Lili" Lowey. That afternoon I walked down to Carnegie Lake, where I used to go with the three children of my first marriage. Thinking by the shore of losing them and of finding Danny, I wrote:

PRINCETON—1945-69

Light on the lake,
Dreams retasted;
I stare back,
Old man from boy:
A whole life wasted—
Into joy.

After a second Santa Fe Fall of work, eased by mountain love—walks with Danny over the Atalaya hills (our two children sometimes in eastern schools), I recall one warm day on the meadow of Thompson Peak how we threw off our duds and danced a glad free dance. Later, when Danny had to go East to decide about the girls' schooling, I climbed the same Glorietta-Thompson ridge to its meadowed peak and wrote:

DANNY

What does it mean for two to have each
So penetrated and possessed the other?—
Not that one lacked loves, and loved
Them too (how else to claim an ultimate savor?),

But that no shared place in the world
Touches without longing: the grass meadow
Near the crown of Glorietta Baldy—gnarled
Aspen, twisted like self-murdered

Shades in Dante, leaf-pocket overgrown
In hollowed granite—and that I cannot pass,
Climbing alone and gray, you flown East now—
Without half swooning to lay you down
And spread your glory under these stunted trees.

But I had no time for swooning. Danny would return, and meanwhile *Symbolic History* was continually heightening its demands on my life: the years, the decades, of monopolized creative time, not only going it alone making slides, buying records, blending them, often with my historical translations, into a text, to be audio-recorded; but more, applying for grants from public and private foundations and even from loyal art-loving friends—a quest for which I had to write a history of *Symbolic History* as a lifelong occupation, an account to be found at this volume's close.

As to my verse output since our moving to Santa Fe, I pick up here with the revisions leading to Persea Books' 1986 publication of *Five Chambered Heart*. Having hit on that title's five-fold ordering from Love to Soul, I had still to decide which 100 regular poems (plus five composite long ones) should be chosen and, more troublesome, by what overview was I to arrange them? Here, a St. John's friend, Fiona Boyd—wife of Stuart Boyd, our tutor from Scotland (and former

Bridge Too Far paratrooper)²—came to the rescue, spreading a large oil cloth on the floor, to be ruled into five columns, down which titles printed on adhesive paper, by successive sticking and unsticking, could be tried in various arrays. Amazing, how a few days of such shifting improvement brought the whole book into an organic and meaningful pattern. This a reader can check by comparing the poems with their five-fold listing in the table of contents.

Of course I could supply Life-ties for many of the poems, but I will open such comment with two: one of soul, called "Gnomic." Having worked late downstairs in my split-level library and study, I lay on the chaise longue and fell asleep. Soon after twelve, I was waked, as by a voice dictating the poem:

> The night each plows
> A furrow of death
> In the field of stars;
> Who calls?
>
> I am nothing,
> But one with the one
> That makes the nothing
> All.

Before long, I learned that an old Princeton friend, John Fleck, of the Parnassus Bookshop in Princeton, had died the same night, around that time.

The other experience concerns "Neighborly," a comical little piece in *Five Chambered Heart* about which I happened, in 1998, to set down the facts:

> There was an apricot growing by the wall which
> bounds our property to the south. It used to bear fruit
> for us, but when the borer killed our branches,
> the trunk spread a fruitful ramification on the
> neighbors' side. They, however, were not avid for

---

2. The epic film was directed by Richard Attenborough and based on Cornelius Ryan's well-known book of the same name. Both tell the story of Operation Market Garden at Arnhem, a 1944 Allied plot to parachute 35,000 soldiers into Holland, some sixty miles behind German lines in order to seize six vital bridges and bring an end to the war. The paratroopers were to be supported by thousands of ground troops, but the operation failed, largely owing to failed radio communications, and the Allies withdrew, suffering severe losses.

apricots; so, sanctioned, one day I opened the gate between the lots and began to pick the fruit of my own tree, on their turf. By a leap of imagination, the above-named poem came to me—to throw me rolling and laughing on the ground. With pocket papers and pen I scribbled the experience, thus altered:

> She's like an apple tree
>> that leans
>>> over the wall;
> She belongs to him
>> but her fruits fall
>>> to me.

When the book was published, I haven't a clue what anyone around here made of that "neighborliness." Most likely, they didn't read the poem at all. Such the probability which supports the old saying that to write or publish poetry is like dropping a pebble into the Grand Canyon and waiting for an echo. Yet from that very piece I was to receive quite a special echo, though, luckily, not from our apricot neighbors.

It was at the graduation dinner the president of St. John's College gives each spring for the senior class. That year, to save restaurant costs, we ate in the Great Hall of the College, decked out for the banquet with tables and chairs. I was sitting with two of my dearest friends, Stuart Boyd, and our great Hungarian, Istvan Fehervary. With the seniors also at the table, we had used up the wine provided. But the meal was giving place to speeches and toasts from the podium. While our lights were being dimmed and those of the platform heightened, students from the work force were going around refilling glasses. Still talking with the friends to my left, I became aware, in the dusk, of a feminine arm, young, bare, and lissome, advancing on my right, bottle in hand, tilted to pour. At the same time soft hair brushed my cheek, and a girl's beautiful voice delivered to my ear: "She's like an apple tree," with the rest of the poem.

Before I could detach myself from friendly

talk, the arm was withdrawn, the hall went dark, and what student it was who had quoted "Neighborly" I never knew. Yet it remains the most telling echo I have had from such a pebble cast into the rarely responsive Canyon of Poetic Utterance.

As I leaf again through *Five Chambered Heart*, so beautifully printed in hardback and paper by Persea Press, house of Michael Braziller (his father an outstanding publisher of art books), I find other poems that need comment or clarification: thus "Speculum Mundi," which I have often read and tried to explain. It should have been dedicated to Jascha Klein, the dean who held the Annapolis St. John's College together after Barr and Buchanan bailed out. Among his moving lectures was one on the Platonic (and Aristotelian) account of perception as a begetting: how the male Form or *eidos*, entering the organ of sight (female) engenders our world of vision. In Latin, the Greek *eidos* is replaced by *speculum*, which can mean either mirror or (related to species) a form or image.

I remembered this as Danny and I sat with the Overtons on a visit to their Illinois country place, watching a splendid sunset. The poem, with its "Mirror of the World" title, delivered itself, and was scribbled down. Of course the first and last word turned out to be "light," with various other word-reflections between, as: "sun," "poured," "cloud," "touch,"; while the idea which informed the whole was that I, the seventy-year-old receiver, by a death-union with nature, should become the light itself—poured into some receiving eye, the feminine "you" of the last line. Thus the poem became for me a love-death hymn to the Cosmos.

With a further poem, "Libations," I have on file a fourteen-line version, as published in "Today's Poets," *Chicago Tribune Magazine*, June 21, 1970 (from which the six-line compression was drawn for *Five Chambered Heart*). But since the earlier form seems now in various ways richer, I here add it to the record:

LIBATIONS

No fire begins at the best. The times
We look for are the twilight stages,
Charcoal embers where we pass the evening,
Talk, make love, stare through silences
Into a glow that is self-consuming.

We pour out wine and spill small libations
That hum in the fire, as we name the old
Names: Dionysos. Aphrodite.

Is it now at last beginning, the wonderful
Slow night of tempered radiance, when the powers
That warm their evenings at our hearts
Take the good of our fire; lean in love
And holy drunkenness, to pour on us
Libations to the quiet above the gods.

There is a comic story also about a poem dropped from position two of the Love, Lust, Earth, Waste, Soul sequence, making room for perhaps my best erotic piece, "Deirdre." The dropped number was a bawdy stomp-dance to the meter and tune of Purcell's catch, "My Dame Hath a Lame Tame Crane." I hated to get rid of it, but it was thought beyond the pale, and I alone knew how to perform it. I'll start the cancelled poem here, and let readers try to sound it to a double stomp-dance:

King Kong has a dong that is long
King Kong has a dong that is strong
King Kong has a dong that's as long and as strong
As the bongo buck's horned prong.

Suzy Wong loves a dong that is long
Suzy Wong loves a dong that is strong
Suzy Wong loves a dong that's as long and as strong
As the sprong of the ape-man Kong.

Let the wedding gong go bong
Let the throng sing the wedding song
And the long strong prong of the ape-man Kong
Rip the sarong of Suzy Wong.

Although I have so recovered "King Kong" here, I am glad its earlier elimination forced me to invent its substitute, the poem called "Deirdre." I took the title from Irish lore as the most passionate woman's name though I had not known a Deirdre. I thought to build the poem on suspended puzzles. Sailing on Italian ships I had heard the joking proverb that for Eros the sum of the ages should be seventy. But what happens as a man nears that age? Deliver us from what Suetonius

reports of Tiberius and the bath-babies he called his "little fishes."
Varying that thought, could not an old man say to a young girl "You're
too old for me?" With off-rhymes and a meter going from four, mostly
through five, to six, what wrote itself is the poem J.V. "Jim" Cunning-
ham, author of such books as *The Helmsman* and *Let Thy Words Be
Few* and our best writer of epigrams as exampled in *Trivial, Vulgar,
and Exalted: Epigrams* and *Some Salt: Poems and Epigrams*, on a visit
from Chicago, called my cleverest and, for him, most exciting piece.

From our first driving up the long prairie climb, through the
Front Range, to Santa Fe—the mountain scene, with the hippie-eased
life of town and college—had prompted jottings for poems springing
from details of the American West that were new to us. Before *Five
Chambered Heart* most of these were published in New Mexico jour-
nals or collections: "Silver Lining," "Echo," "Cañada Corales," "Aspen
Meadows" (Hippie Campground), "Wedding Dance," "Lean to the
Ponderosa" now revised as "Basalt Bowl."

Fascinated in those early western years, we began also to ex-
plore Mexico: past beautiful Oxaca all the way to Chiapas for a cottage
in Trudi (Trude) Blom's San Cristóbal garden—first with our Santa Fe
house well-leased in the summers and Trudi's rented almost for a song,
then on a year's leave (1970-71). Meanwhile I was laboring at my third
novel, especially a core chapter, "Prodigal Father," about a visit the
year before (November 1969) to help my second daughter, Charlotte,
fallen into the famous drug street of Berkeley.

At this juncture, Danny hit on our buying and renovating a
kind of courtyard or cloister house in the east quarter of San Cristóbal
de las Casas. There for ten years we would go in summers, or for longer
stays when I could get leave from St. John's. Indeed, the first dozen
synchronized shows of *Symbolic History* were taped there, using slides
and texts, with cassette-music and a player I had brought down. But
what may redound to the general (even poetic) interest are two Lacan-
don Journals I kept when the renowned Trudi took us on visits to the
Maya ruins and jungle haunts of the white-robed, long-haired Mayan
descendents, whom she had adopted. I even translated some German
and wrote a bit of poetry in those journals of 1972 and 1978 (published,
I believe, in the New York quarterly *Grand Street*). Now I transcribe
them from my own typescript: "Lacandon Journals, 1972 and 1978."
But first let me introduce Trudi (1901-1993) with a commemorative
page I wrote for her birthday celebration at Na-Balom (February-March
1971):

GERTRUDE DUBY BLOM, AFFIRMATIVE SPIRIT OF THE CENTURY

In this year of 1971, we at Na-Balom celebrate the seventy years of Trudi. Her life has almost coincided with the century, and its activity has spanned Europe and the New World. Her point of origin was Switzerland, mixing-center of north and south, Germanic and Latinate. She is the daughter of one of those learned ministers elected by a canton. "A fine growing-up time," she says, "big houses, enormous gardens, the village, the castle, and on all sides the mountains—walking, skiing." A symbolic opening, surely, when she and the other children would steal the key to the tenth-century church, and Trudi would preach to the resonance of a columned nave: those firebrand ideas she was already forming (as if in rebellion against her conservative father). Even the gardening she pursues early and late at Na-Balom (with such gourmet results) goes back to her first calling, when she studied, as she says, "at a very good and very hard gardening school for professionals." And even there (in the exciting years of the great strikes and the Russian Revolution) she joined with other students in the zeal of the Left, though it wasn't, she confesses, "exactly a Leftist school."

In Germany, through the crucial years when the Weimar Republic was being subverted by Hitler's rise, Trudi was there, in Hamburg and Berlin, organizing and reporting. One could make a book of the adventures she lived through in that underground stand for freedom—the hairbreadth escapes, resistance attempts in France, Italy, revolutionary Spain, with a brief spell in a Luxembourg jail as well as one in fascist Italy and a Nazi detention camp in France at the outset of the war; then to England, with Bertrand Russell's League against War and Fascism; so to the U.S., trying to spirit refugees out of the clutches of the Nazis; and in Mexico, femme fatale of the Zapatista rebels, writing their biographies.

Thus her wanderings led to that extraordinary convergence when she and the other European-American writer-adventurer, Frans Blom, romantic archeologist, discoverer of the giant Olmec heads at La

Venta, met in Ocosingo airfield: "I knew about him. I had come from the jungle, waiting for a lost mule in Ocosingo, nothing to do but hang around the airport, reading the newspapers. I read that Frans Blom was in Tuxtla. One day a plane comes down, out steps a tall guy, blue-eyed, blond, Chamula shirt; I went up to him: 'You're Frans Blom.' And he, 'You're Gertrude Duby.'—'Who the hell told you I'm Gertrude Duby?'—'Who the hell told you I'm Frans Blom?' So we went to Yaxchilan." (Though malaria and delirium forced her to get him out of there.)

In 1950 they bought a large property in San Cristóbal de Las Casas where they founded Na-Balom, a Mexican cultural and scientific center for Trudi's life-long attack on the old demons of darkness. Not Nazis here, but subtler destroyers who all over the world are upsetting the balance of nature and poisoning the globe in the name of progress—in Mexico the destruction of the Lancandon Rain Forest.

It was Trudi's extraordinary power to be able to face hideous facts that might lead to despair (the poverty and oppression of the Indians, burning and clearing of forests, erosion of land, looting of Mayan monuments—Chiapas details of a general ecological ruin)—to face that terror and turn it into a program for a future toward which she worked with the experience of age and the fire of youth—a radical program (from Latin *radix*, "root")—going to the roots, but for conservation of the earth's natural and human goods—a Radical Conservative! (A world-party to be wished for.)

Whether dealing individually with the Lacandon Indians, who walk to Na-Balom from far off jungles to sell their hand-woven goods, or collaborating with the government to promote and reward their crafts; whether guiding visitors from all nations into the Lacandon jungle or to the ruins along the Usumacinta, or using her photographs of that beauty and its waste to persuade governor, president, the people listening on television to do something while there is still time—in all this, Trudi remains in my mind the unforgettable, lovable, seventy-year old child-daimon of human energy and hope.

June 27-July 3, 1972, Trip with Trudi Blom from San Cristóbal de las Casas, Chiapas, to Yaxchilan and Najá (my "Journal")

The little plane came in over the daisy field under blue sky, white clouds, limestone ledges. We loaded, strapped in and banked up over San Cristóbal, our house, Francesco's Casa

Grande, favorite walking valleys and oak ridges to the east, then past my range, the plateau falling away to successive great basins of what a few years ago was forest-cropped now in innumerable patches, ragged steep fields of new corn among huge burnt trunks, others a few years older, rock-gray, weathered to stonecrop, knocked out of the forest cycle for who knows how long; and everywhere, in cut-over scrub or remnant forest, thatched huts of Indian colonists living against time on the destruction of the last Mexican wilderness (burn a thousand dollars of hardwood and plant two-bits worth of corn), like all our civilization, on collision course; but what can you do: they're here, they multiply, they can't eat oak.

Each valley falling off deeper, the plane from 9,500 feet easing down with the contour of the land, dodging the cumulus that is building up for the afternoon rains. Now over Ocosingo, in a wide, half-cleared bowl, even the rock ridges bone-gray, burnt out with fires. Rain-muddy streams, scrubby fields; where is the famous *selva*? Trudi yelling from behind, against the roar: "I saw this whole valley (and that and that) when there was nothing but forest."

At last the roads peter out, the land always lower; the true forest appears with lakes green- and blue-clear, wooded shores. "On the island of that long blue one," she shouts, "are ruins." Under the clouds at 4,500 feet, a little rain; scattered huts and *milpa* squeeze the big wood (like the one Faulkner wrote about—the same burning and clearing in the Mississippi Delta of my youth). At 4,000 feet a glimpse of the Usuma-cinta, forest, more lakes. Across it now, dropping down on the Guatemala side, jungle and scrub, then banking almost at the tops of the trees over the river again, great white seibas reaching toward us; suddenly a mowed path and pigs running, the short bouncing airstrip of Agua Azul. (Not the famous water-fall, but an old lumber and chicli camp by the swollen stream.) Down.

THE USUMACINTA

A huge house of tall mahogany planks thatched with steep-sloping palm fronds. A dark interior of insect-buzzing heat. "In that room," says Trudi, "I lay sick a long time with malaria." In the separate kitchen-house behind, an oven as big as a furnace flames away for boiled water, coffee, tortillas. The

Usumacinta flows past, brown as the Yazoo and as swift—the
old scene, except for a shift from South to North and a dream-
change in the dense overhanging vegetation. As if all the
malarial and alligator swamplands around the Gulf of Mexico
had the feel of being one.

Down the caving sandy-bluff path of my boyhood
to the familiar water. The boat, though, not our flat-bottomed
bayou skiff, but a thirty-foot dugout, as for savage wars, cut
and burned from a great mahogany. Take up the hand-carved
paddles, beautifully inadequate; push off in swirling mud-
water; start down between half-cleared jungle banks, huge
seiba and mimosa-feathered guanacastley, under forested hills
screaming with birds—a good current taking us as of old to
the Gulf, north here—the furious Charon cranking away at the
motor with no result, giving up. He and his boy paddle; I pitch
in—a five-hour trip, they say, to Yaxchilan this way. After
about an hour, the old man's cleverer son, paddling with airy
grace across the stream in a light dugout heaped with orchids
(his trade, or fancy?) joins us, leaving his own boat tied. Pappy
rants and scolds like the fool he is, but that son soon starts the
motor. We spin down through narrows, rocks, over banks and
whirls, shooting near-rapids, the river widening as tributaries
flow in; the shores—as in any pioneer land, sometimes giant
forest and again burnt-over fields, palm thatch shanties, mud
slums of new settlement, with eternal *milpa* and sugar cane
among charred trunks, starving dogs, termite nests as black as
buzzards in the remaining trees. None of the hope that must
have touched temperate-zone pioneering—too late in history
for that, and the tropical soil a foreknown disaster, leaching to
sterile brick a few years after it is cleared.

YAXCHILAN

We reach the steep peninsula the river ox-bows around, the
ruins lost in terraces of forest. To shore. Up the high bluff over
a heaped wall of what was once the palatial court of the holy
city, catching at the same time a smell of pigs and fragrance
of lemon bloom. The great walled plaza and ball court has
become, like medieval Rome, a squatting-ground. A round
house made of poles, a square house of planks, both roofed
with palm thatch and windowless. Other open thatched huts,
hammock-swinging roosts for guests: Conrad Hilton Yaxchi-

lan. Chickens, ducks, wormy dogs, sly cats, enormous pigs, captive birds (a black jungle peacock, a macaw, a parrot or two), brown men and women with children, among trees; bitter oranges, pasty sweet lemons, guanabana (guava), mango, played-out papayas; behind, rise the incredible ruins, more incredibly overgrown with vine-covered trees, chicli, cedro, seiba, and (taking over like a reptile wrapped around another tree, encircling it and dropping air roots until it becomes, at last, the usurped tree itself) of the fig family amate; this, the matapalo, or strangler fig.

    We are hammocked elsewhere, removed from the press, under an open roof of thatch, along a jungle trail lined with ruins and carved stelae, figures of gods and warrior priests, then out to the edge of the river, our thatch on the bluff, down which we can slide when the heat, flies and mosquitoes get too fierce—wading out through alligator grass for a cooling dip in the mud-brown flow, a current hard swimming barely holds its own against. We were to have stayed in the Conrad Hilton hutch, but another family was there, as it proved, only for the night; Trudi put on a show of how she had enough of tourists in San Cristóbal, had made her coming known. The others should have been cleared out; we wouldn't eat with them, didn't want to see them around, much less hear them. They lay pretty low after that—though Danny and I preferred our retreat by the river.

    After lunch a guide took us to the lower ruins, those enormous trees, cedro, sapote, and mulatto ignudo growing up and rooting down through massive walls, heaving the squared stones back, springing the triangular vaults—a strangler fig wrapped around a corner like a poured cast—briefly holding what in time it tears apart.

    Back for a swim and a read, the sweat washed off, but the insects so fierce you can't settle anywhere but under dark thatch in the darker zipped-up jungle hammock. I had brought along the Pantheon *Deutsche Gedichte* and a notebook to write in, so I sat in jungle ruins by the Usumacinta translating the classical musings of Klopstock (mocked by Blake in a scatological poem; though his German lyrics voice the neo-classic Europe of Haydn and Mozart, Gray's "Elegy" or Collins' "Ode to Evening": "Like thy own solemn springs, / Thy springs and dying gales"). It was the columned dream my father tried to rear in our Delta swamps, that style of Enlightenment America had loved, and which Catherwood, in fact, applied to the Mayan ruins, when he explored with Stevens here in 1840. I translated from Klopstock's invocation to the buried friends of his youth:

> O wie war glücklich ich, als ich noch mit euch
> Sahe sich röten den Tag, schimmern die Nacht!

> Yet how remote in a tropic riot of birds' and howler
>   monkeys' cries:

> Happy those times when I could behold with you
> The rose flush of dawn; night a silver glow.

We raced a thunderstorm down to the big caoba plank house, where the caretaker and affiliate families live in the old ball court. Stood under the eaves for the downpour, which soon flooded the ancient paved area, ducks going to it in three inches of water, until the old man pokes the original Maya drain with a crowbar, stabbing deeper and deeper so water swirls through, coming out almost by the river at the foot of the rock pile.

Next morning Trudi, with her trusty machete-wielders, guided us to the hill-top ruins, especially the great combèd temple of the Jaguar Man, the painted temple, several carved lintel temples, the temple of the hieroglyphic stair and the rest, sprinkled over various Acropolises, all overgrown like those we saw yesterday, with the holding and destroying strangler fig.

Of course I'm eager to learn the names of everything and the history and archaeology, but Trudi's giant will to suppress any rival eruption on the scene makes it impossible in the end to do more than listen to what she wants to tell. I admire the old girl and love her too, but some Freudian backlash of father-castration makes her the most trying person to learn from I've ever encountered. "Is that tree a matapalo?" or "That huge one on top of the temple must be a chicli." The words have hardly left your mouth when she shouts "No!" and "Don't be a fool!" before she can look. Then maybe she does look, and maybe if what you've said is apparent, she might grudgingly revise, though mostly she shifts to another misunderstanding where she can put you down. Still, there is no grudge in this, nothing petty, just the outbreak of capricious violence, volcanic as the Popul-Vu; as if she were assimilated to the old Maya Gods.

We went slowly up and down the steep rock slopes, and it took us all morning. After lunch, then swim and rest, I ran over the whole course quickly myself, pausing in silence to contemplate the temples, carved stelae fallen in the dirt, split on rocks, buried in leaf litter, figured lintels cracking, painted plaster and stucco reliefs peeling off, making the half-human figures more creatures of the jungle than they ever were.

Tomorrow, from this ritual center, to the tribe which still makes pilgrimages here.

NAJÁ

Thursday June 29: Pepe's little plane came to the Yaxchilan field by 10, lifted us (staggeringly) through the narrow gorge of the river, almost scraping the walls of high trees, then west to Trudi's lake lair, near Na-ha, in subtropical forest, her own Maya tribe (like Tarzan's friendly Waziri in the Boroughs' books I once read and practiced, swinging and leaping through the great Delta oaks of my boyhood)—Trudi's long-haired, white-robed Lacandons, a small inbreeding clan of beautiful forest people (we heard of one youth whose first woman or wife was his grandmother; what a lot she must have had to teach him). The camp is like something from a Tahitian romance, a flower-filled clearing among enormous mahogany, black cork, and chicli trees, their boles buttressed like Mississippi cypress, but maybe twice the girth of our largest, and in the cleared space, palm-thatched rooms with open walls. The insects here have eased off to tolerance, the air is cool enough (at about 2500 feet?), the humorous Lacandons glide in from forest trails for the ceremony of greeting and hot chocolate, which Trudi brings by the bushel.

The lake is a great blue spring in limestone hills. A clear stream runs out of it near our camp. Those snails, intermediary host of the liver fluke, work on its rocks, but the region is so far uninfected, the snails benign rock cleaners. Two Lacandon youths are assigned to paddle us in one of the dugouts over the lake to the village (a few huts together and a few more scattered) or back to the alligator swamp (we didn't see any) or to forest trails and walking places. Also for lake swims.

The days flowed into one another, quiet and beautiful, paddling, swimming, walking, going up to the God Hut to watch ceremonies—prayers for corn, a cure for Trudi's rheumatism, the men drinking a ritual brew, with chants to Mayan gods. By day, it was sprinkled sun and cloudy rain, with heavier rain in the night. But the trots came on Danny and on me, headache, bone ache, some fever (just for alarm, the ten required days of typhoid incubation since Mexico City), with flux and intestinal strife, cause unclarified, one of those nameless nothings that give such pain. I may even be glad when Monday comes round, six days from our flight to Agua Azul, to get out of that jungle beauty and to the metropolis of San Cristóbal de las Casas, the City of Houses.

RECOLLECTIONS FROM NAJÁ VILLAGE

The whole male population, men and boys, out mowing the airstrip, bending down whacking with machetes—a white-robed rhythm working up the long band cleared in the forest.

That fallen mahogany log six feet through, decayed into a humus garden: moss, begonia, sedum, bromeliad, orchid. Say it reaches back five hundred years. Another such cycle, and the Mayas had burned the land and were building their temples on the strength of crops as soil-destroying as now.

Strange to sit half sick in a hammock among post-Maya tribes, open a book and translate from Goethe, the Part II call to a greater Faustian venture:

> Last and noblest, let him wake,
> And come again into the sacred light.

Trudi, mellowed by the fallibility of my sickness, puts her dearest self forward. At night she tells us stories of her expeditions with Frans when most of the Chiapas was uncleared, roadless forest . . .

I hear rain, like rivers in the night, fall on the thousand-year-old forest of Najá. Rain to flood a world. Not a drop moves from where it falls, sucked up by the gurgling jungle, two hundred feet of layered leafy green-elephant-eared plants drinking the downpour with an agonized sound of swallowing.

Here one feels the tension of nature between the arrow of force and the wheel of containment: wild pigs rooting up a whole forest floor; leaf-cutting ants carrying leaves off to their dens on herbicidal runways, devastating an amazing round. It seems the primitive forest could contain it, but can anything except the starry cosmos contain the vector of human power? Theology liberated God from the authorship of evil by a claim of Free Will enticed to its Fall: no way but in Freedom with all its liabilities to shape societies of searching possibility. But nature too had no way to adaptive change but by endowing each parcel of energy with restless quest, the organizing and endangering hubris of evolution. Thus, nobody knows yet whether global or cosmic history will take the form of the arrow or the wheel.

The unchristianized Lacandons chant in the God House to god-flames in god-pots, or to god-pots full of dismal ferment they at once swill and offer to ancient gods—meanwhile, voicing low chants (the ritual language, it is said, different and centuries older than what they speak every day). The first time we watched, it was the corn prayer, then for Trudi, now for a girl bit yesterday by a fat, nasty-looking yellow-and-black-speckled pit viper. She was saved at once by anti-venom. Thereafter as she lay in the house of old Chankin (attended by one of his three wives), each pregnant woman in the village drifted in to tie a new-spun thread around the swollen foot, to keep the soul from issuing there. Today, to do a final job on the swelling, the men shift incense in the god-pots and croon a low musical phrase, punctuated by a grotesque protesting shrill jabber, as if the evil were fighting back, arguing, trying to rally, then being driven out as the healing chant resumes its overlapping waves.

That was this morning. Now thirty Protestant missionary youths training for salvation, Boy Scouts of the Lord, pass Trudi's camp headed for this last village of unredeemed Maya ways, laughing, with the crass eagerness of Baptist young, to wash everybody in the Blood of the Lamb.

While the long-haired white-robed men with smooth beautiful faces slip through the forest, as if they represented a way. And in one sense maybe they do: Chankin, the old leader comes down with his three wives trotting behind. He is in his eighties, but seems half that, a life-center of the tribe. The youngest wife, in her teens or twenties, is nursing a laughing baby. The older wives, one childless, stand protectively around, with the devotion of aunts or grandmothers admiring the child-bride's child. Against the pursed lips of Grant Woods' *American Gothic* or the Baptist missionary couple, the Lacandon simplicity of achieved love throws a queer light on Western monogamy. [An observation which gave me another *Five Chambered Heart* poem: "Two Families."]

SECOND JOURNAL, May 25, 1978:
A Visit to the Other Village, Lacanha

Driving with Trudi from San Cristobal the back road to Palenque (Huistan, Oxchuk, Ocosingo: the marvellous sight of the true Agua Azul, like a blue coral sea turned to a landscape of waterfalls—national park now, for crowds who throw garbage and who crap in the bushes, and indeed, for all those bus-loads there's one overflowed can for trash and not a single toilet—we traversed what was *selva* ten years ago, now horribly cleared and burned. Again, after Palenque, we drove most of another day on a new gravel road through patches of what is still called the Lacandon Forest, for four days at Trudi's unspoiled Lacanha camp, by a little fall on a deep clear rain-forest stream, in a pocket of mahogany, sapote, matapalo (the strangler fig), towering terraces of leaf, bloom, and fruit; yet the day we explored eighteen miles or more out and back through alternate giant forest and burned-over and cropped fields, some scrubby with second growth-where our Lacandons had to machete-clear the always closing trail; our goal a still unpeopled lake also called Lacanha (the rest on horseback, I glad to walk and run)—even there one felt how perilously the wilderness confronts a destruction closing in from all sides.

What we had seen was an anarchy of wasteful assault—that veterinarian with the nervous dark face distorted by a twitching tic, whom we met in his Indian Bureau jeep—the gravel ribbon already an access for Tzeltal settlers invading what Trudi had thought to secure as a National Forest reserve for the Lacandons (though even they, once long-robed and jungle-gliding, mostly Baptist now, begin to live and dress like mestizos in dirty villages with gas stoves, radios and *tocadiscos*—all Indian populations progress, reverting to their paired, earth-cancerous skills: to breed and burn), so on either side of the road as far back as you can see, and on destructively steep slopes, the great charred trunks stand in a waste of earth slashed and fired, the thin soil already eroding to rock—as if it were all planned by grafting profiteers to get Indian migrants to clear-burn, and live like pigs a year or two, until their corn fields leach out under tropical sun and rain (what is happening in all the great rainforests of Africa and Brazil, irreplaceable lungs of the globe)—so that exploiting cattlemen can take over, pushing the Indians on—to turn the whole area into grass pasture—what they have already done and are doing; why else had this vet (as he said) been up there to inoculate some sick cows? When Doña Gertrude accused him of the whole world-wrong as if he were personally to blame, he protested with his cocky assurance and twitching face: "We're going to make this land—*ésta tierra productiva*." A bargain of productive ruin, sealed how long ago?

Here I wrote another poem, "Third World," destined for the *Five Chambered Heart*, but I should have complemented it with a scribbled impression of night noises:

Night sweats in the sagging hammock under the mosquito net,
Enough to make a man think he was in a fever—night noises too:
Birds or tree frogs whoopin' it up around the camp:
"Who're you?"—"I'm queer."—"weird . . ." and "Whew! Whew!"
Then the first begins again, as if unanswered: "Who're you?"

After four days of swimming against the heat and to keep off insects: fleas, three sizes of biting gnats and four of flies, a vampire horsefly so big that half-blind Kayum said I oughtn't to swat it, it was a *mariposa* (butterfly). Kayum, trained at Trudi's Na-Bolom, supposedly as a medical assistant; but come back to the sloppiest house and messiest child-wife of all: the blazefaced chestnut horse dead and rotting in the thickets behind, a dog covered with mange-sores, chickens dropping dead all over the yard, left there to infect the others ("Yes," he thinks, "they have a sickness." Plunge again in that green paradise stream (but don't take it in your mouth lest amoebae fill your guts—as they may do anyway); then out to the gnats and flies, wondering which might be the one that lays her eggs to hatch and squirm in your flesh; we crept again over the long ribbon of rough rock road to Palenque, the others to rest (having done the ruins on the way in), I for a last shot at them, climbing in the heat up the pyramids and palace, my camera

bag swinging on my shoulder until my shirt was open half
way down on my chest—when an intense dark Mexican (was
he native there, a Maya priest, medical student?) greeted me:
"From the United States?"—"Yes."—"Professor?"—"Yes."
Suddenly he leaned and pointed under my open shirt to a
dark lump seated on a red base which I hadn't noticed before
(hardly keeping track of which moles and hickeys pepper my
flesh): "Ésto es malo," he said, "quittarlo!" with an excising
jerk and sizzling hiss, as if an electric needle.

It was a weird moment; but I would have thought less
of it, if from then on, the spot had not grown before my eyes,
until by the time we got to San Cristóbal late the next after-
noon, the lump had doubled or trebled in size. I was thinking
of that colored skin cancer, which once it starts, takes over;
and I knew if I didn't want to worry all night about its being
diagnosed after its notoriously quick metastasizing made it
too late, I ought to see a doctor. But the alcoholic one I used
to know had let his car roll him off a cliff while he was drunk,
asleep. I went to friends, the Woods, where Allan, with the real
and imagined sicknesses of his granny, had medical contacts.
Amazed at the story, he drove me to the hospital—a drab pre-
fab to which I took a dying child a few years back when a wall
collapsed on her in our barrio.

After days of Lacandon rot among anarchic smoke
and flame, I was almost down on Mexico; but we were granted
a consultation at once with a bright and lively young doctor,
blond, red-mustached, I suppose from Mexico City.

"I want to report a strange case of voodoo," I said;
and told him of the Palenque encounter, and how the growth,
as if by that suggestion, was now twice the size. I bared my
chest. He and his assistant looked and fell back, dismayed.
(Something bad? Melanoma?)

"Doubled? In a day?"

"More."

He grabbed his flashlighted magnifier and peered.
Tension gave way to amazed delight.

"It's alive," he said; "an animal." It was a tick,
swollen abdomen, but front end so small, so deeply set in the
flesh—we have no parallel—true, like a carcinoma, an alien
life feeding on my blood; but comical. Dr Leonello scorched
it with his cigarette and worked it out—wouldn't even let me
pay. We parted on waves of tropical laughter. If only Mexico,

weird and wonderful, could so lightly dodge the death wish of our burning world.

In one supplement to the Lacandon Journals I closed with a poem which would become the next-to-last of *Five Chambered Heart*, "Complins of Youth and Age", in which the central verse paragraph, sketched at Little Pines Farm just before our 1949 marriage and called "Evening Hymn," sounds a complin music for an ideal and fruitful earth:

> How the round pearl of a world mothered in air
> Falls quietly turning; and our evening falls . . .

After I had photographed the still smoking, burned-out forests of Lacandon, and used the slides as a dissonance before the closing resolution of my show "Nature: The Perceptive Field," I also framed the glowing middle stanza of that poem in the war and dysecology of a crucified earth, ending with our own complin prayer:

> Fathering fire, forgive; mothering void, receive!

These journals do not mention a poem to be inspired by Chankin and his god-pots, soon to take a Waste position toward the end of *Five Chambered Heart*; namely, "Charm for a Sick Planet." But now I proceed with the gathering of Santa Fe poems (mentioned near the start of this chapter). The order must be somewhat arbitrary. First, one begun in Annapolis and revised here:

WHO WAITS

> Leaves that rustle
> Down a street
> Where one attends
> Footfalls
>
> Lure the listener
> To the door
> For no visitor
> But wind.
>
> Think soul will never
> Find its peace

Till the blue tent fall
And the micro-dance cease.

Next, the shuffle presents one of our mystery pieces, "Last Cry," requiring comment:

      I cannot say with Etheridge's 1676 *Man of Mode*, Dorimant: "Next to the coming to a good understanding with a new mistress, I love a quarrel with an old one"; still, the letterhead of this poem specifies Santa Fe, yet I no longer know what occasioned this so-called cry of flesh and soul:

LAST CRY

Can two
Who made time
Their weaving, entwined

In moon, leaf, stream, and frond—
Oaths undone—call self-deceit
The deepest memories we own?

Less to keep you than hold what else
Melts to the nothingness we are,
This cry of flesh and soul.

      Then a poem fit for the intermittent drinking-streams of our Sierras, dear to hikers, but going dry:

MOCK MAKERS

Young and thirsty, we conceive
The sound of water in blown leaves;
Old and doubtful, we have learned
That sound is nothing but the wind;
And so we sit and mock at dream
In earshot of the actual stream.

      While mockers were being mocked, a little codicil post-scripted itself:

NAÏVE HOPE

Naïve hope is less naïve
Than to forget the world-balloon,
Blown up by the hopeful naïve.

From the same walks and pillowed wonder of our cumulus clouds:

NAP TIME

The heavens conspire to give us rest:
Behold that cloud like a nippled breast.

Another poem dreamed, like some earlier ones, as if I stood at the underworld's fatal shore:

WESTERN OBOLUS

Coin a Greek soul had to pay
Charon for his Stygian ferry:
Soul, at the crowded rail
Waving earth departure,
Is it worthwhile any longer
To tell what we loved?

Summer lupine beds under ponderosa;
Fire-black lava rocks in snow
Rimming la Bajada.

It did not take a third of our Santa Fe years, especially walking, cycling over the beautiful foothills and mountains, past cleared fields along country roads, to note the spreading take-over of aggressive European and Asian invaders, from weeds to trees. The first title was ironic ("To Blossom like the Rose"). Now, since the "Weed Farm" title of *Heart* has been changed to "Burdock," I incline to "Weed Patch."

"Piñon and white cedar:
What are you up to,
Letting Chinese elm,
With stinking Tree of Heaven,

Crowd you out on your
Old desert ground?"

(Flowering chamisa answers:)
"Dish-wash and piss-effluent
Sluiced into our ground
Give such odds to rag- and pig-wort,
That you, peeled-off meddling ape,
Are sure to leave a weed-patch
Wherever you squat down.

No comment on the next:

JOURNALESE

Acres of asphalt, black
With an ash peppering
Of pebbles, a parking lot, lacks
Articulations of the organic stair.

Media prose is like that.
And must we espouse it
Because the world now
Rides on blacktop?

No—
The cloak of naturalism
Cannot always hide
Crimes against nature.

Now a longer poem, begun a few years back in sketches called
"The Word" and "Calligraphs"; so put together recently as a challeng-
ing inquiry in prose and verse:

TRIFORM MEDITATION ON THE SWAY OF
THE WORD—HOW POSSIBLE?

The arts of language labor under the distance of the
word; while seeing and hearing, color and sound, like
their arts, claim an immediacy beyond the verbal.
        Rothko's drowning pools of blue, red,
purple; the soul's sensuous ride down modulating

tones-leave the poet halting on merely conventional
crutches, where "a rose by any other name would
smell as sweet".

Strange then the sublimation (not of image
only, but of the whole complex of likeness,
causality, plot and reason) by which the crucial texts
of act, thought, mystic vision-severed from sight and
sound-sway by promptings of the intelligible word.

.   .   .

Close your eyes against the sun:
You are a salamander robed in flame.
Open them to a coral pool:
All you are dissolves in blue.
The lore of sight is close as touch.

Cheek to cheek, each mouth to an ear,
Voice a scale in sliding tones:
Triad, second, unison
Throb, through beats, to a perfect one.
Symphony puts on flesh there.

How can the hieroglyphic word,
Cold as "fire", remote as "touch",
From its orbit of the abstract—
Gathering to Thor's thunderhead—
Torrent over sight and sound?

.   .   .

Say Water under cloud refracts the light
Of the low sun, amber through green waves,
It is, to an epic watcher, as if his heart
Took that fire-glint in its own sea-caves.
Or when, at the focus of a painter's art,
Some stilled vortex of ruby swirls the night;
Or music, near its cadence throws a look
Of upward poignance from the heaving bass—
Then in the cosmo-chaos of that dark,
Which we perceive and are, we know how light
Contours the belly of its opposite;

While the poor trade of words—how beggarly, how
        stripped,
Spun down distances, of body bereft—
Cries for the fire rock strikes from rock.
Have words answered? By axiom:
What is, is possible!

     Approaching and soon after the millennium, I gathered a typed page of somewhat thoughtful pieces to send to the *American Oxonian*, published in the Fall 2000 issue, as "Rather Recent Poems":

FROM AGING EARTH

Conceive Orion:— south, blue Rigel; north, red Betelgeuse;
Between, three of the belt; at the side, small,
Two, with the nebula, complete the sword, or dagger—
Easy to describe; but wanting the physical,
It is the ghost of seeing.

And now, these winter nights,
As you walk out in age
(And the sky smogged), dim eyes
Scarcely make it out.

Flesh is failing; and what move of spirit
Can reclaim, in light's reality,
Perceptions known and lost?

"Your old men shall dream dreams . . ."
Dream, old man:

Memory is enough: space, too, remembers.

TO SEE

I wake. An inner glow
Lifts me from earth's couch
In consolation and glad praise:
To have perception and response.

But shining minnows glint the same
As they dart up a tide stream
Flouncing off granitic rocks
Outcropping from the sand.

Cosmic jubilation: to see,
Like minnow-play, the dance
And mating of atomic particles—
          I see, I see; perception and response.

CRY OF AN AUGUST NIGHT

If only, on this earth, as in the sky,
That Archer stood, bow bent, and the dart
Pointed at the Scorpion's heart—
Tail-curling threat of world-plutocracy.

A PROSY PROTEST

What is Aristotle's definition of a "natural slave"?
"One who cannot see the consequences of his actions."
And what is wrong with the world today?
Chiefly that it is ruled everywhere by natural slaves.

Now for something almost penultimate, to be thrown down
like a gauntlet:

CONFESSION OF A CORPUSCLE:
CANCER-PARABLE OF PLUTOCRACY
For the Bush Money-Boys

Coursing the life-maze of arterial blood,
On pulse-throbs of the heart, I came
To a realm of growth, a seething brood
Of propagating cells, where the tame

Decorum of an ordered being broke
Into abandoned burgeoning;
There gobs of flesh and tissue soak
In an ooze of lymph. Wallowing
In the frenzy of that blood-rush, I join the race
To enjoy the unreined, rapturous, free
Ardor of that breeding place.
There nudge a dawdling neighbor: "What ecstasy!"
"In such exuberance," his sage reply,
"Of cancerous growth, the organic whole must die."

After that left hook to the jaw, why not a playful close—two almost negligible toss-offs:

LITTLE RED HEN

"What sign has she ever given
That she had better to do
Than sow and reap and grind and bake
For others' feeding?
Leveling pharisee—
Tell her we bring the password!"

"Word? Against that cackle?
Who told you Biddy could read?"

A PLOT

What's to do
With the unrequited
Passion of these songs?
Get a black box,
Stuff it full,
Lug it some afternoon,
Like a time-bomb,
To the police station
In the public square;
Drop it,
Then scram!

I have already announced that my intention has not been to bring this Life through a lean crop of recent poems to the halt of an ironic joke. I must rather lead through "The History of *Symbolic History*," main creative investment of my Santa Fe years, to the script closing its last show: "NOW: The Rooted Future." Here is a logistical account of the history, start to finish.

The story of these 40 + 1 shows, or studies (plus one in German), seems almost the story of my life—where each need has been met by a timely opening of personal or technological opportunity.

Thus, when first astronomy and natural science gripped me, there was the illustrated nature-lore of The Book of Knowledge, aided from my twelfth year by my parents' donation of a 2 1/2 inch refractor, a microscope, the *Scientific American*, and a shelf of astronomy books.

When, at Virginia (age sixteen to nineteen) a boost toward cultural studies was imperative, lo! Stringfellow Barr, with the flung gage of cyclical history. When that pursuit by 1936 required study abroad, behold! Rhodes, with his scholarship. After three years of taking more degrees and building a library of comparative literature, art, and the whole scope of music on records (especially early music), what I sought was a knack for combining projected visuals with sound. That was 1939—the very year Kodachrome was released. Allow almost twenty years of photographing and presenting shows (a blend of slides, records, and improvised talk—aided by teaching posts here and in Europe: Princeton, plus Black Mountain; Chicago, plus Frankfurt; St. John's Annapolis, plus Munich; then St John's Santa Fe—variously backed by grants: Rockefeller, Ford, Fulbright)—until the need was to tape voice and music in a recorded art of sound. Presto! A line-mike-mix cassette deck came to hand.

That would take us about to the summer of '75 when I returned from a Chiapas year of improvised recording: playing music in the room, catching it with a single microphone, into which I also spoke, adding a count-down for manual changing of the slides. A dozen finished, I offered to show one weekly for our Santa Fe Fine Arts Museum in St. Francis Hall. They accepted, so I gave that series to a pretty good audience. Here I should introduce my most essential helper of those years, Dick Reichman, newly come to Santa Fe from New York City. His father had left him with a portfolio of investments and a related broker, so that he could lead, with his own family, a life of modest leisure—which he devoted to music, acquiring a great record collection (classic to modern, complementing my unique stock of rare early music). He also played piano and harpsichord, and was to build the finest clavichord I have ever heard. He had given programs for radio stations and thereafter for television, and for this he was even paid a bit. Well, when I gave my Museum of Fine Arts series, he attended throughout with his wonderfully bright and companionable wife, then pregnant with their first child, Nathaniel, soon to be born—little Nat, who absorbed my shows, one might say, in utero. Certainly, he absorbed them plenty thereafter, propped in an overstuffed chair, at their house or mine, while his parents, often with other viewers, experienced the growing muster of Bell's phantasmagorie. Meanwhile, Nathaniel, though he grew at a normal pace and was clearly alert, for over two years did not speak at all; so that Dick and Christine were bound to worry. Then one evening, down in my study, where I had shown my recently completed "O Western Star—Whitman's America," a long and ambitious achievement, Nat suddenly turned to me and cried out, "Great show, Charles!"—as far as anyone could tell, his first verbal utterance.

When it was time to record master audios freed of my old count-down—as requisite for later film, video, whatever else the future would require—Reichman and the Santa Fe Arts Foundation rallied with a few other early donors. He guided me to an open-reel Revox, with which he skillfully put together audio after audio, working, as later helpers would, mostly on his own time (what foundations call "cost sharing").

All this while I had been driving with Danny to colleges and universities from Santa Fe east, hauling my equipment, carousels and all, to show the shows. In Oxford, Mississippi, where my father went to college, and had been on the board (until Bilbo took over), I met Bill Ferris, head of the Institute for the Study of Southern Culture. I gave shows for him, to which he took a fancy, so that I donated a set to his Institute. In return, he put me in touch with the California Skaggs Foundation, writing a letter of recommendation to their perceptive administrator, Jillian Sandrock. On one of our trips we went there, showed samples of my work and, for years after, received substantial support for the Reichman audio-taping; as also for Phil Chandler, a former student and colleague, to computer-edit the scripts.

Who should then surface, just as needed, but the famous Santa Fe Vasulkas, Steina and Woody, who had seen my slide-tape weekly shows at St. John's and said they knew just how to put them onto video, first dubbing Reichman's soundtrack and then the images on 3/4-inch videotape, to be edited to 1-inch masters of the now forty plus one shows-so dubbed down to VHS, fifty at a whack, for non-profit placement (in colleges, etc.) of more than eighty complete sets so far.

For all this we thought to supplement the Skaggs' generosity. I applied, as I had before, to national and state endowments, only to find their citizens' boards so skeptical or hostile to such trans-departmental daring that they hit on every way to avoid contribution. If I sent to the NEH (Humanities), they said mine was an Arts project, "Send to NEA." NEA in turn sent everything back but my precious sample tapes, saying mine was the province of the NEH.

So it looked as if Skaggs would be our only asset. Ah! But we had a new president at St. John's, Michael Riccards, who became a great benefactor. Espousing the shows, he put himself on the citizens' board of the New Mexico Endowment (which had formerly refused me) and argued so persuasively that for years they blessed the project with twelve or more thousand dollars annually. Only thus were the videos completed.

But the whole thing, from Kodachromes to videos, was still mounted, by necessity, on ephemeral plastic! At this 1998 juncture, how should inventive industry have failed our culminant demand for some better means of archiving and access?

By March of that year, Riccards had given way to a new St. John's College president, John Agresto, who now took up the cudgel for Bell, providing a Polaroid scanner, powerful computer, and fine monitor. Also, by appealing to my seminar and *Symbolic History* friends for donations to a Bell Preservation Fund, he was amassing what came that year alone to more than $12,000. Meanwhile, Ralph Swentzell, loyal tutor, had begun-a gift-in-kind!—the digital transfer of the visuals for the first show, "Nature: The Perceptive Field." Since then the fund has financed skilled computer helpers (chiefly Paul Cooley, alumnus), working with me (another gift in kind) eight hours a day, mostly five days a week, for about fifteen months, digitally scanning and recording more than 15,000 slides, fifty-five hours of audio, and later, for the first twelve shows, blending sound and image on multimedia CDs. Always spurred on by hope! Though the careful scanning of so many slides used up the first year's donation; another Agresto letter, sent also to local private foundations (as Frost and Peters) more than doubled the former sum. Thus Paul and I kept at it, sometimes night and day, until by the millennium I could herald that all 40 + 1 slide-tape shows (thus fifty-five hours) had been enriched, transferred to digital, and stored on computer disks.

One negative result, however, of such fifteen months' day-and-night concentration would be the revocation of my old jesting health-claim: "My only health problem is trouble with micturition when I put my long winter underwear on backwards"; so much so that by July, 2000, I had to send family and friends the following health account, which I tried to keep—as I did the living of it—good-humored.

My "micturition . . . long underwear" boast no longer applies, since I have had a genuine prostate cancer, diagnosed late in March, 2000, and under treatment for more than three months:

First let me share my carefree acceptance and peace of mind with any correspondents. Through several years of erotic "It's no go the rickshaw" (my only real symptom), I had begun to suspect that even I might be mortal, and I cheerfully accepted that, as one must all natural visitations. Second, let me project as lively an account as I have time for, of the background, discovery, and (perhaps entertaining) hormone and radiation therapy.

Remember: those two and a half years, at forty hours a week, plus nights, putting *Symbolic History* onto digital disks. Before that protracted strain, my urologist had noted a gradual rise in the PSA number, but through all that work I quite forgot about him and his advised blood tests.

It was March 21, 2000, before I went to him and learned that the hormone count was 51, and that we should do something. March 30 biopsies were cancerous, though the bone-scan revealed no metastasis. After delays going to Boston for an Alumni showing (and visiting our youngest, Sandra), I started treatment April 14, with a heinous great shot to the left of the anus (made me feel like Scipio Africanus). It was Luperan, to suppress all testosterone, which I had not thought to have produced for years; but I guess the body does it—just enough to feed the cancer cells.

Here a drive with Danny, south and west over the state, to read my poems and to show shows, intervened; then Santa Fe community seminars, with a trip to see our Carola's would-be filming for a New Mexico script of hers, and then a lovely visit from English cousin, another Carola, etc.—until the x-ray zapping began June 1, 2000.

Now I knew I had to entertain the nurses and nurse-technicians by quoting poetry and inventing all sorts of descriptive fantasies about the huge, ton-heavy x-ray head, circling like the spheres over Marlowe's *Faustus*—this above, below, and to each side, gnashing its shutters like teeth, and blasting poor little me stretched out on the central bench (in a loose flowing robe, for all the world, like the ghost of Banquo); so I called that x-ray the Killer Whale, and myself Kipling's Kotick, the little white seal—quoting the song his mother sings him: "For great white sharks and killer whales, are bad for little seals my dear, are bad for little seals." The dear nurses would hug and pet me: "We'll take care of you, our little seal." Another day I tell them: "I'm in second child-hood now; so you kind ladies have got to mother this poor child." They get most amiable, and do a fine, loving job; while I quote *Faustus* again to the tooth-gnashing zapper: "Stand still you ever-moving spheres of heaven!" Then I would pick up more quotes from Uncle Remus, or whatever poetry popped into my head—giving the whole procedure a kind of lively delight. Finally I would tackle the doctors: "Do I have side-effects? Well, I have a sore tail-pipe." I tell them they have to give up that Greek and Latin terminology, and use real names: "The woodpecker pecked at the schoolhouse door / He pecked and he pecked till his pecker was sore." (So from my childhood.)

But that will end next week with another heinous shot of Luperan, leaving us free to fly to visit Sandra and family on their lake in Maine, for almost the whole of August. I will take chiefly Hölderlin's "Brot und Wein" (Bread and Wine) the greatest Western rhapsodic ode, the dactylic hexameters of which I must put into English so that they make something a shade more poetic than Hamburger! (The earlier translator.) . . .
Love, C. Gaffer Bell

P.S. September: I had told the nurse that x-ray killer whale was bad for little seals; but it didn't turn out so; since when we came back after the August stay with Sandra—I still gathering and revising hundreds of my poems preparing for this CGB Collected 2000 + (a labor now making a paper Sargasso of all our surfaces), I had the diagnostic PSA test and the level had gone from the 50s to 0.4, which doctors and all call miraculous. So now, as my Halloween 85th birthday nears, it's time to finish this Bio and poems; back then to my interrupted "Poetic Translation," my "See It Whole" essays, my Goethe's *Die Wahlverwandtschaften* (The Chemistry of Love) and at last, to another life-work—my philosophic "Creative Paradox: The Contours of Reality." Had I not closed "The Brief I Am" with such a projection?

And should I finish these things before I die, surely I will remember Goethe: "If I am restlessly active to the end" (and it was near the end) "nature is obliged to find me some other form of being, when this one breaks down under my spirit." Whether that obligation was fulfilled, we have small evidence, unless one of us should prove a case in point. But when and if my own organon should be completed, how long would I (with Mozart) not have been asking: "What will the little ones do when Don Giovanni has gone under?" To which the opera gives ready answer: "Noi buona gente . . . We good little people will sing the old familiar song."

And even now, for the close of the present work, the last pages of script for that final *Symbolic History* show offer more than an earnest of the metaphysical and scientific synthesis I have hinted at: from my Iowa Thunderstorm Vision, through the Princeton "Mechanistic Replacement," to a longer Chicago essay "Toward a New Organic," published in Borgese's *Common Cause*. Conceive, as you read these "Rooted Future" words, the accompanying images and music noted in the script (as follows):

154) Trefil & Freman 1983, "Birth of the Universe," 1st 10 to 43 of a second.
154a) Triple: Virgo Cluster; Spiral NGC 5194/5, & our Milky Way.
155) Queen Hatschepsut's Temple, c. 1480 BC, West of Thebes, Egypt.
155a) Bronze Horses, St Mark's, Greek c. 330 BC, with c. 1500 Venice.

Here a last dictation seizes me, hardly my own. Call it the Sufi
dance of the cosmos:

If, under the usual shield of antinomy, we go, for the moment,
with the Big Bang hypothesis of cosmic beginning, we have
of course to ask, what is that inconceivable pre-matter, even
pre-energy concentrate of an expanding and organizing space,
time and causality: the mass of at least a thousand-billion-bil-
lion suns, besides dark matter, black holes and radiation, the
self-searching infinity of algorithms that could yield universes,
living worlds, man, the possibility of earth-culture: Egypt, the
Bible, Greece, Dante, Shakespeare, Beethoven, someone writ-
ing this history, you somewhere receiving it—if all that was
strangely present in that no-space—what might that Big Bang
substance be?

> 156a) Chartres. c. 1250, North Portal, God sees Adam
>   in his Thought
> 156) Masaccio 1427, Trinity: detail of God the Father
>   with Christ, Santa Maria Novella, Florence
> 157) Trefil & Freeman, from Big Bang to 50,000 years,
>   atoms, etc.
> 157a) J. Gurche 1985, Horned Styracosaurus. vs.
>   Daspletosaurus
> 158) Michelangelo 1508-12, God and Angels, Sistine
>   Creation of Adam

Mind now presents two axioms: the old of causality,
that the antecedent must contain the result (Descartes' proof
of a thinking God—thus at Chartres the Maker sees Adam in
his thought); and the recent, of emergence, that the moment
is decisive and creates the new (Massaccio's eternal Father
and crucified Son). Since the axioms are complementary, both
apply. If the Big Bang package is what Hegel would call pure
potentiality, as Hegel knew (yet could hardly express in a
logically committed language) the whole concept is mislead-
ing—both right and desperately wrong. Since no potentiality
can generate that organic actuality but as it is itself Actual. The
concentrate (however named—in rational-materialist terms,
energy, measureless-fire) is not only such a physical seed, with
all trans-physical potentialities; it must also be pure and abso-
lute ACTUALITY: creator, mind, spirit, algorithms (information),

whatever has been gathered into the word and notion of God.
That godhead, as emergent, may be secondary to the stuff
and immersed in it, but as cause, it is primary—primal—the
power, form, imagination, act and Word of the whole.

> 159a) Eliot Porter's Africa: slide overlay: Cheetah,
>   cubs, and kill, superimposed on Murchison
>   Falls
> 159) Steven Fuller, photo: Yellowstone Fire, August
>   1988, sun-rayed Beethoven 1825, Grosse
>   Fuge, climax of 1st section; Col M5S677

To which conclude: once such, always such. That presence,
like black-holes sprinkled through a universe, remains every-
where, in each and all, voicing and radiating the triumph of
its being: I AM; I AM that I AM—while at the same time the
whole contrary message is uttered: I am not. Everything runs
down hill and destroys itself; yet in such a blaze as also rounds
the wheel, crying with Lear when he sees at the death-close . . .
(Cut Beethoven at the pause)

> 160) Chartres 1145-50, Smiling Queen of Judah
>   (head); on flames of Japanese 10th century
>   Fudo, Fire Guardian, Shoren-in, Kyoto
>   Perotin c. 1210, four-voice Sederunt, last
>   phrase (Cape) Archiv 14068

the love-truth, that Cordelia lives and breathes: "Look on her
lips; look there, look there."

From the first Springfield, Illinois, 1939-40 presentation of my
searching, sketched epic of culture, I knew that the last resonance had
to leap from the tragedy of our time to Lear's death-vision of Corde-
lia coming to life: "Look on her lips; look there . . ."—returning us in
the play to the betrayal of Gloucester, his wandering over the heath,
blinded by bastard Edmund; then found and guided by his true son
Edgar-Gloucester, who as Edgar has lovingly identified himself, has
also died—by Edgar's report: "twixt extremes of passion, joy and grief
. . . his flawed heart burst smilingly." The tragic loves of two lives—so
"wasted-into joy"—as that line came to me in the little poem of my

Princeton return, looking back to the year when a first flawed marriage failed, and Danny was found:

A whole life wasted-into joy.

So Rilke's *Duino* ascent, as translated by Leishman and Spender, with the Early Dead toward the ranges of pain:

> . . . in silence the elder Lament
> brings him as far as the gorge
> where it gleams in the moonlight,—
> there, the source of joy . . .

Paradox, complementarity, a mystic reality. Like the discovery in one of my "Rather Recent Poems" that energy itself can have shaped a cosmos only by ingredient "perception and response." Let perceptive spirit trust the Cosmos which has brought us here! Such, mind's last stream-panned nuggets of tried gold.

SONGS FOR A NEW AMERICA

Between the dust and dust,
in a little moment of green.

Part 1:

"O land, O cities; and down to the salt sea again."

SONGS FOR A NEW AMERICA
For Adlai Stevenson

1

We rise by the water; all things begin in the sea,
The formless mother, but of such melting beauty,
She draws at the land's heart forever. We
Are banking in the air; the bay and city
Wheel beneath us. That girl holding the lamp,
Timid in style, is a foreign freedom.
But here and higher we have put our stamp
All over the rock island of Manhattan.
Here is our Liberty, a cubistic thing,
Abstract line without face or feature,
Catching the dawn at the tip of the lowered wing,
This beauty no man planned, clean beyond nature,
A crystal of explosive energy—
And this is our land, tall over the shifting sea.

2

We are crossing the Susquehanna. Just about here,
In a farm house by the woods I know a man
Who lives as his fathers did. As far as he can
He keeps away from the city. He dips the clear
Water from his own spring. There is virgin timber—
Oaks and enormous hemlocks—in his ravine;
And he has planted all his hills with pine.
He gathers maple sap in the snows of winter,
Makes beautiful furniture, carves and weaves,
And fashions with wrought iron at his forge.
He is a Quaker, as honest as his streams.
He has no radio, and when new roads
Appear in the forest, and framed roofs
Spread from the city, he returns to his hearth and grieves.

3

For my own part, I think we have gone past
Nature—as past the ridges and cut-over woods
Of the dwarfed Alleghenies, where the roads
Are winding as they climb, and the mired rivers
Bend down to the plain through hills they sever.
Out in the central valleys in an hour,

We have run through a hundred years and more
Of the opening of the West. Here by the Lakes
The midland cities stand, and one that takes
The breath with daring as we bank and lower—
Still brute and butcher, yet you of the wind's towers,
Chicago, is this curse of earth and air
And water, this rearward ugliness the cost
Of every embodied dream and act of power?

4

Over miles of tenements we are settling wings
Through the gray air. I do not even descend.
Against the danger of such forward vision
Familiar voices call and roads beckon.
And what love draws us on? Quiet in the plane
I close my eyes until we resume the lane
Where flight commences. Wait. Again we feel
That great acceleration like a hand
Press us into our seats. The gaunt earth reels,
With a last bound drops behind, and we are things
Of the air. Brief separation. Yet we must dream
It could protract itself, be in our command
So easily to break from the old stem
And leave this shadowed limb of the sad land.

5

The diminishing city vaguely splotched with sun
Withdraws under the mist; we roar head-on
Into a luminous bank of cloud, a thin
Shell of brightness. Then we break out above
Over a clear expanse rippled with tints
Of rose and blue and melting purple, as in
A rainbow, colors in light, all fresh and new.
Over this blindingness the map as we move
Marks where the centers lie, dynamic engines,
Crowds that are traffic in the noontime canyons.
Here, imperceptibly heaving, as on winds,
With the quiet breathing of a peaceful thing,
Under its mottled cover—one great pearl
Of rounding beauty—sleeps the endangered world.

6

Past the Mississippi, clouds are breaking,
Making way. The first rifts are like shadows
Of such deep blue you think them darker cloud.
Then by glimpses, golden lands are shaping,
Stubble and corn, patterned fields of yellow,
Along the winding streams by fall-flecked woods,
Tender through last mist and dissolving scud:—
This earth again. Welcome stranger. It was good
Almost being parted from you. You are one
We have loved too deeply, too much counted on,
Lovers so young, each has betrayed the other.
Now the clouds are gone. Incredibly wide you discover
Your goods beneath us. And always love will burn
Through the sweetness of parting, this sweet return.

7

The great brown Missouri and the shallow Platte—
Following the last, a dry stream in a prairie,
We go up over fields of harvested wheat.
Brown fingers of rock erosion are reaching back
Into the ruled tables. Frightening the very
Expanse and marginal slipping into waste.
A dammed-up lake is a blue promise in the vast.
These men live under weathering rocks
Where the flat mudstone tilts and breaks
To the old outcrop of the Laramie peaks,
They are always gambling on the cold and heat,
Chances of sun and rain, and all their hope,
Under the giant sky, is rooted between
The dust and dust, in a little moment of green.

8

Over the broken teeth of the Wasatch Range
We reach dead center—that sudden dropping away
To the salt basin of an exhausted sea.
Shimmering in the heat. This mineral plain
Is not of our spoilage. Nature left it drained
Before we entered. Now the whole cycle has changed.
From that irriguous ground and granite temple
A new leader rallies his wavering people:
"We are men singled out by destiny

To a high calling. What an age is ours.
It is the coming of our fathers' dream,
This hope and trial of which the weak complain."
Caught in the rush of mind the desert flowers.
We build as we destroy, consummately.

9

Much of this country is more of the moon than earth.
For the pioneers it was days and weeks, trekking
Salt-flats, range on range of the heart-breaking
Desert. Strange they went on. But they made a path
Upward, there where the last rocky spur
Juts to the high Sierra—pine and fir
And orange clumps of aspen as they verge
On the bluest round of a lake, its water stirred
By mountain winds, the cold Tahoe. Then shelving
Valleys plunging in the sky's flame down
To the Sacramento. The naked hills are scored
As with rivers of fire; they shine like burnished bronze.
Here in the valley where the wild light is poured,
In goblets of wheat and vine we drink the god sun.

10

The fog comes rolling in from the long Pacific;
Redwoods tower in the mist where we go down;
Their needles drip into the columned gloom;
The white-skinned eucalyptus are swaying and weeping.
Over the warm hills and bay, fog dissolving
Lets rainbow light play through. Long sunset rays
Touch the mirrored shores glimpsed through haze,
Golden as dream, a melting hieroglyphic
Of all our temporal lands. So cloud and rain
Close the curtain, as banking we descend—
Cycles of rise and fall—where crashing waves,
As slow as heavy, gather weight and pound
The splintered granite of the coast range:—O land,
O cities; and down to the salt sea again.

The Nation, 1953

THESE WINTER DUNES
For Jim Gilbert, painter of the same

I sit over the lake on a hill of sand;
Gold lights and purple shadows, the playing forms,
Weave on the swift shuttles and are withdrawn.
Other hills are carved in rock, these mounds of the wind
Continually melt and change, wakening
The sweet tenderness of impermanent things.

Ridge after ridge, brown leaves on the yellow blowing,
Clumps of dry grass, the bare fabric of trees—
When this detail has melted, vegetation and air,
The sand will lie like rock in the cold unmoving
Before-and-after of the moon's vacancies—
Now love like a vine works round and attaches here.

That far-off smoke is Gary, the steel mills.
Here solitude. Nobody. There is nothing at all,
But the lake and ice-hills thawing, the taller hills
Of sand that quietly shift in the mothering swell
Of the wind and soften into grass and leaves.
Geese go northward; over the water a gull grieves.

A whistle bleats at the last faint line of the woods.
This whole stretch is waiting; it is already owned
By a great corporation; they bide their time.
Soon it will be factories and apartment homes,
A well-fed people, but involved in the doom
Of shifting things, knowing no permanent goods.

If there are strangers still coming to this great land,
Tell them out of pity, and make it plain,
Not to love what they find; or if love surprise
(As we are weak), let it be of special kind,
Quick and evasive; for here all things will change
Before the fruit can ripen on the vine.

That is why I take this place and moment
An image of our being, a man alone,
Loving the shapes of sun in a bank of sand,
And over all landscapes hold these winter dunes—

Gold lights and purple shadows, the heart-breaking forms
That weave on the restless looms and at once are withdrawn.

The Atlantic Monthly, January 5, 1954; and recently in *Rio Grande Sierran*.

PATTERNED EVENING

Spring returns, and I return again
To this valley with its winding stream—
Always return, even if the place is new:
For the earth's rock foldings everywhere
Wear the first beauties of light, form air . . .

Three budding trees, that bend like feathers, fuse
The late bare branches in a haze of leaves.
And hear how the whole earth rings with the stir
And whir of grackles, while from all sides breathes
The transcendental mourning of the doves,
Two notes, the low and high, lapped in an endless
Chord. From wind-spread cloud breaks the dropping sun,
And on the trunks that shield me pours its bronze,
Touching the green spines to unearthly fire.
And the flock of birds, braving the stream.
Veer up and wheel, far as the flight of eye,
Fading at last to motes that group and spread,
How vastly volute in that radiant air!

Image of the world, mirror to all time:—
Clouds, winds, and waves of light, senselessly beautiful,
Moved by the force that moves, borne down the stream,
Flung from the high to low, seeking repose;
And birds, bearers of life, that sing and soar,
Fired with a god-like will, breasters of the wind,
Beating bold wings up a torrent sky,
Feeding the sweet blaze of eternal desire.

This Iowa poem, April 1944, is treated in the Life, Chapter 2, where the closing section,
for its importance as a breakthrough, is repeated.

LONG BEACH ISLAND

Mountains and sea preserve one power of healing—
Sinusoids of eternity, the one
Moving, the other titanically frozen.
Over both rise the stars with far more native
Assurance; they have deep wells of strength they share
Together; never the silent wanderings of
The planets more sagely cryptic, than above
The fossil boulders of some skyward mountain;
Never the moon more prescient in its risings
Than when the red arrows expatiate over
The waves it woos, resurgent to its powers.

Here it is ocean. I stand on these dunes;
And the reddened bay at evening dies in the west
While eastward gleams the long white surf of the sea.
Not even the lure of interfolded mountains,
Mist-breathing from within, can reach me here;
No voice of earth looms more oracular.

The giant waves are hasteless; what they are,
Flows without effort into what they shall be.
Their breaking is implicit in their motion.
Down the sweep of the whole beach one climbs the shoal,
Towering to a smooth green, perilously leaning;
Then in a sudden splendor of foam, fountains
Downward—exultant ocean pours from the crest—
North and south a spreading Niagara—
Boils to the shore.
               Last clouds darken on the glossy
Wet sand. Fishermen's fires brighten over
The wide strand.

             All day long they have stood, lashing
The loud surf with taut lines, and yet no answer;
But now they light the campfires under the stars,
Pinning hopes on darkness. Surely it
Cannot be fish they seek here, but only the breast
Of the ancient mother—I do not mean the sea,
But the sea's mother, whose wave-mark she wears.
Is it strange that love should cloak itself

In foreign habiliments, courting shapes of disguise?
I have known men who could never take to the fields
But with excuse of ball or gun. And one
Who shuns this artifice, wandering to commune,
Is almost held a madman.

                                        Always under
The coppice of earth we veil the deeper longing.
And what is the sea's self but another of our
Devices, by which we raise the unbodied,
A tongue of flesh some spirit will be stirring—
Words out of ken of the waves? How could we live
Unvisited by such ploys of soul in body;
Nor weak the love that needs accessories,
But strong to knit earth-allies in its cause.

Still the lingering fishers cast their lines.
And even I, descending by the shore,
To win for a daughter's hand from the wave its shell,
Drop eyes from heaven, stooping as I pass.

This pentameter meditation of June 1946—here slightly revised—is mentioned in the
Life, Chapter 3, as the chief poem of that summer, when we rented a house just over
the dunes from the Atlantic, midway down the extended retreat of Barnegat Island. The
poem's length probably kept me from trying it on a magazine; but it may be my best early
blank-verse discourse in the manner of Coleridge's so-called conversation poems (com-
pare also Wordsworth's "Tintern Abbey")—works I had memorized on my University of
Virginia discovery of them.

PIONEER FRAGMENTS

We halted the wagon at the maple grove.
The clear stream choked with leaves. I skimmed them golden
Away. Arm to arm we bent and plunged
Our faces. The brook cold and the air chill.
A good Fall. With the tang of smoke in the woods.
Then we pushed on. By afternoon we came
To a fresh water as wide as the sea,
A place of pine and sandy dunes, the clumps
Of yellow spear-grass swaying in the wind.
Russet of autumn. Northward the expanse
Of waves rolling to the smooth hard strand.

We lay in the sun, her head on my arm,
And said: We will build a cabin here
With pines from the farther hill, and raise girls
And boys, a westward race of men. And the wind
Swayed in the spear-grass, yellow against the blue.
And it was good to think of lingering time
And the sunlit wealth of future years.

*   *   *

My father that last year dreamed hills of the west;
Woke with a smile upon him, kissed
In the night by a goddess. They sold the red earth
Of the gullied farm. Three wagons held
Their promise with their past. Night fires and music
Marked them over the plains.
After the desert
And the falling oxen, the last two struggling
To the ridge, just up and over; over
Into evening through the high sweet air,
The Sacramento Valley, green with life—
Wading down into a sunshine sea—
They sang a new song, both the hearts and tongues
Singing. And my father said: This is
The promise, dear ones, it is the place of the dream.
I remember the rock hills and fertile bowl—
Under a rainbow arch and a setting sun—
Like home I have come to, every rock and tree.

*   *   *

Tall, crisp, against the cloud, the swaying pine
On the whistling tuft of the hill. What memories,
My children!

Written in Chicago, October 1949, this poem merges our Indiana dunes with a dream of
the far West.

Compare Russell Lord, *Forever the Land*, 1950.

ANOTHER FLIGHT 609 (1949-1951)
With thanks to Rolfe Humphries

We rose through layers of the crossing cloud—
Streams and bursts of sun, with dark and rain,
A tent of light and then of dark again—
Over low stratus, through rough cumulus,
Into the solid nimbus—out and above—
An Alpine sky, and boiling white below,
And forward and far down our tiny shadow
Racing beneath us in its iris ring,
And out across the wing, two rings of iris
The propellers turning.
                  Then openings of
Deep blue, mountain ridges veined below,
The forest-sprinkled land, this curving earth,
Wonderful, deeply loved, and here first known
At three miles height in color and in form.

Over the Appalachians and the Lakes,
The wooded valleys and the upland prairies,
Blown grass under the drift of cloud. Then the
Rock wall of mountains, snow-capped, streaked with fir;
Over the last high peaks in the purple air;
And letting down, through golden gates of after-
Noon, over redwood trees in the lengthening sun,
Down to shoreward granite, cliff and knoll,
Rounding headlands by the Pacific's bowl.

And we returned by night across a land
Alive with light, those bright far galaxies
Of light, towns tied with chains of roads. And it
Was beautiful in the calm mountain dawn,
The low mist lying in pools of the long ridges,
Coasting down toward the Potomac, through
Woodland farms, in the first clear of morning,
Like a return from planetary wanderings
Safely home, to the sweet and pleasant world.

From high above we saw America
The symbol of its own expanse of spirit,
This good earth Thoreau and Lincoln walked on,

Where men tried perilous freedom, Quakers
and pioneers. And nowhere else in all
The world, such breadth and hope and promise. Who
Can tell what it would mean to man if this
Should fail, this beauty fail? And some of us
Were born to it—what is there more to say?

Perhaps: The impossible future
Holds nothing more impossible than is ours
In this present-out of the fall and rain
Of energy, building of atoms and cells,
Desperate chances of reptiles, mammals and men,
This present given or won, unbelievable,
Our hope, our now.
                    The property of spirit
Is transcendence. We have much to transcend.

For the evolution of this poem, see the Preface to the Life, to which I add here the close of "Turning and Turning in the Widening Gyre," my first essay for G. A. Borgese's *Common Cause* (University of Chicago Press, January 1951) followed by Rolfe Humphries, verse reconstruction of my prose, which was published in *Harper's* (January 1952) as his and mine:

> Not long ago I flew across the country from east to west, the pioneers' years contracted into a space of eight hours. We rose through three layers of crossing cloud, streams and bursts of sun, then dark and rain—over the low stratus, through rough cumulus into the solid nimbus—then out and above, an Alpine sky and boiling white below, with always the shadow of the plane racing beneath us in a circular small rainbow. Then openings of deep blue, the forest-sprinkled land, this curving earth, wonderful and deeply loved, first grasped from that distance in the richness of its form. Over the Appalachians and the lakes, the wooded valleys and upland praries, the blown grass under shadows of clouds. Then the rock wall of mountains, snow-capped, streaked with fir-over the last peaks in the high purple air, down shoreward granite above the redwood trees, rounding the headlands by the Pacific's bowl. We returned by night over a land alive with light, galaxies of light tied with chains of roads. And it was beautiful in the calm mountain dawn, the mist lying in pools of the long ridges below, to coast down toward the Potomac green farms and woodlands in the clear light of morning, like a return from planetary wanderings to our sweet and pleasant world.
>
> I saw America from above as a symbol of its own expanse of spirit, the earth of Thoreau and Lincoln, of Quakers and pioneers, the experiment of freedom. There is nowhere in the world such breadth and promise and hope. Who can conceive what it would mean to man if this beauty should fail? And for us who were born to it, what more is there to say?
>
> Only that America was always a dream, that the impossible future is no more impossible than this present—out of the fall of energy, the building of atoms and cells, desperate chances of reptiles and mammals and me—this incredible present we have won.
>
> The property of spirit is transcendence. We have much to transcend.

FLIGHT 609

Through the three layers of the crossing cloud
We rose, through streams and bursts of sun, and then
Through dark and rain and sun and dark again,
Over low stratus, through rough cumulus,
Into the solid nimbus, then above,
Out and above, into the fullest blue,
An Alpine sky, and boiling white below,
The utter dazzlingness of summer snow,
And forward and far down, our tiny shadow
Racing beneath us in its iris ring
And out across the wings
Two rings of iris, the propellers turning.

Then openings of deep blue, and mountain ridges
Below, that look like mole-runs, and the land
Sprinkled with forest, and more water there
Than ever we knew of, living in our houses
Or driving cars—this precious curving earth,
Wonderful, deeply loved, and here first known,
First felt, first seen, from three miles high, that richness,
Variety in union; color; form.

Over the Appalachians and the Lakes,
The wooded valleys and the upland prairies,
The blown grass (though we can not see it moving)
Under the moving shadow and drift of cloud,
Then the rock wall of mountains, capped with snow
And streaked with fir, over the last high peaks
In the high purple air, and letting down,
By afternoon, over the redwood trees
To shoreward granite, rounding cliff and headland
By the Pacific's bowl.
                        And back by night
Over a land alive with light, those bright
Far galaxies of light, all linked with light,
Towns chained by roads. And it was beautiful,
In the calm mountain dawn, the low mist lying
In pools of the long ridges, coasting down
Nearer Potomac, through green farm and woodland
In the clear light of morning, like returning

From planetary wanderings, safely home
To a sweet and pleasant world.

                         From high above
We saw America, a symbol of
Its own expanse of spirit, the good earth
Thoreau and Lincoln walked on, where men tried
Freedom for once, Quakers and pioneers.
And nowhere, nowhere else in all the world
Such breadth and hope of promise. Who can say
What it would mean to man if this should fail,
This beauty fail? And some of us were born
To this—what is there more for us to say?

This only—the impossible future holds
No more impossible miracle than we own
Here in this present. Out of the fall and rain
Of energy, the building of the cells,
The dance of atoms, and the desperate chances
Taken by reptiles, quadrupeds, and men,
We have won this present, unbelievable,
This gift, this now.

The property of spirit is transcendence.
We have much to transcend.

VISTA-DOME

Our search-rays catch the gray woods as we pass,
Single farms, one near, on the right hand,
Under the ghostly fountain of its tree.

An aerial crowns the roof: in that womb-place
The talking flicker knits them to the clan
Of meta-cells, the unthought destiny.

Lights focus to a town, a moment's race
Of buildings in the night, the reckless span
Of steel and glass, live with electric play;

And all goes by . . . . Then farms dropped in the waste,
And woods again, this world of frost and frond;
A startled owl in the searchlight wings off gray.

And overhead, silvering our bubble of glass,
As strange as far, the moon and slow stars stand,
Beyond the cloud-drift of earth's vaporous sea.

Written on the train to Washington, D.C., March 1952
American Weave, 1953

NOVA
For Isabel Harper, our Libertyville hostess

Two days of rest from the city; they are welcome.
Afternoon: the sky, relaxing, holds the horizoned land;
Fields and oaks are brown, the elms are bare;
One sycamore lifts tattered leaves, gold
In the long light, over the whiteness of boughs.
On gusts of wind, clouds are forming and dissolving,
Through which, in slower recurrence, brightens the moon.

But look: that wood lot, felled; those farms abandoned;
Where commuter houses mushroom: there, and there.
And yet we call it nature and solitude—
All things being relative to what we have.
Across the earth's curve, trails a wedge of smoke,

A new power plant by the Skokie line—
Likely, they say, to become nuclear.

I have also heard—ironic speculation—
That the work of man is to make stellar explosions,
Novae of the night, flashing the record
Of such mad discovery and release as ours.
I call it doubtful; but the truth is no less bitter:
Bacteria too disrupt their habitat;
This waste and overweening is a mark
Of life—nor of life only. If new stars
Are not the pyres of warring creatures,
It is only that atoms can explode without us;
They have their native ways, which we inherit:
The perilous urge and chain-reaction,
From bound to unbound fated flameward.

South and west a freight train rumbles;
A flight of jets crosses overhead.
They are not even gainful wings of commerce,
But trainers of war from the Glencoe base.
Tomorrow we return to the soar of the city.
Two days of quiet on a space-time island,
We watch the winter woods and enduring sky,
As we dream in the eddy of an exploding star.

Chicago, November 1951

This form, trimmed and revised, here replaces the older one used in the 1953 and 1966
Songs. For comment, see Life, Chapter 4.

CHESTNUT TREES
"O chestnut tree, great-rooted blossomer"

When I was a boy, we went up from the flat land
Of the Delta country, to those poor red hills,
My mother's birthplace. The good of that ground
Had been slaked out, bled from the lean fields
By killing cotton, the best part gullied down
To our wide river plain, black earth, water, and trees.

But there was something left of the old hill forest.
For the first time, come from cypress swamps,
Water oaks, and gums with the broad base,
I saw, among yellow pine, on the clean slopes,
In clean virgin stands, with maple and rock oak,
Blossoming over them all, great-rooted chestnut trees.

We ran in those woods. On crisp fall days
When the big limbs were bare we came back again,
Went rustling up the hill, tossing the leaves,
Long-toothed leaves on the ground, and a few falling,
Until we found the burrs, prickly shells
With the sweet kernels, last offering of those trees.

For they were dying. They were a Deep South stand
Of mountain powers. Who knows what subtle change
Of the tamed fields and people went hand in hand
With their slow blighting? Down the Appalachians,
Year after year, you could see them, crowned with vine,
Or else bone-bare, rain-bleached pillars of barkless trees.

Now most of them have fallen; where they were
Is a ring of rotten wood you can walk inside,
And from that center, over the forest floor,
A long mound of humus where strange plants feed—
Indian pipe, horsetail, fungus, the oldest pale life,
Claiming the amber twilight of decomposing trees.

This saprophytic lingering and reversion
Haunts the old place. But I have known too well
The lost wild goodness in the spiny shell;
I close my eyes to quicken remembered vision—

As of fabled giants feigned by folk-tale dreamers—
I dream bold trunks lifting flowers above all other trees.

And still they sprout from the ground every spring,
The young chestnuts. In the woods we watch for a breed
That may come and live. I have only seen them dying.
But the pattern holds in nature; in every seed
Is the form I knew as a boy on the worn red hills—
High and sweet over all, great-rooted blossomers.

The New Yorker, September 26, 1953, without the sixth stanza. For comment see Life, Chapter 4.

Part 2:
"From the bine of the bitter blood"
(Poems of more personal memory and passion)

BLOODROOT

I walk them in my sleep, those woodland trails
Of the Ragged Mountains. Often when milk-trucks roar
Or garbage cans are gathered in the dusk before
The gray dawn of the city, I stand at the old place
By the tulip tree, where the path bends with the hills,
And a clear spring breaks out cold from the rock face.

It was a long way from the town, a day's tramp
To reach it and return; but the forest there
Was almost virginal, the moss on the ground
Dense as a carpet and scenting the clean air,
And that was where in the spring I always found
The strange white flower with the bitter stem.

Bitter and dropping blood. It seemed a sign,
That pure loveliness out of the bleeding frond;
And at the same place, in the shelter of the hills,
Brown leather mushrooms grew, the great morels,
That we called devil's fingers, a hideous brood,
Mingling with those flowers as evil with good.

From the tulip tree a trail went up to the ridge,
To a run-down mountain house in an apple grove,
The apples hard and bitter; a wagon groove
Led down the other side to the valley road.
A man lived there of no particular age,
A good-hearted man, but with a rough edge.

I did not like him at first, he had a bride
So beautiful you could think only of her.
Men are slow to learn they must beware
That kind of lonely-eyed excess of beauty.
She left the man one night and their young child
For a boy going in a big car to the city.

The man lived on, nursing his child a year.
He was joined at last by a woman so plain, I thought
Her his sister; but they said otherwise.
I used to camp out overnight quite near.
They would come down with some good surprise,
Sit by the fire while we ate what they had brought.

And something of nature's paradox I learned
That last spring from the man. I had never heard
Such things were edible. He brought them stewed,
Those devil's fingers—"the best food in the wood;
But never you taste," he said, "the bloodroot's blood,
Unless you want your heart and bowels to burn."

So I learned it waking, and afterwards with pain;
But still in sleep I come to the place of the dream,
And trampling the devil's fingers in my old mood,
With the joy of the first sighting, pluck and admire—
The eight long petals yearning like a star—
That pure white beauty from the bine of the bitter blood.

January 1953.

For Galway Kinnell, then with us in Chicago, though the memories go back to 1933-36
and my University of Virginia himes.

SPRING INTERVAL

Again with branches to the stream
The willow of the waters welcomes spring,
And in the haze of afternoon
The upland field surrenders to the sun.
Only the beat of planes brings me in mind
The season's peace is but the peace of time.

Many things from earth are gone
By a quick parting, wait a slow return.
And we require some little span
To mend the shaken destinies of man.

Princeton, April 1947, from V-Day to Cold War, just before the sequence of Loss and
Love. Misplaced in earlier editions, let the poem now introduce the break of a first mar-
riage and joining of what endures.

THIS LITTLE VIGIL

Between the first pangs and the last of love
There is no difference, but that the first
Are bittersweet, the last are merely bitter.

Here in the waste of fore and after desert
The brief oasis of a trysting passage
Lures to the longed-for and regretted joys.

See the "guns of personal loss first spoke for me" passage in the Life. This June 1947 poem, penned when I hitchhiked from Princeton to the Delaware Water Gap, after receiving an announcement of infidelity, fictionally disguised in *The Married Land*, though the "little vigil" or "brief oasis of a trysting passage" (my first marriage) had lasted more than ten years. See also the related "Aurorean Prayer" from that August, at the same place in the Life, and, from the Black Mountain involvement, my hopeful "Forfeit Good."

Rolfe Humphries, *New Poems* (Ballantine, 1952) and *New York Times*, July 2, 1961.

LETTER FROM NAPLES
March 1948

Standing above the straits of Dover, evening,
Twilight of the world, Arnold willed
One to the window, where the wave receding
From the shingle, curled off the ribs that build
The sheer blind reaches of the godless sphere.
"Ah love, let us be true to one another"—
The only hope that broke his darkness there.
A time we too disdained him. Night now over
The rounding ocean gray. I lift eyes from
War-fallowed fields, furrowing this dark shore,
And my cry shatters on the rocks like foam:
"Love, love, let us be true." I have no more
Prayers to waste on the dead gods of the gloom;
The prodigal heart has this last hope of home.

The New York Times Book Review, September 23, 1956.

Refer here to the Life, end of Chapter 3, where the whole Loss and New Love sequence, with the Rockefeller Grant travel and its poems, especially from Florence, and related to "La Giostra"on the following page. Thus the above cry is called: "a fart kicked from a dead donkey." Here I add the Matthew Arnold, the poem's literary source:

DOVER BEACH (1867)

The sea is calm tonight.
The tide is full, the moon lies fair
Upon the straits;-on the French coast the light
Gleams and is gone; the cliffs of England stand,
Glimmering and vast, out in the tranquil bay.

Come to the window, sweet is the night air!
Only, from the long line of spray
Where the sea meets the moon-blanched land,
Listen! You hear the grating roar
Of pebbles which the waves draw back, and fling,
At their return, up the high strand,
Begin, and cease, and then again begin,
With tremulous cadence slow, and bring
The eternal note of sadness in.

Sophocles long ago
Heard it on the Aegean, and it brought
Into his mind the turbid ebb and flow
Of human misery. We
Find also in the sound a thought,

Hearing it by this distant northern sea.
The Sea of Faith.
Was once, too, at the full, and round earth's shore
Lay like the folds of a bright girdle furled.
But now I only hear
Its melancholy, long, withdrawing roar,
Retreating, to the breath
Of the night wind, down the vast edges drear
And naked shingles of the world.

Ah love, let us be true
To one another! for the world, which seems
To lie before us like a land of dreams,
So various, so beautiful, so new,
Hath really neither joy, nor love, nor light,
Nor certitude, nor peace, nor help for pain;
And we are here as on a darkling plain
Swept with confused alarms of struggle and flight
Where ignorant armies clash by night.

LA GIOSTRA

Upon the terrace gave the expected door.
Florence below saw late-found lovers meet,
Greet, be silent; silent at our feet
The city took the twilight as before.

"To hold this beauty, with your hand," I said,
"Makes me a part of ages gone so far
That only love remembers what they were."
She answered, "Without future, love is mad."

"Observe your city," was my blood's reply,
"Built here in life and beauty; and each one
Who sent these singing towers to the sun
Forgot in love more wrinkled cares than I."

"Tomorrow you must go." She turned
Full-face her sorrow. I spoke: "Against your peace
I cannot work, such is the time's weakness.
But in some other dream, or life, we learned

That beauty is the valley between harms."
Her eyes flared up with such a wild sad light
As flamed all years' forgetting. Fell the night;
And the burning Simonetta filled my arms.

See the discussion of this poem in the Florentine account, etc. of May 1948, near the
close of the Life, Chapter 3.

THE LOCUS OF LOVE

However friendly the peace of general ideas,
It is body clips our passion, burns the caress
And lost regret of enfleshed memories.

When religion had also body it could wake such images.
There were rival dreams of the night watches,
Sensate as ours, less frustrate of consequence.

Now every spirit melts into generality,
Lust only holds the siren of its body,
To which not Virgil nor Beatrice opposes.

We too would dream of god could we shake this temptress
Who clings, eyes narrowed, stirring to our loins.

But our shaking only sends through the willowing frame
And lifting lids a more voluptuous tremor.

And the void scale lifts and pan of flesh settles;
Images of day and night rehearse dear torment.

Having given Mildred sole title to our house and been told to leave, I moved into the loft
of the Parnassus Bookshop, September 12, 1948. This veritable nightmare waked me
soon after. Then, remembering, from the boat, Danny's talk of her parents at Little Pines
Farm, Darlington, Maryland, I wrote her, asking to visit and meet them.

WOODBIRD
For Diana

Woodbird softly trilling from the maple spray;
Red leaves above quiet waters
In the webs of sun.

This fall is my spring; down lost forest ways
Your frank eyes guide, the daughters
Of laughter run.

When I forget, my love, image of the light and spray,
Forget, eyes, earth and waters
And lose the sun.

Written on the train, Sunday evening, October 17, 1948, returning to Princeton after a
first weekend stay at Little Pines Farm, meeting Danny's parents, and walking the farm
and woods with her.

THE SUN SETTING IN PISCES

Good that winter is out of step with the sun:—
The leaves of fall cling to December trees,
While late snows warm in the lengthening rays of spring.

Our love's deep night and solstice day
Passed over when the leaves
Hung brown above; we said goodby
Under the shadowing trees.

Now the low bright sun on the snowfield world,
A distant bell beats five;
It is the last of winter's months,
And still love is denied.

More winter lies before us, but the sun
Later declining golden burns through the trees
And, over vacant white, rays the slant promise of spring.

Of the February 1949 parting.

SUB REGNO DIANAE BONAE

I wake by night to the sense of wandering city
Streets, out late and alone. Drinking dies
And voices and lights close. The empty ways
Stretch before and behind, with only the swinging
Of a shuttered door. There is the dread
Of returning to the old houselessness of heart.
And I lie in the calm while knowledge comes like dawn:
Now north and south are known, and goal and home.

ON A BALTIMORE BUS

Observing point by point bare instances
(As lice a courtesan) what can you see
Beyond this valueless: that what is, is,
And if flesh move, that's just its tendency?

A public carrier may be sold to some
Who fill a private purse; then ads press
From every surface, dentifrice and gum;
Last radio's installed, public address,
With the hourly lechery of melodic sale.

Have all the annals of old tyrannies
Told such pervasion? No quiet interval
Of private peace from prying enterprise?
Such usurpation?
                    These are the letters spread
That read the corporate virtue strumpeted.

TOUCH-ME-NOT

"It was wonderful. The cruise boat stopped at the stream,
And there they brought a barge and put us on.
We had the deck with curtains; just below,
A marimba band played the whole day through.
So we went up the river. It was nice.
They have beefsteaks at fifty cents apiece,
And frosted drinks."
                              "I guess you docked in Cuba?"
"For three days."
"We were there; the ceiling's made of glass.
And we drank daiquiris, I think it was,
At forty cents a throw."
                              "Fancy that.
I bought banana liqueur."
                              "And on the boat
There was something every hour. Cocktails helped.
And when we went ashore we never walked."
"Did you see them lick cigars with their tongues?"
"Sure. I got two boxes, but they were strong."
"Sounds interesting."
                              "Only the people are queer,
Unfriendly, you know, and beggars everywhere."
"And did you see the small plant touch-me-not,
That when you touch it, it withers all up
Before your eyes?"
                              "No, that we did not find."

Go back; it is the essence of the land.

Conversation overheard on a Mississippi-to-Chicago train, December 1951, as I returned
from a visit with my mother. The last line is my spoken thought.

TREMEZZO

In a walled garden over the Lake of Como,
Having eaten and drunk well of the rose-red wine,
Under the spring-thaw sun and gray of olives,
The whole world now (as bees buzz in the bine-flowers
And rivulets, coursing down from snowpeaks, murmur)
Dissolves in perceptive pleasure: the young shadows
Of plane leaves lie double on the ground; and I think,
What if all other mortals—these natives here who laugh
In their chattering, and the dark lovesome barmaid
Bearing full flasks and a belly six months showing
(Here in this garden enclosed where a gargoyle's smile,
Of old church granite mortared into the wall,
Spouts sparkling water)—what if all others live,
Carefree partakers of this present time,
Which I, withdrawn into shadow, miss, and therefore
Blue reach of Como waters just glimpsing from above—
At once both rich and poor, a god creating, sing.

April 1952, Danny, with Carola, visiting English relatives; I photographing in Northern
Italy on the way to our Frankfurt teaching.

VILLA CARLOTTA

Summon three like memories, from past to now:—

The plain brown nightingale singing at dawn
On the slopes of Mount Athos where once we climbed
From the Greek light of islands to witness that home,
In the darkness that followed—of the Virgin and Son—
How he leaned to the stream on a tendrilled spray
And trilled out his heart in his ecstasy . . .

(Or the nightingale caged on the point of Sirmione
Where olives and moon silvered dark ruins—
Paene insularumque—his tragic rune,
Again and again: tereú and tereú;
The rest forgotten or never known—The joy trills
Only a caged cry for lost forest and stream . . .

(And now over Como in the day's lingering
The garden villa, as we lie in a close ravine,
Our late prime of life, and hear from the Western tree,
Sequoia of towering heights and eternal green,
Over laurel banks the full-throated roll,
Grief with celebration, voiced by a like bird, free . . .)

Think thus of separate moments, three in a row,
And ask what bridges bind into one,
What dauntless adventure of love can hold
Moments and patches, which always move,
Flashes as they are, to scatter and dissolve?

I, still by Lake Como, en route to Frankfurt.

LICENSE THEY MEAN

On the bridge of Frankfurt over the ruined town
I saw our careless soldiers, three drunk men,
Chasing the already too-much-tempted girls;
But these passed on, having been hissed and pawed,
While natives reproved in German, not understood.

The fat-jowled man, the hilly-billy brawn and bone,
The pimpled snob from the city, three assumed
A face of all, that I surprised them, speaking:
"You disgrace us over the world. Think what you lose.
We are here to make democracy, not break it."

One laughed, the others swore. "Democracy?"
In his snide tone, "Can you tell me what that is?
I thought, aim at the highest— "Yes," I said,
"It's where men have freedom, but still they show
Respect for other men and for value and law."

A growl from the jowl: "He's out of this world;"
A whine from the bone: "Can't come in from the rain;"
From the third a squeal: "Do you go to Harvard or Yale?"
Taking me for young. "Look here," I said,
"I'm thirty five, have a wife and kids and I've

Been teaching the likes of you, with small success,
For thirteen years, and I know more of the world
Than you ever will; and I'll tell you again
What democracy is, but just for you, so you
Can understand" (like one who weeps and speaks:—

"It's what has set you damned fools up where you
Can talk to your betters. It's what I build and you
Kill, and you have the power, and God help us all!"
And so I left them and walked back alone
To the bombed walls, while they came after

Whistling and calling names. I was deep in wrath
And sorrow, having held in absence a vision
Of the country loved. Poor spendthrift land.
I felt the Psalmist's mood, to summon God
For vengeance on offenders. And then it came

To me (blessing returning its quiet way)
All of this was only to see—being forced
From the center toward them; so punishment
Could not be worse than to abide in that waste
And that blind would not see from without, but be.

Frankfurt, April 1952.

KÖNIGSTEIN

Rooks cry over the walls. The great state rooms
Are broken shells—only the vaulted spring
Of Gothic. This tower was well made
For a poet to climb and work on his loom
Threads of the Rhine country; knights at arms,
Girls rustling in the court below, the blond
Youngsters of barbaric blood, growing
Into courtly love, singing the new songs:—

"Take this wreath from me, lady—the flowers I have;
But I know where all colors blow, and birds sing;
Come, let us gather flowers." Blushing, she came.
Until dawn took me from my laughing dream . . .
And Frankfurt there has fallen, the Goethean town.
You see the new frames rising, to melt again
In such flash and fire to later shards
While tragic love reshapes what strife destroys.

Those woods of Taunus are growing, green, dark green.
But terrible the reaches and unplanned pain
Of the slow building, and here a while
We crown the conquered world, and can no more
Answer spirit's why than weeds that flower
Out of every crevice of the old stone,
Or rooks that in the last light of the sun
Fly on banked wings, screaming around the tower.

FROM LE HAVRE

The tug pulls, tightening the steel strand. This harbor
Water churns oil and chunks of bread. Slowly,
Slowly the great ship moves. Strong is the land's
Hold. And the wharf is lined with waving hats
And hands. Strangers to me. And strangely sad
I wave—though the call of the West is calling me home.

Houseless home of our wandering—vacant fields
And tall inhuman cities. I would not turn.
But eyes go east and a face meant to be glad
Is quietly pensive, and the hand waves—as if
I were myself, waving myself goodbye,
The new waving to the old, and both alone.

Thought wins me back to a day closing a ride
Through German forests, wheat and vine, at cloistered
Maulbronn, where a crescent moon, the pearl
Of sunset—down the mingled glow of pointed
Windows—lights from bowl to bowl that murmuring
Fountain, and the mystery of Gothic and water are one.

Birth and chance determine our home. But the harvest
Valleys and tender towns, the laughing virgins
Carved in stone: Oh they wrap round the heart;
(A few months only) and on this art-rich land,
Like a remembered love, we could wish to hold,
Hold her forever, love fastened here.

Now the waving arms are gone, and the clay chapel under
The hill. A destiny of power takes
The hull. Whirls of water drive us on.
And the course is westward, where steel towers loom
Larvae of the future, along confluent streams,
On the leafwork of a continent, axil and veins.

For the earlier sailing from Le Havre, Friday, July 9, 1948, the docking at Southampton
when Danny came aboard, see Life, Chapter 3. On this August 1952 sailing sequence,
with Danny gone home the month before to bear Sandra, our second child, though we
docked again at Southampton, of course, no Danny appeared. Yet I penned a second "Is-
land Greeting." For the first, "Humanist Island," or that second one, see the Life, Chapter
4. (The above was one of Rolfe Humphries' six Ballantine Press choices.)

PART 3:
"obedient to the general law"

DIRETRO AL SOL

Over the gulf and soaring of the city
We came to dusk to the roof-garden rail.
Darkness flowed in the streets; the sheer beauty
Of towered steel rose in the violet air—
Bands and heights of light under the sky's plumes;
Cars to the suburbs burn the long road lanes.

Here on the terrace, drinking wine and eating,
People of every nation, hearts unquelled
By the encroaching shadows, mingle, speaking
Tongues of kindred lands. Their voices tell
Of customs and of needs, of the fools who rule;
They are loose in talk and laughter, slurs and dreams.

And the clouds relinquish the sun's brown setting.
Twilight deepens as the city glows.
Out of the past of another world-evening
Spirit has suffered, a great voice looms;
It is Pericles—with Athens at the bourn
Of her adventurous sailing into ruin:

"We are the school of Hellas. Wonder unending
Of after ages will be ours. We have
Made sea and land the highway of our daring.
If now obedient to the general law
We invite decay, the greatness we have known
Will be some break of beauty in that gloom."

These words echo in the mind. From dark flashing
Along the gray shore and the wash of waves,
Towers, and cars streaming. Up vibrant air reaching
Cones of light catch at the destinate planes.
The roar west and east. Here in the hum
Of mingled voices, careless freedom sings.

And we too have lived the dayspring and daring
That all time will remember; we have seen,
Over the earth-foreclosure of our wasting,
Still the incredible brightening of the dream . . .
Now promise is almost presence under the dome
Of night stirred with light and the rush of wings.

September 1951.
New Poems (Ballantine, 1953)

AUGUSTINIAN WISDOM

There are more parts to wisdom than suffering,
But that is some beginning.
We who have seen the first crack in the wall,
Our fellows buried, though ourselves secure,
Crouched in this (at the best, inglorious) corner—
What have we borne?—Crime and Punishment,
Waste Land, the Lower Depths.

Think: our slum squalor, stench, and sores
Have not passed over us as over Lippi
To leave angels inscrutably smiling.
We have wept more, believing less.
And this? What Bolshevik claim?
"TO GOAD THE WORLD TO ORDER!"
Such is the last spun thread, and when it severs?
Comes the timeless trial, the pure affliction
Until we die in wisdom.

May the powers to that end give faith, their ingredient,
With as liberal a hand as man for his portion,
Will pour on torment, sorrow and suffering.

January 1944

My taste, clearly, was to turn Spenglerian prediction toward spiritual affirmation. I paraphrase: two wars have shown the late cycle crack, burying my fellows (T. C. Shields, my best high school friend, killed in Normandy), while I was teaching, in Iowa. Yet how could teachers escape the evidence of *The Waste Land*, etc.; even worse, of hearing colleagues say the Communist State was to "goad the world to order!" which I, expecting the fall also of materialist tyranny, here pray ingredient faith may alchemize suffering into wisdom . . . ?

BALSAMUM

We of the hunger,
Crouched in the last cave
And high cranny
Of the earthly mountain
And thin air,
Have fleshed wish into answer
But the flesh fades,
A putty god,
Our own device
And idol.

We struck rock
And thought water,
Closed ears and felt paces
In the stone's shaking,
The high hope and advent
Of our God.
There is water
Or we would not dream it;
But this is dream—
While the giant steps dwindle
Over the hills.

He who has waited and lost
The God's coming
Endures last trial.
Faith there and patience,
Then the subtle air
Creeps into the hollows,
Even as the Messianic
Tread dies.

The God has myriad forms.
Not in thunder only
But the slow dew
And upwelling
Of unperceived
And unpremeditated
Power.

To have lived
And suffered is enough.
In dearth and suffering
To have worn faith,
Eyes on the stars
Is and becomes guerdon,
The reward
Of known oneness
With the one
And the all-shaping
Lord.

This short-lined poem is from my Princeton time (October 1945). No doubt I was teach-
ing, yes, reading T. S. Eliot; but what spoke here was inspired by the German I was
memorizing: early Goethe ("Prometheus," "Gesang der Geister . . .," and "Grenzen der
Menschheit") with late Hölderlin ("Blinde Sänger" and "Patmos").

IN THE TIME OF THE ITALIAN CAMPAIGN

Come from the breathing beauty of the hills,
Distant, rolling, the bacchanal of leaves,
Of winds and waters, racing, inebriant, eager as wine,—
Home to the evening news and to its world,
Less home indeed than all the farther fields.

How many more in the course of the day,
Once great cities, have melted in ruins?
What new pile of rubble is crowned with the title,
And ironic honor of liberation?
Italy, you of the fatal beauty,
Garden of the world, it is yours to answer,
Despondent mother of a child-like people.

What comfort is here? I am too much embroiled in these issues.
Would you ask the blade of grass that browns and withers
How its russet builds to the landscape's beauty?
But no clump or cluster, not the lushest, greenest,
But bears its tips of desiccation,
Blending in struggle, weed on weed.
I lay in the gourd-bed, flowered, fruitful,
Slipping curved fingers down the tendrils
To feel the clutch of subtle runners,
Weaving a noose for the throats of grasses.

To some all-seeing eye is this our landscape
Lush by its murders, hued in destruction?
Here is the boundary of mortal conception,
This the limit of Job and the whirlwind;
After a thousand turns and gyrations,
Wanderings, discoveries,
Still the stream bears us back to this granite:—
To deny it, denies purpose, to affirm it, condones;
One kills distinction, the other incentive.
Remember this and give thanks for enigma.

Tomorrow back to the fields again,
Where rival plants engender blossom,
And russet builds into the landscape's beauty.

This Iowa poem of July 1944, the last Iowa one to strengthen my Songs volume, was first called "Friedrich's Brown," making Caspar David Friedrich's russet stippling of green meadows (with blades of desiccation), a metaphor for Job's moral problem: why such death and outrage on God's earth?

FOLD OF FRIENDS

Philadelphia, fold of Friends—grown now
To the great-towered trading town
Pouring smoke on the April air;
And rock-ridged Schuylkill, sliding stream—
Defiled with oil and foaming brown.
And yet your waters, far off, go sky-blue,
And the warehouse of the *Daily News*
Distended in the surface strangely shows
The gleam of ivory and flush of rose.

Across the way a scaffold stands
Where wagons laden lug the town's refuse.
They back above a barge and tilt their frames
And all goes crashing in an ashen cloud
That sets the gulls with wimpled wing a-reeling
And wraps the cursing Blacks in filth's coiled skein.
And then the barge slips streamward to abuse
The incalculable ocean with its stain.

Garbage, bottles, ashes, rusty cans,
Those haunted devils in the smoky shroud,
Stench, dirt, damped souls, the ceaseless trains
Of battered lorries and of broken wains—
Welcomed in the stream's reflecting arms
Grow quietly beautiful. And look, one roan,
Hard backing under bit, curvets, rears,
And for a moment all the grandeur bears
Of his old fathers in the Grecian frieze.

And I who came to see the art museum
Have spent an hour on this river's brim
While Botticelli waited, and I have seen
In this sad spectacle the earth grow green:-
We only blight by parts; the whole they form
Evades the withering of our ghastly charm.
When we have laid our last curse on the land,
That curse burns beauty in the everlasting hand.

March 1946, a hopeful deflection from the above-mentioned art museum visit. But has today's dysecology shifted our curse from parts to the globe?

MOUNTAIN CLOSE

Upon this crown of metamorphic stone
Soul spans the mountain world and waits alone.

In the far valley steel things sweat and stir
Ditching and hauling for some later war.

About earth's ruin reflective spirit wreathes
A garland of vine over the bone-blanched tree.

An offshoot of those August 1947 hikes with Galway Kinnell above Black Mountain
College, North Carolina.

FALL OF TROY

The woods are burning. Under mournful light—
Amid long reeds—by the red banks of water—
Stoats and foxes run from slaughter
While a pattering of rabbits fills the night.

And was it all for this, the years of nurture,
Rearing the shoots, and terracing with skill
The downward radiance on the hill,
For this, the sudden suicide of nature?

No sensual trace remains. And yet one ray,
Blood-red of flame, like the last flush of sun,
Caught on the pool the imperiled swan,
Mirrored the pluming breast, and wings that day

Would greet in the new land by the unfired river;
And on that dying world woke such a song
As melodized immortal wrong;
And this has wrung the heart of God forever.

I have written of this poem toward the close of my Life, Chapter 5, Annapolis time,
where I return to my Delta ties with Shelby Foote and Walker Percy—with Shelby espe-
cially when the above poem, written in Princeton, September 1946, was included in the
1952 *Mentor Selection of New World Writing*, which also picked up a chapter of Shelby's
then unpublished *Civil War*; so Shelby wrote me about the coincidence of our leading the
"New World"—he in history and I in poetry. For the last line, compare Euripides' "*Trojan
Women*" close in Gilbert Murray's translation.

PROTEUS' SONG

I who cursed my age and cowered on
Under wrought shadows, shall go down
In voiced hosannas for the glory shown
The lurking spirit in this bag of bone.
Never on earth has soul so grown
To self-perception of its own.

We stem from dark; but we have witnessed dawn
Plant ruddy hopes on shoreward stone,
Felt globed earth spin beneath us, mounting sun
Spread spacious air, paling its mirror moon;
And we were made sun, moon, air, earth in one.
Never in all time's ages gone
Has spirit so possessed its own.

If night now gathers, if the earth and moon
Plummet into the swallowing sun,
Has not day flowered—lifeless stone
Quickened in petals, golden air with song?
If beauty break, has soul not known
The embodied world, not made that world its own?

We saw all-spirit spread a glimmering zone
Up shores of man, and washing on,
Bind every star in one perception;
And we in that wide sea have soared and flown
In the flight of the alone to the Alone.
If now we blaze extinction, shall we moan
The partial loss by which that whole has grown?

Sing glory for each act. Most for the boon
Of rueful knowledge, for this crown
Of mortal splendor, our foretasted wrong.
What is death when have learned us one
With the starred universe we fed upon?
Never in ages past has spirit known
Such amorous surrender to its own.

This poem also has been dealt with in the Life, Chapter 3. It was in October 1946, after
my return from Long Beach Island to teaching, while the family stayed a spell by the
ocean, that I experienced the solitary, midnight, pantheistic outpouring of "Proteus'

Song," its thirty-three lines all sounding the assonance of *on, own, moon, sun*—"as loving a hymn to the cosmos of life and dying as I have received."

Later, when I sent a copy to Danny's English aunt Evan Middlemore, soulful lover of art and poetry, she (then in the throes of cancer) wrote me: "It is glorious—and fills me with courage—Poets are prophets—and it is good when their message uplifts us. I shall keep it in "Fear no more" [her notebook of treasured quotations].—Love, Ev."

NEGATIVE RESURRECTION

Blind in the night, remembering times of vision,
From the unseen dark horizon thunder wakes
Lost images of lightning; flickering streaks
Of flame reform on the retina's prison
Empires of brightness, soul's indwelling. Risen
On the world the god of thunder shakes
The drowned heart in the leaves. Blindness seeks
The fountain of fire, destroying intercession.

Dark. Wind runs in the trees, depicting cloud.
Sense gropes by shadows, as the sick desire
Moves to the storm. Now two shapes gathering spell
Our past and future:—day-spring up torn shrouds
Of the tomb; and here on the great west hill
An old man, arms to the lightning, seized by fire.

In my marked-up Berg edition of this Chicago, February 1951 poem, I have penned a
bracket: "cf. Hölderlin's 'Blind Singer'." That great, late Hölderlin ode: "Der Blinde
Sänger," with a fine J. B. Lieshman translation (in Huntington Cairns' superlative anthol-
ogy: *The Limits of Art*) is to be taken up in my volume "Poetic Translation: A Mythic
History"—where the Blind Singer prays the Thunderer for Visionary Lightning, which
(beyond communication or understanding) becomes a death cry:

> O nimmt dass ichs ertrage, mir das
> Leben, das Göttliche mir von Herzen.

This I translate:

> Take from my heart, that I may bear it,
> Life, the godlike, take from me!

Hölderlin's poem is mysterious enough to beget a prodigy of mysteries—among which
mine seems to stretch Western civilization, from the archetype of Christ's Resurrec-
tion through our global conquest and dysecology—to this poem's "old man, arms to the
lightning, seized by fire."

TO DICK WENDELL
Who died of multiple myeloma, February 27, 1951

Grief strikes. Foreknowledge is no shield against
the impingent act. The teacher is dead.
Two years ago he answered from the bed
Where he lay all that summer, and green leaves danced
At the wide window. There was one bending branch
Where he saw figures sparring, and he said
He kept his heart there, for it seemed his life.
So the fall winds came and the leaves were shed;
The tree stood bare, all but the single branch
Love held green. And then one day he glanced
And saw it cut as clean as with a knife.

So he by faith fought through, and now is gone,
Past miracle, on the same wind that bears
To its all—winter, plants, the earth and stars.
Our age also is wasting, struck to the bone
With want of what he was—truth's champion-
Incurable as he;—which yet our prayers
Hold green a while, with spirit's hope complying
As he grew noble through two martyred years.
Good Saint Richard, in what present dawn
Of time or timelessness you work your own,
Smile on us here—who still in life are dying.

I have also written in my Life of this Iowa State teacher-friend, who read Dante's Italian
with me the near six years I was at Ames. Later I fictionalized him in *The Half Gods* as
head of a college like St. John's above Ellicot City and the Patapsco. He was also a liberal
scholar of the Bible, who deserved the appellation here given him of saint.

TO BORGESE, KAHLER, AND THE UNKNOWN THIRD

> *. . . Ben v'én tre vecchi*
> *ancora in cui rampogna l'antica età la nova . . .*
> *Purgatorio*, XVI, 121-22

Old men, the few, that had their roots in deep
Before these blusterings, do not give with the time.
They are oaks among reeds. The worst they suffer
Is the nemesis of the strong, thunderbolts
Of an angry and always eminence-threatening sky.
When all else is shifting and sliding they keep
Proud fixity, landmarks over the scrub
And chaff that hisses driven on the winds.

One such, Antonio, you stood for me
When I, taking the easy patriot's side—
Defense of today: tomorrow's compromise—
Sanctioned the course of violence we hold,
One of the needless many, cheering what is,
Forgetting what should be, however a dream,
Which dreamers still must claim (and I, once young,
In the dawn before these storms, might have cried the same)—

Answered: "No, no, no! The apologist's need
Is filled by all, the drift of the time; we side
Too with our own, but as it works our vision.
What we serve is the country of our hope,
Which we now prove in the act of freedom, hating
Lies. Love crowns the new land as the old;
But not to knuckle. Weighing such world-wrong.
We are left one only word: No, no, no, no."

I thought of Princeton Erich and wished a third,
Remembering Dante: "Three old men there are
In whom the last age chides the new." While vision
Opened on a wind-swept scene, the willows beat
And the grass blown, a field where three oaks took
The storm. They have more risk than praise. Yet in
The shelter of the earth they hold, I saw
Oak saplings root—the scrub and chaff whirled by.

As translated by Charles Sinclair, the epigraph reads:

> There are yet indeed three old men
> In whom the ancient times rebuke the new.

This passage is followed by a naming of the three worthy Lombards, who, without Dante, would hardly be known today—any more than my two, in a media-ephemeral age of "glass-belly" trash, are likely to have held their own.

BRITANIC EPISTLE

Gaius of Britain to Cinna of Gaul—Brother:

Here we stand at the northern waste of the world.
Our season's course is gray. It is no place
For leisured living. There is neither wine nor oil.
Most of the country lies in fens and forests,
Savage, inhospitable. Above the lowlands
Shoot bare arms of the moors like land through waters.
Here a little life feeds on the stonecrop acres,
Made almost as savage by the wind and cold.
Our towns are walled with stone, guarding the imperial
Ways; our villas dark, closed to the damp air;
And we conduct hot flues of tile in the walls.
We sit shivering through the long winters. The poems
Of our fathers are without place in this land,
And the women strange fish of the northern seas.
When spring returns I weep for Sirmione,
And the sweet warm days in the wine of Gaul.
Then comes a grunting savage whose wit is alien,
And I must bend to his state our high Roman laws.

Brother, if you may pass a good word to the
Favorite of Caesar in his turn through the Province,
Speak of my condition, call me from these shadows.
I have lost enough years holding moorland roads
Over the desert of oak-darkened fens.
I fear that it will never turn to good.
We are building baths west of the central downs,
But never Rome in this sun-forsaken land.
Brother of my youth, let Gaius be enlarged.

I recall it was the Thames yacht scene at the start of Conrad's *Heart of Darkness*, where
Marlow, looking at the brooding shadow of London, says: "And this also has been one of
the dark places of the earth"—which touched off this poem, gathering (July 1950) a body
of European memories. *Beloit Poetry Journal* published it, early summer 1952; from
there the *New York Herald Tribune* took it up in "A Week of Verse," June 29, 1952.

GENERATION

After the picnic we stretch out on the blankets,
Old people resting while the children play.
They are climbing over rocks. We catch the voices,
Ripples of laughter, vanishing and high.
And we are no longer lying as we were,
But climbing over rocks in the bright air.

On the clear winter wind this laughter sounds:
"Look where I am, I have climbed, I am here;
See, I am standing on the highest stone."
We do not need to look, we are already there,
Heedless always of the times that are,
Breaking with time, being born again.

Leaves that fell to the ground return in the tree:
The old harvests are pressing at the limbs—
Fat buds waiting the fountain spring—so we,
Lying in the forest where we lose our names.
Children over rocks climb the topmost spur,
And our voice is the voices: "Look I am here."

This poem is dated February 1953, but I think it was sketched the Fall before. It seems
we had been taken by our friends, the Von Simsons, west of Chicago into the forest belt
to a picnic place with a pile of glacial stones.

Atlantic Monthly, October 1953; *New York Times*, January 31, 1954.

THE WHEEL

Life is a wave that moves by breaking.
Always at some point the tumult of motion
Forms the future. Behind is the broad peace
And undulation of exhausted water.
Through us now lies the charge, pointing the peril
Of self-conceiving thought, the aspiration,
The white churning of disordered foam.
It asks courage to endure—more than courage—
Daring to the high hope and fountain of manhood.
Always the summit breaking spends its power,
Dies in the wash and the wave advances.
Hardest to hold both: the vision at breaking,
And resignation of the promise broken—
It is knowing the bulk and bond of all ocean,
Crest and calm, the rounding of the wheel,
That it turns in beauty, and its ways are good.

After Indiana had accepted my book, I wrote a number of poems of thought (1951-52?) to strengthen the close of the volume.

American Weave, 1952

THE RIDER

And look, along the green bank of a stream,
Under the wind- and light-refracting trees,
A black horse is running through the sun and shade;
The rider bends forward, loose is the rein;
They go as one through random breaking waves
Of earth and air, light, molecules and leaves.

He is not guiding—only that now and then,
Watching his time, responsive to the need
(As through this network and determined chain
Of blind force we master, will intercedes),
He leans into the wind and twists the rein
Ever so slightly, relaxing it again.

See, he depends on the stable form of things
To hold the intervals entelechy leaves:
The beautiful beast along the winding stream,
The plummeting hooves, the dark flanks quivering—
Through whirls of earth and air, the gold and green,
Perceptive spirit rides with loosened rein.

Beloit Poetry Journal, 1953; Borestone Mountain Poetry Awards, 1954.

HERACLITUS IN THE WEST

"The way up and the way down is the same."

And the raying sun from behind breaks out east
Over the sea, opening a river of light
Into the dark of cloud and wind-tossed gray;
Against that drop, the unguessed wheeling gulls
Burn silver sparks of search, volitional fire.

Once we looked west over sea to the golden
Oblate and beckoning sun dropping without cloud
Behind the fired earth's verge; and the call was sunward,
Burning rooks and gulls of the dark eastern land,
Stirred wings west up rivers of light from the gray.

Here the great sun drops at our backs behind us;
The call has been followed to the last verge of land,
The light struck and the wave rebounds; into dark
We burn down rivers of fire, re-entering cloud,
Gulls to the gray-walled close by the eastern sea.

Sunlight before or behind are tides of one motion;
The way up and down currents of a single sea;
Beyond east or west rounds the gulf of one darkness;
And every flight of spirit burns rivers of fire,
Gulls to the landless drop of the wind-gray cloud.

I had been reading the pre-Socratic fragments in translation. As I looked east, April
1950, over what was in fact Lake Michigan, with gulls lighted by the evening sun, the
poem, based like an informal sestina on word repetition, delivered itself—as if one had
pioneered from Europe to America, then to the Pacific, to bounce back to our Atlantic,
facing toward Europe?!

New Poems #3 (Ballantine, 1953)

FLOWERING PEACH

This is the site, the viewpoint I remember:—
As far as you could see it was all woods,
That long fold in the mountains, unfelled timber.
But evening and dawn from the ledge renewed
Such light over Arkansas, the plain and river—
We bathed in light, the rock pool empty of water.

There was the remnant of a hand-heaped wall
Behind the camp, a fallen chimney of stone,
An old orchard, a peach tree never pruned,
Growing above the ruins of a dry well.
The lizard lay in the sun and ran rustling.
They said Jean le Caze lived here, who gave his name
Of Little Jean to this isolated range.

We went once overnight to the head of the bowl,
A mist-hung valley where a fall came down,
Hollowing a cold lake in the circling stone.
We camped out in the woods under the spray;
I swung a hammock from the trees and slept well,
Though listening at first for the voice of Jean le Caze.
He died here, and we heard haunted the place.

The Reign of Terror ruined him. He was one
Who believed in liberty, though nobly born,
A French aristocrat who fought for the dream
Of a free people, found himself betrayed
By the blind hardening of the many freed.
Imprisoned a time, he fled from France exiled,
To find a dying freedom in this wild.

Now warplanes cross from the Delta. The rock at the fall
Is mined for the flying metal; the forest is torn.
The whole bowl glints with houses; the people rule,
And loyalty is the law that all must learn.
The experience of freedom is a hard school.
Only the ridge remains. I walk away,
Back to the camp where I came as a boy.

Into the orchard ruin. The peach still leans
Above the fallen well. And spring has come.
The brave tree is a mass of sweet bloom.
Many great dreams we have had and will have,
And all unfulfilled; the circling year
Fails of its autumn; no fruit matures;
Yet every spring this beauty startles the air.

The perfume diffuses as the winds move.
Timeless work of limbs and net of leaves,
Enduring patience, flowering its first love,
Without hope of end or fruit or seed;
Dusk and dawn return and the world is changed,
But over the ruined wall and abandoned well,
Look, how this fruitless tree is blossoming still.

In my poetry notebook of 1953, I have, with an early typed carbon of this poem: "Flowering Peach," a letter from Ernst Levy (February 21, 1953) who we had met one evening at the house of Otto and Lulix Von Simson in Chicago. He had mentioned a peach tree, growing and flowering, but without fruit, in the garden of his house near Paris. I thought of such a tree by a ruin on Mount Petit Jean in the Arkansas Ozarks, where our YMCA had a camp; but it was only when Beethoven's great Opus 111 Piano Sonata was put on the gramophone that I wrote the poem. When I sent it to Levy, he answered me: "Your delightful poem to the beauty of 'useless blooming' really moved me. I imagine that the little peach tree of mine must have died the day you wrote the poem."

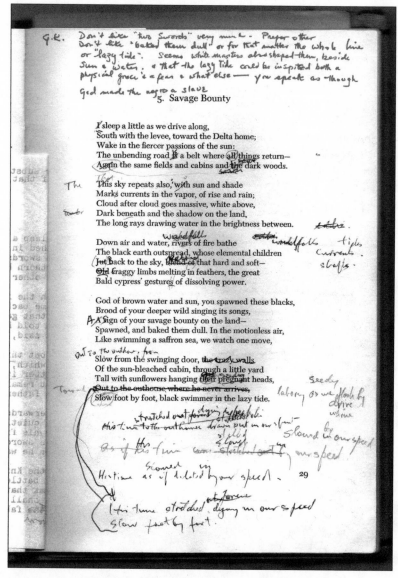

5. Savage Bounty

I sleep a little as we drive along,
South with the levee, toward the Delta home;
Wake in the fiercer passions of the sun:
The unbending road is a belt where all things return—
Again the same fields and cabins and the dark woods.

This sky repeats also, with sun and shade
Marks currents in the vapor, of rise and rain;
Cloud after cloud goes massive, white above,
Dark beneath and the shadow on the land,
The long rays drawing water in the brightness between.

Down air and water, rivers of fire bathe
The black earth outspread, whose elemental children
Jut back to the sky, blend of that hard and soft—
Old craggy limbs melting in feathers, the great
Bald cypress' gestures of dissolving power.

God of brown water and sun, you spawned these blacks,
Brood of your deeper wild singing its songs,
A Sign of your savage bounty on the land—
Spawned, and baked them dull. In the motionless air,
Like swimming a saffron sea, we watch one move,

Slow from the swinging door, the track walls
Of the sun-bleached cabin, through a little yard
Tall with sunflowers hanging their pregnant heads,
Out to the outhouse where he never arrives,
Slow foot by foot, black swimmer in the lazy tide.

29

DELTA RETURN

I will sing with the spirit, and I will sing with the understanding also.
I Corinthians 14: 15

TO DANNY
FROM THE JOURNEY OF RETURN (1953)

Absence wakes memory; I remember times:
Trees, rocks and caves, the bright small streams
In the woods of Wissahickon, those first days.
I mind how we lay once after a light snowfall,
Where the low sun of winter dreamed toward spring,
The distant purple softening the tips of trees;
And as the hemlocks thawed, showers of small
Crystal flashed in the air like bells, and from
The earth and sky that warmth and peace rose in us.

Lovers there are who strike like birds of prey
To catch at the melting pleasure; be it so.
But we will lie at our ease and wait the good
That wells for us like water, comes and goes,
Blesses or passes by—in either case
We smiling; not that earth's sweet is not worth running
For, but running spoils the sweetness. Remembered
Smiling eyes, slow, slow, now gently close.
What is so good as sleep in the arms we love?

FOREWORD

> As I lay and lenéd and lokéd in the water . . .
> Langland, *Piers Ploughman*

These poems arose from a trip I made in June of 1953 to visit my mother in my hometown of Greenville, Mississippi. I had sent off my first book, in which the title poem, "Songs for a New America," celebrated the tragic daring of the flight west. Here that Promethean theme yields to the water-death and ebbing of the motion south and home. Though, as with other underworld journeys, what is sought is not death simply, but some ambivalent, regenerative sign. As Rilke says of the endlessly dead: "They would be pointing to the catkins . . . or to the rain that falls on the dark earth in the spring of the year."

I began scribbling as soon as the bus left Chicago, and I went on through the days in the Delta floodplain of the Mississippi and the Yazoo, a landscape made by water and still, it seems, half floating; I kept it up on the Rebel bus over Alabama and Georgia and north to Maryland, where I rejoined my family at Little Pines Farm. It was my custom then to write the first draft of a poem as fast as my pen would move, and afterwards to pore over it until I had discovered its implicit form. But whenever I took up those sketches in the hope of doing that, I was caught by a new idea. This continued in Maryland and on the train ride back to Chicago.

Some days after we were settled again on Woodlawn Avenue, I opened the frustrating bundle to a barely legible page about our old servant, Lethe, and saw that what had been written as prose fell into pentameter, and that five lines revealed themselves in each of five stanzas. Now I studied the other jottings, and found that every one bore in latency the same shape; moreover, when they were arranged in the order of the journey, that first dictation formed also five groups of five poems, thus:

I: The Road South: 1. Leaving Chicago, 2. Over the Wide Ohio, 3. The Hills, 4. Gulf Memories, 5. Among Ruins;

II: This Low Delta: 1. As a Stream Flows Home, 2. Air- view, 3. Liquidation Sale, 4. Savage Bounty, 5. The Tower;

III: The Queen City: 1. The Local Whiteway, 2. Known All Over the World, 3. The Oaks, 4. The Columns, 5. Lethe;

IV: The River: 1. Of Water Come to Water, 2. The Flood (i.e., The Break), 3. Cotton, 4. Baptism, 5. The Gar;

V: The Dead: 1. The Memorial, 2. The Fig Tree, 3. The Beacon, 4. Moundbuilders, 5. Homeward Arms.

Starting with five feet to the line, it was an array of five to the fifth power.

For a year I resisted altering that. But my university editor, Sam Yellen, would not call twenty-five poems a book, and I would not make them part of another random collection. During the fall of 1954 I began to write poems consciously in the form unconsciously given. By the next spring, teaching, and writing mostly after midnight, I had completed a triangle or Delta, of such five-by-fives—more sensory and meaningful, with a middle section like a dialectical pillar for the whole. So the University of Indiana Press published it in 1956.

In the fifteen years that have passed since that edition, I have variously set myself to revise the book—especially for Norman Berg's 1956 edition and for the present *Collected Poems*. The modern way to clean things up is of course by excision, and no doubt a free verse poem could be calcined from this more formal discourse; but how could I violate the symbolic homecoming, or its original, multiple five-fold form? Has it not been suggested that sliding pentagons are the clue to the liquid state, to water, which is also the well of life?

Santa Fe, N.M.
June 1968

I. THE JOURNEY DOWN

Behold now the hope and desire of returning to one's own country or to
primal chaos—like the longing of the moth for the flame . . .
Leonardo da Vinci, Notebooks

A. THE ROAD SOUTH

And in the dusky twilight where I moved, burned
The shadowed woods and the yearning brooks of home.
Hölderlin, Patmos

1. LEAVING CHICAGO

The pole star is high; the others circling
Sweep the cold lake. Dawn spreads across that sky.
The bus heads south from the city of towers.
Wind in the elms quickens the fine lace of spring.
Cars go north where the center wakes into day.

The other motion is ours. It has been long
Since a boy came to master that Fair of a World,
The Hall of Science, the Temple of the Arts—
An age of mastering, while the friends at home
Slept at the sun's hearth like peaceful dogs.

South, south by water, heat shimmers on bar sand;
Lazy the land rustling in the bees' drone . . .
To climb is self-possession; to go down
Yields to the homing tide. North, I said,
Is human hope and daring; and so I found.

They say the ice age stirred us to be men;
And I have seen this city when breaking waves
Stretched into crystal on the steel-gray wind;
And I have been one of the muffled faces, leaned
To the blast for the wind-driven prizes.

World-promise melts like cloud when evening brings
Again the low music of the slackened string.
Deeper than the will and before the will was born,
This hunger for night and void where I return
And soft surrender to their welcoming arms.

2. THE HISTORICAL MOTION

We learn it is no longer time and space
But space-time in one motion; so we plumb
The tensile field where years change with place-
Toward past or future, who knows?—time is round:
Backwardness is the shape of things to come.

In the last light, hills gully and go bare;
Scrub growth fills the bottoms, a world of scrub,
Human and vegetable. We put off the robe
Of day, the ordered rule, strip to failure,
Sure homecoming that is always ours.

Like a remembered omen that frame shack
Undermined by the caving clay, a woman
Barefoot at the weathered rail. It is southern
Illinois, and already shadows trace
Round columns on the hill . . . We seek the deeper

Layer, catacombs of the fall, a face
Where eyes widen to mystery as the flesh
Decays-not memory only, not this crop
Of sighs, this homeward visit of four days
In the sweep of north and west, and even that home

Caught in the forward rush . . . Wait: time is round;
Return is now. What water-rich birth and passive
Way opens through these tattered hills?
Like lovesick brooks of the homeland we go down,
Seeking what past or to come, what gulf, what sky?

3. CROSSING THE OHIO

At the day's end of dwindling towns and farms
We are still in Illinois, but as sunset fades
We creep on the trestle over the wide Ohio.
The glacial lakes are behind; down this stream
My grandfather took a proud wife to a Delta home.

If the South is always in my blood, it is not
A life-force only, something as well of the old
Miasma bred in her swamps. Return home.
Full-leafed branches merge on the darkening sky;
We stop in Paducah, Kentucky, first of the South.

Under magnolia trees two waiting rooms,
The black and white, warn of the lingering plague.
Long ago when yellow fever struck in June,
Those grandparents with my father fled past here,
Seeking safety. Where now shall we flee?

The wrecks of southern summers rock, lolled
On the porches still. In the white restaurant
I eat, and the bus is called. We roar to the South.
Quieted by the night, protest dissolves.
Sleep sings the remembered beauty daylight mars:—

Walking through the heavy dusk of colored town,
Past porches of honeysuckle, the swooning smell,
And rich as song those throaty waves of laughter,
Rain-forest rivers fluted under the moon,
Where we paused listening-Listen, drink, be drowned.

4. REDBUD

No country is drabber than ours and none more glancing
With willful beauty; of both, love is the solvent.
As we rode south one spring, clouds thickened;
Under the dark of fog, trees in tassel
Lost in the gray the flush of leaves advancing.

The whole Delta was a dripping March-cold blanket.
Vague in the dimness we sensed the spring was wasting;
Then the darkest day of all, the vaulted closure
Broke in mother-of-pearl, at whose center—
Was it the source of that word and open sesame

Of welcome summer?—on a leafing limb,
Scarlet as flame a cardinal was singing:
"Bright world, bright world, bright world"; and all the others,
Mocking bird, thrasher, and the blue jays flocking,
Waked into voice and color; and under racing

Clouds in sudden sun, the great flowering
Judas tree, not in the branches only, but
Down the foot-broad bole, erupting wanton-
ness, gushes with bloom, as honey oozes
From the honey comb; and bees hum

In the petalled haze; and high above, bridging
Smooth limb-to-limb of the crape myrtle grove,
Wisteria hangs like grapes, where a jet-black squirrel,
Through lavender clusters, on the azure swing
Of the sky, leaps, leaps to the redbird's song.

5. THE ROAD UNTAKEN

In the dark at Memphis we cross the Frisco line,
The road that was not taken. When first ambition
Stirred in the blood and manhood of my father—
Fat smooth faces from cigar boxes and razors:
"Make friends and influence people," the time's calling—

He dreamed one night of the West, booming surf
On hills of the great endeavor, sunset peaks;
Woke in the dawn of vision, as men will,
When the future comes to the hand like a tame bird
That sits and sings—the wish almost fulfilled.

He planned in a moment, got up, packed his things—
Then walked outside the promise, as when walls
Of the room return, the mere habitual.
He stayed in the broken South; before long,
He met my mother, and they grew to the known.

Strange this taking root in the here and now:
The present leafs out in the unperformed
Like destiny in freedom. I have thought sometimes
How changed all this would have been, had the low floor
My childhood sings me been that plunging shore,

And he, his southern failures turned to western
Gold. Fool's gold. Time is unalterable.
I am only I, chance child of the actual;
And what might have been is a measureless field,
Where self, lost to the self, goes blind, unreal.

B. NATIVE STATE

The Earth spread forth her table wide; the Night a silver cup
Fill'd with the wine of anguish, waited at the golden feast.
Blake, "Valla"

1. THE HILLS

A night in Memphis, then the last stand of the hills;
They veer off east and south with the curved Yazoo,
Return at Vicksburg, closing the Delta bowl—
Red bluffs and gullied slopes, a leached-out soil
Of meager farms and men, hill-billy towns.

When we went to Baldwyn my cousins were stringy and long,
Not able to match me wrestling; they could not swim,
Knowing no water but in shallow streams,
Chest-deep under the clay bank at the bend,
Where they would splash and blow and marvel at one

Who came from lakes and blue-holes, child
Of a more opulent nature, floating its tides;
Though their upland sky arched clearer stars.
Such, one bonus of that hill terrain,
Sloping north to Shiloh's outcrops stone.

There is no simple motion. Up or down
Are ways of loving, each going a return:
In the flood we sought the refuge of this ground;
And what our Delta is I have not learned,
But the fluctuant earth we own and do not own.

Post-war stoic hills were my mother's home.
Right her inwardness should have its source,
Deep and smiling, a well of timelessness
(Still the angel's "Ave" in these gullies)-
To flow as I flow, down the time-wreathed valleys.

2. GULF MEMORIES

Yes, in clay hills, 1882, my mother was born,
Like a spring to flow through the Delta south to the sea.
I remember a summer in Gulfport after the flood.
It was when I had learned that stars are other worlds.
I would climb a tall pine by the house and gaze into space.

One night I looked down and saw her standing below
At the trellis window, and she was gazing too
At the same stars. She had no need of climbing,
Or even to ask what kinds of worlds those were;
Enough for her that they and all we see

And we ourselves spring deeper, strangely grow
From that same ground. I climbed and reached, she stood;
It was mother and son. The fountain holds all things
For which it longs. So I saw her from my tree
At the honeysuckle window beside the sea.

I remember too those walks along the shore
On the long spits of sand when the tide was low
And slow evening dissolved its cloud, its dream;
I see her still, poised on the last point of land,
My brother and sister playing about her, small—

She tall and gowned, like a woman of the Greek islands,
Looking south to the darkening sky and water . . .
Spirit of that quiet-pool born in the hills-
Holding the mountains and sky and rooted in the sea,
You rest a while in this Delta, wait to be one with these.

3. THE SKELETON

That summer on the Gulf in a live-oak park
We met a man whose hair and beard hung white
On shoulders shrunk in their Confederate coat;
He told of Lookout Mountain and Shiloh wood,
And sang us Rebel songs, hate's mummy food.

(In the park by the water a fabric of bones
Sprawled, the relics of a storm-beached whale,
Where we would play, crouching between the jaws,
Or crawling in the roofed cave of the brain,
Dry defiles that had rushed with life and blood.)

To the trial of the Wilderness quaint honor came,
Bullets whistling in the wood, crunching the trees;
Then the charge of gray-coats; men dropped like flies . . .
(Mosquitoes, I remember, as he spoke,
Settled in swarms from the coastal swamp,

And buzzed in his white beard and round the face
Of the lamplike hollow eyes.) In the lazar house
He lay in the fever of wounds—smell of the dead
And dying flesh—and on such insect clouds,
The yellow fever came, and men died and died.

Soldier, you were too earnest in your talk,
And I too old to have asked you, like a child
Talk had ravished to your war-death world,
The question you thought mocking: "Did you die?"
You turned and limped off, snorting in your beard.

4. SPIRIT OF THE NORTH

My father was the spirit of the North—
His blood, come down with the river, sought return:
Vacations it was cities, war-fields, the coast of Maine.
On his wedding trip he chased the midnight sun;
The trophy was a seal-fur stole he gave my mother;

It hung in the cedar closet unworn; we children
In the scented dark would rub our cheeks across it.
And before we were born he had gone with her abroad.
Recounting that time, through Sunday dinners
Of a long life and in the heat of our summers,

He would dwell most fondly on a moment told
As if we had shared it with him: how with a guide,
Climbing from Zermatt, one August season,
Over the Gorner glacier, he had found in green
Ice, a melted punchbowl of clear water.

They were hot and tired with climbing; he had bent
And plunged his face and drunk the eternal cold.
While he was speaking our fan would groan as it swung,
Raying a feeble beam across the room;
The ceiling fan was ambling its lazy round;

Sweat oozed from our faces, as down the table passed
The silver pitcher brimmed with water and ice,
Its surface beaded with a cold dew. We would fill
Our glasses and, with throats strangely dry, drink
From the glacial bowl, the father-well of force.

5. AMONG RUINS

South, where the hills return, we had our great
Plantation—an old world without profit of age:
Gray moss hung from the trees, roads were deep rutted,
Black helpers kind but shiftless, the old house a ruin,
Vine-grown reminder of what they still called the War.

It was not a land to make money of or acquire
For any cause but madness, those myths of the past
That renewed planters in the South's cotton waste,
And roused young men who were doing well in practice
To the more destructive dream of public office.

My father in the governor's race went down in those
Same hills; Bilbo was theirs, who later died
(Well-chosen scourge) of cancer of the mouth.
We heard a speech he made once in full dress.
"You folks think I'm getting rich in Jackson," he said;

"But I tell you, I'm so poor," (histing his tails)
"I have to patch my pants." He spun his rump:
In the new cloth were patches of bright red.
The crowd roared, and one spat, shifting a quid:
"That's a slick bastard; I'm going to vote for him."

Blind republic, torn by these pampered hounds,
Till the best withdraw in the cyclic change
That hardened Greece to Rome—you floundering on
In a world of desperate need; this I learned
Under broken columns—strange to live young, and in ruins.

C. THIS LOW DELTA

A gulf profound as that Serbonian bog
Betwixt Damiata and Mount Casius of old,
Where armies whole have sunk . . .
Milton, *Paradise Lost*

1. AS A STREAM FLOWS HOME

Down the last hill . . . The road lies white and long
Over the marsh-streaked, cypress-bearing plain,
Cabin-dotted, brushed with remnant woods,
Melting always to a wave of green
At the flat horizon—a strange place to be born.

I remember once from the settled beauty of Princeton
I came south in late winter, and snow fell.
The next day thunderstorms and a steaming rain,
And everything was water, turgid and brown,
Creeping from bayous into garbage-littered yards.

I went back east and was telling of it all,
All the compelling horror: in flooded fields,
Cabins leaning, propped with poles, a thin
Smoke from the chimney, rooster on the ridgepole,
Shingles roughed like river-splintered board,

And still the lean hound baying at the door;
When a compatriot, teaching with me there,
Spoke, to the laughter of those northerners:

"What are we doing in this God-forsaken hole;
Why don't we go back South where we belong?"

Recurrent urge of the tide-abandoned blood
For the fluid gulfs and shiftings; I have come
Over and over again, and still I go down
To this low basin as a stream flows home,
Its night of birth and ending, and to the sea's arms.

2. AIR-VIEW

I have also come by air and seen the signs
That every landscape wears of its origin.
Water has sealed this with a double curve:
Down the midst the mile-wide flood turns and reverses,
Flings off on either side new lakes of green;

Beyond and older, flanked with cypress, the beautiful
Blue lakes bend, where settlers steamed through chutes
Of muscadine to flood-raised shores and built
Slave homes; and farther, older still, I trace,
Filled lakes, now swamps, in inter-curving bands,

Or loops of darker wood, all swirling, emblem
Of the change, where earth flows with water,
Here outward, from the river; its lakes are wells
For bayous that wander east and south to the hills,
Then back with the brown Yazoo to the river again;

And these in the same image put off little whorls,
Brush marks of water, arcs of swampy wood;
I have seen the whole Delta-built by yearly floods
Before the Irish with barrows or Southern lords
To give them orders heaped the long earth mounds

That divided the elements, fixed land and sea,
A firmament in the waters-patterned still
On the spiral shapes of melting, infinite seal
Of home-returning time on the transient floor,
Under star-cloud night, first matrix of that swirl.

3. TUTWILY

The beginning is motion, a stream with somewhere to run;
Then the current spreads and meanders, backs into bogs,
Doldrums of the quest. From the bus window
I glimpse at a dirt side-road, as we drive past,
The specter of a sign: "Tutwiler, ten miles."

A childhood ride comes to me, dim recall,
Without beginning or end, in those slow days
When roads were dust or mud, and—why, God knows—
Going somewhere, Tutwiler lay on our course.
We asked an old Negro the direction, being lost.

"You go up here a middlin piece and you come
To a fork in the road; you bear left. A little bit more
And you turn right over a bridge. Now that road
You hold to. It winds here and it winds there,
But you hold to it; it'll take you to Tutwily sure."

After an hour we stopped and asked afresh:
"Tutwily? O Lord, it's a fur piece to Tutwily.
No sir, boss, I don't know; I never been there.
But you on the wrong road. You got to turn back
And ride 'twell you come to a bridge at a fork . . ."

At the bottom of that wandering I see a log-road
Through a swamp of gums, over water, under rain,
The logs bumping and sloshing, the old man's refrain
In our ears: "O Lord, it's a fur piece to Tutwily."
Wherever Tutwily was—place I've never been.

4. LIQUIDATION SALE

From the fields and far woods moving as we move
We come to a little town with its cotton gin,
Beulah or Boyle—no matter, each the same,
As weird as familiar. How many hours
Have I sat in an oven car by those clapboard stores?

That was in the Depression, a time between
The flood and dust, the earth and people drained;
I would drive my father then, from town to town,
Wait, while he talked, encouraged, farmed the claims.
He was known to all and honored as the Judge.

Well, he deserved some honor. He saved their skins
Often when city firms would have had them sued,
Eased them along to his peril, gave up his fees,
Himself the most in debt, and the life-dream torn
By politicians and a failing farm,

Private loss and Hitler—our world betrayal.
At night I have seen him when he could not sleep
Sit up in bed to light his pipe, the weak
Flame rising and falling like the pulse of his hope,
Revealing a face whose lines make me weep.

So I live it all again in the sun-baked towns,
The scourge of bitterness which must return,
As rust from these tin awnings, painted now,
Where, like a token, the great "Liquidation Sale"
Blossoms in red on Solomon's old store.

Commentary, 1955

5. SAVAGE BOUNTY

I sleep a little as we drive along,
South with the levee, toward the Delta home;
Wake in the fiercer passions of the sun:
The unbending road is a belt where things return—
The same fields and cabins and the dark woods.

This sky repeats also: sun and shade
Mark currents in the vapor, of rise and rain;
Cloud after cloud goes massive, white above,
Dark beneath and the shadow on the land,
The long rays drawing water in the brightness between.

Down air and water, shafts of fire bathe
The black earth outspread, whose elemental children
Jut back to the sky, blend of that hard and soft—
Old craggy limbs melting in feathers, the great
.Bald cypress' gestures of dissolving power.

God of brown water and sun, you spawned these Blacks,
Brood of your deeper wild, singing its songs,
Sign of your savage bounty, on the land-
Spawned, and baked them dull. In the motionless air,
Like swimming a saffron sea, we watch one move,

Out to the outhouse from the swinging door
Of his sun-bleached cabin, through a little yard
Tall with sunflowers hanging seedy heads-
His time stretched out, dying in our speed-
Slow foot by foot, black swimmer in the lazy tide.

D. THE QUEEN CITY

... my most kindly nurse,
That to me gave this life's first native source
Spenser, *Prothalamion*

1. THE TOWER

We near the town; first of all I see the tower
That brought the electric lines from Arkansas.
We had climbed trees and hung ropes for the plunge,
One best of all at a blue-hole, where we would swing
And drop to the smooth water like a stone.

The courthouse was next; we had no peace
Until we had scaled the roof and spire and pole;
But the three-hundred-foot tower was a challenge still.
The pillars were sheer cement; we cut a tree,
Propped it in the mud and worked to the steel.

There the ladders began; I say we climbed
Until our earth was round and its air thin
To reach a platform shaken by the wind.
Current hummed in the wires, incredible power
Of the fire-liquid spilling across the stream.

And we were there at the copper veins of that blood.
It was not heart leapt only; I climbed the last rail,
Hung by my knees over reeling earth and air,
Daring the comrades, who would not take that dare
From a fool whose eyes loved danger like a girl.

The river coiled beneath its triple coil.
The flat land breeds a hunger for such heights;
And what is climbing and the work to climb
But a moment of vision, at the last verge
Of the wide water, dreaming of the flight down?

2. THE LOCAL WHITE WAY

In such a great flat land it is all sky;
The earth is waiting here with a slow patience
Under the rain-gathering vault; at night it dissolves,
A mere darkness hid in the universe,
And nowhere else is being earth-bound stranger.

One night long since, returned from overseas
To this bottom of the world, knowing the heart
Could not rest wholly here, no longer free
From the domes and spires of Oxford through the cloud
Taking an aureole light in the meadowed land;

Or upland wheat fields of Bavaria,
Clean stands of fir under mountain snow;
Or down those mountains south to heart's best home,
Nest of the migrant wings, the Tuscan town
And singing towers of the Western dawn—

Remembering now that beauty, spirit in form,
Clear voice of the past, never to be lived down,
As I, come back that evening, stood alone
Over this landing, on the levee's crown—
West the wide river, Venus, and the moon,

And east three lighted blocks in the Delta's dark—
I felt the strangeness of being localized:
By an accident of birth to be held and to hold
This poor spot of earth on the turbulent flood
A center always of the wheeling stars.

3. KNOWN ALL OVER THE WORLD

"Queen City of the Delta"—we slow through shaded ways.
It was here at this corner, when I was a boy,
I saw an old man sitting under that oak tree
A white-bearded black man who went the rounds
Begging, or working, if work was required.

"Howdy, Uncle!" I said, and he: "Whose boy are you?"
"My father's Judge Bell," I told him. He raised his hands:
"Judge Percy Bell, known all over the world!"
When I reached home I found my father there.
It was the climax of his life, that election time;

We had him little then, for always he traveled
In the proud trust that sent him to the masses
With his vision and reliance on their voices.
Now it was over. He was shaving; his face was lathered.
I stood at the mirrored door of the bath; and mother

Came from the telephone bringing the latest
Returns. He had that tragic flush of power
Before our youth is broken. His half-broke then:
His voice was shaken, hearing what pious little
Good effort had garnered. And I a schoolboy, thought,

Though not with the words of thinking: What else
But failure comes of a temporal undertaking?
At best an old man with eyes to the sky: "Known
All over the world." What worlds to conquer. No cause
To end the search, only the heart's aching.

4. THE OAKS

Water oaks of the house, on buttressed stems,
In winter green, and tender in spring with tassels,
You have grown; swifter than elsewhere are
Our trees. The cypress god of colored town—
Twenty arm-span we measured him—is gone.

But in Greenway Park, once forest, houses now
In the broken grove, a great swamp Spanish oak
Is lord of the east and south; there I go,
By the black funnel of trunk, and under the high
Prehistoric branches worship with head raised.

Yet even here are marks of a greater power.
The upper limbs are shattered and re-formed;
And the gnarled white arms of the basket oaks
Bear the same signs. Well I recall that day,
And lived it afterward in marvelous dreams.

Though there was pity in walking the wood when half
The trunks were down, roots in the air, with all
That circuit ground; in a gum, their splintered home,
Small flying squirrels were leaping everywhere,
Recklessly; for life laughs at destruction.

And during the storm, climbing our own tall trees,
As ever for the wind's ride, I had felt them swayed
And looked off south, where down a cumulous sky
That dark dissolving funnel cut through the wood-
The greater god, to rule and be ruled in my dreams.

5. THE COLUMNS

Through trees now gleam white columns; the old South
Beguiled itself in that façade of Greece—
Vision, as always, shadowed by its harm—
These doubly so, built when the First War boom
Launched a lawyer who intended justice and peace.

They were his gesture of Enlightened faith
In a world of human good; their classic form
Clothes the romantic heart; they are Faustian towers,
Crumbling of their own weight, like Beauvais spire,
Flutings of freedom, cloud pillars of our science.

No human condition is more set for sorrow
Than that which asks embodiments to mirror
The hopes of spirit; it was the way of my father.
His failed; and when he died (hard broken death
Of one who dreamed too fondly), I myself

Began to tear pilasters, like limbs of me,
From his library and mine, an apartment now,
Where people come and go; for the great house
Shelters my mother with a tenant crew
Who pay for the blunders of that tragic man.

Promethean father, child of the westward pride,
You beckon from these columns, white on red
Behind the green oak shadows—you whose end
Was bitterness, beckon and smile. And I climb the wide
Porch stairs under a roof tall and blue like the sky.

E. FABLES OF HOME

> The days gone by
> Come back upon me from the dawn almost
> Of life. . . .
> Wordsworth, *The Prelude*

THE CIRCUS

Where all those houses are was a wide field
Filled with goldenrod; across the canal
The canebrake began and stretched to the wood,
Dark reaches of swamp oak; and every fall
The circus came and set up in that field.

The train arrived by night; we heard the whistles;
At first dawn we could see the painted carts
Rumbling along the street in front of our house,
Swaying elephants, cage-pacing lions,
And curtained vans with the still sleeping stars.

In a little while a tent with many flags,
Rose, like a cloud city, in that field;
And our sidewalk was lined with Negro stands:
Fried chicken and biscuits, cold drinks, cakes and pies.
Then the leaping life of acrobats and clowns.

Lion-tamers with curled whips, moustached and proud,
Beautiful ladies on horseback, in diamond gowns;
So on into dark with music, lights, and crowds.
It was a concentration of all the fire
Down roads of time, the pageantry of man;

And then in the hush again the rumbling wheels,
Rattle of hooves and swish of elephants,
Dim in departing night, and with the dawn,
The empty field, the trampled goldenrod,
And a boy standing alone as dusk returned.

2. THE HOUSE PAINTER

He does not know me now, that old deaf man—
With face like Einstein—stumbling in a daze;
Yet I was formed by him: Past twelve I was
A hunter. When spring grackles came, settling
In all the trees, with a rustle of iridescent

Wings, I dreamed of a bead on a distant shape,
The rifle's crack, black feathers falling limp.
One day I shot two dozen, heaping a pile
On the back porch table by the mackerel pail.
That old deaf German was painting for us then.

As I came in carrying a couple of birds,
He was standing at the table stroking the dead,
Lifting the purple wings and letting them fall,
Saying over and over in his hollow voice:
"Poor things, poor things." I slipped out of the house.

Sentimental fool!—But the pie I planned
Was never baked; I buried the grackles in mud.
If we relive the race, our changes come
No less by revolution; to drown his womanish
Words, I ranged in anger through the woods.

The mother thrasher in a thorn was laying eggs;
I shot into the nest and tore her wide.
As I lifted up those quivering brown dregs,
The old man's spirit caught me in its clutch
Of pain. I did not play with death again.

3. THE SAILS

We slept on a high screen porch among night and stars.
All winter long, the rare snows that fell
Would sift fine flakes across the eider down;
Summer, trees were rustling dense with leaves
In the close-scented dark where cicadas jarred.

We lived in that world; there was no choice
What frames the mind would take; taken by force
It flowed in and out on waves of dark
Or merging glints of the moon. It was life in all,
Romantic meeting fashion could not change.

I recall one August how we drove home late,
Drowsy with warm lake water, went to bed,
Fireflies lighting, bats gliding, last swallows in the air.
Midnight we waked, oaks wrenched and torn—
My father calling: "Pull up the tarpaulins, son."

We pulled each on a side; the canvas rose,
Bellied in the wind, cracked; we lashed it tight.
On to the next, then the last. In bed again,
Wrapped in a crazy quilt for the sudden cool,
I heard first thunder, felt a mist of rain,

Smelled how foliage and earth received the damp
Under blaze of lightning. So sleep returned.
And always in my ear like an ocean charm:
The flap of wind in canvas, yawing sails—
Where to, mariner, in so deep a storm?

4. BROTHER

A shade haunts the house, of the father's name
And proud disquiet, the mother's tenderness,
Self-tormented blend: "Sweetest the fruit
The worm feeds on, the soul preyed on by woe"—
Blake wrote it, brother, and you proved it true.

Gladdest born and saddest grown, you took too soon
The vicarious burden of earth's wrong—too gentle
For that weight that falls, falls, like a stone.
When I was swimming the river and climbing trees,
You, younger, painted and wrote grieved mysteries.

You were a poet when I studied science,
And spoke the free-verse voice of modern pain,
The broken person, heightening to that harm
By which we lost you and you lost the spring.
Had I been what I am, could my being

Have eased your trial, and both now be singing?
Or is that battle always fought alone?
At your death I was abroad; I crossed
The ocean to a sad home. A grief unhouseled,
As from beyond the tomb, settled upon me.

I found myself, odd times, sketching figures
For poetic lines: "Bound on a wheel,
Of fire . . . tears like molten lead . . . ." So I
Received your spirit. Brother of my blood,
You haunt not this house only, world-wounded shade.

5. LETHE

Having seen my mother and aunt, I go the first day
To visit Lethe, named for the dark stream
Of forgetful water. Of all those who slaved
For our childhood, only she remains, the oldest,
Born a slave, now nearing a hundred years.

The roof is rotten, the porch has fallen in.
She does not answer. Mother has feared for her,
Not having come for the weekly gift of food.
The neighbor says she is working—incredible!
We leave our presents there and drive away.

After sunset, in another part of town,
She rings the bell, having heard Misser Charles has come.
I open the door. She gathers me in her old arms.
Ah, Lethe, Lethe, dearly we have loved
This dark devotion daylight conquers now.

She is thinner every season; I count the bones.
Her shoulders are bent, but the lined smile is the same.
"Lawd, Misser Charles, how long you gonna stay?"
We are passing semblances in space and time;
I could ask her the same, but I answer, four days.

After a few minutes she questions me again:
"Lawd, Lawd, Misser Charles, how long . . . ?" She has drunk
Of her own oblivion-melting stream—you too
Are my homecoming. Come—I will walk her home.
We go out together into the great sky under the stars.

II. DIALOGUES OF THE MIND

Be it life or death we seek only reality.
Thoreau, *Walden*

A. DIALECTIC OF LOVE

Love that is seed in you of every good
And of every action which merits blame.
Dante, *Purgatory* XVII

1. TWO LOVES THERE ARE

Home to the bed of youth and manhood's returns,
By the river of my birth, passions and times
Come back upon me, dreams subdued and worn
To the solemnities of paradigm:
The poles of being interpenetrate and breed

As man breeds on woman; all things reveal
The mingled essence: night wears a starry braid
Of broken day cut out in little beads
By which her beauty goes more darkly veiled;
And day by the grace of shadow rescues form

From vacancies of light, recurrent waves
Of breath and passing, man, mother, shape and void.
Two loves have called us, alter and return
In age as in childhood, rich with shade or stars,
And yet themselves, not merging, dark and fair.

Your name I think was Angela. It is long past
A schoolboy brought your books and loved the face
Of the frank smile, gray eyes and gentleness,
Soft light hair, wide forehead, widow's peak,
To be treasured again and again under many names.

Then the night hayride by the river, star-
Strewn fall, when the nameless dark newcomer
Whose breasts grew sharp, whose lips and eyes were lures
Of the tropic sea, shook down ship-launching hair,
Currents of black night in which hearts drown.

2. OF COMFORT

From that Icarian plunge you sheltered me,
Form-building and benign, second love of day,
Mary, so much ideal I had no power
To touch or handle, though the perilous fire
Yet will mount in our serenity.

Sunlight falls down terracings of lawn
Above the luminous waves of Austramere;
Wings of colonial brickwork close the yard
With shadowed red; tall windows, on the green
Of live oaks and magnolias, an orchard beyond,

And then perspectives of a grove of pecans.
Grown-ups on the terrace drink muscadine wine.
Your father is speaking, his face half-raised,
Poised in the light as a hummingbird sips sun:
"Where shall we go," he says, "shapes of the dream?

Let us retire gently from the world."
We came with a burst of laughter from the lakeshore,
Where cypress, out of a labyrinth of knees,
Plumed the evening, and you, Mary, full of grace,
Stepped forward with our string of speckled perch.

He turned slowly with mild distant eyes.
What years, tossed on the torrent of our days,
Have we kept this scene of twilight gentleness—
Though he, its center, from the silver age we culled,
Sought what other gardens, in what mist of gold?

3. AND DESPAIR

For what comes after, chide those shapes of air,
Leafwork too lightly buttressed against fire;
That love of light and Apollonian calm—
The waking vision over depths we are—
Stirred worse hunger as unfleshed, half-real.

June, when the mockingbird sang in the dusk,
And locusts and frogs were loud, through head-tall weeds
I would walk to the river, when summer stars
Clustered the vines of night, and crooning sounds
From shanty porches and the jasmine smell

Leaned like breasts against me:—I could have cursed
This northern heart and reformation blood
That hold us from such yielding, and would have sold
All birthright of the day for a mess of dark:
"Melisande, Melisande, laisse tomber tes cheveux noirs."

You combed your raven hair by the river of waters,
Your eyes so with grief; you had always known another,
And lonely from those arms invoked desire
To ride the winds of hell, recurrent love;
Four times I took you by four shapes and names:

At New Orleans where the long river slows; by Thames
As war-dusk knit on the world; over cypressed Arno
Drinking the wine-cup of love; and dark Iseult,
I brought you home at last to this brown stream,
Where we engendered on each other's pain.

4. LIGHT AGAPÉ

Now the nightmare has passed; I have thrown my heart
In enough whirls of drowning, and all the stars
Have burned to ashes in the phantom hair.
Polarities in mingling generate
Each on the other the new embodied birth.

So I sing islands in the wasting flood,
Fixed and moving, of which earth is one.
Whelmed in the jet waves, I felt firm sand
Rise to my feet, and there your blessed shore
Of fair daylight lay in the beauty of pearl,

The discrete dews on the leaves, water charmed
To feed and nourish; and frank eyes revive,
Admired Miranda, girls of the good reign.
We ruled over halcyon seas and soft mist fell
And washed the smoke of burning and eased the wounds,

And in your island I have set my heart,
And here we grow together like tree and vine.
Let us walk by the river, love. Even in this
Night land, of rising waters, we rear homes,
And only on that sureness—validation

By antithesis—I brave the songs
Of death and void to which loved-forms return;
At the house-hearth feed Heraclitean fire:
"Whoever would sound the peace eternal
Must tune his harp in the war of its fibers."

5. DARK CARITAS

For love is the fable only and myth of wings
To plume the nameless wish and name it with names,
And from love to love we span on arcs of quest
The prolific void where pole and pole enlaced
Like mating birds creating beauty clasp.

So all things grow from love and by love's stair
Descend or climb, and as their space is curved,
Again and again meet and cleave, dying and born.
The living world transcends itself, evolves:
It is from the heart of dark that light flows.

One evening far from home and that last Iseult,
I walked volcanic hills over Baia's Bay-
Nisida, Ischia, Procida, Greek islands in the sea,
Land-roads over sunset water—and under trees
Watched lovers stroll, and small bats in the air.

I thought of the lost image and deathlessness of love,
And so returned to Naples, in the dusk, alone,
Dreaming of the face of night and our blond brood,
To stand at a restaurant window weighing scant funds,
Where a dark-haired girl was begging, lean, in rags.

Faces meet and mingle, hers was the dream;
And on her shoulder she carried a fair little child,
Blond out of dark, like any of my own.
I gave her what I had with the blessing of God,
Which is sometimes ours to give, by the power of love.

B. THE BOOK OF KNOWLEDGE

Still climbing after knowledge infinite.
Marlowe, *Tamburlaine*

The eternal silence of those infinite spaces frightens me.
Pascal, *Pensées*

1. THE PRISIM

Our house was full of books; there was one shelf
This age does not forbid, though it tempts like fruit:
The Book of Knowledge. When first the wine-ripe skin
Yielded to my touch, Newton was the man
Who stood at the darkened window, prism in hand,

Cleaving white light, which fell in rainbow glowing
On the facing wall. That thing I desired,
And wrote to Santa Claus, but Christmas morning
Found among toys and marbles no such glass;
Until my father, hearing the tearful case,

Took me down to our reception hall
By the arched door, where the rising winter sun
Struck through leaded windows' beveled panes,
Painting the walls with rainbows, often seen,
Though not considered. "All these colors," he said,

"Are spectra of such prisms." If they were dim
Against the colored print of Newton's room,
It was enough; I stood wordless in wonder
At the disguise of things: white or color?
If both, how much of truth is metaphor?

From red into violet the patterns played.
I was standing at the fall, where forms go down
In a bright veil of mist, and found myself
With all I called my own, of such endurance—
Appearance of the moment, mere appearance.

2. THE VOLCANO

It was the fall, the melancholy quickening,
Call to aspire and plan. Cold wind and rain.
I sat turning the book; the volcanic world
Opened like split fruit, where central fires
Broke through the crust, red lava, scoriae.

To counterfeit that force . . . The rain blew over.
In the tool shed were blocks of roofing tar
I took a spade, heaped up a mound of earth,
Hollowed a foot-wide crater, kindled fire,
Laid on asphalt; it melted, ran in a blaze,

Filled a lake of lava, overflowed the sides.
Eruption was at hand. I poised a stone,
Heaved it in the middle of the boiling pool . . .
Men say the elder Pliny went ashore
To observe Vesuvius, and what sights he saw:

Day dark with cinders, night bright with fire;
Earth shook, stones fell, while from ground and air
Hissed the ash and fumes by which he died.
If he shared any of our Western mood,
Did he judge that murderous knowledge good?

So a boy, touched by Promethean flame,
Sat again at the book, turned another page:
Rockets and aeroplanes, the coming wars
That wither our aspiring, sear such scars:
We learn the cost, but find our fate unchanged.

3. HOLY FEAR

None is himself apart, but time on time
Renews old myths like changes on a theme.
I seized on the universe and stared in its eyes
As at a cat I tried once to hypnotize:
Worlds from the sun, life creeping up from slime.

On the rock of ignorance where ancient seers
Built by a drowning sea, worships holy fear;
While knowledge, glorying in the fertile miles
Won from that ocean, scowls at the broken tolling,
The chapel bell's eternal bim-bam-bonging.

Extremes beget extremes; opposing fools
Tempts to converse folly. By common truths
Of space and time one became a Faust in the simple
Town. "Religion," I cried, "must be destroyed;
Nature is opening; like an oyster, it will yield."

At a summer camp I was talking late one night
In the high-flown style of Southern oratory,
Discoursing cause by cause how the world was made;
I railed at Eden—that last slavery
Over the mind of man, the altar of his god.

"We are almost at the secrets of life, and how long
Shall we be bound?" A gawky red-haired fellow
Spoke: "From the Bible I learned just one thing—
Fear of God is the beginning of wisdom." I fairly
Roared: "Fear is the beginning and end of folly!"

4. THE BOMB

One joined the dark conspiracy, strange son
Of a wandering father, with a stranger name,
Lear Nigssen—where are you now? What flight or ruin
Has drowned you with the monster that we made?
We planned to loose the atom and bind the world.

We invented socialism, thought ours the first:
All men to work and share. How ultimate hopes
By promised goods have hardened into loss!
That year the Academy failed; it was locked and barred.
We climbed the second story. In the chemistry lab,

With a high school text we spent our afternoons
Exploding nature, discovering how all things
Are balanced in destruction: hydrogen flamed,
Chlorine coiled its poison, magnesium flared.
Our greatest day we unsettled glycerin.

In the nitric bath, heaped up its molecules
At the frightful verge, poised to decompose,
Ten thousand times their bulk; it was our Bomb . . .
Appalling hours nursing the bottled doom,
Fearful of heat and jars. At the cold day's close

We stole to the river, poured the yellow oil
Out in the sluice of nature whence it came.
The quest of knowledge had led back to fear.
Over what gulfs we fruit and flower. You moved
From town. Where are you now, strange friend, lost Lear?

As the poems of my Delta homecoming, landscape, and life required, the treated events
are real—even this of a dangerous chemistry. My conspirator, anagrammed as Lear Nigs-
sen, has been rightly named Earl Sensing in my Life, Chapter 4. His later life remains a
blank to me.

5. SILENCE

After the titan revolt and world madness
Imagine one last survivor. As a magnet draws,
He is drawn to the lidless eye of Palomar.
And could he not stare his life away in the star—
Flamed silence where earth's wars were waged?

For the beginning is the end. Knowledge that sprang
From wonder to wonder returns. A boy, I opened
The book at worlds in space; that night, stole out
Under a sky burning with worlds, first seen
When day's new knowledge taught the night to loom.

Later, from the wranglings of camp, I took my glass
To the midnight field and scanned in sacred wonder
The star-streamed Milky Way. Or years after,
When worse knowledge had blighted hopes of progress,
When Spengler fell like wormwood to the sea

And the sea was bitter, while all human power
Turned in the rusty wards to reveal a grave—
Sick then of the forward motion, yet grieved to kneel
At the backward altar, having read most of the night
Some terrible pages of our modern waste,

I would climb the dark Observatory Hill,
Knock and greet the teacher, and there till dawn
Poured robins' song in the bowl of Albermarle,
Guide the great refractor, or quietly gaze
Into the star-spaces where this dust-world dies.

C. THE LAW

Men of Athens, I honor and obey you, but I will obey God before you.
Socrates, in the *Apology*

1. CHILD OF REVOLT

I think we are born the children of revolt—
Not that our fathers or grandfathers broke the law,
But that Blake, Thoreau, and Nietzsche hated rule,
And as the bay-tide lags behind the moon,
So in our shoals of spirit the wave comes slow.

A flashlight searched the dark of the oak's limbs.
Like playing a game I clung to the high stem.
Acorns showered on the passing cars
Had brought the despised police, the invited
Chase. The search beam took me: "Hey boy, come down!"

I worked my way up higher. "You get him, Sam,"
The old man told the young. Both of them came
Up the ladder to the crotch; then the young one climbed
Lighted by the ray. I reached the crown
Where branches in the moon weave into one.

His voice beneath me: "Come on, I've got you now."
My answer was a leap, out and down.
I knew the crossings blindfold; limb to limb
I swung the tree's great circle, hand over hand
Down the last low bough and off to the ground.

On a garage roof out of range I paused,
Beat my chest and gave the bull-ape cry,
Defiance to all constituted law,
Priest and custom, whatever limits and binds;
Then leapt blind in the night and led by the blind.

2. THE GREAT REVERSALS

We had many leaders, a whole age
Of wishful titans, ravishers for man
Of transcendental fire. The stern myths changed:
Restraint and reason became the tyrant powers.
While impulse ran like sunlight on the hills.

And the wide world's chorus, lark in the rustling corn,
Spirits of earth and air, of plant, beast, and bird,
Were singing: "Take your joy, for everything
That lives is holy." Erected by the voice,
Faust and Satan proclaimed the golden feast.

And all whom superstitions of the dark
Had thundered down for daring-Icarus
Sun-melted, Phaeton Jove-destroyed, Prometheus
Titan fire, Lucifer of morning,
Niobe made tears and Semele love-burning—

All rose divinely, winging west with the dawn:
Timbered mountains, grasslands wide as the sea,
With bison shifting under mountain-clouds,
Cloud-shadows they in moving magnitude—
That was a land for giants and demigods.

To act again Shinar and Pelion . . .
We feel the fatal angels strike the tower,
Or, through slant rifts of the rock-hurled hail,
Glimpse dreads of distance where our running kind
Shot with his lightnings fall, and the mountains drown.

3. THE FREE ANTITHESIS

Or have the timid cried at every scare
The perpetual reversal of their fear?
Like Knox of Shay's Rebellion: "Give us laws
Fit for the beast that is man"—to whom Jefferson:
"An occasional revolution is salutary."

And Tocqueville warned: Democracy leans most
Not to freedom rashly bold but leveled, lost;
And what remains for us of the liberal hope
If we go over to the other camp?
Better the wild sea than that slavish coast.

I had a Quaker friend in the last war
Who went to prison as a testament.
Like Socrates, he was the state's betrayer;
Or do they worse betray who toe the mark?
Another man I knew put country first.

He came from the war with every medal and cross.
Now he runs his father's firm, a pillar of strength.
He lately addressed a graduating class:
"The 'isms' are out; we shun the brainy pink;
There are regions where it is better not to think."

I rather choose the free antithesis.
Even the worst radicals, an outward risk,
Assert the latitude of environment—
Are chiefly dangerous as they come full force
Back where the timid were, to the cult of the mass.

4. IMMORTAL GARLAND

For freedom lives in tension-perilous mean
Between excesses mainly to be blamed
In the smart perversions of the self-deceived—
Most of all who assume the prophet's robes,
Poets, heirs of Delphi, seers gone wrong,

Saving lawlessness or ruthless law
Under the fashion of a world disease.
But beware of falling to the other side—
Conservatives with nothing to conserve.
Hardest to discipline the open mind.

Hardest and best. My father was of these,
And two like later fathers, Sicilian and Jew:
You taught faith and boldness, Antonio,
Planning beyond all nations for the time,
Never and always, artwork of the dream.

And you, sage Erich, wonderful droll man,
Pot-bellied Silenus of the great wealth within,
Apostle of transcendence, pacing the floor,
You serve that world—what if the world ignores?
Remember the proverb you would quote those nights—

"And surely night is the fairest time of day"—
As we walked gray mountains and your reigning voice,
Like moonlight on the midst, pearled in radiance
The high vision where law has become self-rule,
And each wears the crown and mitre of his own soul.

A celebration of Giuseppe Antonio Borgese and Erich Kahler—both dead now—also appears in *Songs for a New America* under the title "To Borgese, Kahler, and the Unknown Third" (with an epigraph from Dante: "Ben v'èn tre vecchi ancora / in cui rampogna l'antical età la nuova" (There are yet indeed three old men in whom the ancient times rebuke the new).

5. BEYOND GOOD AND EVIL

Open your ears to the clamor of this crescendo.
If you thought Europe was enough, wait, we have
Seen nothing yet; all heaven-stormers, from
The builders of Babel down, dwindle to shadows
As the pride of the rising East breaks waves across us.

Madder assertiveness, more ruthless law,
And the flowers of self-rule blown on the wind
Down wastes of the world, steppes of the mass-mind;
Now the Western gardens blanch in the same blast,
Is free vision a thing of the gentler past?

When the mechanized Germans were rolled from Russia
With a force like avenging nature—"Vengeance is mine,
I will repay, saith the Lord"—, who did not respond,
Whatever his finer scruples, to that assertion
Of the cosmic word powered by brute passion?

I do not mean surrender to such madness,
No wave-of-the-future jettisoning of value;
But that nature is not our little academe,
No Julian Huxley park and art museum
For the cultivation of private gentlemen.

If it is Bergson's machine for making gods,
It makes as many devils and gives them power.
The urge that brought us may have its wilder aim.
To which we fighting fall, what good we discern
Drowned in its infinite, the law past law.

D. WORLD AND TIME

One of these now am I too, a fugitive from the gods and a wanderer, at
the mercy of raging strife.
Empedocles, *Fragments*

1. GOD OF MIND

We have brought with our blood this brief crown of earth
And captive power of sentience—victim gods
At the burning focus of the universe.
I gather space and time and revive the waste,
Swept east from Delta—South to world West.

Canvas blown from the bridge wings the night;
Resonance of the invoked gale sweeps the boat;
I set my face to the wind, satanic compact.
In that Europe a Wagnerian screamed for thousands:
"Like a somnambulist I go the way God has chosen."

—Clouds to the hunger of storm. I called myself
A man of art and peace. Gentle evasion
Of those Oxford days: flamboyant music
Lifting poignant threads along the groined
Vaults of the past, rich to the point of tears.

War would exile me home . . . Iowa: cycling
The bare corn plain I had not learned was mine,
My life stretched before me like a weary dream;
Riding, it seemed, past Wytham over the Thames,
I searched now the drab Valley of the Squaw,

And took smokestacks, far off, as spiry towers.
Brooding Spengler's Fall I wrote those years:
"Caught in a festered calm we shall go down
Old rutted hulls of ships that never sailed."
Crown of the stars' kingdom, mind, crucified god.

This poem reflects my 1936 storm sailing on a cargo ship from New Orleans to London
for my Rhodes scholarship. The Wagnerian is, of course, Hitler, whom we heard by short-
wave radio in a German I could understand, having just finished a thorough year of Ger-
man at the University of Virginia. As the foaming madman announced the first of those
seizures that would punctuate my three Oxford years and (just after my homecoming and

first marriage) precipitate the Second World War, he took up the German God-calling of Luther, who, when he tore up the Papal Bull and threw Europe into centuries of war, said, "So hilf mir Gott, ich kann nicht anders"—So help me God, I cannot do otherwise. So, believe it or not, Hitler's words were "und jetzt wie en Somnambulist"(And now, like a somnambulist, I go the way God has chosen). But why marvel? Since the most dangerous president this country has ever had has just pressed, without United Nations approval, his own unilateral invasion of Iraq by claiming for himself the same God-authority.

2. WHIRLIGIG

Birthplace cities of the Gothic dawn,
Tender aspirers, planted along the Rhine
And wine-rich Mosel, over the plains of France,
Or trade-routes of the Danube opening south
To the spires of Po and Arno, jeweled crowns—

I had seen you before, now after, when the last storm
Romantic recklessness involved you in
Broke upon you, and your Atlantic children
From verges of the west returned on the wind
Like nature's backlash clouds of detonation.

Beauvais and Ulm at poles of the cross-axis
Widen before me, image of them all:
Fire-scarred gaunt cathedrals out of ruins—
First and last skeletons of the flesh
Time fed and consumed—steeple the ash-acres.

Beauvais and Ulm—in both it was carnival.
On rubble fields a carousel was whirling,
One of those crack-the-whips that bedevil riders
Through giddy loops of speed. And tattered children,
Crept from cellar holes and patchwork shanties,

Clung on for dear life, scared, with blood-drained faces—
As their parents had those war-nights of terror—
Yet wild for another fling. And a boy, a cripple,
Leaned on his crutches, told me, kicking the rubble:
"Next time I'll be flying above, dropping the bombs."

3. MEDITERRANEAN

Sailing to Crete, once the cradle of Zeus,
A spent land between Damietta and Rome,
We passed the fabled strait of the whirl and rock,
Fields seven races have plowed. Where has the human
Harvest burned such sacrament: wind-wrought

Stone and olive out of the azure sea?
The shores dissolve in vision, recessive time:—
On the cliffs of Capri, Gothic towers, and bards
Mingling a music of the North and Rome . . .
Then classic villas of the imperial peace . . .

Helenic light reversing to its clean
Pre-Doric wells, back to another dawn—
Achaians of the golden hair; and they too found
In that earth of conquered beauty caring hands
Had framed, man's half-remembered Odyssey.

What old Sirens of the Minoan trade
Taught these Hellenes by the Trojan fires
Fables of song so sweet and perilous?
Vision precurses vision like the blur
Of dusk and dawn, until great forests run

From glacial ice, and plains of Africa
Are a peopled zone from which eyes looked north,
Over the water, where this middle earth
Waited unshorn and pathless, that is now
Wrought stone and olive out of the azure sea.

4. SPACEFLIGHT

Waves of the living journey break through time;
But the greatest climbs to the future: I have served
Diodes of the clockwork from whose crown,
At the beat of the bell leaps the bird of flame,
Launching the earthly cycle toward the stars.

I have seen man reduced to a hand, an eye,
Stripped of person, caught in the radar net
And feedback relays; I have watched the film:
From the whirling tail, beyond the thrust of fire,
Earth contracted under its mist of air,

Visibly curving, the forsaken limb of land . . .
It seemed a deposition when men learned
This central world is a grain of dust down space.
Intrinsic radiance left the human face;
The covenant was broken; life returned

Of loss take comfort; as our hope grew small
So small is our betrayal. When the dawn
To a casual recurrence where each stormed
A fitful fever . . . We now who wait the fall
Of our own fire to consummate the past

Glitters the ashes, the imperial vast
Of the blue air will vague its million stars,
Round which—more self-destroying Lucifers—
Burn living worlds and waste, and all goes on
As it must go and has before time gone . . .

5. UTMOST SAIL

All is purposeless to the outward view,
Idle change and recurrence, vanity
The preacher preached; only from within
Where dependence falls to the pool of being
Some "aching void" reverses entropy.

This is the farthest journey we pursue,
Past the door of every moment, through anywhere
Taking the skyway of life's gossamer.
Learn the subtlety of revelation.
The world is like those shelves of the Looking Glass

Where search negates the presence that is sought.
So with spirit; wherever we look it retires,
And again at the rim of sight it is restored,
Phantom periphery of the examined void.
The vague transcendencies by which we breathe

Have no place of being; they dissolve
Under the wise dissection of our science.
Yet in all the universe there is only the dance
Of entelechy through a veil of dissolving.
Therefore not only the things of man, but the whole

Construction of space-time is nothing but spirit,
Absolute, entire—which from without
Is the cancellate of blinded material.
It is not part on part, but each and all;
And this is the wave-mark of our utmost sail.

This poem may well be read with an eye to the following passage from my essay, "Mechanistic Replacement of Purpose in Biology," *Philosophy of Science*, 15:1, January 1948:

The axiom here is only this, that the sum of any interacting and organized thing, from the electron to the cosmos, transcends as a unity the parts which construct it, and, if examined rationally, must be found to exist as well in toto, in essence, in spirit (a shocking word) as in the no more solid particles, the relationships and dependencies. If this is metaphysics, make the most of it. It is only what physics presents us, in a world where, without this, not only we ourselves but the universe throughout dissolves into nothings within nothings, every substance to the last [quark] melting into mystery, a trail of manifestations only [the essential] void crowning a phenomenal field.

E. TIMELESS CREED

Our heart is restless until it rest in thee.
Augustine, *Confessions*

1. THE BIRTH OF MYTH

Flight and sail round homeward; but if our home,
Like this low land signed with the water's seal
And landlessness we are, swims with denial,
How shall we hold the great house of dream?
Only by the myths that come in another name.

The will that buttresses enduring things
Against the fall that menaces their being
Appears at every vaulting of the spire
In new devices of constructive power,
Harnessing the daemonic rush of fire.

Waves of the pervasive yet vague event
It binds into particles; and these head-on,
Plus and minus, orbit in their descent;
And carbon and oxygen by the force of flame
Dance the inverted burning of earth's green.

Ours is the work of nature; in formative mind
Emerge the archetypes that transcend man:
Knowledge and law, justice, philosophy.
Yet all these are tame; they do not ride
The fire-stream of love. Caught in the brunt

Of all-denial, the leap through death and beyond,
Morality is poor. Hurled to his knees
Man seeks some Coming; and in his humbled flesh
Receives the myth, the Word, the embodied faith—
As true as the doubt whose partial truth is death.

2. THE ROMAN

We are consumed with a longing beyond the world,
That answers by denial, gives what we are
To the fierce hope of becoming. Gauged by pain
It should be our worst sickness, and yet the cure
Is across that dying to the other shore.

Why not rest easy here? We do not choose.
In the cup of selfhood lie the sensual dregs
That drive us from all calm; the heart's goad
Is the act of satisfaction. Witness in Rome
The pampered patrician who became so bored

He left the feast of life, trying all creeds
Of painful offering. Stripped to the skin he crawled
In a makeshift grave, was covered up with boards;
They slaughtered the bull of Atys over his head.
The god's red rivers fetched him from the dead.

He rose incarnadined as if reborn,
But lost, as before. Then a Cynic came,
His hair freaked with knots, a filthy rag
His sole debt to the world, and cried to all men:
"Look at me, look at me; I am your king and lord."

The Roman followed, put off clothes and land,
But not the self. As he turned at last
To the Stoics of death, a Christian caught his hand:
"Take up this Cross." That Easter he was burned
In the Colosseum, a torch that writhed and sang.

3. THE ALTAR

We have seen omens of the Western future,
Self-haunted faces of the busts of Rome;
The features loosen while the widening eyes—
Barometer of longing, storm-precursors—
Gaze from the remnants of late-Classic rule.

Under the Dark Age church of San Clemente,
Closed by the mosaic apse of spaceless gold—
Bodies stiffened against the flux of things,
Eyes vacant and strange, transcendently cold,
The monogram, the wellspring, cross and vine—

And under the lower church of that first zeal—
The City of God throned on the earthly ruin—
We follow an excavation along the wall
Of the prehistoric town, Cyclopean stone,
Where a wandering Roman water with a lost sound

Runs forever through the buried hall,
And reach a vaulted room: four windows above
Where seasonal light once entered are darkened now
Under meters of silt; the walls are carved
With seven signs of the days of seven gods.

In the center stands an altar, also carved:
Between raised and lowered torches of the sun,
The god Mithras, his face to the fire-orb,
Drives a knife into the crab-pinched bull.
Come tourists, bend, taste the sacramental blood.

4. SANTA SABINA

Fleeing from Naples where the reek of war
Was on the breath like the belch of rotten food—
Less from the random gutted walls than the bruised
Complex of man (they say a gangrenous wound
Will glow in the dark)—such flashes from Naples too:

The slum-hole restaurant in the Tribunale,
Crowds pouring by, the blind singer, two girls
Standing in the door, down the skirt of one
A trickle of milk, their laugh, the lifted blouse,
A folded rag laid on breasts overflowing—

Too fecund city: (a boy of thirteen, unlucky
Age, no hands, one foot, one eye blown out,
One bleared—rising like a hydra from the crowded
Way, imploring stumps of mortality:
"Bombardimento . . . tutta la fammiglia . . . morta")—

Fleeing to Rome, I climbed the Aventine
That morning of Palm Sunday, entered the serene
Retreat of aisles and alabaster panes,
Holy Sabina, of the columned calm,
From the cloister heard the procession of the palms,

The responsive phrase, the knocking at the gate,
Its opening and then the lingering chant,
"Libera me," a green eternal island:—
From the crushing of Rome this peace flowed like honey;
But what ripens on our tree of pains past or to come?

5. DELAYING NOT FORGETTING

Before the war I expected a Dark Age
From war's event; in Solesmes one spring
I stayed with mystics who hailed the decline
And second coming; meanwhile to ease desire,
They slept with each other's wives or the men with men.

From Augustine and Spengler we seeded the waste
With a hard kernel of light—sheer creed in a time
Confirmed by that denial in the civil fall.
And all was the blind conception of our wish,
Out of the romantic self by loneliness.

We were deceived; that peace comes late, and at
A world-consuming price. But our world beckons,
As last light climbs pillars of cloud. We are
Not Rome but Greece. It is man we love and earth—
Transiences—light in the rainbow, mirrored

In water, stars. As Socrates for the outward
State, unveiled the forms whose mystery
Reduced that outwardness to shadow-play;
So we, in the radiant nature of our West,
Linger between time and timelessness.

It is no Apocalypse the present needs
But a temporal mastery of the relative;
Great wings of hope, Daedalian plumes—
Over the dark Delta of our birth and grave,
To bank in the golden light, suspending creed.

III. PERPETUAL CLOSE

Thou hast seen these signs,
They are black vesper's pageants . . . indistinct
As water is in water . . .
Shakespeare, *Antony and Cleopatra*

A. THE RIVER

By the rivers of Babylon, there we sat down, yea, we wept, when we
remembered Zion.
Psalm 137

1. BAPTISM

We drive this Sunday south in the country
Where a white frame Gothic church stands at the levee.
The Negroes, dressed in black, glistening with the heat,
Come early, carrying lunches, and stay late
In the steaming little church where they sing together.

Across the levee at the old landing they still
Hold their baptisms. A live religion deals
In living symbols; so they prefer the river,
Their untamed font of darkness. I recall one evening
When the red sun broke through colonnades of cloud,

And the two tides met, brown and golden, of earth and air—
Light calm and pure, and that violence of water—
How they went down in white and moaning lamentation
To the mud-brown flood and under, then broke up singing,
Rolled on the earth, reborn out of death and nature.

Here at the Christian crossroad we note the cleavage
Between the enlightened few with their stoic wisdom
And the hungry soul of the many whose new Mystery
Is the beat of this spiritual jazz, the loved return
Down to the brown river and wounded Thammuz' blood.

Through all aseptic channels of the modern
This wild release is pouring; and we who listen,
As the brooding ground and single imploration
Break in waves of answer, group-homing passion,
We Whites, listening, are baptized in our tears.

2. COTTON

In long perspective rows the cotton now
Is blooming. Better to come at the end of summer
When the warm insistence of that more liquid than air
Billows to its cumulus, and the flat land singing
Under cotton, white as its clouds, pours fruitfulness.

There are men whose most casual word or gesture
Is a function of their nature and full of meaning;
It is this that we love in those of personality.
So too with a land: therefore our allegiance
Was less to the nation or state than this bowl of the Delta.

Even its crop has the softness of air and water:
Flowing in white merging streams to the Mississippi,
Fleece pillows of the gathered bolls in tall wagons
Drawn by mules over roadways, piled cloudy puffs,
Where we would lie cushioned as we swayed through the town.

Greenville was the center; bales mounted on its wharf.
The stern-wheelers would dock with barges, and black
Stevedores, with a roll of muscles and rippling oaths,
Would load them, and always in the night distance
The low whistles were moaning as they churned down the river.

Sometimes we would ride them to the foot of the bend,
Cross the neck to drift with the stream, the ten-mile
Sweep and back where we came; and at dusk from a floating
Log, I have seen them go flickering, down and down,
Bright bearers of cotton into those mirrored glooms.

3. THE BLUE-HOLE

The swirl of water dominates the plain
Where water is held back. They thought also
To straighten the river like a man-made thing.
When I first left on my grown wanderings,
They were cutting the necks across the oxbow bends.

I stand on a spur of the old levee now,
Where it broke for the great flood. The river, wide
Before me, banked with new willows, is curving
Again. The current down the straightening strikes
This shore, takes it visibly, slide by slide.

The double blue-hole that it broke and made,
Dug in the flat earth as a token well
Of waiting beneath all things, parting the veil
Between the waters of the ground and sky,
Deep and filled with fish, tree-shadowed now,

Where the live river eats at the buckshot mud,
Attends that union-give it a year, or a score,
The last bank will settle, the heavy brown
Pour in the green depths and make the severed one,
Homecoming always to the mother flood—

Not father of waters, deeper, deeper far—
I was born of your dark dissolving, waited years,
Firm-formed and clearing, for the night's return,
The melting of all things, under cloud and rain,
And recessive evening milky with star-spume.

4. HOME-CROSSING

I meet a young fellow on the street, sleepy eyed,
Who calls my name. He was at camp, he says,
When I last counseled there. "You did a thing
That struck me more than all the things I've seen.
It was on the ferry that night coming home.

Across the river; the current was bad. A stranger
Said he dared anyone to swim. You stripped
And stood at the stern. I thought, 'My God.' Then you
Went in, swam with the ferry, caught it, climbed on
Again. I'll not forget it as long as I live."

For me, I had lived too long. "What? You mean you
Don't remember, at all, a thing like that?"
And I: "I've done so many damn fool things
In my time, I can't keep them straight;" and to myself:
"What a stupid act to celebrate so long."

And then like water widening the gap it has made,
All that poured back through the crevice of his words:
I saw the river heaving under the moon
In lighted turbulence and liquid sound;
Once more I took the dare—both man and boy;

For night and water cried to unclothe what we are,
Breathe a time in the moon, then out and down . . .
Mother of waters, may no turn or flinching
Mar the clean line of the plunge, when on the home-
Crossing we dive deep in the river of stars.

5. OF WATER COME TO WATER

Before the flood that year the rains set in,
Pouring all day, with thunder in the dark.
Our cook came complaining to her work:—
The roof was leaking; the shingles were half gone.
We went with Daddy to see what could be done.

Our house is like the body, the place we live,
A shell against the unforming. Theirs was dark,
The windows patched with boards, and such a smell
Of mould and woodsmoke, body-fumes, it seemed
A liquid, lymph and blood of a savage life.

Black babies rooted in the dark like worms;
The grown boys lounged, peering at the doors;
And a man—not the husband; he had changed
Years since in the fluid shiftings—smoked at the hearth,
The strong blue vapor around him like a pool.

Everywhere cots and pallets. Where one slept
The rain came through, a dark place on the covers;
The other beds were moved to miss the drippings;
Rusty cans caught the slow drops rattling,
Or with the sound of water come to water.

That night in a dream I slept on such a bed,
Under that rotten roof, where rain came through,
As to a corpse dissolving in the ground.
Next week the levee broke and loosed the flood.
Strange, to love these hints and meltings home.

B. THE FLOOD

All things come from water, by water all is renewed;
Ocean, grant us your eternal sway . . .
But look, Homunculus, whom Proteus misleads . . .
Now he flames, he lightens, he dissolves in the sea.
Goethe, *Faust* II

1. THE BREAK

To yield, to flow out with the elements . . .
We went one night to see them hold the levee.
The slope burned with torches; in light and dark
Men struggled, brown and white, with bags of sand,
Building the top, or below, where it seeped in a boil.

Fires hissed in the rain, a steady rain
Blown on gusts of wind from the raw west.
The waves lapped at the ridge and as we watched
Reached higher and higher, fingering the crest;
In two days it broke and the home sirens screamed.

School was finished; farmers poured into town.
The protection levee was being closed. No one
Thought it would hold but the engineer, a man
Who was always sure and always wrong. He had built
The city streets with bouncing thank-you-ma'ams—

His own device for drainage; in a flat land
They could never drain themselves. Widow Archer called
From her yard: "D'ye think he can hold the water, Judge?"
"I doubt it," my father said. "He should," she cried,
"He's held it in these streets for twenty years."

Harder to keep it out than in; the river came,
Sat a while at the gates, and then crept through.
Who could forget the waiting of that night,
Or how at the break of morning, down the street,
The silver lanes of liquid slid like dawn?

Chicago Review, Fall 1954

2. THE BARGE

"Camp the blacks near the land, to plant as the flood
Goes down; the whites, all but the men, evacuate
To the hills." There was no road but the river of
Our harm. As Dante made for the hell-stream of tears,
We rowed to the wharf. The streets were swirling under

Five feet of water, plowed by crosscurrents.
We saw small boats capsized, and everywhere
Drenched men struggled to save themselves and theirs.
But the other flood was worse, that clotting tide
Of mortals on the levee. It is good to discourse

Of love and sympathy; hard to enact
For a calamitous and swarming mass.
On the southward barge we slept on gunnysacks,
Women and children; we owed the beast no fur—
Humanity stripped off to the common core.

Mother dozed, I waked. "Hey you, hey you,"
Tow heads of the northside were calling. I answered
"What?" They took it up in chant: "What, what,
Chicken butt; come around the house and lick it up."
The force I prized in nature, bared in man,

Shook me from kind moorings. I slipped to the prow
Where the river voiced its life in roaring mouths.
Sometimes Apocalypse seems the only road:
To join the Avenger, pour this human form
In the blind occult, world-nature, storm.

3. THE CATCH

At the down-set of the wheel where earth flaunts
The lie, bitterness rounds on itself, as the stern
Bard wrote, the worst returns to laughter. So too
With the lie called Death—nethermost point
Of the turning wheel—ground of resurgent life.

As formlessness ebbed from our works and acres
Melons in the sun swelled to prodigious size;
The lake swarmed with fish, birds darkened the sky;
Earth's cycle began again, breeding in the tangles
Flesh with spawn abundant, living soul.

We drove the shore-road by Lake Austramere
That incredible fall, scanning the mile-wide water,
Where all at once a radius of a hundred yards
Went silver with striped bass running the shad,
Lashing the mirror surface: "There they are."

And my father; "After them, boys!" We swerved the car
Off in the ditch, climbed the fence and ran.
There were boats among the cypress, but they were chained.
My father carried a hammer; he swung broadside
At the rusty padlock; a crash, and it sprung wide.

We rowed out amongst them. Fore and aft
They bumped in a welter of life. A trotline trailed
With spinners took them, three or more at a haul.
The leaky boat was loaded; we made for the shore
Deep with earth-gain, flood's miraculous draught.

4. CRAWDADS

Blind and groping, automatons of life
Begin again in the slime; the strangest birth
Was of crawfish congregations. I had seen
Crawdads enough, by ditches and swamp shores,
Bent claws working in the mud-heaped lairs.

But as the ebbing waters left the town,
Flowing in gutters still or after rains
Rising to fill the streets, those crawdads came
By thousands from the sewers; and what was weird,
They kept their beastly worship. The god they served

Was brazen light; by night arcs'glittering
They flocked like insects in slow clacking swarms
To the dazzling holiness, all waving arms,
While we with buckets and shovels scooped them in.
For days we ate them with every kind of sauce,

Keeping the surplus in the guest-room tub.
Lord, I can see them yet, one on another,
Scrambling, loathsome things, in their own vile water.
We could not eat them all; one night they died.
By morning the stench had crept into every wall.

Clawed and fighting fools, as you abandon
Our lord sun by the waters of earth and air,
And in the town and dark of the moon adore
A guttering lamp, you die in the tile-white pen,
Idolaters of the flickering arc of man.

5. THE CARCASS

What the river left behind was a dying swamp
In which life sprouted. Only this question remained:
Are you of the living or dead? Sunk off the bar
Or down the mud-flat where, knee-deep in mire,
We would leap and flounder, you could feel how shrimp

With fine pincers were nibbling at the skin,
Testing the firmness: is this one ripe or green?
They leave the green to ripen in good time.
That fall on a poplar knoll in no-man's land
Outside the levee, we built a cabin of logs—

A view across the river; the autumn rise
Filled the hollows with brooks going back to pools.
Where water ran, we drank and called it clean.
One day, walking to the place, thirsty and tired,
I bent at the river itself, where a brown eddy

Circled a fallen tree, and drank my fill;
Then rose to smell corruption, sick decay;
Stepped over the stump and saw, caught in the snags,
Legs out stiff, guts like long seaweed
Washed in the current-water in the belly's cave

Gurgling and out again to bathe the point
Where I had bent to drink—a long-dead mule,
Bloated and sloughing skin, carrion of the flood.
I walked on, a transmuting horror into pride:
"I have drunk at the bowels of death and remain whole."

C. THE LIVING

All visible objects . . . are but as pasteboard masks . . .
If man will strike, strike through the mask . . .
Melville, *Moby Dick*

1. THE GAR

Shorty, the minnowman—first settlers gone to seed—,
Calls me to fish in Lake Lee. We drive in the dark.
By dawn we are tied at the willows. The sailors' warning
Flutes the green depths with red. Soon rain is falling.
We sit in a steady drizzle as corks go down,

And bland white perch come slithering through the air.
And now I have hooked the fish I strangely admire,
Silurian reminder, one of the family of gar:
With armor plate and tooth-armed bony jaw,
Who steals the bait, sweeps off, and breaks the line.

The fishermen all hate this fossil sign
Of the swamp past we share. My father would stave
Their heads, or if they were small, crack the bills
In his hands, cursing them as the devil's spawn.
And once near here we found old Foster seining.

The big net filled with spoonbill, catfish, drum;
And in their midst an Alligator Gar,
Twice the size of a man, was plunging wild,
Ripping it all to shreds. They hauled to the shore,
And Foster stood, a shape of violence,

The revolver crashing in his lowered hand
As he pumped the slugs into the dark wallowing form . . .
Now all around us the water works with gar
That rise and belch, sweep oily tails. Demons
Of the South, you are strong; time is yours; you will endure.

What steals the fisherman's bait and is sometimes (if seldom) hooked is either the long-nosed or the short-nosed gar. The alligator gar, largest relative, tremendous thing, was what we saw in Foster's seine.

2. THE REVIVALIST

The tent bellies in the night as if the words
That preacher belches blew it up like wind.
Itinerant antichrist, have you returned?-
You who years ago to swell your coffers
Sermonized on a boy? Reason endeavors

To forget these things; they are the food of song,
Which makes a cult of anger as of love.
So I revive the past:—we were veering to war,
When I, a pacifist seeker, in a Bible Hour
Unburdened my young heart; and all the wrongs

Of black by white, poor, rich, truth by lie,
Were tallied in that count. Conceive the storm:
Fury in the barber shops, veterans alarmed,
My job foreclosed, our councils of despair,
Streamlined mobs, distilling hate and fear.

Much was saved by a fighting father, in whose
Walls non-violence sheltered, as always, proclaiming
Peace, though involved. It was this preacher then
Who raised the rabble to cry around our house,
Until my father stood forth with his gun.

Old wind-bag, what are you spewing in that tent?
The same gall as ever? You are true to form.
A long history is yours, almost the history of man:
Trafficking in the madness of the blind,
You sow self as god, earth reaps the whirlwind.

This occasion surfaces in my Life, Chapter 3; though chary anent details of the Holy
Roller and his crowd gathered in the dusk before our house, threatening to paint swasti-
kas on the brick work, until my father, flinging back the upstairs study windows, leaned
out with his double-barreled shotgun. Like the yelling mob in *Huck Finn* come to lynch
Sherburn—but confronted by a loaded gun—these po-whites melted away.

3. HORSE-AND-RIDER

Here in the drugstore comes a tun of a man,
Gut distended, red face wreathed in a grin,
Holding out a hamlike hand. Who are you then
Under that mask of tallow? Can you tell?
You are harder to guess at than Yorick's skull.

Old Studs, is it you? Here's a mammoth change.
I could almost weep—but they are laughing tears.
You have laid a saddle on since the days I rode
That broad back and shoulders. What cushions here!
My faithful beast, Lord, how we two would lunge.

I was four when I went to school and undergrown.
But I had my skills; horse-and-rider was one.
This Studs was the toughest dunce in the whole class.
Every recess he would charge like a whinnying horse,
Boost me up and gallop on the fields of praise.

He ran, I ruled, invincible brawn and brain.
(I think with half our people the town of Chartres
Built the great cathedral; a few more
And Athens schooled the world. There is no goal
Man cannot reach under spirit's rule.)

Now he shakes my hand and mumbles in his jowls.
You have gone to pasture, you and the whole town,
On earth's fat field, black horses of the soul,
Unvaulted by lofty dreams—foundered beast—
And the horseless rider—single, powerless.

4. A CLOUD-CHANGE

After a close warm day under sheltering cloud,
About the hour of sunset, from the west,
A lifting wind opens a slip of blue;
The low roof of day breaks everywhere,
And night, deep night, widens the old mystery.

There are three men in the town, I think of now,
Who move a single way, as these clouds clear:—
Barry deals cards, lets others guess at the face,
Sums the chances, tallies, hopes that way
The laws of mass will dissolve like limits of day.

Matthew has gone fanatic; he always reads
The Book of Revelation; in the "walls of wrath"
Surmises symbols of atomic blast.
He goes to all revivals, gets up to stand,
Crying, "Beware, our judgment is at hand."

And bright young Sams, who used to stargaze with me,
Is gazing now for saucers. He has a perch
Built on his roof, and tells how a year since,
In the red dusk of the sky he saw a disc
With lighted flange, implying things from space.

Through the last arms of cloud I look, and see,
Swirled from the Swan to the Archer south and down,
The great sun-clusters of the Galaxy;
Now reason bows to wonder, is this the way
The world melts: on the wind suffers a cloud-change?

5. BUZZARDS

They still circle the sky, these black buzzards.
When I was very young and that blue was heaven,
We had a colored maid who said those birds
Were as big as houses, with furnaces inside,
Where red apes roasted little boys and girls.

We did not quite believe it, but from that time
It was taunting evil powers to lie in a field,
As still as death, until a spot way high
Would drop and widen into ragged plumes,
Then more and more, till the round sky was full,

Circling, descending; and we would leap and scream,
Cheating the darkness, which scattered on quick wings,
Gliding and beating the mild ethereal blue.
But I first felt all the horror of those things,
Heaven's hyenas, eaters of the dead,

When we were hunting once, and far in the wood,
We found a hollow stump with a nest of the young,
The old bird circling above, hooked beak and claws;
They were fluffy things, pure white, looking around
With innocent strange eyes, whom the vulture fed

On strips of carrion torn out when flesh dies.
We had cut our way through canebrake; one of the boys
Raised the machete; he would have cleft the brood.
But a man stopped him; the law, he said, was theirs,
They were protected. He did not say Whose law.

D. THE DEAD

O here
Will I set up my everlasting rest . . .
Shakespeare, *Romeo and Juliet*

1. THE MEMORIAL

At the end of the town by the levee is a new monument
To a free country and to those who died fighting
In its last great war. Flanking the stars and stripes
Are plaques intended for the names of the fallen.
They stand an empty white, the colorless all-color.

Troubled by the incompletion, I asked its meaning
And learned the shame of the whiteness:—a cotton broker,
My father's enemy and mine (his ranks are legion),
One who has served our paleness under the hood—
Mark of a cloaked malignance that grows among us.

Accusing by red or brown all uncloaked persons—
This man, I heard, with others of like vision,
Denied the dead black names a place by the white ones;
Therefore the roll is mute and shall remain so,
Government not permitting a partial monument.

There are times when one doubts the benefits of progress,
Yet serves it still, if only by revulsion
From this wrong. I have not much cared for war either,
And am seldom stirred by battle monuments;
But this featureless sign at the melting river

Moves more than wrath:—Old hater, you have done well.
The god of time is a god too of the whiteness.
You have raised a monument to your own vacancy,
And to all the hearts of the world emptiness,
Nameless names in the masked terror of your voids.

2. THE FIG TREE

They say the fig is the symbol of life. The largest
Fig trees in our town grew behind an old
Frame house; it was two stories high, unpainted
Wood, with gingerbread porches all around.
A family of seven lived there not far from us.

One night it burned and firemen brought from the flames
Four small bodies and laid them in our yard
In scorched bedding, went back to fight the fire.
They salvaged what they could. It was very little.
What was left of the family moved out of town.

That was in winter. With spring the leaves came,
And as summer advanced, weeds of all kinds grew
And took the yard head-high, and the great fig trees
Bore as never before, the purple and green
Turning to sugar on untended boughs.

Birds came flocking but could not eat the half;
And I, who lived that part of life in the trees,
Longing to reverse the descent of man,
Would steal out through the grass by the charred ruins,
That grown-up secret yard, and half the day

Swing in the branches and from tree to tree,
Gathering the ripest harvest as I swung.
I thought of that night of fire, eating the fruit,
Almost an ape again, in the tree of life,
The fig that will ripen on the ruin of countless worlds.

3. THE BEACON

This is the quietest place. I have come
At dusk to measure for my mother's grave.
She says the time draws near and the family ground
Has gathered friends and foes, and she would lie
By her last born, my brother, the first one home.

Having measured I sit at a neighboring tomb,
An Italian wife who died young. Beyond
The trees grain elevators climb. The sky
Is low, the boggy earth not solid; yet we
Are drawn in the same proud life from which I have come.

Back of the cemetery a four-lane road
Runs east and west where Rattlesnake Bayou flowed;
It reaches out in space for the river bridge
Nerve- and blood-net of the life of time.
Yet time is what it was; here we go down

As a leaf in darkness settles to the ground.
The great oaks take the shadow, small leaves mingling;
The moon pours a melting light on solid things;
Tree frogs billow the lonely dark with cries.
Between black cedars, peaked as in Val d'Arno,

Gleams the white angel cut of Carrara. O dark-
Haired mother, child of Palermo, what old hunger
Of blue waves and olives sent back over far seas
For this girl of home, you homeward, here to stand
The phare and beacon of your waveless harbor.

In my slide-accompanied selection from *Delta Return*, I use photographs of this Green-
ville tomb of the Muffuletto (Sicilian, hotel-and-restaurant) family, with details of its
Announcing Angel of Carrara marble. It has also been introduced into Chapter 17, "The
Graves," of my first novel, *The Married Land*, but that fictional treatment should yield
to this prior "Beacon," near the close of *Delta Return*; as to a six-line verse paragraph
from the 1945 graveyard sketch with which I close the Midwest (Iowa) Chapter 2 of my
Life—identical source of the last six lines above.

        Though the novel adds something observed in my youth, when we would
take flowers, Sundays, for our family graves, how my father would select a branch, and
walking across, lay them before that angel—the marker, as my father told me, for a Muf-
fuletto daughter or bride (I forget which), who was to die young (again, I am in doubt

whether of consumption or in childbirth), a girl who had helped him with Italian when he, home from Ole Miss, was planning a trip abroad. I wondered sometimes what might have been between them—the promising young lawyer and the lonely Sicilian, bending heads together, joined in deciphering Petrarch.

4. MOUNDBUILDERS

In an Indian burying ground where the spade turns native
Bones we coffin our outnumbering dead.
They by the river cleared a few fields in the great
Web of forest where bayous pulsed and returned,
Overhung with trumpet vines bright as cardinals.

A little way to the north is a group of mounds,
Pyramids of earth where the temples stood
On tiered heights around which they danced in plumes—
First stirrings of form against these shifting floods.
We dug there once and uncovered giant bones—

Cattle no doubt, but for us they were ancient men,
Looming through dusk like myths of dawn. And what
If they (touched with Mayan fire), had conquered
The forest for another day than ours?
They were too slow; we came and took the future.

Now far to the south I have seen in a cypress swamp
On a dwindling reservation tired Indian husks,
Empty of meaning as their gullied cairns.
Gringo destiners, take up the proud yoke,
Not proudly! We are the moundbuilders now.

And say, like Herodotus' Libyans, we come to sleep
For divination, on our fathers' tombs,
How can their ghosts but point us on and on:
Over poisoned fields, up a strand of steel,
Where a spacebridge arches a river star-coiled?

5. HOMEWARD ARMS

Midnight of the last day I am still with the dead.
Waiting a word to redeem the lost returns.
I stretch on the ground beside my father's grave.
The subtle stars are above me: Coffin, Lyre;
In the grass dews whisper like a thousand ghosts.

How long in our anticipated world
Have we been seeking mystery as a tide
To lift the stranded vessel . . . The waters rise—
This little village glimmering down the stream
And yellow sweeping flood by gibbous moon

Drop in the shift of leaves, sad withered time,
And all turns to one; my father's ghost am I,
No longer of these hands or touch of skin,
But sheer non-sentience through the vacant shores . . .
There is no word but being, this life we are.

The rest is like a death into whose womb
We are not yet engendered to be born,
Nor home to return until all time's time turns.
Then homeward rather to the stranger place
Whose columned fluting bore my stranger days . . .

Well, we shall not live always in the frail shell.
Who has seen the walls once waver knows they are staged,
Till curtain, and they fade, or drawn away,
Leave night forever, all ablaze with stars,
And I who dreamed home, melt into homeward arms.

E. TOMORROW

Tenderly-be not impatient
(Strong is your hold O mortal flesh,
Strong is your hold O love.)
Whitman, "Whispers of Heavenly Death"

1. THE FALLING STAR

Out of the Virgin comes a falling star—
Strange things are born of virgins—; golden and slow,
It drifts north in the heavens, showering sparks,
And dies in the Dragon. That is the eternal war.
My mind goes north and back to another year:

Lying in the August park . . . and music sounds.
The pavilion plumes the night like a spread of wings.
Above us stars, and the golden great ones fall.
What more star-compelling than this music of
The old Beethoven in the new time of the gods?

We had come up racing from the waves to the sand,
Spirit in flesh, melodiously unclad;
We had eaten under the trees and poured out wine;
Now we stretched on the blankets, women with the men,
Flesh fitting earth's curves, embraced, or hand in hand.

To put off inhibition—good to be freed
Of the past, children of Bacchus, all races, white
To brown, under the city while music sounds.
We have sullied fact and dream; but still the moment
Bends the tree of time with fruit of promise.

We are singing from our wind-city of towers
Over the far-winged emblem of our ways;
We are singing, forgetful of the night of the soul.
Men have not enjoyed many days
Of free humanity; let them sing while stars fall.

2. THE GARDEN

Cadence of the song:—The Buddhist tale
Says spirit haunts the body fourteen days,
Skimming the dross of deeds. Here on the grass
Of three generations composing, flesh of my flesh,
I haunt tomorrow, which resumes the past.

Building eternities in time, time broke
Eternity. We too were born of the Virgin,
Creed of Grace; we have crossed the zenith showering
Freedom's sparks; and behold, the Dragon, crude
Denial of our last hope, the natural good.

It is little enough that we know any longer
Of the suffering god who took his cup of anguish
In the starlit self-surrender of a garden.
Not from the cross our cry of desolation;
From the hunger of plenty this *lama sabachthani.*

But it is with us still, that ground of atonement
Of the proud West of the world; for this Michelangelo
Turned on titan failure of his marbles;
Rembrandt broke mass and color for this, ah, terrible
Lean Christ at the column. Have patience only . . .

In the garden of innocence we have remade,
The fruit tempts again and again, and man exiled
Plants a new garden with the bitter seed;
On the serpent's tree we exalt the mortal god;
The star dies in the Dragon; long live the star.

3. INTERMISSION

So the journey to this home, this night, this grave,
I make in space once yearly; but in soul
It is the perpetual orbit where I move
At every moment, my conceiving soil
And October earth of these recurrent leaves.

Clear water shelving down the granite race
Of the world's boldest mountains, charged with light
Of the purple sky and sun-needled spruce,
In that incisiveness is water still,
The liquid mystery of every pool

And quiet to which it flows. So, by the city's
Towers, we lay while music played—as lulled
As here, remembering, on the grass of the graves—
Young lovers joined in their tomb, the rose and briar.
Under what timeless music we mortals drowned,

Float in the gathering sea, that always in spume
Breaks on temporal shores and hurls us dry
Up the bare sand and shingle, music's close.
And like the Judgment painted time on time,
At the world's end, from dark ground these uprise,

Strange stirrings out of earth, poor living things.
It is only an intermission. The music will resume,
This resurrection pass, the fitful stir;
We will stretch out in the warm night again
And lie hushed and dying in each other's arms.

4. THE SUBWAY

Such is the journey north tomorrow brings,
And these my yearly (and hourly) homecomings.
You will see me there in the rush of the streets one day
Caught in the whirlpool of a subway stair,
The pit that insacks the evil of the world:—

A muscle man swung from the clutch-bars, pawing,
Ape-glints at all women; the hungry-eyed
Religious girl, grown into groping—on what
Lean pasture will the boughs drop fruit?
On what bare altar falls the sacrifice?

You will see me sitting as the moments pound,
Thud of feet, beat of the blood; you will see
Me rise, giddy with faces, bellies, groins—
Our hate and love—whirled as blind a span
Through the earth—passage run, crying aloud for air:

"Tickets, no; we have paid, we have paid!"—and then
I shall pause, thinking how stars in the clear sky burn
Sagas of light. Are they gone? I knew them once.
With the gods I grew, the Olympians, calm;
And dying saviors who took upon them man:

Osiris of the earth, Thammuz of the stream,
And gentle Christ of the spirit spring. You great
And lowly ones, be with me now and always.
Tomorrow in the city when I am dust on the wind,
Come like stars in water, assuage my need.

5. IN MY FATHER'S HOUSE

I turn away. In the ultimate shade is a tomb
I played at long ago—a table of stone,
Carved on the top a draughtsman's compass and rule;
Beneath is a name with only this inscription:
"In my Father's house are many mansions."

My own father, whose grave I leave behind,
Told me the story: it was his boyhood friend,
Who had set his hopes on being an architect,
Sketched great façades and died in his teens.
Are we not all bearers of such designs,

Getting nowhere with them?—Architects
Of the unbuilt city, we die more or less as children;
And happy the one who can carve on his coffin
The fable of that hope: "In my Father's house
Are many mansions," and go with a good grace.

For my part, I cannot tell. It is hard to think,
In this ground of the dead, something endures;
Not to think it, harder still. We cannot hold
Life's boundary stone: each day we die with the sun,
And our dream-sleep is a web of dying and return.

Therefore this dark of the water-spilled gray moon
And oaks by the river over the watered plain,
And moon-gray sky and sky's legend of stars,
Are the ebb and flow where we go up and down
The swirls of Delta night-space, place, haunt, home.

Five Chambered Heart

FIVE CHAMBERED HEART

To
wives, loves
mamas, daughters
granddaughters

Consider the ways of clouds:
A cumulus by growing
Dissolves at the crown;
Shapes mingle and part—
Limbs that fold and unfold—
Glad in the play and dying
Io learned from Jove.

Praise age, sacred teacher
Of permissive desire,
A wantonness that smiles
As its claspings yield;
Blesses its own abroad
To quicken in other lives . . .
Nestlings I have loved,
Nestle with love's gods.

The poems in *Five Chambered Heart* form twenty numbered waves which move recurrently through five archetypal states of love: Love simple; love narrowed, as in Lust; attached to things, Earth; perturbed or reversed, Waste; transcended, Soul. Longer poems, imaging the same states, surround each sequence of five such waves.

I

FIVE CHAMBERED HEART

The first begins to beat like a drop of blood
On the egg-yolk of the world the fifth day
When vessels reach to guide the coded wave
Under brooding wings in the dark of LOVE

A second cleaves the wish, one on one,
Mounts to spool and gender on its own:
Ruling reptiles upreared in a world
Of electric LUST and cycad palm.

The third, of two and one, admits a space
Between self and other, EARTH manifold,
Where love meanders the sensible,
And what it sees and meets with calls its own.

Four chambers pound with use gone wrong,
That all time, seas and saurians, beast and man
Kindle WASTE by everything we loved;
And lost the flower-turn from four to five.

Heart, infold again, world—fire infold,
SOUL cradled in a spiral swoon;
Still desire in cerements five-fold,
And do not ask of the all if up or down.

1a

RAINBOW

The passing caught and held—*percipio*:
An evening once in white-domed Mexico.

The sun, long set behind volcanic peaks,
Had flecked the clearing vault with salmon flakes.

Sunset was enough, a sky full;
But what we saw passed that: brighter than all,

A double rainbow, far up, out-flamed the cloud
Twenty-five years together, and we stood

Almost in doubt, how loves so far gone
Crown a present less believed than known.

A wonder-of-marriage poem, after 1970, from our time in Chiapas, place of
extraordinary rainbows.

1b

LITANY OF WOMEN—with Analogies Mythic or Actual

I have forgotten the names of women I lay with in those days,
And yet they come across me, nameless distinctions:

One all flesh, who beached from primal water
Prehistoric or Annapolis Hippie

To be mounted in the ooze—sprawled, like saurians;

That lost empress who rode hard to the kill,
Then turned, still crouched, agape for the rearward monster;
Messalina, wife of Claudius,
the Lynchburg bawdy house

Grower of grapes and grain, mother of tranquility,
Sun-burned, ox-eyed, in the Tuscan vineyard;
Ceres, with a vineyard
daughter, Austrian in fact

She whose purity, by London's sullied river,Appeared a weeping babe
tendering its pale flower; ·
a troubled Blakean image:
Matron, in the strict English girls school

You of the stately house, whose love reached through us,To weave a
custom, fireside, children, fine old fabrics;
Juno, and cf. my own Diana Mason Bell

And one who tore all fabrics, by Easter starlight
Virgin Mary, with the mystic Praying, in fierce humility,
to be God's mother; soul of Simone Weil

And that high lonely thing who calls all hearts forever,Proud on the
tower, over towns and beached ships blazing.
Helen, and cf. my first wife Mildred

Poetry, August 1969

1c

RAINSONG OF FISH AND BIRDS

A long drought. In the heat this afternoon,
Unaccountably, the birds
Begin to sing.

I go with mask and snorkel to the pool. Plumb
Fish come round me: black bass, goggle-eye, brim
Flowing and retreating, expectant among
The water weed. When I come up to breathe,
The interface is dimpled with white spume
Rustling on the water; thunder shakes the trees;
The birds are singing in a gust of rain:

How cause and wish,
Foreknowledge, chance and deed
Rustle around us dark and luminous as rain.

To experience and write this poem at Yaddo, Saratoga Springs, summer in the 1960s, I
had to buy a diver's mask. I deducted the mask from my next Income Tax Return. An
auditor tangled with me: "Mr. Bell, what is your profession? You're surely not a diver?" I
did my cause little good by the claim: "My profession is being Charles G. Bell."

New York Times, June 13, 1965

1d

HIGH TENSION

My life in strange places.
Night. I climb a bank,
Try a short-cut through some trees.

The hum in the dark increasing.

(In New York yesterday
I saw my crazy Charlotte
Penned up, ranting.)

They loom in dim light, fenced with warning,
Ringed tails upended, barbed
Hornets, buzzing.

(A jet zooms over, somewhere fire is falling.)

I think these Martian wasps hatched our civilization;
And I go past as she, past a policeman,
Muttering against the curse, steeled against the sting.

Walking out from Rochester, NY, Spring 1967. Grim time of Vietnam; I sight the
city-transformers.

Quarterly Review of Literature

1e

VOICE OF THE CHAMBERED FIRE

Moments, when the heart
Fills with unconnected burning,
A black-body rounding
On itself; when mind,
Almost part sharer in the fire,
Lays the treasured word-hoard on the hearth:
"How we two leaning in a certain window"
And "Come to the window, sweet is . . ."

Pours on memory's oil:
The bee in the blossom, beyond the castle,
Over the slopes of Tyrol.
Remember? The songs of Wolkenstein?
When our youth sang with the world?
Though all that birth of love
Leaned to a century of wars, the timeless
Twisting of the human child—

And we play the record maybe:
"mit lieber zal . . . das in dem Wald erklingt,"
Knowing in the darkness nothing moves outward,
All things return on the windowless
Close burning (if through the glass window there
The blade-thin shape of a moon puts off its cloud),
The chambered fire, that murmurs as it dies:
"Forbid that any love should doubt its own."

"Black body" is from physics: the perfect absorber and radiator. The first "window"
quotation is from Augustine's Confessions, the final scene with his mother; the second is
from Matthew Arnold's "Dover Beach"; compare Chapter III of the Life, my "Letter from
Naples."

Out of War's Shadow, A Peace Calendar, 1968

2a

WAKE ROBIN

To see the summer stars, Scorpion, Lyre,
The clustered Milky Way—with Venus now—
Rise before winter dawn,
Brings a softer breath down mountain snows.

I, Hiem, and you June: what glints of love
At the dawn rising of your summer stars
Over my snow fields,
Stir, sweet shimmerer, these April airs?

2b

DOGWOOD AND FLOWERING JUDAS

Cornel, a Florentine profile,
Snow-maiden
Quatrefoil dawn-flower;

Redbud, Venetian putana,
Spilling the
Wine of noon's orgies;

In the garden of the heart—
God said—
Let them bloom together.

These trees were growing together on the St. John's Annapolis campus.

St. John's College Magazine

2c

GIANT SPRUCE

To climb that liquidly resilient up the air,
To take fixed and swaying all year the wind and rain,
To point branch over branch the sky—bone of the spire
And trail for the nurture of light sun—terraces of green,
Through centuries to unfold the template we are-
Dreams the earth-conqueror as he kindles fire,

The allusion is to a hundred-foot Norway spruce by the Yaddo artists' retreat, Saratoga
Springs. In summer months, a climb to its swaying top would leave biting flies and mos-
quitoes below, though I would think there of our global burnings.

2d

WHITE ROOM

A high window, a white room.
Paper, pen, table, chair.
Of the longest life, half is gone
Cars on the street below are a blur.

Strange to write and no one to read
There is my mother, her wits are with God
That will save postage. Journals, friends
Answer with smiles or blank returns.

To work as if the working were a trade,
Knowing it will not leave the windowed room,
Knowing, almost desiring. Another fall
Turns to winter, gray-brown under cloud

Is the vigil or the word
At a cradle or a tomb?
And how to work the will of God
With God alone, in the white room?

The Life, Chapter 5, treats of my St. John's Annapolis white-walled garret office, where
a mostly solitary struggle with my first novel also prompted the question of this poem. I
have found other testimonies in prose and verse to the trials of the same room, which—as

they are quoted on those pages of Life, Chapter 5—need not be repeated here; though I should stress that the best of them, extends the crisis, through the image of a squirrel in a blighted oak, to our rather scurvy age. (The same Life passage then closes with setting to right everything by the inverted ceiling of the room)

The next poem here will tell how I was transferred from that white garret room to the windowed tower over the Annapolis St. John's mall.

2e

RESONANCE OF TOWERS

Tonight in the lighted tower
I have outwatched the Bear.

Think of Dante in banishment
Climbing another's stairs by candlelight,

Collins in the clouded hut,
Rock-walled Jeffers, embattled Yeats.

Rats with electrodes in their heads
Jump on the treadle for a charge

The night web of soul in the world
Leans from tower to tower.

In the same Annapolis Life, Chapter 5, I tell how my St. John's garret was needed; but I rose higher, to the windowed octagon above our central towered hall. As "The Brief I Am" would record: "Tower poems now sprinkle the Five Chambered Heart. The Life mentions four, spread over different 'archetypal states.' Indeed my recurrent sequence of Love, Lust, Earth, Waste, Soul has somewhat challenged the poems. This tower piece (1964-65) has been drafted into Soul.

Quarterly Review of Literature, 1972

3a

A WIFE GATHERS

Is it for one
Such meanings stir
To elations
Of despair
You walk dry fields
In the last sun
Gathering blue thistles
Hedged with thorn?

This 1964 poem, standing in for Love, voices Blakean sympathy for a troubled
wife in a Washington, D.C. seminar I was leading.

3b

DANCING MOTHER

The palm shack bellies—
Strings and gourds—
Mother and all are dancing;

While frogs from vines
And flame trees take it up:
"Coquí, co-co-co-quí."

Sweep breadfruit breasts
Down laurel hair; under
The mangoes hanging, weave your loins,

Woman of the night and frogs,
Ishtar, mother of flesh,
Gaea, mother of gods.

Whereas the search for Lust drove me back nine years to a Puerto Rican poem
I had been hoarding, c. 1955.

3c

THE BERLIN TITIAN

Where Venus in the lap of flesh,
Subdued by music, turns her thighs,
The lover plays; only his eyes
Pursue those generous valleys, flank and breast.

But in a landscape broad as dream,
Brown fields and mountains in dim light,
The curtained carriage of his thought
Drives to a stable, drawn by a plunging team.

Being, on its downward course,
Delays in music, delegates the act;
Love unentered is the root
Whose flower is beauty, whose seed is force.

For the third position, Earth (or Nature) I was seduced rather to the landscape background
of Titian's wonderful Berlin Venus, mentioned in the same Chapter 5 of the Life, but
earlier in reviewing our Fulbright year, 1958-59.

Quarterly Review of Literature

3d

TERMITES

A friend writes from the temperate zone:
He has a fourth child, a gold-haired girl.

Here the termites are swarming
Through unscreened windows
They drift in whirls to the light;
Dropping wings,
Pale worms on the table,
They pursue and mate;
Then eat into the books,
Blotting the word.

Procreation wraps us like a spider's web.
How shall I write my friend
Blessings of the occasion,
From this lush land where breeding is a curse?

More strikingly, for Waste I have searched further back, to the Puerto Rico year
of 1955-56.

Rolfe Humphries, *New Poems* #2, Ballantine Press, 1957

3e

INWARDNESS

Close your eyes against the sun.
In the fire-vault, look, a man-
Fearless-among flaming lions.

Hard-pressed for the leap to Soul, I took the flame experience of looking through
closed lids at the sun—as if it gave me a vision of Daniel.

4a

FROM HEIGHT AND SILENCE

How shall I, who
From childhood have lived
In the recklessness
You fear, know what you have
To forget, what to forgive?

But that we being as Blake
Said on earth a little space
Have learned how saints kiss
In the Angelic Brother's
Paradise

Who will believe
Their innocence
Is lack of touch?
They have put off the weight
Of shame, not flesh.

I do not trust desire,
Much less regret.
At home in love as in air
I wait. Incommunicables
Why confess?

For this return to Love, I fix now on one of the Annapolis tower poems.

New Mexico Review, November 1969

4b

EURYDICE

Orion and the Dog are lifting
Over the east; the dew has fallen.
We have come late
To bivouac under the stars.

I see you at dawn among the early dead
Who walk by the river on the other shore,
And far off and cold to us
Are our love-glances.

An imagined poem of a stolen night out, with its cold waking to dewy dawn.
Hardly Lust but Love narrowed—as for Orpheus.

4c

DUNGHILL HARBINGER

Only the poor keep roosters.

In the dark before the dawn
From every moonvine porch
And shanty ridgepole breaks
The raw confirmatory cry.

The suburbs of the rich are silent.

A Mexican distillate, holding the position of Earth.

Anthology of Humor, Ashland Poetry Press, 1972

4d

CHICAGO TWENTY YEARS AFTER

The city always taller over the shore;
The sirens of its promise heavier;
I almost caught in the dream rush as before.

Ask the manikin whose mythic hair
Slogans a costly tweed: "Was the Western star
We pledged with life, tinsel as you are?"

Smiles lewd, smiles last: "What Promethean lure
Set your soul to sell, in a mortgaged store,
That three-piece suit of freedom, profit, war?"

From the antecedent "Diretro al Sol"—affirmation peak of *Songs for a New
America*—that Chicago dream falls here into the state of Waste.

4e

SILVER SABLE

On the lake pier, at the end of winter,
Under a moon of mist, trailing my feet,
I look back to the city I almost hate.

Lids half close; through tears and lashes,
That moonlit shattered world goes silver-sable:
Lanes and extensions of star-drift work

Live cross-hatchings in the spaceless
Dark. "The eye rubbed," says Plotinus,
"Sees the light it contains—truest seeing."

Here that Waste Chicago is turned to Soul though by Plotinus' withdrawal
to inwardness.

Chicago Tribune

POLLY'S WINTER TREE

A stone lintel like a grave . . .
I remember leaves
She gathered casually,
As over a battleground
A goddess of death and return
Stoops for the noblest slain—

To be pressed between book—
Leaves until the dark
Of the year, when at her
Voice and hand, the russet
And purple and tawny leaves,
Shaken from their graves—

Maple, tulip, linden,
Flame red, umber, black-veined,
Fledged to a beech limb,
With lost fall fill the room;
And I come where Polly Persephone
Is love in her garden caves.

Back to Love, for Polly Hanson, poetic resident and secretary at Yaddo—after
my fall visit, a Christmas return.

Chicago Tribune

5b
ENCORE

Marianne:

I swear, if Eve seduced Adam to eat the fruit
(Or Lilith—to whatever gauds she lured him),
It was not by brow or breast or the dear hoarded
Slopes of belly, but by the tongued and breathing flute
Of song. Witness yourself, just old enough to be
My second daughter; and when you sing that song by Schubert,
Your lips parted for the secret savor
Of lost romantic passion, you so confound me,
I forget wives, loves, whores, daughters, granddaughters,
To lie in the falls of your Lydian laughter.

If ever poet-lover plunged
Off the deep end, it is the drowned
Yours forever,
Charles

Here Love slides to humor for a precious singing ward of Yaddo; this message
laid on her plate the morning after she sang Schubert.

Quarterly Review of Literature

5c

DOCTRINE OF SIGNATURES

Through entropic December of shifting total fog,
Blurs to the branch of the barely discernible apple tree
A condensing shape: scarlet, crested, tail-perked, winged.

Whatever cleaves the blank and nebular immensity
With the self-proclamation of a bounded thing, name-bearing,
Jocund, smug, gives the password—one with me.

So to the third state: Nature, affirmed by kinship with what seems to have been
a winter cardinal.

New York Times, August 8, 1970

5d

A FLY THROWN INTO THE FIRE

The small body shrinks and hisses
Fringed with light—
What stretched the neck, what preened
Head and wings,
Changed to incandescence—
All flesh grass,
In the hands of the living God.

Now the burning of a fly raises Waste almost to Apocalypse.

Chicago Tribune, August 8, 1969

5e

MAN

Two, subconscious of each
Other, one waking
While the other sleeps.

To reach out and touch
The double above our waking,
The one who sleeps.

Here, Soul's haunted attempt to contact some higher self.

II

WAVE PLOTS IN SPACE AND TIME

1
Two loves have brought me to a cold March shore:
The old of ocean and another new;
Gray eyes paired on the breaking Gray;
Lips as changeful as the sea.

Tell those who love you, when they look at you,
To leave possession; for your face will shift
With banished Eve from smiling into grief.

Like sandpipers, up and down with the wash,
I follow the wave-play of those lips.

2
From the windowed house Atlantic day
Renews, you with me, flower-gowned.
After thirty years to watch the dawn rose
Throw petals on the waves. We have no better
Teachers than the gods: ocean, sun
Squander tides of unconditioned love

For kind, who cares—and who cares not?

3
Grass stems mark the turn of day
By the shadows' conjugate curves;
Wave-concaves, toward noon, focus sun.
Small ones, down the beach, crack musket fire;
The thunder of the great, carried higher,
Thins to a whisper as the surf shoals in.

On the strand of now time's motion rides:
Wind in the grass over migrant dunes,
Sand-ripples shadowed from the low sun.

The most ephemeral most of all endures.

4

Motorbikes barrel the strand oil slicks;
Surf brown; sludged foam. Washed no more
In the limitless, illimitable blue.
To float a dream
Of lawns and houses down the Main Line
We slag earth's ocean to a dying pool.
Good times end it sooner; give us good times.

To ride the love-surge of your youth
I could almost pioneer another westward death.

5

The finite effluent takes the sky.
Change rounds on itself, the lift and lean
Crashing always to a shoreward spill,
Restless as the molecular sliding fives
By which (some say) the fluid state obtains . . .

I sit face backward on the time train,
Hours and miles of distance clacking to more
Every paired Bosch bubble turns to dream,
Whether of earth of woman.
                              Cry the other
Sea: cosmic tongues of flame, wider
Than the lost, more changeable-unchanged

Here the longer, five-section poem recovers a never-consummated relation of an attrac-
tive coed to an older tutor, invited to join her on the Atlantic coast for an afternoon swim
and surfing, then a night in her parents' beach cottage The five-sections have been faith-
fully adapted to a chaste variation of the "Love, Desire, Nature, Waste, Soul" chambers
of the book. The whole justifies a frequent contention that poetry has less of recorded
fact than of visions—is more imagined than recalled. This is the Robin greeted earlier in
"Wake Robin."

6a

LEAVING BAVARIA

Gentian waters down from snow,
Restless, as my thoughts to you,
Probe a space of temporal valleys
 For the rock-pass of solace.

The eye to see can only scan,
Fingers wander for the form;
Face of absence, foundling, come,
Weep the landscape of return.

To a Munich traveling companion after the Fulbright year.

Quarterly Review of Literature

6b

SAND AND SNOW

You lie on dune sand
How sacredly
Your bare hip swells
The air—hill
Of my desire, cool
In the grass-blowing wind

Snow falls. Lost
From your love
I have the taste
Of death under my tongue

Desert Review Anthology published these as two sketches called "Nude"
and "Il gran Rifiuto."

6c

SILVER LINING

Give me a hill, that when it rains
Commands some far-off corner of the scene—

Mountains lighted by the sun
With all the cloud-washed air between—

Sandia, Jemez, Taylor, through the veil,
To keep one life-illusion real.

The Santa Fe scene.

Saludos (with translation into Spanish); also *Puerta del Sol*, Vol. 21, 1.

6d

FLY BAIT

Stung with sweat and flies
I strip for the rock pool. Dive
When I come up rock-clean,
Black swarms on my clothes
Flout me. Like all the world's fools—
Sold on the leavings of a man.

Saturday Review

6e

SURSUM CORDA

In cold night
The crooked log
Spouts fire.
No more asked
Of death-loves than this:
That punk at midnight
Bleed like stars in space—
How fiercely vindicated
The earth that wrings our hearts.

New Letters: Reader II

7a

ENGENDERED IN THE EYES

"You are old;
Forego the love
Of women and the world."

"To the world
Old and loveless
I quit claim;

"But to women hold
While their eyes
In mine

"Plead the world
Old and loveless
And love unclaimed."

.

7b

ALPHA AND OMEGA

She turns for shame, her
Ripe Omega
Mirrored in the water

Striptease of the pool, turn
Again, reveal
The sacred Alpha, cuneiform.

To Danny, 1948: our New Hampshire honeymoon summer.

Quarterly Review of Literature

7c

HEROES

A pair of gray mallards,
Almost invisible,
Move in the distance;

Only their ripples
Catch the sunset;
And those birds—

Light into darkness—
Ride the still world
Ignorantly glorified.

c. 1960, viewed from our Annapolis house.

New York Times, March 3, 1969

7d

VICTOR-VICTIM

Read your SONGS:
The publishable flash;
Better these, hopeless—

Dystrophic youth
Crutching to class,
El Greco eyes—

Manikin world, to fling
Once in your teeth
A statement like that.

7e

POOL OF TAO

I waited the fullness of time.
As sunset deepened
The wind died.
In the hush the pool
Was an iris of trees
Fringing a sky—

Motionless, until
A flight of geese passed over;
Then I heard the sound
Of water, a stream
That falls to the pool,
Lingers, and falls away.

When the geese were gone
The sky gave over
The motion received;
But heart was full,
Holding flight and water,
The arrow and the wheel.

New York Times, April 5, 1962; published with a first stanza, I'd since cut;
I add it here for the record:

> I looked into the pool
> And the pool was troubled,
> Broken images of earth and sky;
> I said: Let calm
> Perfect what is revealed.

8a

QUEEN OF NIGHT

All night I have kept you waking
In the wreathed unrest of love;
We have seen the gray moon streaking
The warm hills of home,
The long moonlight probing
The fringed lake and grove.

Now day is breaking
And day birds are shrill;
Reason comes creating
In the blind depths of the will;
And to the world of making
I follow the day's spell.

But you, my love, will shade you
Deep in the sepia grove.
Sleep, my soul's soft shadow;
I would not have you move;
Until the moon and I shall wake you
To the wreathed unrest of love

Ladies Home Journal, May 1963

8b

BANANA

Unexpectedly, from the highest shoot, a huge
Thing detaches itself, leaving the sheath
Slowly like a stallion's appalling member.

Curling, purpling, thrusting out an emergent
Flower that lifts from day to day petals
Like loin cloths, revealing the genitalia:

Enlarging fingers of banana capped with cream,
Dropping nectar, to which small queenbirds fly, and sing
The shocking abandon of fertile and phallic bloom.

Rolfe Humphries, *New Poems* #2, Ballatine, 1957; also *Erotic Poetry*, edited by William Cole, Random House, 1963.

8c

BARN SWALLOW

A swallow skims low over the field,
Turning and darting as insects rise.
I see the blue back, orange breast, forked tail;
Pursue the motions, the bank, the dive,
The swerve in flight that nabs swerving flies.
He sees me also, bends his course
To skirt my presence, flutters, cries.

I like that fluttering; I only guess
At what he likes, beyond his prey.
I do not take the invisible world on trust;
Probabilities remain, and this is probable:
The flight of his outwardness, the stance of mine,
Harbor like visitants, some angel I,
Banking in timelessness, intrinsic, free.

Observed in Vermont, summer about 1960.

New York Times, April 18, 1963; also *New York Times Anthology* and *Poetry of Azatlán*

8d

TIRESIAS SPEAKS

"Odysseus, stern guard,
Put up the sword;
I am the prophet;
Let my tongue
Blossom in speech."

I wake, my mouth filled
With the salt reek of blood

Given to me in sleep; first called: "On the Shore of Birth." ·

8e

STRANGER

From towering darkness,
Flash and thunder;
The lights go off together.

The old woman
Understands a moment
Then forgets, gropes
From lamp to lamp
To flick them on,
Bewildered
Calls the cat.

(To bring the years'
Stray kittens from the storm.)

A door slams in a gust,
Trees brush the window,
Rain in sheets goes
Solid on the screens.

She trips and stands smiling,
Lost but not worried
(It is we
Who draw back in fear);
The smile on her lips.
She calls into the darkness
Further than drowned light:

"Here Kitty, Kitty, Kitty;
Come Kitty, Kitty;
Come Kitty."

Written as observed: Mother in the Greenville house, one of my last
summer visits, August 1962.

New Mexico Quarterly, 1969

9a

THE FIRE

The fire was slow kindling; it was damp wood.
Twice I rose, to mend it, from your side;
Stirred the wet sticks and blew the smoldering ends.
Then in the cold night-clearing of the wood,
We two, not young, and wet with time's worse rains,

Forgot the fire; until suddenly it was there,
Point kindling point to take us by surprise;
A majesty of light, a living blaze,
That sent up sparks to coil across the sky,
Earth's poor matter assaulting the dark.

On this ground, the shore where we are bred,
We watched the lattice of transfigured wood
Slough films of gray ash and renew its glowing,
And in the clear space of the dew-cold forest,
Saw the last sparks waver among the stars.

On this poem from our first Annapolis Fall, September 15, 1956, see Life, Chapter 5—with a quotation from my mother's letter.

Ladies Home Journal, May 1960; also *Doubleday Anthology: Modern Love Poems*

9b

GIRL WALKING

Here comes a girl so damned shapely
Loungers stop breathing. Conceive how subtly
She works those hips. She is all sex, she knows it.
Lace shows the bubs; she is proud of notice—
Head high, back arched, long braids, wide crupper—
Walks like dancing, calls the gods to tup her.

Her mother goes before, full as a tick,
A trundling hill of flesh, a breeding sack,
Swollen with stoking of all appetites.
She stirs her buttocks too, but not to our delight.

Body of flame, how can you stroll
With such impulsive beauty, admired by all,
Your destiny waddling before you down the road?

A frequent sight on the street in Mayaguez, Puerto Rico 1955-56.

Rolfe Humphries, *New Poems* #2, 1957; also *Erotic Poetry* (Random House, 1963) edited
by William Cole; so I put it in my Lust category.

9c

NOVEMBER TOWER

The big wind rattles the glass of the eight-sided tower. It has
Blown down all our fall, all the late lingering of those leaves.
Bring the fur-collared coat, castoff of a hunting friend;
Bring the fleece-lined brogans, lug table and chair
Here where the pale sun slants through southwest panes.
On all four quarters the stripped expanse of cold-shrunken land
Circles this self-center. Bite down on that now. Until time
Smiles, swing—a bulldog at the focus of the bare earth-wheel.

1964: from my St. John's tower office, Annapolis.

9d

PTERODACTYL

I sang the vine of beauty on the slopes
Of terror, hungry for reaches
Of the reptile seaways—Niobrara . . .

In despair even of cleaning the bottles,
Cans, wrecked cars from our own back yard,
We take wing and glorious
Rain fire and poison on far-off
Margins of the world . . .

We chose it in theory:
Night after night in prophesies of flame
Acclaimed the world-commitment
Where it seemed our greatness to burn;
Hated the funk of reaction,
Withering earth's call to globaloney.

Now we wake to the Midas touch of fire,
Where do we go to be human again?

Response to Vietnam, from our Santa Fe house, on a ridge which might have
faced the Mesozoic seaway.

Poetry of Azatlán

9e

ROSE OF SHARON

Women I have seen ripe as fruit
In the green hills on the low horizon
When the voice of the turtle was heard in our land,

Withered in the pantry; and the men of my youth
Gristle and fat. Who calls from the waste country:
Like a roe or hart upon the mountain of spices?

Yet Shulamite-Magdalen at the dying fire,
A crumpled bone bag, sings against the darkness:
Until the day break and the shadows flee away.

And at the deathbed of a loved woman
I have found the last silence charred with sighs:
Stay me with flagons, for I am sick with love.

How all these cold days of the weeping spring,
Crouched at the fire, this gaunt flesh sings:
Rose of Sharon . . . as the lily among thorns.

Approach, Rosemont, PA

10a

DEUS FORTIOR ME

Beyond your husband at the church service
Your folded hands and face raised
Preach the greater law; to find a way,

Gothic, tender, total, dark, and
Skyward, as when flesh possessed
Breathes "I love you" in its rutting thrust.

The title is from Dante's *Vita Nuova*, where he, a youth, first sees Beatrice, a girl by the Arno, and speaks or hears (in Latin) "Ecce Deus fortior me, qui veniens dominabitur mihi."—"Here is a god stronger than I, who coming shall rule over me." It is true that Dante's sublimation seems swayed here by another passion; still, the poem (Annapolis, c. 1965) stands in the first position, of Love.

10b

BE SECRET

Is love simple? What if mothers
Come to kindness lifting conscience
Gownlike to the touch of lovers?

Is love partial? Have not husbands
Won the glory of their wives
By the toss of a girl's thighs?

And who knows if everybody loves best
Where the need of love is least
And Eros like Agape gives itself?

While for Lust (Annapolis, the same 1960s), we yield to sophistic argument.

Quarterly Review of Literature

10c

TWO SCALES

For the Greeks the natural succession was Orpheus descending;
Gold into Iron; Phlegethon, ground of passion;
Post and lintel of tragic song.

Our scale rises, Gothic vaultings,
The grave that moults the angelic butterfly:
Its third is love, its seventh pain, its diapason fire

My first years at Annapolis, Victor Zuckerkandl welcomed me into the music course he
was shaping for the St. John's program. My records, from Graeco-Roman and Gregorian
to Gothic and later Western, plotted the drama of "leading tone." So this poem, of about
1960, takes up the category of Earth or Nature.

10d

ECHO

Nearing the Halloween that nears three score,
Century of our ruin, quit the town;
Past piñon hills spider-webbed with roads,
Thread Arroyo Moro up Atalaya's bowl.

Cliffs of Precambrian metamorphic gneiss
Mottled and folded with dark Vishnu schist . . .
More than old trees and almost as much as stars,
You have always loved and hankered after rock.

If then the amorphous jelly of the tongue
Take voice: What seeking? What its own? Does not
This cleft gorge of the flawed earth, weatherings
Of pink and gray, give back the answer: stone?

Santa Fe, c. 1970; following our 1967 move west, Santa Fe poems begin to sift into the
collection. Appropriate—at the rate development was invading our mountain back-
ground—that the first should settle for the designation Waste.

10e

DARK TRAIL

Bare your feet old man, that once
On midnight mountains, for a wife—

Yours of another's erring—
Searched the dark

(How love's lost follies burn
Remembered youth, as if desired);

Dark again and mountains,
The worn touch of the ground—

With creased feet bare, Tiresias,
Grope the deeper trail.

Santa Fe poem, but remembering Black Mountain.

Five poems in five languages, each with my English translaion. For a critique, compare my forthcoming "Poetic Translation: *A Mythic History*," Chapter 1.

III

ARCHETYPES WITH TRANSLATION

1.

Victor Hugo (past eighty years old): AVE DEA: MORITURUS TE
SALUTAT
A Judith Gautier

La mort et la beauté sont deux choses profondes
Qui contiennent tant d'ombres et d'azur qu'on dirait
Duex soeurs également terribles et fécondes
Ayant la même énigme et le même secret.

Ô femmes, voix, regards, cheveux noirs, tresses blondes,
Brillez, je meurs! Ayez l'eclat, l'amour, l'attrait,
Ô perles que la mer mêle à ses grandes ondes,
Ô lumineux oiseaux de la sombre forêt!

Judith, nos deux destins sont plus près l'un de l'autre
Qu'on ne croirait, à voir mon visage et le vôtre;
Tout le divin abîme apparaît dans vos yeux,

Et moi, je sens le gouffre étoilé dans mon âme;
Nous sommes tous les deux voisins du ciel, madame,
Puisque vous êtes belle et puisque je suis vieux.

HAIL GODDESS, WE WHO ARE ABOUT TO DIE SALUTE YOU
To Judith Gautier

Death and beauty are two somber loves,
As deep in blue and shade as if to say:
Two sisters, alike fecund and destructive,
Bearing the burden of one mystery.

Loves, voices, looks, tresses dark and fair,
Be radiant; for I die. Hold light, warmth, solace—
You pearls the sea rolls in waves up the shore,
You birds that nestle, luminous, in the forest.

Judith, our destinies are nearer kin
Than one might think to see your face and mine.
The abyss of all opens in your eyes—

The same starred gulf I harbor in my soul.
We are neighbors of the sky, and for this cause,
That you are beautiful and I am old.

2.

Goethe: SELIGE SEHNSUCHT

Sagt es niemand, nur den Weisen,
Weill die Menge gleich verhönet:
Das Lebendige will ich preisen,
Das nach Flammentod sich sehnet.

In der Liebesnächte Kühlung,
Die dich zeugte, wo du zeugtest,
Uberfällt dich fremde Fühlung,
Wenn die stille Kerze leuchtet.

Nicht mehr bleibest du umfangen
In der Finsternis Beschattung,
Und dich reisset neu Verlangen
Auf zu höherer Begattung.

Keine ferne macht dich schwierig,
Kommst geflogen und gebannt,
Und zuletzt, des Lichts begierig,
Bist du, Schmetterling, verbrannt.

Und solang du das nicht hast,
Dieses: Stirb und werde!
Bist du nur ein trüber Gast
Auf der dunklen Erde

SACRED LUST

Tell the wise; the many lour,
And make ignorance their shame;
Say I praise the living power
That hungers for a death of flame.

Love-nights breed us as we breed:
In the candlelighted cool,
Feel the gates of dark go wide
For the moulting of the soul.

From its woven bed of shadows
Mere enclosure falls away:
Love spreads new wings to the meadows
Of another mating play.

Tireless, upward; spaces dwindle;
Nothing hems declared desire;
God is light and light will kindle,
And the moth wings leap in fire.

Know, until you learn to weave
Each flame—dying into breath,
Everywhere you haunt the grave
Of the shadowed earth.

3.

Petrarch XI, IN MORTE DE MADONNA LAURA

Se lamentar augelli, o verdi fronde
mover soavemente a l'aura estiva,
o roco mormorar di lucide onde
s'ode d'una fiorita e fresca riva,

là 'v'io seggia d'amor pensoso e scriva;
leicha 'l ciel ne mostrò, terra n'asconde,
veggio et odo et intendo, ch'ancor viva
di sì lontano a' sospir miei risponde:

"Deh perché innanzi 'l tempo ti consume?"
mi dice con pietate: "a che pur versi
degli occhi tristi un doloroso fiume?

Di me non pianger tu, che' miei dì fersi
morendo eterni, e nell' eterno lume,
quando mostrai di chiuder, gli occhi apersi."

AFTER LAURA'S DEATH

If birds' lament, green leaves' or tendrils' stir
To the soft sighing of the air of summer,
Or through the wave-wash at the petalled shore
Of a clear stream, crystal's liquid murmur
Sound, where I sit bowed to the forest floor—
Her, whom heaven showed and earth now covers,
I see and hear and know, as if the power
Of her live voice responded from afar:

"Why do you spend yourself before your years?"
She asks in pity. "Or wherefore and for whom
Pour the wasting river of your tears?
You must not weep for me. My life became,
Dying, eternal; and to eternal skies,
The dark, that seemed to close them, cleared my eyes."

4.

CATULLI CARMINA XXIX

Quis hoc potest uidere, quis potest pati,
nisi impudicus et uorax aleo,
Mamurram habere quod Comata Gallia
habebat uncti et ultima Britannia?
cinaede Romule, haec uidebis et feres?
et ille nunc superbus et superfluens
perambulabit ommium cubilia,
ut albulus columbus aut Andoneus?
cinaede Romule, haec uidebis et feres?
es impudicus et uorax et aleo.
eone nomine, imperator unice,
fuisti in ultima occidentis insula,
ut ista uestra diffututa mentula
ducenties comesset aut trecenties?
quid est alid sinistra liberalitas?
parum expatrauit an parum elluatus est?
paterna prima lancinata sunt bona,
secunda praeda Pontica, inde tertia
Hibera, quam scit amnis aurifer Tagus:
nunc Galliae timetur et Britanniae.
quid hunc malum fouetis? Aut quid hic potest
nisi uncta deuorare patrimonia?
eone nomine, urbis opulentissime
socer generque, perdidistis omnia?

Catullus, 29
ATTACK ON CAESAR FOR HIS FAVORITE MAMURRA

The man who can face this, the man who can take it,
Is whored himself, a drunk, a swindler. Mamurra
Laps the fat of crested Gaul and farthest Britain.
Pansied Romulus, you see this thing, you take it?
How he struts his way through everybody's bedroom,
Like a white dove, a white-skinned soft Adonis—
Pansied little Roman, you take it in, you bear it?
You are like him then, as drunk, as whored a swindler.
And was it for this, Rome's only great general,
You conquered the remotest island of the West,
To feed this screwed-out tool of yours, Mamurra?
See him spend, twenty or thirty million? First were
His own estates, then the loot of Pontus, then of Spain—
Hear Tagus, the gold-bearing river. They say the Gauls
And Britains fear him? And you love the mongrel? Both
Of you, Caesar, Pompey? While he swills oil of patrimony?
For this, like in-laws, father and son,
You have sluiced wealth and all of the world-city.

5.

San Juan de la Cruz:
CANCIÓN DE LA SUBIDA DEL MONTE CARMELO

En una noche oscura,
con ansias en amores inflamada,
oh dichosa ventura!
sali sin ser notada,
estando ya mi casa sosegada

A oscuras y segura
por la secreta escala, disfrazada,
o dichosa ventura!
a oscuras, en celada,
estando ya mi casa sosegada

En la noche dichosa,
en secreto, que nadie me veía,
ni yo miraba cosa,
sin otra luz ni guía,
sino la que en el corazón ardía

Aquesta me guiaba
mas cierto que la luz de mediodía,
adonde me esperaba
quien yo bien me sabía,
en parte donde nadie parecía

Oh noche, que guiaste,
oh noche amable más que el alborada,
oh noche, que juntaste
Amado con amada,
amada en el Amado transformada!

En mi pecho florido,
que entero para el solo se guardaba,
allí quedó dormido,
yo le regalaba,
y el ventalle de cedros aire daba

El aire del almena,
cuando ya sus cabellos esparcía,
con su mano serena,
en mi cuello hería
y todos mis sentidos suspendía

Quedéme y olvidéme,
el rostro recline sobre el Amado,
cesó todo, y dejéme,
dejando mi cuidado
entre las azucenas olvidado.

THE ASCENT OF MOUNT CARMEL

In the dark of night
With love inflamed
By luck, by chance
I rose unseen
From the house hushed in sleep.

Safe in the dark
By a secret stair
My luck, my chance
And night for a veil
I stole from the house of sleep.

By chance of night
By secret ways
Unseeing and unseen
No light, no guide
But the flames that my heart gave—

Led by those rays
Surer than day
I came where one waits
Who is known to me
In a place none seemed to be.

Night that guides
Purer than dawn
Night that joins
Lover and loved
And the loved into Lover changed.

In my flowered heart
That is only his
He lay in sleep
Lulled by the breeze
The fanning of my cedars gave.

Down turrets that air
With hand serene
As it stirred in his hair
Gave my throat a wound
That took all sense away.

I ceased, I was gone
My face to his own
All passed away
Care and all thrown down
There among the lilies where I lay.

11a

THE PLACE

Where moss banks the stream
His running stopped;
Palms catch the temples'
Fluttering.

The nearer to dying we are
In the forest of loss,
The more wish makes us
A nest of wings.

Recognizing the place of some earlier forest Love.

11b

TWO FAMILIES

In rain forest Chiapas, at the table of Chang,
American Gothic exhibits right from wrong.
The Iowa mission sends this virtuous couple
To demonstrate imperatives of the moral:
Hobbled, who gazed and scratched together
Thirty years without breaking a tether,
Exhort through lips like a pursed-up bag
(Categorical sabotage)
Our old forest Maya with his child-wife and child
And his old wives and children—and look, how they smile!

At Chankin's Naja, 1972. See the first of the "Lacandon Journals," Life,
Chapter 6. (Call it Love, not narrowed but widened.)

11c

DAY OF CAMBODIA

Always far off, the soft assurance: the first
Note tentative, a second rising, in question
Or alarm, three then of comfort, breathed, subsiding.

Thunder darkens over the woods of error
Where I walk listening, slow to fathom
The five-fold tones of a dove's covenant.

For me, in Washington, DC, with students, for a Kent College protest, a dove's
five-tone sound, affirming our Earth.

11d

ORGANIC SPECTRA IN INTERSTELLAR DUST

When we drive up a long road slanting a little toward the sky,
I see beyond the clouds space sowed with worlds.

Over all civilizations we flushed and disinfected—
Wishful eyes on progress.

Punctual—disaster kindling in our bounty—
How life's fierce radicals,

Hydroxyl, methane, cyanogen, ammonia,
Sow the stellar void with wishful poisons.

Given our dysecology, may not the life-radicals through cosmic space hint
somehow at Waste?

11e

WORLD-CAVE

I light the torch
And lift it to inscribe in smoke
My curse, my warning on the wall.

Is it rock crystal
Shining? Gold mosaics? Shapes
I have known: Cross, Lyre, Crown!

For the metamorphic states of this poem of Soul, see Life, Chapter 5.

12a

THE POOL

There is a valley in that forest
Green with siftings off the leaves;
Water with a low sound down the stone
Gathers to silence, where a pool
Floats the lights and shadows of the grove.

In the wavering, I cannot tell
Which is better: if sight alone
Surface where leaf-shadows move,
Or body plunge into the deepest
Sway and lapping of the water's hold.

Only from every day's appearance
I take the path down to that pool;
Watch, where the slow drop from the stone,
In its trembling tear-shape mirrors
Two forms laced in a forest dark as love.

The closing word, Love, speaks this poem's placement.

Desert Review Anthology, 1974

12b

HOUSEMAID'S KNEE

"When he was live and had his feeling,
She was on her back and he was kneeling"

How have I contracted housemaid's knee?
By devout kneeling to housemaids,
Schismatic loves, womb-liberators,
If you overturn the service at that altar,
It may ease my chronic malady.

At the Santa Fe St. John's, my box in the postal array is so low I have to sing the Christ-mas carol "Fall on your knees . . ." to get my mostly junk mail. Once, on that flagstone floor, this lusty ditty came to comfort me.

Desert Review, Fall 1971

12c

MICTURITIONS

From the flickering dark of the mezzanine
I reach a porcelain room marked MEN.
In mercury light I see as strange
The stream that was me, from my flesh,
Leave me, this seeing nothingness.

I water in the moonlight on the grass,
My drops, globed on grass,
Moon back at me—delight's
Deliquescent light.

Two short sketches, "Paramount" and another, merge here, desperately fulfilling the Earth-Nature requirement.

12d

FATHER OF LIES—Time of the Vietnam War

Paid again, peace talker,
The tax that bombs and flames.

You enter the bedroom door,
Your shadow on the wall.

The door slams behind
Blotting you out.

Shut in the dark
With the shape you have become.

Through those years, each payment to what some then called "The Infernal Revenue
Service of the United Snakes of America" posed a moral crisis.

12e

THIS BREATHING HOUSE
(Coleridge)

Music, always reaching in the flow
A seat of permanence . . .

The hermit crab, distinguished
Less by solitude than wandering,
Readiness
Among shells of a beach pile
To go on shifting ground.

I do not understand the juncture
Between timelessness and time, the hunger
For an actual home, requiring homelessness.
Being of that foreclosure, I take it
Like bread and wine; I call it incarnation.

. . . Listen to the viols:
Indwelling soul, homing, down the shadows.

My years of playing viola da gamba with an Annapolis group suggested this Soul analogy.

13a

TE, DEA

The well
That floats the leaf
And flower
Drowning them;

The flame
That folds itself
In flaming
And is still;

Well-flame
Where all spirals
Leaf-dying
Fire-renewed.

"Te, Dea" is from Lucretius' invocation to Venus as the mystery of atom-linking Love.

St. John's College Review

13b

HOUGHMAGANDIE

Even the Romans in the decadence
That loamed the fallen world with monuments
Of their gloom, and when the bitterness of sex surprised them,
Sought it, loved it, prized it.

Out of fabulous crypts of the Dark Ages
Issue nameless voices,
Avowed monks on their knees declining
To the dear socket of a girl's inturning.

Sanctimonious Puritans
Warmed beds with bundling, Victorian
Dames veiled under bustles of silence the same fesses,
Smooth, indented, thighs spread for caressing.

Body, naked, cloven, supple, swaying—
Here, where the great cloud waits at
The sun's horizon, shall we not mate and slumber,
Our foldings wreathed again on the leaves of Indian summer?

Title: a good old Scottish word for what is here talked of; note: the feminine
ending prevails.

Quarterly Review of Literature

13c

WINDOWED HABITATIONS

East, over the water, nothing but trees,
Green shadowed nature. At sunset suddenly
A light appears, a torch, a star,
Another sun, pouring through dark leaves.

We are leaf-shadowed here; give us reflections:
Something not ours to image, that over water,
Someone, far-off, will say: "Surely
That is one of soul's windowed habitations."

In our Annapolis house, we often caught such reflections from houses across
Spa Creek. (Revised from a fourteen-line poem.)

Rolfe Humphries, *New Poems* #2, Ballantine Press, 1978

13d

GLOOMY DIS

It was not in ignorance: again and again
We mounted time's slope; though time
Had given proof romantics rifle virgins—
This round of sea and land soul so loved
That eyes still westward take through tears
The heave and crashing of those sullied waves.
To have her young again—Proserpina

Driving the Pacific coast of southern Mexico, where the waves fling filth
and garbage up the strand.

13e

GNOMIC

The night each plows
A furrow of death
In the field of stars
Who calls?

I am nothing
But one with the one
That makes the nothing
All.

See account of origin in the Life, Chapter 6.

14a

BLEIBE DER FLAMME TRABANT
(Stefan George: Hold to the Flame)

Where they rose in the woods by the water
she painted the bay and shore

Caught in a flagrance of loss that made
the land all fire—

Orion's burning sea, love's old nebula

Half a world away, he frames it
on the wall

In a rainbow of tears, always earth's
water sign

And airy cry at dying: trust the fire.

About a parting and a landscape expressing grief. From Annapolis to Santa Fe.

14b

TWO CENTERS

Full-face! Arms spread, legs spanned!
Sex marks the center of Vitruvian man.

Only from above—vertical view—
Head focuses our radial play;

And that blind worm, poking below,
Comic appendage, points one way.

Curious, the pact between sex and comedy.

14c

WESTERN DRAGON

Lights, along the tidal reaches
Dark—cities—I see you lovelier
And lonelier than ever in our days
Of hope, your beauty rooted
In your loneliness.

Dark by day, clouding
The embayments of your streams,
Breeding hutches of the overpopulating us,
At night you constellate a coil of flame
Along the roads of water.

And we, airborne through night,
Catch by the bay the renewed
Dragon of fire. The old snake
Casts his skin: cities of light,
Spangled in our tears.

Technocratic Earth, its wasteful brightness seen from the air through tears.

New York Times, September 25, 1961; close so revised.

14d

WORLD CHOICE

Our freedom death, our life-road
Regimen . . . Soul, spinning itself out
In matter, plant, beast, bird—
Was every turning point as desperate?

When nature took the habit of fixed laws,
Attraction deadened into gravity—
Did all stand then as now in such love-doubt
Where the blind longing would lead?

Is not the first sentence a dire enough pronouncement of the choice?

14e

RESONANCE

When I see the world reduced to sky
And rock and a bare spacing of trees,
Perspective rhythms choir in standing waves.

Love does not count on man;
In space and time extension weaves
The celebration of its magnitudes.

The need of Soul to affirm gave this poem its first title,"Still Choiring"—as if
space, self-perceiving, were enough to make a cosmos.

15a

DA UNSER ZWEITER BETTE WAS

You, smiling from the ground, a Chartres angel fallen—
Mothwing lids on eyes preternaturally blue—
Are you ingredient in the secret landscape?
Or must I wake some day, the sun as now a furnace
In the gum trees, this moss-bed crushed beside me,
And know you for the phantom seen since childhood:
Fair-haired Sainte Modeste, Queen Cunegunde, smiling Uta?

The title is from Walter von der Vogelweide's most fetching lyric, of the couple "Under the linden, on the heath," in their bed of gathered flowers. Here it raises the question of all passing loves.

15b

BABY BLUE-EYES

Paired with eyes as luminous as blue
That break in glances over a swelling sea,
A student stands before me, lips inquiring:
May her thesis be of love, on which she is knowledgeable.

Sight swims with blue:
Where waves crest white
On purple, there the reef
Down swinging fans unfolds
The coral of its caves.

Once we go far enough
Into the element, fear
Turns to desire, the green
Eel withdraws, we follow
Into deeper water.

"No doubt," I tell her, "that will be satisfactory.
Relate it if you can to Penelope and Calypso."
How peerlessly her swaying leaves the room,
And leaves it swaying, like a tide-pool, blue.

It took this student to change that smiling love to a tropic caricature, recalling
our Puerto Rican coral seas.

15c

CAÑADA CORRALES

Sacred, in dry country, every stream.
This, from Atalaya, down a black sill
Of outcrop marble, carved at the rim
A bowl for flesh to bathe, in Eden's truth:

Chest-deep, worn for two, female, male,
Chastened in cool water and close stone,
Rippled through the clear to harvest miles
Of rock and canyon, sky and valley pine.

Until a new buyer made a cement dam
For a swimhole, crazed the gradient;
The first flash-flood brimmed the rock bowl
With gravel, where shoal water slides.

Forcing nature is our life and death:
Oedipus plows the mother, to their pain;
A risk with love and knowledge; wanting both,
Defiance flung to the boomerang.

Nietzsche tied the myth of Oedipus to man's shift from idyllic food-gathering, as in pastoral Arcadia, to agriculture, that plowing up of mother earth for our fruits of sustenance. Here, I tie a stupid landowner's spoiling a favorite rock-pool south of Santa Fe so a boomerang, ignorantly flung, could have veered back at him, and at us.

15d

BURDOCK

"Take a truck-jack after rain,
Wrap the corded stalk around,
Heave back, levering to a ton;
As if a devil groaned
     'Karrunk'-
Feet of dark bull-pizzle jimmies out."

I, so, from Vermont; Kinnell then from Plaquemine:
"Peace-marchers, clubbed and jailed"
I fling the burdock, twist the next, heaving
For the death-groan-Ah-
     "Karrunk"-
As mad as wrong or right to purge the earth.

In this poem, called "Weed Farm" in the 1962 edition, I have had to clarify the polarity, that summer, between my uprooting cockleburs on our lately acquired Vermont property, and the clubbing and jailing of my best Princeton student and lifetime friend, the poet Galway Kinnell—on civil rights marches in Louisiana. Alas, I, as "purging Right," seem in the poem (superficially, I trust) to resemble the mad "Southern Wrong" of that clubbing. Surely, I took out on the burdock what I felt for Galway's clubbers.

New Letters II: *Reader* II; since revised

15e

LOVE OF NUMBER

ONE

The point alone-
Dilated now: birdcall, waves in a pond,
Circle and sphere (in the gravity of oneness, raindrops, stars)
Cleaves an in from out, other from same,
Self-reflecting

TWO

Since every actual round
Stretches on some yoke, oblate dividing star,
Breeds the antimony of poles. Fix on the void between—
In turbulence the axis mounts a thrust
Bisecting: pyramid of

THREE

Timaeus' flame
From there to four asks toil: vertex
Split apart; asks skill, to draw them equally, balance the post
And lintel temple of the year, Roma Quadrata,
Circumscribed

FOUR

Too perfect.
Reason's limit. Beyond is miracle
Return imagination to the sphere, the wave four had stilled:
Golden section, curling vine, petals, starfish,
Undulant and dancing sea-born fluctuant

FIVE

Love would rest there
But in rest; knows the cold descent of rule,
More than quadrate order where all waters close,
Lost to love and play, tyranny of bees,
The radial crystal

SIX

From that ice cage
We reach out any way. Numbers
Infinite: seven music's dynamics, rounded in the octave;
The god's ennead nine; three threes
And one, Gothic

TEN

Endecasyllable
Hourly market dozen and the haunted
Gulf thirteen . . . But all of them born of Pythagorean five
By the breeding on female two of male
And numberless

ONE

For an account of this poem and the longer one, "The Number of My Loves," which
follows, see second half of Chapter 5. The long poem—four major sections, plus a final
line—was published in *Epoch* (Cornell).

1V

THE NUMBER OF MY LOVES

1.

I have one love in the city of Florence.
When we were young we might have married;
But our language was not sufficient
For us to come to terms with each other.

How could I tell her:
"If you love me recklessly now,
You will have me for as long as husband"
Or if I had? Florence lives by custom.

That bargain was made with another. Platonic
Love is rare and not always rewarding;
But for twenty years, like brother and sister,
My Florentine and I have gone on loving.

She runs the mansion and sees to her parents.
Only at evening when the flower looks westward,
She climbs the balcony and takes the blazon
Of towers singing in the cypress valley.

And once in five years, say, I come to that city;
I kiss my Florentine and escort her on the river.
She is beautiful in face and language.
We canoe among the rocks.

I think she hardly braves the sun but then.
"You know," she says, "once in so many years,
From around the world you come like Perseus, caro,
And stay a day—to take me boating on the Arno."

2.

Of my dark love I have told enough already;
But how should dark withdraw into its darkness
While the night flashes with intrinsic fire?

One can suffer years and learn little.
What I learned came afterwards and looking back:
That hate and love are one; that love burns forests;

That lightning kindles what the cloud-dark rain
Balanced in slow love against love's burning;
That these are poles of being: leaf and flame—

For which there are times and seasons. I have learned
We are herdsmen now and harvesters, not hunters.
It is not profitable to burn the grain

To singe a few rabbits and call it tragedy.
Do you remember when those first affairs wounded
Us and others—Europe under fire?

No skill masters the labyrinth
Of hate coiled into good. The walled garden
Wilts with blessing; burned-off barrens

Mantle with wild roses. Yet who but
The spendthrift of a jaded age would put
A torch to the world on a chance of flowers?

Must we, in love's plurality, still swear
By that star-brand ripping a sky of thunder?—
"No matter what's lost or destroyed, I want you to suffer."

3.

There are loves of fact and loves of imagination.
I have been blessed all my life in the love of women.

I will praise loves like angels who kiss entire,
Mingle body and soul and unpossessing,

Drift apart like clouds, break bread of passion
In charity of flesh, not promiscuity.

I could wish for loves in every part of the world,
And be a traveling salesman hawking pleasure:

Look, I have fall days here; I have spring flowers;
Limestone ledges and the limbs of swimming;

Wheat is golden in the palm of my hand;
And the shade of beechwood slumbers on my belly.

You who are queen of silence will come without calling;
We will go into the night, hierophants of nature;

And all our sounds as we are poured into each other
Will be like birds and waters, lappings, sighs;

And you will sleep, and wake filled with a secret,
That love is a drop that lingers to its pool.

You will not mind our coming or our going,
Any more than dreams, or the drift of wings or seasons;

You will get up smiling for the event of day,
And at night, holding another:

"Let him take me again when he passes this country;
Meanwhile, what is love but a gain?"

4.

And there is the wife of my heart, for whom I regret
None of the other chances; for when I return
From my travels, she takes me in the kind
Arms of her wreathing, and I look into eyes
That have no shadow in them.

Like a mountain lake she is a good place
To bathe in on a sky-blue day, or drink
At the rock shore of every evening;
She is a cabin built high in the forest,
In wilderness, a fragrant house of balsam.

Our children laugh in the doorways; she is all
Neatness; she rules with order. And when I am off
On my wanderings, she writes in her brave small
Hand, my hearth's keeper: "We had Chinese
Cookies for supper with fortunes in them;

"I took one for you. It said: 'Make use
Of every moment.' And for me: 'This is
A night for love and affection.' Come soon."
Sometimes I wake under the moon or stars,
As now when Venus is comforting the east,

And think my loves before me.
I am one who has been greatly favored—
Most in her, to whom I send this greeting,
May she keep her fortune a day or two, not doubting:

5.

Love will come home, again and again, forever.

For an account of this poem, see note to preceding poem.

Epoch (Cornell)

16a

MOSS-GREEN

Far in the spruce wood, through the stained
Twilight over the needled ground,
A space opens, as under water, brimmed
With sky and green, where a spruce tree has died.

To stretch out on the cinquefoil of that ground:
Wood sorrel, bunchberry, goldthread,
A walnut gnawed, a robin's egg,
Coil of a snail, gray feather of a dove.

Child of death, come with me
Over the brown-stained ground
To the round place of birth,
Love-luminous, moss-green.

The spruce wood must have been near our Vermont summer place. The closing invitation was meant for my oldest daughter, Nona, born 1940 (the recently published artist of *Nature and the New England Seasons*) on the occasion of her first marriage, to Mark Estrin, author of an acclaimed weird fiction, reviving Kafka's cockroach for amazing 20th-century adventures. They had both lived through troubles, Nona from my divorce in 1949. Now they had ridden on a motorcycle from California to the Danby Four Corners summer place, where the wedding was to occur. I have lost a short envoi applying the "Moss-green" place and poem (in the spirit of the *Five Chambered Heart* dedication: "Nestlings I have loved, / Nestle with love's gods") to that union.

16b

POST COITUM NON TRISTIS

And when we have done:
The loved form
Stretched on the world-floor
The round O flared
Parted lips
Speechless with adoration . . .

Probably took off from Donne's "Post coitum tristis": "Since each such act they say /
Shortens the length of life a day"—of which I published, in my third Oxford year, an
analysis in *The Times Literary Supplement*; whereas, here, I invoke every sensuous
counter-argument, culminantly, the flared round O of parted lips (applicable either to face
or loins) "speechless with adoration."

16c

PHOSPHORESCENT BAY

The wake lightens; fish scatter
Like stars; painlessly
I dip my hand in flame . . .
Our youngest daughter nestles to us tired

Venus trails in the west; I call
Its name: "A world like ours." She looks
And sighs. "And each of those Seven Sisters
Is a sun." Her eyelids fall.

The boat comes round-home
Over darkened water. Dying fires
Shine from islands where night fishermen are
The small soul we cling to sleeps in my arms.

This luminous bay, La Parquera, near the southwest corner of Puerto Rico, here joins a
wonder of Earth to astronomy and generation—our small Sandra in my arms.

16d

ON TELEGRAPH AVENUE

When you were love's towhead I was the father.
The breakup hurt you worse than the others.

Years I was God in the garden: "Beware the fruit"—
Your brown eyes hungry for love and for death.

Child-marriage, heart's ease of trust and children,
Mistrusted, loosed you to the cauldron

Of Fillmore and drugs. I preached salvation
After the moral mouthings of our nation.

Dysecology and war have silenced that:
Global wrong the fruit of righteous right.

Take your guitar, sing the songs of loss:
Mind dissolves in the sway of the voice.

Crazy Jane of blues and rage,
Wrapped in a halo of heroin and rags—

I crash your spitty pavement, schooled
By the queen of the most broken street in the world.

Before the San Cristóbal year of 1969-70, I went to Berkeley, California, to sit for several days with Charlotte, second of my first three daughters—she fallen from teen-age marriage, first to People's Park, brief Hippie refuge, then to heroin and the infamous Street. I carried a little tape recorder and would stay up all night, copying and composing from the day's talk, what became a searching story, "Prodigal Father," bought by *Harper's*, only to be edited out; abandoned also as core of a third novel, though it led to Charlotte's Christ-call, new marriage, and liberation from drugs and the Street.

16e

MIDSUMMER NIGHT IN ASPEN MEADOW

Winding down three valleys from fir mountains,
Converging pastures, flickering fires in dark now—
I see the world like that: multi-dimensional
Comet-slug, shaping time-space lendings as it goes.

And by each eye of fire, in the cave of Nativity,
Krishna dancers, bongo hippies, single acid brooder,
Spin cocoons of vision, inwardness as always
Reaching out-to be the whole earth-river,

Glacier of merging soul-fires down black mountains,
The comet filled with eyes, it cannot be—and is.

Peak of the Hippie invasion of Santa Fe and our Sangre de Cristo sierra.

Saludos Anthology, 1995, with Spanish translation by Consuelo Luz

17a

TO GALWAY

I dreamed of you tonight, your liver
Doubling you up like a shrimp in bed
I waked, the Yaddo scritch-owl
At it on the sill. Death-devoted
Singer-you, not that damned bird—
Something more than poet, a man:
For God's sake, mind yourself.
You are too sole to leave us here
Among so many cruds, the worse alone.

The dream and waking of another Yaddo stay.

New Letters Reader. II

17b

LAST SUPPER

I taught him first. Years after, in another place,
Lay with his wife, beautiful, proffered, theirs asleep;
He, intern, hunting acid and like-sex. No hope,
No ease blessed the divided search. She told, of course;
Took the prick for that. Later, in another house,
He, doctor, knocked at midnight, mine (and wife) asleep—
To expose the teacher-false-friend who broke him up.
"We tried love and failed; your move," I said. He passed.

Lean and bearded, children, ex-wife, joint loves, hers
And his, camping in communes, dispensing medicine
For rip-off welfare, they stop. He cites Kennedy,
Test case: to praise the shot that did false promise in.
At table his eyes find mine; in mine the saint face blurs.
Crushed to mystic squalor, he loves and praises me.

Died since of AIDS.

Past eighty-five now, I can answer as Sophocles did when asked at that age whether he
regretted outliving amorous play, and he said: "I feel I have been delivered from
grievous tyranny."

17c

GILBERT-SWAMP-BLACKBIRD

Squall. "That fatal and perfidious bark"—a canoe
Built by the wife's father for himself alone, sunk
To the gunnels, wobbly as quicksilver—what should I
Care?—having with me again our master painter, neglected
Don Quixote of the brush. Mopping water from the bottom,
My shirt for a sponge, we came, as rain cleared,
To the overgrown creek's end: beneath a rock-oak slope
And flanked with pine, a blue-green swamp of reeds, tide-
Flat surface hatched with alizarin dead stems. Across
From the crabber's shacks and long sleek boats, by a bridge
Some quirk of decay strips to the heirloom of a Chinese
Pen (where a redwing blackbird flies from the swamp nest,
Creaks like a hinge that opens into music, rupture of gold
And vermeil from black flight and the spilled rush of the trill),
We gain the wooded shore. The painter squints for a focus;
I withdrawn to a hummock of moss, lean against a pine
And write—nothing, to celebrate but the fact of sharing
Again the thunder- and sky-reflecting tide-swamp world
That is ours, and the rusty creaking of a coal-black bird
That flying breaks in wings of flame and-yes-song.

Our house is still brightened and adorned with watercolors and oils bought—over his protest—from Jim Gilbert (1899-1970?), University of Chicago. Our "living Old Master" and early teacher of Spanish-American Esteban Vicente, Gilbert was himself a lifetime pursuer of the "Cezanne problem"—to reaffirm nature and man by representational depths, surfacing over the canvas as abstract color forms. So I have shrined him in *The Half Gods* and (with color images) in the final *Symbolic History* shows. It bespeaks our media blindness that Gilbert has not been recognized and featured in national art museums. When I told him that he had conspired—by his avoidance of exhibition and sale—to remain unknown, he typically cried out: "I have succeeded beyond my wildest dreams!" Small wonder this Annapolis visit, before his Chicago retirement would bring him to us as St. John's artist-in-residence, produced (Princeton, c. 1960) a poem of such gratulation.

The English Leaflet, Spring 1960

17d

BICENTENNIAL AT HALL'S RESTAURANT

Shore up this place—old bar by the waterfront,
Copper spit-trough like a urinal,
Gilt and steamboat gothic—patch it all;
Fix the back stair senators would mount,
After state gambling, for a venal cunt;
Spot the old picture on the facing wall:
Eve sluiced out, Adam up from the Fall,
Pounding his clutched head, vain penitent.

Exhume all trust-betrayers who like him
Cursed losses here, feared what else acquired
Subpoena dead and living to this bar:—
Now charge them: "Swill and spill! Enact the dream
That leaves a screwed-out planet, pimped and hired
By Johnson, Nixon, Ford, and worse, and more!"

I was taken there several times by friends who knew the history of the place—also
something of my history as Radical Conservative (from *radix*, roots, going to the roots to
conserve the world fabric), the only sensible party. I wrote the poem facing the huge post-
Romantic *Fall*, looking like a Böcklin.

From Annapolis to Washington, c. 1965.

Washington Anthology

17e

WINTER CAVE

Starnbergersee, a cold remove, ice from the eaves,
Snow banked from the lake almost to the double panes;
Heart driven back to a stove-center,
Pursues the prayerful quest of images:
"Be like an arctic whale wrapped in its blubber."

Call back another winter, that shack at the Dunes,
After Adlai's lost election: how the old painter
Gilbert, fierce poet Kinnell, and Bell
(Prophet verse betrayed) heaped the chunk-stove,
The city far-off lowering through its cloud.

When the first blizzard flung the waves in crystal,
We almost lost the insular illusion.
By night, from shook bedding, lamplit dust
Wheeled and melted south: external wind
Blew through the clapboard space a horn of judgment . . .

Death on a bulldozer followed after . . .
Until this German stove-room windows Now:
Ours is the wilderness beyond the city,
Along the lake that signifies all water—
Three gathered in one loss, past overthrow.

Defiant immortal profection of a triune fellowship, from the Munich year,
remembering Chicago and two treasured friends.

Quarterly Review of Literature

18a

MARCH SNOW

My love is out of town
And the March snow
Like grit bevels around
The four-quartered windows
Of the tower.

I dream of a spring bank
Where moss revives
Earth's precursive
First attempt
At flowers.

Not likely,
Dream being free,
A man would stretch out
Alone, under the conceptual
Beech tree

While the horizon tilts white planes,
Traveler, I give you leave;
But come with the thaw:—
Our flower-rites
Ask flesh not dream.

A rather pure Love poem, though the last two lines voice the Spring-thaw
of desire. Another of the *Annapolis Tower* poems.

18b

NEIGHBORLY

She's like an apple tree
that leans
over the wall;

She belongs to him
but her fruits fall
to me

For the story of this Santa Fe poem, see Life, Chapter 6. In my copy of its first book
publication, I have noted this poem as going with "Moonrise" on the next page.

Contemporary Poets, St. James Press; and *New Mexican Review,* September 1969.

18c

MOONRISE

I rise and climb the dunes. A waning moon
Breaks over an ocean shore it washes clean.
I am content in the ruins of nakedness.

Sleeping or waking, listen, all I have loved:

The heart of an old man wants nothing more
When the dead moon spills its yellow seed
In the heaving and sighing salt furrows of the sea.

As we camped on the Carolina beach, driving back from Annapolis to Mississippi.
Ocean and moon give substance to a number of my Earth-Nature poems.

Contemporary Poets, St. James Press; also *New Mexican Review,* September 1969.

18d

LATE

The earth still has trees
Green-leaved against
The blue of day,
Stirred at night over stars—
Poignancies.

I dream earth tonight,
Its soul-pool round it
Like a swarm of bees
Darting in for birth,
Taught by us displaced
The crisis of the hive . . .

I wake wide of the mark.
Impossible the spaces
For another start.

An ecological fancy, holding the fourth position, as Waste—here of the globe.

18e

SPECULUM MUNDI

Light through cloud now poured from the spent sun
Receiver I to the childing of your touch
I who next will be the very light
Poured down cloud for the receiving eye
Great either way sight cloud and sun
You into me with the same spending touch
As I then into you with the child by my light.

The Life, Chapter 6 gives the occasion of the poem, with Jasha Klein's account of the
Platonic doctrine of perception as a mating and begetting; also, my own notion of being,
in my death-union with nature, light itself—eidos—the male principle of seeing.

19a

LIBATIONS

No fire begins at the best, the times
We look for are the twilight stages,
Charcoal embers where we pass the evening,
Talk, make love, stare through silences
Into a glow that is self-consuming.

Is it now at last beginning, the wonderful
Slow night of embered radiance, when the powers
That warm their evenings at our hearts
Take the good of the fire, sit down in love
And holy drunkenness, and pour on us
Libations to the quiet above the gods?

This poem, cut to the last six lines of fourteen by the *Chicago Tribune Magazine*
in 1970, is given in its full and richer form on in the Life, Chapter 6.

19b

WEDDING DANCE

Strobe light green: trumpets, drums;
Hips flared, crotch front flung;
Red light: tuck twat, snaked up arms.
No fuck, fuck-dance; stab-light green;
Rum-tuckers, strobe strutters, old on young.
Hey old mother-rutter, rub a tub o' bubs;
Stoke that trombone
Fuck-dance, daughter, shake your little thing.
Plug a bugger, gap-face, ruck that drum;
Plump those strings.
Green tongue, red prong, long-haired balls;
Follow your guts and strut your holes.
Gong it solo, boom to boom.
No fuck, fuck-dance; beat my strobe;
Suckers and whuckers are flesh of God
Red bang-green bang-horn hot hole;
One God-swot in the all-God whole

The reality was sketched on a bill-pad at a St. John's wedding celebration at La Posada,
Santa Fe, Spring 1968—my first experience of strobe-dancing. Penned revision deci-
phered from bill-pad, August 1969. First, second, and third type slowly worked toward
this printed version.

19c

THIRD WORLD

In the burning selva waiting weeks for rain,
When the sky clouds over and wind comes in gusts,
Under the forest tent you hear a mournful rustle;
It is leaves, not drops, leaves of the rainless
Winter, that fall from the terraced roof.
And you wait in a smoky wood where fire creeps through the brush;
Listen for the sound to change, from dry to a liquid spill—
Globed water gurgling to rain-forest rivers green and full.

This poem—originally published with my "Lacandon Journals" in *Grand Street* (1944);
see the Life, Chapter 6—was taken over to serve in the third, Nature-Earth position at this
point in *Five Chambered Heart*.

19d

BASALT BOWL

We loved this country and we came to it,
  in too great numbers and with too many cars.

This landscape, roll with it; flow out over lava
Mesas, first smog creeping from Albuquerque
And over the Chama gap from Farmington;

This landscape that was fire and will be smoke—
Poison (we agar-plate bacteria), feel now
Its soul in the rock, springs in the rivers;

In the basalt bowl lifted over the world, sit
And wait chastened; not hate . . . not even pity;
Wonder, at a being whose fatal flaw was love.

Called "Lean to the Ponderosa" in the first edition of *Five Chambered Heart*, this poem
holds in the nineteenth, five-poem sequence of that book, the fourth or Waste position-
waste, of our Western world.

19e

SUNDAY ON THE WALLBERG

From the cloud of Munich in a bubble chair
We reach a height where it is autumn clear;
Stripped on crystal cobbles in bright air,
Dream the garden aether of beginning.
Wake—to muffled music: organ, choir,
And faint as under water lost bells ringing.
From dim churches and mist-vaulted towers
In the passion valley of our homing
We take the Lethe of the vesper hours.
Tears plant flesh upon us. Great with longing
We sink in darkness toward the fallen singing.

This poem, from the Fulbright Munich year, was published in a looser, twenty-five-line form by *Approach*. The title here replaces the "Waldberg Lift" of the earlier *Five Chambered Heart*—though I hold to the book's revised text.

20a

WHAT LOVE SHAPES

Wishing a presence time and space withhold,
I walk the twilight of a settled road;
Far off, one appears; I call the name,
Start forward to a likeness which is dream.

Must three hundred years of seeing still rehearse
The Cartesian axioms of the universe?

Winter grape arbor behind the house,
A cesspool under, winter odorous;
Remembering vintages I dwell on shapes
Of frost-brown vines: what I smell is grapes.

How often with others have you closed your eyes,
Felt their being in you, and known it mine?

An attempt to invoke love as stretching the deterministic limits of Cartesian and Newtonian cause.

20b

DEIRDRE

By the Roman fable, for perfect luxury,
The sum of the ages should be seventy.
Beautiful married women, blown and mellow,
How that doctrine cheered a wandering scholar;
Cheered from year to year an aging tutor,
Playing for younger nymphs Silenus satyr.
Seventy nears; I think with reluctance
Of old Tiberius and his infant sucklings.
Deirdre, youngest, warmest, all accurve
You're too old for me—forget it and let's love.

20c

LAKE-DUSK-PINES-MOON

The water holds the brown sky of dusk.
Who set that little fire by the lake?
Who let the twilight through the pines
Fold this crescent sliver of a moon?
Who made dimensionality ambiguous,
Eye's mirror-lake of pines, dusk and moon?

The answer to this puzzle-poem is: Caspar David Friedrich, north-German painter of
the time of Beethoven, master of the transcendental landscape. The picture described,
in the collection of Dr. Georg Schäfer, Obbacht bei Schweinfurt, is Plate 56 in George
Braziller's monograph, New York, 1974.

20c

CHARM FOR A SICK PLANET

Fill the god pots with god-brew:—

Call Truth the spinner of the world—
The dying need it, the new-born need it;
Hold it together as long as you can.

We who tore the earth-robe
Crying still the birth of God,
Gather at the spring of paradox.

Motion is its own, not for a goal:
The jet of time in the pool of now.
"I am" speaks the gravity of stone;

"I am," the levity of wind;
"I am," the rip-saw of fire;
"I am," laps water as it flows.

Think water, fire, air, earth will hold
On the sun-terraces of the world
(As long as they can) rebellious soul:—

Then spill the god-pots to the ground

This poem could have been mentioned in my "Lacandon Journals," Chapter 6. The neo-Maya ceremony of god-pots is described in of that chapter.

20e

COMPLINS OF YOUTH AND AGE

From earth hung in space, as from a ship
Heeled to the blue gulf rayed with light—
Mutinied, cannoned, bloodied, tongued with burning—
Repeat the hymn of the first evening earth:

How the round pearl of a world mothered in air
Falls quietly turning; and our evening falls . . .
Fields of wheat or barley, standing or
In swaths, or shocks like random trees, and trees
That close the fields in somber sheaves—fuse
A complin music down the depths and shoals
Of the atom-weaving, spirit-breathing worlds . . .

If oneness with all-ocean cannot save
The ship mind overreached, it may seed starry space.
Where the spent light-bearer spreads his arms,
Himself the flesh he nails, the cruciform earth-shadow,
Down and down, sounds through the complin wave:
"Fathering fire, forgive; mothering void, receive!"

The generation of this poem, with its 1949 ideal center of a fruitful earth, surrounded by images of a burned out and crucified globe, is also described in the Life, Chapter 6 at the end of the Lacandon visit. It is used, besides, in *Symbolic History*, toward the end of the last show—40: *Now: The Rooted Future.*

V

WATER-FIRE-AIR-VOID

Birth by WATER always, liquid love:
You have seen oceans moving, tides and waves
That leap at breaking and are air, cloud-foam,
Then drops, whole-seeking rounds, each hungry
For the next, quick-silver joined; from space
How green all globe an earth sun-glanced,
A bay at evening, where the level rays
Bleed amber through the blue concaves;
So love refracts in your translucent mould
And turns its ash, breath, moisture into fire.

The cosmic masses are not earth but FIRE, kindled
In void, space-crystals gone to liquid, vapor, heat;
Until the plunge is stayed, a stilled blaze—

Plus and minus balanced into dance, fondled
In passion, as the groove and spool of rutting tame
The Deirdre flame: loins for all asplay, the red lance

Reared for all: as I with you, you whet for me
The craze of flesh, lust-gorging ways—
Dandled at the faithful hearth of play.

Stilled almost to the ambience of AIR,
Almost beyond its nature,

As clouds at sunset,
Even of thunder, fold to the light

Rapt limbs of pleasure
Wind-caressed, or water laves a shore

Or thought pervades the limestone of a land
Held in all its breathings, sight and sound.

What is this EARTH-concretion Dante spread, a last
Periphery of the point of fire, as basalt crusts
On lava, salt from seas? Genesis could only risk

Fall by freedom, nature the destruct of quest.
As Leonardo in a mottled wall, we trace
In schist the stilled orogeny of every earth.

Maelstroms of light, black holes, star-sinks in space;
VOID only chambers the death-birth of all;
Fire, air, earth and water, act and word
Mirage from the zero-flexings of all void:
To hold that calm and aching mothers god.

To the Greek four elements—in our physics, the states of matter: Water = liquid,
Earth = solid, Air = vapor, Fire = our plasma—I add Einstein's curved void, matrix of the
rest, thus shaping a five-fold close for this poetically structural volume.

Subject Index

Title/First Line Index

The long slow twilights of July have fled, 82–83

The man-trained willow, 171–72

The man who can face this, the man who can take it, 531

The March wind shakes the soul's dark house, 137

The mile-long freight rounds the great plateau, 195

The night each plows, 298, 544

The night is quiet, 240–41

The note is high, Master, beyond all compass, 182–83

The old must have incentives, 163–64

The order you observe is broken: they bend, 164–65

The palm shack bellies, 496

The passing caught and held—*percipio*, 488

The Patapsco scummed, 290

The point alone, 551–52

The pole star is high; the others circling, 404

There are more parts to wisdom than suffering, 377

There is a new place of concentration in the American home, 236–37

There is a valley in that forest, 537

"These Winter Dunes", 341–42

The shadow of a cloven stick, 189

The small body shrinks and hisses, 504

The solitary makes his soul a god, 192–93

The sudden screech of a bird fills the night wood, 176

The sun goes under the dark wood, 243–44

The sun over the bay sets shrouded in vapor, 189

The sun setting at his back, he looked in the window, 238

The swirl of water dominates the plain, 460

The tent bellies in the night as if the words, 469

The tug pulls, tightening the steel strand. This harbor, 373

The wake lightens; fish scatter, 558

The water holds the brown sky of dusk, 572

The way up and the way down is the same, 395

The well, 541

The young beech leaves dance gold

against the darker, 174–75

They say the fig is the symbol of life. The largest, 474

They still circle the sky, these black buzzards, 472

"Third World", 570

"This Breathing House", 540

This first, a choleric fool, swollen with pride, 113

This garret, where for three years I, 260

This is the quietest place. I have come, 475

This is the site, the viewpoint I remember, 396–97

This is the water that bathes three continents, 260–61

"This Little Vigil", 358

"This Low Delta", 414–18

This, my children, is steel in the heart's sanctum, 106

"Threshold", 265–66

Through entropic December of shifting total fog, 503

Through my study window, 263–64

Through the three layers of the crossing cloud, 348–49

Through trees now gleam white columns; the old South, 423

Through two wars I have watched this city. No bombs, 171

Time and matter hatched a plan, 290

"Timeless Creed", 451–55

"Tintern Revisited", 173

"Tiresias Speaks", 515

"Titan Chained", 113

To, 486

"To a Wishful Wife Who Took Flight", 142

"To a Young Girl", 288–89

"To Borgese, Kahler, and the Unknown Third", 389

To climb that liquidly resilient up the air, 494

"To Danny", 242

"To Danny from the Journey of Return (1953)", 400

Today we walk the sand-dunes where a fire, 203

"To Dick Wendell", 388

"To Galway", 560

"To His Fair Mistress", 59–61

"Tomorrow", 479–83

Tonight in a lighted tower, 495

Charles dancing at the wedding of Carol Moldaw and
Auther Sze, Santa Fe, August 3, 1997.